Pusan Kyoto

Taipei

Hong Kong

Bombay

Bangkok Guam

Manila

Kandy Yap

Koror

obi

r-Es-Salaam

SAFARI BY JET)≣ THROUGH AFRICA AND ASIA

BOOKS BY SISTER MARIA DEL REY

SAFARI BY JET

DUST ON MY TOES

HER NAME IS MERCY

BERNIE BECOMES A NUN

IN AND OUT THE ANDES

NUN IN RED CHINA
(UNDER THE NAME SISTER MARY VICTORIA)

PACIFIC HOPSCOTCH

SAFARI BY JET

{()} *THROUGH AFRICA AND ASIA*

BY **Sister Maria del Rey** OF MARYKNOLL

CHARLES SCRIBNER'S SONS }≥ *New York*

To MOTHER MARY COLMAN

WARM, WISE AND WITTY

CONTENTS

vii

TAIWAN

KOREA

JAPAN

TRUST TERRITORY OF THE PACIFIC

PREFACE

ONCE in a blue moon it happens.

To spend eight months in the world's most jittery spots, talking to people of all social stripes, being really at home in their homes, what journalist would not give his right arm for this? To see new nations rise up, to hear old nations groan, to see the puzzled quest for Truth—few missioners can make such a world-wide survey.

When Mother Mary Colman broached the subject late one night (all Mothers General work late at night), she was killing two birds with one stone. Church law requires that a Mother General, either in person or by delegate, visit every house and talk to each Sister. To Mother, head of sixteen hundred Sisters scattered in one hundred and twenty convents over the globe, this is a large order. She did not intend to do it all at once; we would simply go through Africa and Asia. My part was, ostensibly, to carry the baggage but, more often than not, it was Mother lending me a hand with typewriter, camera, notecase and gadget bag. Like all efficient people, her luggage was nothing; mine was stupendous.

Some of the places were old stamping grounds for us; some were new. Both of us had lived for years in the Philippines; we both knew Japan and Hong Kong. I had traveled before in Korea and the Caroline Islands. Africa, Ceylon and Taiwan were new territory. In a sense, though, we had good background for all of them, for Maryknoll headquarters near New York is the hub of a mission network. Reports from the world's hinterlands go across Mother's desk constantly; Sisters of every complexion and hue are being trained in the novitiate. Missioners come and go constantly. And in the parlor, there is always a hopeful Bishop from some unknown nook or cranny on the earth, coming to Maryknoll to ask for Sisters.

Being a Sister, I think, is an advantage. People take you for just another Sister; they talk out as if they had known you all their lives. There are no preliminaries to be got over; no ice to break. They know right off what you are, and like you or dislike you accordingly. Language was no problem, for the Sisters kept up a running translation.

Jets brought travel time to a minimum. A few hours at most lifted us from one culture and dropped us into another. We spent little time in big cities. Notes were punched out by the light of kerosene lamps or scribbled in windowless huts. Transportation came by jeeps, buses, small planes or by two sturdy feet. In fact, at one point I was tempted to name this book: "A World of Maryknoll Sisters, or How I Got Bunions."

At any rate, traveling with a swift-paced Mother General I do not need to ask an astronaut how it feels to be in the nosecone of a rocket. I know. I have been in one for eight months.

SAFARI BY JET 〗 THROUGH AFRICA AND ASIA

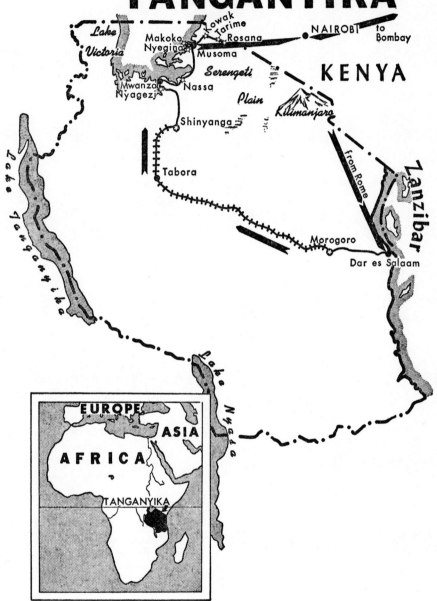

TANGANYIKA

≋(1)≋ *The "Boy" Has a Golden Coin*

As night fell, the sky reddened. Drums rolled; chants rose and fell. We went to the front door to see what was up. With a howl a crowd of dancers, one hundred and seventy-five of them, swarmed over the slight rise. They waved coconut fronds and banana branches. They tossed armloads of flowers into the air. They leaped and writhed and twisted. Some had stripped off banana leaves and tied them around ankles, neck, waist and arms; others had loose necklaces of some sort of spikes. They surrounded us, a howling, shuffling escort, gyrating around and around, gradually edging us toward the glare in the sky where flames reached for the stars.

It was melodious howling and the drums kept up a rumbling beat. Toughened bare feet scraped against the earth with the sound of sandpaper. Every now and then, the noise died down; then a lone voice piped up and soon the crowd was bending, swaying, tossing again.

Where were the friendly dark faces and flashing smiles I knew? Many of these were plastered chalk-white with fantastic markings. As we walked toward the glare in the sky, such a face would often break away from the others, rush toward us, bob and woggle close to ours to frighten us, and then flash back into the crowd that circled around. Twisting, tossing, leaping, shuffling, they yet managed to sing and clap hands and beat drums all the way to the fire. The words must have meant something, but all I could get was "ayee, ayee, cha, cha, cha" over and over again.

We had known all day that something was cooking; now we began to hope that it would not be us. Early that morning, the girls had gone up the mountainside for firewood. In holiday mood—dancing and singing and swinging their great crude machetes. Their gay kangas, wrapped around and knotted under the armpits, made a line of bright dots against the tawny grass. I watched from my window until the string of dots disappeared into the green trees far up the mountains.

I was often—too often—at the window, face to face with the most beautiful mountains God ever made. The earth is red, like Hawaii's; the grass is lion-colored; the mountain sides are scarred like a giant file and their jagged tops cut into the blue sky with saw-tooth precision. The

3

Uluguru mountains are plunked onto a flat plain with no undulations to get you ready for them.

For I could step across the hall into Sister Paul Catherine's cell and see for miles and miles across a valley striped with rows of sisal, a sort of spiky plant like a huge pineapple. Bluish-greyish mountains bulged on the horizon, seventy-five miles away, they tell me. Cutting across the sisal rows wound a narrow black line like a zip-fastener. From it, occasionally, came a puff of smoke and the hoot of a railroad engine. This was the Great Central Railroad, put in by Germans at the dawn of the century. It follows the old slave trail from Ujiji on Lake Tanganyika on the west, to Bagamoyo on the east coast, seven hundred and eighty blood-stained miles.

In the late afternoon that day, as the ridges of the Uluguru were sharply defined in deep shadow and strong sunlight, the girls came single file out of the forests. Forty of them, like a caravan of camels, treading into the school yard. Their bodies moved forward smoothly, their heads were on an absolutely even keel beneath fantastic burdens of firewood. Some of it was shavings, some twigs, some branches and more than one girl carried a sizable log cushioned by the soft kinks of her hair. Yet they laughed and passed jokes along the line, and often one took a quick sidestep to evade a slap in banter.

"What are they up to?" I asked Sister Dolores Marie.

"A campfire, I think," she said.

A campfire? My idea of a campfire is a mild affair where kiddies throw twigs on well-prepared charcoal and roast marshmallows.

African girls have no such ideas. This was an all-out conflagration. They had built up the pyre to at least ten feet, the flames topped it to twenty or twenty-five feet. As the tongues leaped, the African's enthusiasm for life leaped too. There were twenty-six tribal dances—that is, twenty-six on the program. Any number of impromptu affairs and on-the-spot solos filled in any blank moments. It was so easy to see where the old soft shoe dances and the Charleston and Lindy came from. A gap was unthinkable. When nobody could wait for an organized dance, someone would stand in the fire's glare, hold out her hands, start to talk, then to chant and at last to shuffle. In a rush, forty or fifty joined her, and around they went shouting and leaping and doing everything you could possibly do in a dance. And there wasn't a scrap of any music but the drum and the chant.

There is quite a technique to beating African drums. I tried it. It sounded fine to me, but the drum beaters said, "No, no, you make it sound like this." They use fingers, knuckles, the heel of the thumb and the palm itself to vary the sound. From time to time, too, the drumhead had to toast near the fire. The heat tightened the skin and thus raised the pitch. There was always a line-up of drums facing the blaze.

The dances covered Tanganyika and a little of its neighbors, Nyasaland and Uganda. The Bahaya girls did Bahaya dances; the Bakuria, the Basukuma; the Hehe, the Mfipa; girls danced as they did at home. They all told a story; the words are essential to the dance. Here are a few:

A farmer was digging for potatoes and he found diamonds instead! Oi, oi, very lucky! He went to town and bought a motor car.

Poverty is not in one house. Even the queen has to borrow food sometimes.

A man in our village of Kigarama notices that another man had very nice teeth, so he made up a song about it.

When the elephants pass, they leave a wide path. If they go through a forest, they take the leaves off the trees; if they go through the tall grass, their big feet beat it down.

Mother is the person who will help you when you need something.

The people are all very happy because they have received some good hides (the same word means clothing) from America.

Oh, what a nuisance chiggers are!

Kind Mary, be the protector of your children.

A man was walking during the night and he stubbed his toe, so he is dancing about.

The heavy rains are over. The bullfrogs are happy now that there is so much water.

Four Ngoni dances have odd themes: 'Don't forget me!' 'I have a dish full of rice.' 'Will you give me a drink of water?' and 'I don't want to marry a teacher!'

Almost any event, from blighted love to stubbing a toe, can rate a dance and song. Not happy with a mere statement of the theme, the dancers repeat it until even the stupid European on the side lines knows what is being celebrated. They had one, "I like Coca Cola. This is how I take off the cap." It took five minutes vigorous de-capping before I leaned over to my neighbor and said, "You know, I think they're taking off bottle caps." She withered me with her glance. "Yes, you got it."

The Hehe dances took the prize. Two dancers faced each other, backed by the flaming pyre. Each had a police whistle between her teeth. As the flames roared, they danced faster and faster and blew the whistles shriller and shriller. They leaped so high, so close to the fire, they seemed like flames themselves while the whistles screamed above the chant and drums. All at once they were two sodden heaps at our feet. The dance was over.

The Africans dearly love to spoof the Europeans. Two lines of dancers opposed each other; one was European, the other African.

"We are very clever people," chanted the Europeans.

"What are you so clever about?" said the Africans.

"We can blow horns." So they do with utmost pomposity.

Again, the Europeans boast: "We are extremely talented people."

"Oh yes?" ask the Africans. "What can you do?"

Well, they run steam engines and fly planes and play the piano and read books and so on.

At last the Africans call out: "We, too, are very knowledgeable."

"What do you know?" asks the other side.

The Africans fall into hilarious laughter, rocking and rolling in glee. The implication is obvious. The Africans can laugh at us all. This gift has pulled them through two thousand five hundred years of slavery under Arabians, Chinese, Indians, Frenchmen, Portuguese and in our own Southern States.

"Who is that girl?" I asked about one who was laughing uproariously with head thrown back and body twisting from side to side. Her face was plastered with white; a cap of banana leaves set crooked on her head.

"Oh, she's Felysia Burton."

"Burton? Where did she get that name?"

"Her father was from Texas originally, one whom we call a white hunter. That is, he was an expert on big game and used to organize safaris for wealthy men out here for a thrill. Her mother was African and they seemed very happy together. During World War II, Mr. Burton was in charge of a concentration camp set up for Germans and Italians in British East Africa. Soon after the war Felysia's mother died, and not long after that her father was killed by an elephant. The Italian Consolata Fathers took her into the mission and have given her every advantage; they are grateful for her father's kindness to them when they were in the concentration camp."

"What will happen to her now?" I asked. "She's finishing High School this year, isn't she?"

"Her future is bright. Almost as bright as she is. She'll go on to higher studies and eventually perhaps to Makerere University in Uganda. After that—the world is her oyster."

I looked back at Felysia in her banana leaf decorations and white plastered face. Here was a girl who could sail away with an English Literature examination that would toss many of our college graduates for a loop.

"And that one?" I pointed out a short, chubby girl with a drum under her arm. She had just picked it up from where it had been toasting near the fire and was testing the pitch with her fingers, like a violinist with his strings. Suddenly, she gave it a whack and started up a wild dance. Others took it up and the whole crowd was off in full cry.

"That's Elizabetti Mwaggi," Sister answered. "A born leader. She's a Mchagga. Intelligent. Has lovely manners and speaks beautiful English. We got a scholarship for her; she will go to Marymount College in New York next September. In the meantime, we will brief her on what New York girls do, so that she will not feel too out of place."

The night deepened; the fire flared, died down, and flared up again. Agile toes had stirred up the red-brown dust until it rose in a cloud. I could feel the grit of it between my teeth; it lined the inside of my nose; it caked our veils and habits.

The girls should have been exhausted. But they gathered in a close group, one hundred and seventy-three of them, and sang their school song with all their hearts. Then—the national anthem:

> *Tanganyika, I love you with my whole heart.*
> *My country, Tanganyika, I love you.*
> *When I sleep I dream of you.*
> *When I wake up I sing praise for you.*
> *Tanganyika, Tanganyika, I love you with my whole heart.*

It's typical. No reasons why—no praise of beauty, size, importance, ancestral home. No, just "I love you."

Once again, the drums throbbed, the chant rose, the weird faces where white plaster ran off in streams of sweat opened their mouths and sang. The crowd in tattered banana leaves surrounded us and danced us back to the convent. "Thank you so much for coming to see us!" they chanted over and over again to Mother Mary Colman.

As Mother stood at the doorway and turned to smile, they burst into, "For she's a Jolly Good Fellow!" and left us.

As I went to bed to spend what was left of the night with drums throbbing in my head, a paragraph I read long ago leaped to mind as if from printed page. In 1869, Sir Samuel Baker was sent out by the Khedive of Egypt to put an end to the slave traffic. He traveled all over the Great Lakes Region, meaning, of course, the Great Lakes of Nyasa, Tanganyika and Victoria. He didn't stop the slave trade but he did write a book. Says Sir Samuel Baker:

> I believe the safest way to travel in these wild countries would be to play the cornet, if possible without ceasing. This would ensure safe passage. A London organ-grinder would march through Central Africa followed by an admiring and enthusiastic crowd. If his tunes were lively, they would form a dancing escort of most untiring material.
>
> I would say that the chief qualifications of a missioner to the Africans would be: 1, skill at conjuring; 2, surgery and medicine; and 3, the ability to play the bagpipes, preferably in full Highland dress.

You have something there, Sir Samuel, you have something! As a team, perhaps, Mother and I could qualify. Mother is good at conjuring. At

least for some years she has succeeded in conjuring up Sisters to satisfy
Bishops who want them for missions. I can't play the bagpipes but I can
grind an organ. All we need, then, is a bit of surgery and medicine. I fell
asleep and dreamed of myself in full Highland dress grinding an organ
while Mother played card tricks with one hand and healed the wounded
with the other, as we marched across Tanganyika with a "dancing escort
of most untiring material."

I have never seen such an energetic enthusiastic people. Thirst for the
new civilization, love for their own old culture, these are priceless in a
student. Surely, no one can doubt that Africans will lead the world in
time.

Next day, you could have heard a pin drop. Those same girls who had
chanted and clapped, swayed and shuffled in complete abandon to the
rhythm of drums—those same girls were "sitting for Cambridge examinations" on Shakespeare's *Henry V*. And lest you think them easy, let me
quote you a question or two:

> Referring closely to relevant scenes and speeches, contrast the behaviour
> of the French and English armies before the Battle of Agincourt, and show
> how the conduct of the Dauphin and of Henry helps to emphasize the
> contrast between the two sides.
>
> What, according to the Prologue of Act I, is the function of the chorus
> in the play? Supporting your answer by close reference to the Prologue to
> Act III and the Prologue to Act V, show how far you consider the chorus
> carries out this function.

And here's a geometry problem:

> ABCD is a parallelogram. X is the point on the side BC such that $BX = \frac{1}{2}XC$, and Y the point on the diagonal AC such that $AY = \frac{1}{2}YC$. The line
> through D parallel to AC meets BC extended at Z. Find (1) the ratio of the
> area of the triangle CXY to that of the triangle CBA; (2) the ratio of the
> area of the quadrilateral AYXB to that of the parallelogram ACZD.

Examination days are quiet anywhere in the world. The only reminder
of equatorial Africa here at Marian College in Morogoro, was the sight
of a girl walking majestically from building to building with books piled
on her head, topped by a bottle of ink. Considering how those heads are
packed tight with the accumulated lore of both the African and European
worlds, they can probably take heavy weights on top without breakage.

This "sitting for Cambridge"—in fact, the whole educational system
in Tanganyika—requires explanation. To take girls from forty-six different tribes with forty-six different languages, born and brought up for
the most part in mud huts far from even the smallest city, whose parents
are tattooed and adorned with ivory they have personally won from an

elephant—to take girls such as these, rich though they may be in their own special culture, and to turn out High School seniors who can talk and write on Shakespeare's *Henry V* as well as, and often much better than, High School seniors of our own country—well, this takes real teaching from the educator and solid intelligence from the student.

At Morogoro we saw—of all things!—a production of *Pinafore* with clipped British speech, real relish for satire of the Royal Navy and a Little Buttercup who was cockney straight back to her tonsils.

The secondary education system of Tanganyika is very simple—just four Senior High Schools for African girls exist in this nation of nine million people. And they are quite new. The first was a government school opened in the center of the country at Tabora in 1952; the second was Marian College in Morogoro in the east, staffed by Maryknoll Sisters. Five other schools, including Rosary College at Mwanza in the northwest, will be complete High Schools by 1964. Their combined enrollment would be under a thousand. In all of Tanganyika's nine million population, fewer than one hundred and fifty African girls have finished twelve years of schooling.

Small wonder that they and their parents strain every nerve to get into a school. At Morogoro I met Imelda. A girl about sixteen, she started out from home one hundred miles away in February when the school year began. But floods had wiped out the road; the buses to Morogoro would not run. So she and her father walked seventy-two miles to the nearest railroad station. That took three days. There she caught a train for Dar-Es-Salaam, two hundred miles away. From Dar she took a bus one hundred and twenty miles to Morogoro. When we saw her walking up our dusty road from the bus stop, with her wooden suitcase on her head, everyone ran out to meet her. She was only a week late for school.

This is quite a change from twenty-five years ago when Franciscan Sisters began a Primary School here. The parents asked how much the Sisters would pay them if they let the girls come to school. Why not? they reasoned. No one at home to tend cattle, get firewood, carry water from the river.

You may have an idea gleaned from the word "college." To most of us, it connotes a campus of venerable trees with several ivy-covered buildings, a gold dome or so, and thousands of students poring over books on the lawns. Good enough. But try to visualize such a college when the founders had just hacked it out of the wilderness . . . like Fordham up in the wilds of the Bronx . . . or Notre Dame when the first boys drove in from the farms . . . or Santa Clara a hundred years ago.

Marian College starts off with sixteen buildings which might have been ordered wholesale by the dozen, exactly alike. One story, concrete, corrugated iron roofs, 100 by 30 ft. One is an auditorium; several are dormitories; a number are classrooms; one is the chapel.

The two hundred and thirty-three girls are between fourteen and twenty-two years old from forty-six tribes all over the country. The custom is dying out but some still have teeth filed into scallops and points. Some have no lower teeth at all; they were taken out with an ice pick when they were little girls. Many braid their short hair tight into strips which run from front to back, so that their heads look like striped watermelons.

Many here are from the Chagga, Haya and Nyakyusa tribes. These tribes, although their territories lie nowhere near one another, have three things in common: they eat bananas as a staple diet; they grow coffee and are prosperous; they are crackerjacks in school. Nobody can decide if they are smart because they eat bananas, or whether they eat bananas because they are smart.

At Marian College, education supplies are sometimes a problem. Sister Marian Teresa tried three times to get a vertebra of a cow for demonstration in her biology class. She explained to the butcher what she wanted; he always sent it so hashed up with a cleaver that it was useless for class. At last, she got a whole backbone, boiled off the meat and put it out to dry. In the morning, it was gone. Somebody during the night had needed soup bones.

But things are picking up in Morogoro. By the way, the name comes from "mgogoro," a nuisance, because a certain chieftain used to levy a tax on anyone crossing the local river. Germans found it hard to pronounce mgogoro, and gradually it expanded to Morogoro. So we really live in Nuisancetown.

The beginnings of a good culture are here. Already, the plant enthusiasts have put their heads together and formed a Naturalists' Club. Africans, British government people, American Sisters and a Dutch Brother are banded together to preserve the flowers and trees. They held a show. Nothing much, but it was the first step forward. I thought of the flower exhibits in Hawaii, the botanical gardens in Ceylon, the plazas in Manila, the orchid growers' clubs in Hong Kong. It will come to Tanganyika in time. If Morogoro with a population of sixteen thousand has a Naturalists' Club, the orchid fanciers are on the way.

Another harbinger of civilization is a lone piano tuner who lives in Dar and travels the length and breadth of Tanganyika caring for his little charges. He coddles every piano in the country. There are two in Morogoro; one is at Marian College.

Land is what Tanganyika has most of. The nine million people rattle around in it. Back in 1883, when the Dutch Holy Ghost Fathers came to Morogoro, the local sultan offered the Bishop "as much land as a man can walk around in one day." One of those missionary giants of the old generation arose early one morning and took quite a constitutional. The result is a long thin tract of land between the base of the mountains and the railroad. The Fathers were commissioned by the German Government to catch slave traders. The wily sinners used to sneak behind a certain hill in the daytime, thinking the Fathers would not leave their aerie halfway up the mountains. But the padres often sallied out to hide behind the other side of the hill. At nightfall, they caught the traders red-handed when the caravans began to march again. The Fathers have many certificates of freedom for individuals thus set free and sent back home again. Some of them are dated as late as 1903.

The land has been put to good use. Primary, Middle, Secondary Schools and a Teacher Training College are erected; a church and catechetical room, a maternity hospital, and our own Marian College, are strung along the railroad like beads on a string. Also Sister Hildemar's dental clinic. The only dentist in the Morogoro district, Sister has been fixing teeth for twenty-four years in a little white cottage on the mountainside. The patient can take in a breathtaking stretch of land whenever he closes his mouth long enough to do so. Sister has a waiting bench outside her door. Very often she finds it occupied by monkeys who swing out of the mountains to steal mangoes and perch on the dental clinic bench to eat them.

"Twenty years ago," Sister says, "the Africans had beautiful teeth. They were constantly cleaning them with 'mswaki,' a piece of bark they used to chew or rub over their teeth all day long. Now they think that's old-fashioned. They don't see Europeans chewing mswaki. Too bad. Their teeth are deteriorating badly."

Wild life around Morogoro is on the wane, although while I was there, a woman came in saying that three miles outside town, she saw three lions eating six cows. She banged two "debbies" (four-gallon gasoline cans) together; the noise frightened the lions away. Another time a lion was accused of swallowing a dog tied to a pole in somebody's back yard.

Yes, civilization—or what we call that—is crowding in on Africa's interior, seeping in from the coast. We drove from Dar-Es-Salaam to Morogoro, one hundred and twenty miles due west along a paved road. Very easy going in a light green station wagon which has rolled up forty thousand hot dusty miles since it arrived four years before. Its versatility goes beyond even the ads for it. It has served as pick-up truck, as school bus and even as ambulance. An African priest was sick, supposedly dying, out in the mountains. They brought him by litter to Morogoro. He went on to Dar in style on a mattress laid over the turned-down seats of our station wagon with a Sister-nurse on duty during the ride.

With such a background, the British efforts to educate Tanganyika deserve nothing less than a deep salaam. Language was the first knot to be unravelled. A loose figure of one hundred and twenty is given to the tribes in Tanganyika. The figure is loose because no one can quite decide what a "tribe" is. There are close to a million Basukuma; less than four thousand Basonjo; yet each is a tribe. Each has its own language; English is useful for contact with the outside world.

Forty-four percent of African children go to Primary School, having lessons in their own tribal tongue in the villages and learning Kiswahili. At the end of four years, they take examinations sent out by the Province. The twenty percent at the top are permitted to go on for Middle School. Here, they are taught in Kiswahili and learn English. Again at the end of Standard VIII—examinations. Again only twenty percent may go on for Secondary School. Only one percent of all African children make it. Territorial Examinations weed them out again at the end of Form II. Those who have leaped all these hurdles are permitted to "sit for Cambridge," at the end of the twelfth year, known as Form IV. The Cambridge exams are sent out from England even though Tanganyika is now independent. Their very appearance strikes dread into pupils and teachers alike. A huge envelope, heavy with sealing wax, stamped ON HER MAJESTY'S SERVICE, sewed around the edges with bright green thread, with full instructions as to the day, hour and minute that envelope is to be opened in front of the class.

The Cambridge survivors can go on through a sort of Junior College course called Forms V and VI; to date this is available only at Tabora. Only three or four girls in all Tanganyika finish Form VI each year. Persevering further, they can attend Makerere University in Uganda. Tanganyika, as soon as it was born a nation in December, 1961, started University College in Dar Es Salaam. So far, this is only the beginnings of a law school. Makerere specializes in Medicine and Agriculture.

Anywhere along the line, from Form II onwards, the student can qualify as a teacher, although he is graded according to the preparation he has had.

Teachers switch around. Two of our Sisters went to Tabora to "invigilate" as they call it, and correct other schools' work. Six teachers from various boys' and girls' schools from all over the country came to Morogoro and tackled a pile of one thousand eight hundred Standard X English Exams. All the English papers came to us; the math, history, and other subjects went elsewhere. I went past the room where they were working and marvelled to see these English men and women silently contemplate the syntax, composition, spelling and poetic ability of one thousand eight hundred trembling Tenth Graders throughout Tanganyika.

It might be good here to give you an idea of Swahili; we are not used to prefixes to change a word all around. It's a concise language. Put a single syllable in front of the root word and you can save yourself quite a bit of breath. Take the root word, "hehe," the name of one of the tribes, for example. An "mhehe" is a single person of that tribe; "wahehe" means the tribe as a whole. The language they speak is "kihehe" and their territory is "uhehe." Using them all, we could say: "He is a mhehe. Wahehe are a progressive tribe. Kihehe is difficult but once you have lived in uhehe it comes easier."

The Africans love to spoof the European's efficiency. "Zungu" is the root word for "dizzy." In Kiswahili, "mzungu" means a European; "mzunguzungu" is a very European European; "uzungu" is the European section of Morogoro.

Swahili itself is not a real African language. "Sahil" is Arabic and means "coast." The language is a potpourri of Arabic and the coastal Bantu.

Studying Kiswahili, the Sisters make errors, of course. Sister Anthonita, in charge of the kitchen, tried out a new recipe for the Sisters. Later she was telling one of the teachers in school, "It was a great success. They all died." Just a matter of a single letter. "Kufa" means "to die"; "kula" means "to eat." She meant, "They ate it all."

"Colonialism" is a bad word which speakers sidestep nowadays unless they intend to inveigh against it. Certainly, a missioner can hold no brief for it. Nevertheless, it seems to be the first painful process toward good things. I can imagine a Briton around 1100 A.D. looking back on England's history. Rather bleak. The Romans had come, seen and conquered. In four hundred years of colonial rule, they must have given the Britons a clear idea that the natives of England existed for the economic benefit of Rome and of nobody else. Imagine a party in a Roman bath. A rubicund old Roman who boasts of thirty years "out in god-forsaken Britain" snaps his fingers at the "boy," and orders him to take off his sandals, bring a basin and towel and wash the lordly Roman feet. "And be jolly quick about it!" Then he turns to the other Romans to show his superior knowledge of the savage tribes of Britons, and says, "These fellows are slow enough when you give them an order, but they could knife you in the back in a split second."

And the poor Briton no sooner saw the Romans crumple and roll into a corner, than he fell prostrate under the heel of Saxons, Angles, Danes, and lastly Normans. He was well kicked about for a thousand years. The cry of "Uhuru" (Independence!) must often have risen to his lips only to be squashed by a new invader. The contempt of each new conqueror must have galled him to the soul. They called his fair hair and blue eyes "barbaric." They said there was no use educating him because his mental capacity was incapable of learning. They used him as a beast of burden and said that was what God made him for.

But! The Romans left their roads and bridges behind, and their code of law. All the unwelcome guests, in turn, handed the "boy" a golden coin.

And the "boy" watched them closely, stole words and ideas from their languages, learned how they did things—and came off the richer for his humiliations. When his own Uhuru came and he started putting the conqueror's foot on other lands, he used everything he had learned, the good as well as the bad.

So it is with Tanganyika. Greece and Rome knew this coast. Indians, Arabians and Persians have been coming here for two thousand years. The Chinese, too, seem to have paid several visits. Traders came for ivory, wood, spice, rhinoceros horn and tortoise shell. They left behind them glass, cloth, metal, and two priceless gifts—the coconut tree and sugar cane.

In 1945, the Colony became a Trust Territory administered by Great Britain for the United Nations. In that year, two Africans were appointed to the legislature. Tanganyikans are proud that their gradual process toward independence has been peaceful. The furore over Congo's emergence as an independent nation has served as a warning to other Africans. "We don't want that to happen in our country," they say.

In 1958, the elective seats in the Legislature were evenly divided between Europeans, Asians and Africans. Two years later, seventy-one seats in the Legislature were elective, ten for Europeans, eleven for Asians and fifty "open" to candidates of any race. All fifty could be African candidates. Julius Nyerere's TANU (Tanganyika African National Union) won seventy of the seventy-one seats. His call is not Uhuru! but Uhuru na Kazi (Freedom and Work!)

The *Tanganyika Standard* (published in Dar es Salaam) gave a good idea of how rights of the individual are protected, in this story of a cattle-thieving trial. It seems that a Masai chieftain claimed that a certain Kamba tribesman had stolen four hundred cattle from him. Indeed, he said that over the years, he had lost five thousand four hundred and fifty-five cows in Kamba raids. The Masai are pretty good cattle thieves themselves and can be presumed to keep tally on their own herds as well as on their neighbors'!

A British counsel was appointed for the Defense and another for the Prosecution. The two learned barristers brought to bear all the centuries' experience of Common Law upon the case. Something like this happened:

> Defense Attorney: 'It's jolly preposterous to suppose that this charge is true. Why, the Masai tribe cannot count; this old fellow would not know if forty or four hundred cattle were stolen.'
> Prosecution Counsel: 'Quite wrong, dear fellow, quite wrong. The Masai can count quite well. But they object to counting. It goes against their superstitions and their tribal customs. Moreover, when it comes to cattle, a Masai with ten thousand head can immediately tell you if even one is missing. It's positively uncanny—their feeling for numbers.'
> Defense Counsel: 'A statement, I would say, quite safe to say since we

can hardly bring ten thousand cattle here to prove it! I wonder if the complainant is willing to count something else.'

Prosecution Counsel: 'What, for instance?'

Defense Counsel: 'Oh, just about anything. Or rather, nothing much. How about a bowl of beans?'

The old Masai, utterly befuddled by this legal interchange, agreed to count the beans. The counsels sat him down at a table, poured out the beans and let him go to work. His dark fingers with broken nails pushed the beans one by one into little piles; his heavy lips muttered Masai figures slowly. For two hours and forty-seven minutes, he bent over the small table keeping doggedly to the task.

At last, he straightened. The court came to life. The judge mounted his bench; both counsels brightened. How many beans?

'One hundred and eighty-four,' announced the Masai.

'Wrong!' exulted Counsel for the Defense. 'There were two hundred and forty-three beans in the bowl. This proves that the complainant has no idea how many cows were taken nor even if any were taken. He is completely unaware of how many cows he had to begin with.'

'On the contrary, my honorable opponent,' shouted the Counsel for the Prosecution. 'Your conclusion is invalid. It proves, rather, that my client has underestimated his losses. He has lost probably five hundred or more cows in the dastardly Kamba raids.'

Such is the sense of fair play embodied in Tanganyika's inheritance of British law. Both Masai and Kamba are entitled to have clever men press their claims even when the arguments are beyond their comprehension.

But, I asked, why have British lawyers? Why not Africans? Ah, there lies the rub! In all Tanganyika, there are but two African lawyers in private practice and two in government posts. In 1960, among the country's five hundred and fifteen doctors, only fifteen were Africans. That is why Julius Nyerere says, "We are for Africanization, but we would be foolish to deprive ourselves of the services of educated Europeans. Until we are able to do these services for ourselves, we shall ask them to stay with us." Just how long this quiet voice of moderation can be heard above the shout for power, is a question.

The type of educated African we met, gives one a good idea that the day of Africanization of the professions is not far off. The Sultan Patrick and the Sultana Bernadette, reigning monarchs of the Waluguru, for instance.

They bounced up our rutted road in their European car and unloaded themselves from the front seat and Princess Dolores and Prince Christopher from the back. Then the Sultan Patrick straightened his European style suit, tightened his necktie and took the Princess Dolores' hand; the Sultana Bernadette bundled Crown Prince Christopher in her arms. Together they advanced to the convent door. They had come on a state visit. Also, a friendly get-together.

The reigning family of the Waluguru sat in our small parlor talking small talk. Princess Dolores took some time deciding which color gumdrop she liked best. Prince Christopher (let's give him his full name, Alexander Paul Christopher Anthony, to appease many family friends) drooped under such a weight and howled his head off. He is Christopher at the convent because we suggested that name. He changes his name to suit his surroundings.

Sultan Patrick Kunambi speaks perfect English. A small man in a washable suit, he has a definite air of authority. Not yet forty, he says with a hint of a smile, "I am the senior of our tribe." His position comes from heredity and also by popular election. His perfect English comes from Makerere University in Uganda. He was one of Makerere's first students when it opened just before World War II.

Patrick's uncle was the Sultan until 1959. Then he retired and the job was up for election. Patrick, by that time, was one of the fifteen African members of the Legislative Council. He put himself into the Sultanate race against sturdy opposition from a man of the same family but of different political persuasion. It was up to the Electoral College to decide —that is, elders of the Waluguru tribe, men who were over twenty-one years, had completed Eighth Grade and who earned $420 a year.

In November, 1959, Patrick and Bernadette were crowned in three distinct but succeeding ceremonies. The first lasted for eighteen hours in their home village; the second one, his crowning as the African chief, took all morning in Morogoro's public square; the third was his installation as a Sultan with ceremonies deriving from Arabia. This used a long Arabian coat, a hat of monkey fur and ostrich plumes. Bernadette had a cape of the same. The Royal African Rifles, Tanganyika's crack regiment, marched; the school children sang; the Bishop gave his blessing; the tribes danced; the English Governor made a speech in perfect Swahili to match Patrick's perfect English. Later there was ceremonial beer drinking which installed Patrick as head of his tribe.

"For I," said Patrick with that smile, "am the first Catholic Sultan of Morogoro. All the others have been pagan or Moslem. I found, however, that religion was never an issue in the campaign."

He had pictures of the whole affair. Indeed he ran back to his house to get them for us. Taken by the Public Relations Department of the British Commonwealth, they showed the Sultan, arrayed in his monkey-fur crown, silhouetted against the Uluguru mountains. In the dead center of all this barbaric splendor is Patrick's sensitive face, his steady eyes, his highly civilized half-smile.

And now that he is Sultan, what does Patrick do?

"Well, one of my traditional jobs is to be rainmaker. However, I don't spend much time trying to do that. My district, where the Waluguru live, covers 5,200 square miles with some two hundred thousand people. This does not count Morogoro itself, which is under its own government.

"I travel through these beautiful mountains going from village to village. I settle disputes for I am the Supreme Court of the district. I uphold or correct the local chiefs. I explain the laws and try to show that they are reasonable and wise. Such is my work with my people. For the national government, I serve on the Committee on Education which chooses overseas students. We are sending one hundred and twenty to foreign universities this year; twenty of them, I think, will study in the States."

"Is your job for life?"

"Yes, for life. But," with a spread of his hands, "who knows now in present-day Tanganyika?"

So much for Patrick. What does Bernadette do as Sultana? Like her husband, she is a former teacher. In her late twenties, she is a happy sort of person, pleasingly plump, a homey wife and mother. Bernadette is up to her ears in work for the Girl Guides and Catholic Social Guild. She visits the hospital and prison in Morogoro regularly. But her biggest job is keeping up her very modest ranch-style house on a side street, doing her own housework.

As they were leaving, Bernadette turned to Sister Margaret Rose. "We've been crowned two whole years," she said, "and people want us to move into the Sultan's palace. I suppose we'll have to do it pretty soon. But, oh dear, I hate to think of it. The place is so big it's hard to clean. And there's no electricity."

As they whirled away in a cloud of red-brown dust, I realized that Bernadette had shattered forever a cherished illusion. A Sultana is not an Arabian Nights' houri; she is a housewife worried about her toaster, percolator, vacuum sweeper and floor lamps.

◄ 2 ► *The Irishman and the Tsetse Fly*

HE was one of those long-legged Irishmen you meet all over the world. They spend thirty, forty, fifty years running plantations, railroads, waterworks and such in god-forsaken regions, but they are as simple as when they kissed Mother good-bye and set out to make a fortune in a cruel world. Some of them have made it; others are still looking. In either case, they're usually very good company.

This particular one, Tim O'Neil, was leaning out the train window, resting his elbows on the lowered pane and gazing with lacklustre eyes at Tanganyika's flea-bitten landscape. The rest of him completely blocked the corridor along our compartments.

He straightened as we tried to edge by. Then, waving his arm out toward the baked, parched, burned, excoriated earth, he said, "There's no part of Ireland like it for sure. All I can think of is Texas in a bad mood."

Not a bad description. For a day, a night and a day we had been crawling through the desolate land at the impressive rate of 17½ miles an hour. It was like traveling across the United States, a year or so after the last spike of the Transcontinental Railroad had been driven in. Already, we had chalked up thirty-seven stops where there was a small station, a painted house or two for railroad personnel and several small bushes struggling to spread their perfume on the desert air. Many other stops were out in the wide open with nothing at all to mark them.

The East African Central Railroad is one of the engineering feats of the German regime in Tanganyika at the turn of the century. It is a single track stretching five hundred and fifty miles from Dar-Es-Salaam on the eastern coast to Tabora, two-thirds across this square-ish country. There it breaks into two branches, one continuing two hundred and fifty miles west to Lake Tanganyika where boats are available for the Congo, the other heading north for Lake Victoria.

Tim O'Neil used to be on the police force at Nairobi in Kenya, a far more westernized place. "Too settled for me!" he said. "I got me a job on this railroad." He has been in charge of this crack flier for the past seven years. "In charge" is a vague title. His duties were just as vague. I gathered that he talked to the European passengers, kept the corridors free of boxes, bags, bundles, babies, half-eaten mangoes and bits of curry and rice, saw that the sleeping-cabin porter did not fall asleep himself or suddenly take off in some deserted spot, and generally kept morale high among passengers and crew.

This particular train runs three times a week—Tuesdays, Thursdays and Saturdays. The East African Railways and Harbour Company operates boats on the lakes and buses on the dirt roads, as well. With the greatest courtesy, each branch of the service waits for the other branches. Furthermore, amicable relations tie it up with boats, trains and buses in other countries, so that you can buy a ticket in Cairo in Egypt, for Mombasa in Kenya, a junket of twenty-three days by railroad, boat and bus, to go about two thousand five hundred miles. Want to try it? The train leaves Cairo every Wednesday at 8 P.M. As Tim O'Neil put it, "The motto of the East African Railroad is: If you're in such a hurry, why don't you walk?"

Tim O'Neil was master of quite a kingdom. His First, Second and Third Class coaches held thousands of people. We saw them at every stop of importance. Many were African students going home from schools as much as a thousand miles away. A week jogging along in trains, buses and boats was nothing to these boys, although most of them seemed to be only twelve or so years old. Then there were dusty ragged African men and women who had climbed aboard at some desolate place and who would slip quietly off at another. There was nothing to see at these stops but the flattening out of a path through the grass where they had walked to the railroad track and had camped a day or so awaiting the train. They would get off at the same sort of place, settle their small baggages on top of their heads and pad through the grass to the far horizon shimmering in the heat.

The First and Second Class coaches were filled with Indians. Whole families of them. Mama, quite chubby, wore a short jacket, a bare midriff and a wrap-around skirt of filmy stuff. A gem in her nostril, gold kid slippers, a caste mark on her forehead, elaborate earrings, and jewels on fingers and toes, did not stop her from being the complete mama through the trip. Indians do not patronize the restaurant car (as the diner is called); they prefer to cook their own food in their own compartments. The results tantalized Sister Margaret Rose who loves Indian dishes and had to take herself back to the mild English fare in the diner.

The Indians are the rich people of Tanganyika. The Indian boys were coming home from school, too. They wore immaculate turbans of pastel colors, white shirts and very short shorts. You would never suspect that these little dandies had spent two days and nights on a train. One lad in particular had a bright pink turban which brought out the dark beauty of his face. Most of the time, as he strolled up and down beside the stalled train, he fiddled with a tennis racquet. He was itching to get on a court. Others hopped on and off the train whenever it slowed down, and ran alongside until they could run no longer. Having a turban over their long black hair dampened not at all their Huck Finn wriggliness.

The Indian girls, too, linked arms and strolled along the platforms—when there was a platform—their long black braids swinging behind at every step. The equatorial sun glinted on their nose-gems and earrings as they whispered and giggled like school girls all over the world. As often as not, they pulled on straws in Coca Cola bottles as if they had been brought up on it. They probably were.

Our conductor was also an Indian—tall, dignified, with white turban, gray mustache and beard. When he descended at a stop, it was a signal. Passengers could also get off and stretch their legs. When he set foot on the bottom step to mount the train again, all passengers hastened to do likewise. As Sister Juan Maria said, "Keep your eye on Mr. Whiskers. When he gets on, you had better hop on, too."

But it was always a penance. We had a First Class compartment and we had paid four shillings (56¢) extra for bedding. The porter, a small man in ragged khaki shorts and bright red fez, had brought us each a big canvas bag, much the worse for wear, containing blanket, sheet, pillow and towel. We could have ordered a mattress too for just two shillings more, but you have to place the order several days ahead. Anyway, with the mountain of baggage traditional to Maryknoll Sisters, I don't know where anyone could have put a mattress. As it was, we spent most of our time and energy shifting suitcases, handbags, airlines bags and parcels, so as to get floor room for our feet.

Tim O'Neil paid a state call soon after we met him. He floated into the compartment with the experienced trainman's indifference to lurchings. He sat on a suitcase, propped his feet on another and rested his long legs on the baggage between them.

"Yes," he said, "wild animals are often a problem. Not so long ago, a giraffe came to grief in an argument with this train. Giraffe are stupid, you know. Their only weapons are their hoofs and they can pack quite a wallop in those front feet. It was an odd sight, really, to see this big fellow rear up and smash into the oncoming engine with his two front hoofs. Of course, he came out second best. We had to clear the track of his carcass, report the matter to the game warden by radio before we could shove on again.

"Giraffe, by the way, are one reason why I'm not so fond of little cars. I keep a big American car with a steel body. I know a fellow who has a small car. He met a giraffe not so long ago. The animal lifted a front foot and came crashing down right through the roof like an ice pick through a tin can. Silly giraffe! He didn't know what to do then, with his hoof caught in a trap. Tom took one look at the hairy leg going through the seat beside him and decided it was time to make for the nearest exit. As he ran off, the last he saw was the giraffe trying to shake the car off his front foot."

He let that story sink in and changed the subject.

"Lions come out just about dusk. The enginemen see them often. But the whistle scares them off and by the time the passenger coaches come along, the lion is off into the tall grass.

"However, we had a nasty incident at Kasikasi a few weeks ago. One of the switchmen went out of the station a distance of just about fifteen feet, so as to throw the derailer for a coming train. In just that fifteen feet, a lion leaped upon him and dragged him off before his companion in the station could help him."

"We were hoping to see some elephants," we said.

"Not in the day, that's for sure. And there aren't so many elephants around any more. But this ought to be elephant country around here. See that baobab tree?"

He pointed out the window at a most peculiar tree. It seemed to shoot out of the ground with a mighty roar as if it intended to be a giant sequoia, but twenty feet or so up, it ended with a fizzle of scrawny branches. Like the man who started to build and had not wherewith to finish. Baobabs and mangoes were the only trees we had seen for miles and miles.

"Baobabs and elephants go together, the Africans tell us."

"What about the mango trees? What goes with them?"

"Slaves! This railroad was built along the old slave trail to the coast. Slave traders planted mangoes in clumps a day's march apart. I must say those old boys were great business men! They had the slaves carry the ivory and gold; they fed them free with mangoes enroute, and sold the whole kit and kaboodle when they got to the coast."

Tim jerked to attention suddenly. "Put down your screens," he ordered. "We're getting into a tsetse fly zone." He left the compartment quickly and we heard him rushing down the corridor, slamming windows shut, and calling into the compartments, "Tsetse fly zone! All screens down!"

It was enough to set the whole train a-slam. The tsetse fly is Public Enemy No. One in East Africa. He has made two-thirds of Tanganyika a lonely wilderness. Not only does he hit man indirectly by killing off his cattle, but he attacks directly by communicating the germ of sleeping sickness. Oddly enough, wild animals are immune to the tsetse. This gives hope that some day a vaccine may be found to immunize domestic animals, too.

The tsetse is a little larger than the usual fly. He is much less energetic and can be caught easily. You know how flies cling in muggy weather? That's how the tsetse is. I caught one hanging around me once. As I stepped on him, I felt that I had done something worthwhile for Africa.

If this wretched little pest did not dominate wide tracts of land, the African could raise cattle even though there is not enough water for agriculture. But the fly makes it impossible even to keep cows in some parts of the country. This is serious to Africans, especially, since theirs is a "cow-economy." For large sections of the people upcountry, cows are the medium of exchange. Yet, I never saw a cow around Morogoro; and in all of Africa I saw only one horse. He was in the Maryknoll Fathers' back yard in a small village. The priest who rode him said that he produced a sensation—not to say, terror—whenever he entered a hamlet. The people thought he and the horse were one beast and nearly died when he dismounted.

Tabora is a long stop on the Central Railroad. It was dusk; we welcomed a chance to stretch our legs in the cool of evening. Everybody else
seemed to have the same idea. It's an event for the transnational train to
come through and most people in town were at the station. Besides the
motley crew and passengers, most of the town's peddlers were out with
baskets of mangoes, trays of cheap jewelry, bits of cloth—just about everything—for sale. A huge King's African Rifleman strode around with an
Aussie hat turned up on one side of his strong black face; other police
were stationed here and there wearing broad belts and fezzes of dark blue.
Stringing through the crowd came a tall White Sister, one of Cardinal
Lavigerie's French Sisters, head and shoulders above the people, and
dressed in flowing white. Arab traders, Indian school boys and Africans
in smart business suits, circulated here and there. Several blind beggars
patiently went up and down the train tapping on compartment windows,
not realizing that practically everybody on the train was strolling along
the platform.

A tree full of white birds stood just beside the station. There must have
been hundreds of birds all over it so that it seemed loaded with big
white blossoms. In the uncertain light, it seemed to me that these were
souls of slaves come back to haunt the place of their dying.

For Tabora has a long and iniquitous history. For a hundred years and
more, it was a main stop on the Arab slave trade route. Here ivory and
slaves from the north, around Lake Victoria, met ivory and slaves coming
from the west. Here the Congo products from across Lake Tanganyika
were re-packed and re-evaluated. Here the chiefs of African tribes brought
their prisoners of war to sell them to Arab slavers. Intertribal wars were
a rich source of slaves. For that reason, the traders were not slow to foment
trouble among tribes. Estimates say that forty thousand slaves a year came
here. Four out of five of them died between Tabora and Arabia. But
even so it was profitable, for a slave worth twenty to fifty shillings in
Zanzibar brought one hundred and twenty shillings in Arabia. The Africans have a proverb, "When the piper pipes in Zanzibar, the people
near the lake dance." The slave markets in Zanzibar decided whether the
tribes around Lake Victoria would live in peace or not.

We said good-bye to Oscar here. Oscar is a handsome boy, about fourteen, with white teeth, chocolate brown skin, beautiful English and a
load of artistic talent. He is in Middle School near Dar es Salaam and
travels to his home in Albertville in the Congo. It takes about ten days
if he can get a boat across the lake in time. Oscar and his family have
a struggle to make ends meet. They dress as best they can, practice good
manners and cultivate resourcefulness. Someday, please God, Oscar will
be a force for good in Tanganyika.

"There's Whiskers with his foot on the bottom step," said Sister Juan

Maria. Oscar ran off to his section of the train due to head west; we hurried into our own part bound for the north. We were due in Shinyanga at 2:30 A.M.

Bishop Edward McGurkin is one of the highlights of Maryknoll. He stands 6' 4" in his episcopal boots and, with a mitre on top of that, he is impressive as the Empire State Building is impressive. In the dead of night on Shinyanga's casual railroad station, he wore neither. But he could look over the intervening populace and get quickly to where we were struggling with bags and boxes. We kissed his ring, greeted the Sisters and went home to bed.

The official population of the Sukuma tribe is:

1,000,000 Africans;

2,000,000 cows.

The cow figure does not mean cows, entirely. Officially, five sheep or goats equal one cow. This is the scale set in the exchange of cows when they are used for money.

The African loves his cows. He knows each one. If one is stolen he can identify it among thousands. There was a fellow in Shinyanga who lost a cow and, five years later, identified the hide stretched over a seat in the thief's house. However, lest the law not recognize such identification, some farmers notch the cows' ears in fancy designs. It serves as a brand.

The Shinyanga District, or "Shinyanga County" as we would call it, is ruled by 15 kings. A beautiful $90,000 building was erected where each king has a ceremonial chair. He is in charge of about twenty villages and appoints a headman in each. Kings must work for their jobs. They are responsible for collecting taxes, judging minor cases, settling disputes and making minor laws. They also build primary schools and maintain dispensaries in their territories. It used to be that Europeans in the Education Department could attend the Kings' meetings whenever they discussed schools. Not now. Europeans are not invited and have no right to speak at these meetings.

Shinyanga, which literally means "a manure heap under the baobab tree," is nevertheless quite a prosperous area. The major crop is cotton; most of it is sent to the United Kingdom or India for weaving. In spite of the fact that all Tanganyika is clothed in bright-colored cotton cloth, there is but one weaving factory in the whole of East Africa and that is in Uganda. However, I understand the farmers do quite well selling cotton through cooperatives, managed locally.

Theoretically, all land belongs to the chieftain and he can force its return at any time. But in practice, it is as if every man owned his own cotton patch. Hides and aromatic gum are also produced. Many told me, "Nobody is starving in Shinyanga."

Shinyanga market is fascinating. I squandered seven cents on five beautiful big mangoes at 1.4 cents each. It was the mango season; every tree around was laden. The market is a large open square with the entire area, you might say, paved with mangoes. Around the edges were stalls with just about everything—housewares, dried up cow skins, little heaps of peanuts at ten cents African (about 1½ cents) a heap, new wooden pounders for grain, sieves made of wicker and gaudy jewelry guaranteed to last all of ten minutes.

Many a seller squatted beside a small camp stool; displayed on the canvas seat was crudely dried tobacco, matted into hard lumps almost like putty. You could buy a big or little hunk of this or, if you were new fangled, you could buy a single puff of a foreign cigarette. A gay young blade, dressed in bright green trousers and heavy black coat like an undertaker's, bent over the camp stool, picked up the cigarette, took one long draw, pressed a coin into the seller's hand and walked over to a counter to get a hot meal of boiled peanuts.

The meat stalls were fascinating. Have you ever seen the fur stores in lower Manhattan? Iron mesh and double locking doors make life very difficult for hold-up men. In Shinyanga, the meat stalls are fortified with wire mesh and screening. Also, the easy way those butchers swing their cleavers would make a marauder think twice. Business is done as with a bank teller—through a small window in the fortifications. You line up at the window, point to the part of the animal you wish, and hope for the best. The butcher tells the boy to hack off the piece as it hangs from an iron hook. Then he stoops to the floor, picks up an empty cement bag, shakes it out a bit and wraps your meat in it. This is one way to get a hard crust on meat without using flour.

There is a parish, St. Mary's, across the street from the market. Father Smidlein at 6' 5" looks down even on Bishop McGurkin. His parish in this city of less than three thousand occupies a spruce collection of buildings—church, rectory, parish hall, and a smallish building on the main street bearing the sign, "St. Mary's Reading Room." It is the only library facility between Tabora, one hundred and sixteen miles south, and Mwanza, one hundred and four miles north. Even at St. Mary's, books may not be borrowed; anyone who wants to read may come in and sit down quietly.

Most of the books are in English, for English is a passion in Africa now. Two young men were hunched over a table. I peeked over their shoulders. One was reading Common Errors in English; the other, How to Write Letters in English.

Sister James Eileen holds forth in the parish hall lined with posters in Kiswahili. They show clean houses and dirty houses; clean yards and dirty yards; good food for children and things they should not eat; how to avoid the common fly and the fearsome malaria mosquito. But I happened to be there on a sewing day. Women with bare shoulders and arms, wearing their bright kangas bound tightly under the arms, bent their shaven heads over nice little dresses for children. Sister has a system of combining several scraps of material and getting a baby's dress or even a woman's skirt and blouse. She gets samples and remnants from the Indian merchants. The whole effort is to improve living conditions in African homes, showing that one need not be rich to be healthy and wear attractive clothes.

Sister commutes to town every morning, driving the little German car, an Opel, from the suburbs, three miles out. This is Buhangija—literally "The Place You Don't Pass By" or "A Stopping Place." Bishop McGurkin is here and his episcopal throne in our little church is almost as lofty as himself. Besides the "cathedral," this compound has several small buildings, a Primary School for two hundred and fifty boys and girls, a Middle School for one hundred and fifty boys and a very new Middle School for Girls, just beginning. Also a dispensary where Sister Ann Geraldine carries on the healing arts and a school for catechists.

The convent is still in the pitcher and basin stage of mission development. And a highly comfortable stage it is, too. For a shower, you lock yourself up in a really palatial shower room with cement floor. Rather, it would be palatial were it not also a storage room for soaps and toilet supplies, extra ladders, pitchers not used right now, several stools and a locked cabinet containing something only the Superior knows. You lock yourself in this chamber of mystery and steel yourself to tackle the thing that hangs from a rafter. It is a pail of water with a hole in the bottom, a pipe coming from the hole, a faucet attached to the pipe and a showerhead at the end of the faucet. By standing on tip-toe, you can fumble the faucet around and get a trickle of water. The soaping-up process is a time of deep prayer. "Please let the water last until I get this soap off." The water runs across the room and out a small hole in the corner where it escapes into the great out-of-doors and helps to water the lawn.

In the Shinyanga area, you can't help but be careful with water. Every drop of it is brought in a wheelbarrow from a quarter-mile distance in four-gallon "debbies," originally meant for gasoline and kerosene. I was there in December; the rains were three weeks overdue. Fields were dry; everything was withering; the trees hung limp; roads were choking dust. Cattle did not care if they lived or died. Mother Mary Colman was introduced to people of the parish. "Mother is from New York," said the Sisters in Kisukuma. An old man leaned toward Mother and said with such concern in his voice, "Tell me, Mother, have the rains come in New York yet?" Another asked, as he would ask any traveler in Africa, "What is the food situation in New York?"

Many were praying for rain; others would just as soon have it stay off for a while. These latter are building houses. Made of mud brick, they are apt to slough off and collapse in rain. Most of our convents are mud brick, too, but they are covered with a layer of cement, which helps.

Shinyanga has no electricity. We use pressure lamps and Aladdins which burn kerosene. They're good for the health. If anything will get you to bed early and insure a proper eight hours' rest, it's a kerosene lamp burning hot and humid in a town 3½ degrees below the equator. A half-hour under its benign influence and you say to it, "All right, you win. I'll go to bed and finish this in the morning."

The convent stove is wood-burning, coming from Montgomery Ward three years ago for $120. It's marvellous. You keep stuffing wood into a small compartment at the side and it heats four burners, an oven and a huge hot-water well. Shinyanga boasts a kerosene iron, too, which the Sisters claim far surpasses an electric iron. One can't be sure that this is the plain unvarnished truth; I find that missioners are apt to think their country has the very best of everything. It's an occupational failing, evidently.

But if Shinyanga mission doesn't have modern conveniences, it has beauty. Siamese cats are all over the place—all descendants of the original Hannibal and Mabel which Father Brannigan brought with him in 1954. We have their daughter Mitzi at Shinyanga and, more or less as a permanent guest, old Hannibal himself, who has worn out his welcome at the rectory and slips over to the convent for comfort. All the out-stations of Shinyanga diocese have a plethora of Siamese cats; the record so far is Sayu-Sayu where nine of them dispute ownership of the rectory with two priests and a Brother.

On a First Friday morning, I knelt in the back of church for the High Mass. Women stayed strictly on the left; men on the right. The church was crowded. The women were wrapped in their kangas—those large squares of bright cloth covered with pictures and lettering. One showed a motor bike in the center of her back; under the picture was the word in large letters, S C O O T E R. Another had Kiswahili words meaning EVERYBODY LOVES SATURDAY NIGHT. A blue and yellow one said, AFRICA IS YOUR COUNTRY.

The kanga is Tanganyika's billboard. If ever Madison Avenue wanted to sell an idea or product there, they would be smart to give away kangas bearing advertisements.

Patriotism has already used the medium. Julius Nyerere's picture adorns many a kanga; the map of Tanganyika walks down the street; the national flag, the national emblem, the national animal (the twiga or giraffe), and many a patriotic motto are displayed to edify the populace as an African woman shops in the market.

One of the women in church kept her kanga wrapped securely around her head. She is Laurentina. A year ago, she and her husband staggered past our convent having a knockdown-and-drag-out brawl. They had imbibed too freely of beer. The next morning Sister Ann Geraldine was called to see Laurentina. The side of her head was a bloody mess. "My husband bit my ear off," she told Sister without much emotion. "And what's worse, I can't find the ear so that you can sew it back on."

"Never mind," said Sister. "It would not do much good anyway."

Laurentina came to the convent every day for dressings. On the fourth day, she brought a withered piece. It was the ear; she had found it on the floor. "Please sew it on again," she begged.

The wound healed in time. Laurentina was eternally grateful. Both she and her husband promised never to drink or battle again. Now they are model Legion of Mary members.

It was only some months later that Sister connected Laurentina with a woman whom she had rushed to the town hospital for a premature baby about a year before. The baby weighed only two pounds and died in a few days. But she was baptized Ann Geraldine. Maybe little Ann Geraldine won this grace of real conversion for her parents.

I noticed another woman in church that First Friday. Blind Juliana. With assurance, she tied her baby on her back and led her small son up to the altar rail for Holy Communion. "She never needs help," says Sister Joan Michel. "Really doesn't like it at all."

She has a story, too. Some years ago Sister had noticed this blind woman passing in front of the convent on her way to market. She told her Legion of Mary group about her. "She might need a little help in the house," she suggested.

Two neighbors responded. They offered to sweep her house and draw her water at least once a week. Juliana let loose. "Get out!" she said. "I'll sweep my own house, if you don't mind." The ladies withdrew.

But she came around to the convent to see what it was all about. Sister explained. "A good idea," said Juliana. "I'll join the Legion." She had to become a Catholic first, of course.

To start, Juliana's assignments as a Legion member were easy. She did them and made up some of her own. "I pounded a sick woman's grain for her," she reported several times.

Susanna was there, too. She sat in front of me, all absorbed in the Mass, singing her heart out. The Ordinary has been translated into Kisukuma and the people sing it to Gregorian Chant. These magnificent voices roll out the age-old melodies with all the strength of Faith new born and vigorous, strong enough to raise the roof and carry us all on a cushion of sound straight to the Pearly Gates.

Susanna is tattooed; a blackish line runs down her forehead and nose

as if she had been split apart and sewed together again. The design is like
the stitches on a baseball. She used to be a witch doctor. "Oh, Susanna
is just the nicest person! We all love her!" says Sister Juan Maria.

After Mass we had Benediction. With the Blessed Sacrament exposed,
four men who had acted as cantors during the Mass, stood up and chanted
in Kisukuma:

"What do we do when we see Our Chief?"

The whole church stood up. Clapping their hands, they bowed—the
men bending at the waist, the women crossing their ankles and sinking
to the ground. This is the deep obeisance reserved only for the highest
kings.

Saturday is clean-up day for the Middle School boys at Shinyanga. At
rosary next day, my eye caught a lad draped in a once-white cloth with
the corners tied around his neck halter style, walking up the main aisle
in church. Then in came another and another. Most of the boys wore
khaki uniforms. Who were these apparitions in white? Well, it seems the
church bell had caught them in the process of washing their one and
only pair of shorts and shirt. So, not having a barrel to jump into, they
wrapped themselves in their bedsheet and came along. They have only
one sheet and it's skimpy. It serves as pajamas as well, and also ironing
board.

Later, we walked over to the Middle School to observe the process at
close range. Some one hundred and fifty boys were in their dining room,
a large open shed, ironing their Sunday suits. The process was complicated.
They spread a sheet, folded many times, on the concrete floor, making
sure the pad was smooth. They heated a charcoal iron. Then, on the floor,
they ironed their shirt and pants very, very carefully, shifting on their
knees around the ironing pad. Small wonder they look like Eton scholars
when they come to Sunday Mass!

The Shinyanga diocese is in the heart of Sukumaland. The Wasukuma
are by far the largest tribe in Tanganyika, twice as large as the Nyamwezi,
runner-up at less than half a million people. Their territory in the Lake
Victoria Province covers six districts, a matter of twenty thousand square
miles, twice as large as Massachusetts. The Sukuma tribe were very con-
servative until recently, but are now awakening to leadership, politics,
and the possibility of bettering themselves economically.

Their soil is poor; it can support only one person per $3\frac{1}{2}$ acres, or
one hundred people and one hundred and eighty-two cows to a square
mile. The Sukumaland Development Scheme has done much to restore
fertility to much of the territory. Better farming methods and grazing
schemes, the building of small dams to conserve what water there is, and
the use of imported bulls for breeding are slowly making the Sukuma

tribesman aware of what the future can hold for him. The program is under local authorities and is paid for by local taxation.

We drove out to Busando in the little Opel, fifteen miles along a washboard road which can shake the very breakfast out of you. Sister Bridget Maureen put her foot hard on the gas; she claims that at a good speed you hit only the high spots of the road. Sounds good, but I hit some pretty low ones, too.

This is Father Daly's mission, he who once trekked in the New York area. The subway rush was no fit training for this. In Busando there is plenty of space and nobody much to put into it. But Father's sights are set over the horizon where many a Sukuma hut dots his far-flung parish.

With him is Father Bergwall. A young M.D. from Marquette, he went to Maryknoll and was ordained. Just about a month later, trouble with one leg was diagnosed as muscular dystrophy. Knowing well the future, Father went on to Africa to use as priest and doctor what mobility is left to him. I found him full of plans and ideas. With a cane he walked around to show us his small leprosarium. He finds it hard to convince Africans that steady treatment is needed to cure or arrest leprosy. Their only concern is to get the sores healed for the present. He dismisses his own troubles and says he will get along pretty well with a golf cart his friends in Milwaukee told him they would send for Christmas.

Sister Bridget Maureen is one of those perky little Sisters who can whip any class into shape. The day I saw her in action at Busando she had quite a class. They were about 20 men catechists in all stages of outlandish dress. She had them lined up like kindergarteners learning a song:

> I am not like a stone; I can say Thank You to God.
> I am not like a river; I can say Thank You to God.
> I am not even like a cow; I can say Thank You to God.
> Thank You, Thank You, Thank You, God!

The men loved it. With the African genius for on-the-spot variations, that song was made into a full-blown choral for male voices in no time. It is so easy to see how the Negro has enriched American music and deepened our contemplation of God with spirituals. Long ago, the Church learned that the same words, repeated slowly and often, stretch the soul far beyond the world's narrow vise.

Sister Ann Geraldine meanwhile took herself to a tiny house of mud brick with about twenty-five women and girls. They were to learn simple hygiene and sewing. All African women want to make Western clothes. So Sister spread some gay material out on the concrete floor, put a pattern on top of it and then cut around the edges, walking on her knees as she did so. Try it, sometime. It does wonders for your arthritis.

Sister took the roll call. "Three of my girls are not here today," she said. "They weren't here last week, either. They went to attend a wedding."

If you want a real fuss over your marriage, come to Africa! A young girl, when she starts to mature, goes into seclusion in the house and her grandmother instructs her on the duties of marriage. No one but the grandmother can do this. Emmanuel, a man we know at Morogoro, had to take his daughter Konstansia seventy-five miles to his home town, so that she could stay with his mother during this time.

The girl does nothing at all; she is not to work, nor to play, nor even to leave the room. She is just to sit still and eat. The child gets to be the size of a house. In some places, she is forbidden even to walk. We saw a man on the road once, a little bit of a man, carrying his daughter, who was chubby to put it mildly.

After six months, a big "coming-out party" is held and the girl emerges into sunshine. The father is now open to offers from young men around. This is the time for bargaining. Around Nyegina, the papas are so grasping that brides are out of price range for most young men; they are getting their brides from other tribes. Which leaves the Nyegina girls stranded. Prices vary, but you can usually get a good Christian wife in Shinyanga for sixteen cows. Up in Rosana where people are rich, the price is thirty-five.

The payment of cows is required by the government to make the marriage legal. Ten cows is the minimum but few girls want to marry for so low a price. Who wants to be known as a ten-cow bride?

Cow payments are approved by the Church, too. It makes the marriage stable. Fortunately, in Tanganyika, a girl has a good deal to say about the marriage. It is not at all a case of being sold for so many cows; she can put her foot down and usually Papa pays attention to her. But if she agrees to the marriage and then, after the ceremony, runs away from her husband, Papa sends her back. Otherwise he would have to return to his son-in-law the very same cows he was paid. Papa doesn't like that. Besides, probably those identical cows have already been paid out for his son's brides. Sometimes, five or six marriages would have to be re-adjusted so that the cow with the brown spot could go back to her original owner. What price divorce!

Marriages are not casual, even though they may be based on very little courtship, as we know it. Not long ago, a young soldier from the Royal African Rifles, stationed in Shinyanga, came to the mission asking if we could get him a good Christian wife. Sister James Eileen went to

Agnesi, a good girl and still unattached at twenty. Agnesi agreed and her parents agreed. Then the meeting took place.

Agnesi braided her hair almost out of her scalp and arrayed herself in her gayest kanga. She and her parents came to the mission. Up drove the mission car with Father and Damianus the soldier.

"This is Agnesi, Damianus." Agnesi turned her back to them all. Damianus looked at her and walked into the mission office. In a few minutes, Father emerged.

"Damianus agrees," he said. It was over and both parties prepared for a bang-up wedding.

After the ceremony, all the guests repair to the bride's home and the feasting begins. It may last a week or more. Then the guests go to the groom's house and start all over again. The only way they know it's time to go home, is when the cow's feet are served. That means there isn't anything left.

Recently a touchy case for the Church came up. The bride's father killed a cow, maybe two, and put on a big spread. He was a pagan, but his wife and daughter were Christians. After much feasting, the wedding party repaired to the groom's house. Horrors! The groom's father had killed only a goat.

Enraged, the bride's father went out of the house and took with him the bridal party, including the bride but excluding the groom. He killed another cow to show that he, at least, was a good host.

For a while it was nip-and-tuck as to whether this marriage would ever get going. But in time Father was able to start the young couple on the right foot.

Cows are estimated at $50.00 each. The exchange of even ten cows is quite a contract; a Wakuria bride bringing thirty-five cows can make or break the family fortune.

But the cow economy brings difficulties to the Church. If a man has many daughters and few sons, he accumulates so many cows his own wife is overburdened with work. He is severely tempted to buy another wife for himself. There is really nothing else for him to spend his cows for. His old wife urges him to get a younger woman, too. It divides the work in the fields and gives her companionship.

Christianity's stand for monogamy accounts somewhat for the success of Mohammedanism in Africa. The Biblical custom of a man taking his dead brother's wife obtains. It is understandable. It gives the woman a home and tribal standing; it gives her children a new father. The laws of the Church are hard to make clear.

African village life is set up for polygamy. Wives seem to live together with no more arguments than other women. The husband apparently plays no favorites or, if he does, it is his first wife. Everyone else accords her first place in the household. Many a time, a young woman comes to our maternity hospital at Kowak, and with her will be the faithful First Wife to help as best she can this Second, Third or Fourth Wife.

However, outside influences are seeping through Africa fast. Young men in towns are a little ashamed of polygamy. They know that the rest of the world looks down on it. It is a "backward" trait, they read. Also, in the towns, it's not so easy to have another wife. She is an expense, not an economic asset. In the country, a man can put up another house with very little trouble; in the city, he would have to pay rent.

The old folks, however, have real trouble understanding monogamy. A hoary tribesman listened carefully to the instruction on marriage as Sister explained it. Then she summed the lesson up.

"Supposing a man married the widow of his dead brother and later met a woman he liked and married her also. Which is his real wife?" she asked.

The old African pondered some time. He raised his head. "The wife he married first; the one who belonged to his brother. She is the real wife," he said.

"What about the other one?" Sister asked.

"The wife he married because he liked her—she is not the Real Wife. She is the Very Real Wife."

Sister sighed and started all over again.

⧼ 3 ⧽ Young Nation, Young Leaders

"Ach!" Bishop Joseph Blumjous pulled on his long extinct cigar and ran his fingers through his almost extinct hair. "I told a priest what I am going to do and he wrote to me, 'We did not do things this way ten years ago.' So I wrote back to him, 'If you expect to do things in Africa as they were done ten years ago, my boy, then you are a hundred years out of date.' "

We were sitting on the edge of a cement porch overlooking Lake Victoria. There was no railing around the porch; if one stepped off he would drop twenty feet to rocks below. But the Bishop seems to like to live dangerously. He does not go in for settled security. Someone of our party said to him, overlooking the small city he has built on the heap of giant boulders the government gave him, "This is quite a step you have taken, my lord."

The Bishop of Mwanza laughed a laugh which shook all through his loose white cassock straight down to the mud-stained boots which had tramped through fields all afternoon. "A step?" he questioned. "I'm not afraid of taking long steps provided I think they are forward steps."

Indeed, he is not. And results prove it.

Although White Fathers have been in Tanganyika since 1878, the society's main effort for the Church was in Uganda. Priests visited the southern end of Lake Victoria sporadically whenever possible. Not until 1930 was a diocese established in Mwanza, port city at the southern tip of the lake. There were twelve thousand Catholics then scattered over an area that took in practically all the northwest corner of the country. Lack of personnel and transportation kept the numbers low. In 1946, Bishop Blumjous was consecrated and took possession of his huge see. In the last ten years, Catholics have reached the seventy-five thousand mark and some fifty thousand catechumens are studying. The course before Baptism extends over four years. Together, they make up about thirteen percent of the population.

"These people are the solid peasant type," the Bishop explains. "They're not poor. They are very conscious of the forces changing Africa today. They want a 'dini,' a religion. And we have it for them."

We had had an appointment with the Bishop at 4 P.M. that afternoon, but a flat tire made it all of 5 P.M. before we drove up to the seminary at Nyegezi, just outside Mwanza. This is the center house in a fantastic collection of rocks like huge pebbles which some prehistoric stream has tumbled down and left piled up. The seminary, which serves as Bishop's residence, priest's retreat house, chancery offices and whatever else is needed at the time, is surrounded by many other smaller buildings to house other projects of the Bishop's fertile brain. They are all put here and there on rocks, sometimes hiding behind them, sometimes set right on top of them.

We had hardly pulled the brake when the door was flung open with all the episcopal energy Bishop Blumjous is noted for. He came down the stairs in welcome, with his cassock flying and his small pectoral cross all a-flutter, glinting in the equatorial sun.

Have tea! It was a man's household. The Bishop waved us to a huge room lined with books. The shelves were neatly labeled—Theology, Missiology, Church History, Biography, etc. There were German and French, Italian, English and Latin books. Some were ancient tomes; some had shining wrappers, just published. In a magazine rack were the latest in American magazines, Catholic or secular, as well as African, Dutch, German and English magazines.

In the center of this library was a table taken, surely, from the Mad Hatter's Tea Party in *Alice in Wonderland*. A white cloth decorated one end and an assortment of tea cups and plates was scattered on it. A plate of cheese, a loaf of bread on a wooden platter, tin cans of condensed milk, a pot of some sort of jam.

"Join me for tea!" said the Bishop, waving his hand and chewing his cigar furiously. So we did. One of us poured the tea, another cut the bread, somebody else started on the cheese. We served others and helped ourselves. No ceremony at all. The Bishop in gay good humor laughed a hearty Dutch laugh throughout. A bearded White Father with a rosary around his neck joined us. Several others passed through without a word. "They are all on retreat," the Bishop explained.

The delightful, informal tea—which was really a hearty Dutch lunch —ended. We went out to our miniature car and the five of us plus the Bishop squeezed in. The Bishop waved from right to left, pointing out the new Social Hall, the new Domestic Science School, the dormitories, the buildings meant for the School of Social Development. All are concrete block, one-story, painted blue and pink and faint purple. All have shining—yea, blazing—aluminum roofs.

"The road, Sister! You're going past it!" called the Bishop. To Sister's credit, be it said that the road was barely discernible with the naked eye. Just a faint track across the tumbled rocky terrain. We jostled along it for a while until we came to an open field. Quite a surprise in this country of piled-up boulders. "Stop!"

We all got out. Waving his walking stick, Bishop Blumjous pointed here and there into thin air. "This is the two-story classroom building; over there is the dormitory; the dining room is here and the kitchen is right behind it. Over by that clump of bushes is the convent."

A man of vision—almost, of visions—he could see it all. Then he ran over to a space bare of grass. "Like this!" He grasped his walking stick with both hands and used it as a pencil. Scoring the dry earth, he drew a ground plan of all the buildings and floor plans of most of them. "The front entrance is here. The second floor goes like this. The roof will jut out here to form a shaded area, etc., etc." He was showing off Rosary-College-to-be.

"Date for opening? Six weeks from today. Buildings up? Well, none at present but you can use some I have for another project until yours are up."

Here is a man of immense vitality. He feels Africa pulsing beneath his feet. He sees young Africa with its mouth open, thirsting for education, equality, status among nations, independence and God. He is ready with something to put into that open mouth.

His School for Social Development is meant to train two hundred lay people—married couples and single men and women—in the Church's principles of social action. A two-year course taken right there at Nyegezi should make them spokesmen for the Church in labor unions, legislatures, factories and business offices.

A few years ago, Bishop Blumjous looked over the streets of Mwanza, filled with Indian shops and Indian residences. He could never reach these people except through prayer. That's it, prayer! He brought in a convent of Poor Clares from India so they would pray for the Moslem people in his diocese.

Rosary College is another long step forward. A Secondary School for girls, it should give many of them a chance to be educated women, able to take part in Tanganyika affairs and perhaps in the world's.

A young country uses young people. Julius Nyerere, the leader, is not yet forty. Bishop Otunga when he was appointed in 1957 was thirty, the youngest bishop in the world. Women too can change overnight from school girls to national figures. For instance, Mary Kasindi, now a scholarship student at St. Mary's, Indiana. She was one of the first women to go through Standard X, equivalent to our Grade 10, one of the first qualified to teach Middle School, and at twenty-two she was one of three women in the National Legislative Council, the lawmaking body of Tanganyika. This is her story:

> I was born in Iringa in southern Tanganyika in 1934, and brought up by the Italian Consolata Sisters at the Catholic mission at Tosamaganga. From them I learned Italian; they still write to me in that language. Very young, I started at the mission primary school and had private classes in the afternoon. Middle School followed along easily, also at Tosamaganga. This is one of the oldest Middle Schools for girls in the country, established in 1931.
>
> In 1949, the year I finished Standard VIII, the end of the Middle School, the mission began a girls' Junior Secondary School for Standards IX and X. This and the government school for girls at Mbeya (Loleza) were the first two to open in Tanganyika. Tosamaganga had had a boys' Middle School for many years. There were six of us girls in the first class at Tosamaganga. We and the Mbeya girls were the first African girls to start what you would call High School. Two years later, I finished Standard X, which was as far as any girl could go in Tanganyika. I was the only one of our six who passed the Territorial Examinations.
>
> In January, 1951, I started at the Teacher Training School at Tosamaganga. It was a boys' school and I was alone. So the Government told me to transfer to Mbeya to go on for Teacher Training. We were the pioneer class at Mbeya. I was there for three years; only nine of us finished out of the fifteen or so who began. How proud we were! We were the only women in Tanganyika qualified to teach Middle School. I was nineteen years old.
>
> That was 1953. The next year I taught in a new government school near Mwanza but I asked to return to the mission at Tosamaganga. A Training School for 'Grade Two teachers' had opened—that is, for Standard VIII

graduates who would qualify to teach primary schools. For two years I
taught there.

In 1956 and 1957, I served on the Legislative Council, one of three women
in the sixty-seven-member lawmaking body of the country. The governor
appointed me; I have often wondered how he knew anything about me. I
was then twenty-two years old.

In the Legislature, I realized the need for an intelligent understanding
of government, so the following year I enrolled for a civics course at
Makerere College in Uganda. Then I followed my first love, teaching—
feeling that in the classroom I could best serve God and my country. I went
to the faculty of Marian College with the Maryknoll Sisters. Through them,
I was offered a scholarship by the Holy Cross Sisters at St. Mary's, Indiana.

Education is so new for African girls. The marvel is that they measure
up to it so easily. Some of their facility may be due to women like old
Sister Hildegarda. I heard her story in Mwanza and knelt behind her
at Mass in the White Sisters' convent there. It's a stopping place for our
Sisters who often have to come to Mwanza for shopping or dental attention or whatnot. The White Sisters, with real missioners' hospitality,
throw open their doors to us at all times.

I knelt in one of the back pews of the white-washed chapel at Mwanza.
In front of me was a wheelchair; over the back of it, I saw the hunched
shoulders and low head of Sister Hildegarda, eighty-nine years old. A
German prayerbook with very large type was in her hands. She tried
to read it with a magnifying glass. And it seemed to me that an aura of
history glowed around that wheelchair.

I learned her story from Sister Matthea who apologized for not knowing it all. "I've been here only thirty-two years," she said. "So there is
much I don't know."

Sister Hildegarda entered the White Sisters' convent in Holland in
1893. A year later, she went to Algiers and there was professed. Not long
after came the call for Sisters to go to the Congo. Sister Hildegarda was
one of the first group. In 1894 she landed at Mombasa, lowered in a
basket from the ship to the lighter. There was a large caravan ready to
go inland—traders, missionaries, adventurers. It was mostly a walking
job—nearly a thousand miles. But they made it all the way to Baudouin-
ville in the Belgian Congo across Lake Tanganyika.

Sister was sick much of the way and she got no better as the years
passed. So it was decided she should go back to Europe, and off she started
again on the long, long safari to the coast. But they stopped at Ushirombo
where the Sisters had an orphanage and school. And then to Mwanza.
In 1907, Sisters were needed at Tabora, the old slave trading market
and Hildegarda asked to go. It meant walking all the way. Even so, she
wanted to volunteer. So off they started on foot. It took three weeks to

go the two hundred and forty miles in 1907, for the railroad had not been completed on the northern branch which now runs to Mwanza.

In Tabora the main work was ransoming slaves. The Sisters used to buy girls from the traders. Then, when women slaves in town saw the healthy fine girls the Sisters were teaching, they were incited to run away. And when their masters came to settle with the Sisters, the women pleaded, "You should not ask much for me, master. I'm very old. I have no teeth." It was all illicit slave traffic but the arm of the law often did not reach to Tabora inland.

Often, too, the Sisters were asked to treat women in the harems of the Arabs. There were double locks on these enclosures.

In 1914, at the outbreak of World War I, Sister Hildegarda was on Ukewere, a large island in Lake Victoria. Here she was in charge of a leprosarium. She was regarded as a doctor, so clever was she at treating the lepers. She was not interned as other Germans were. For twenty-five years she stayed on Ukewere and even now, the Sisters at Mwanza tell me, her old patients and the children born in the leprosarium come to Mwanza to see her.

In 1939, she was too old to continue. Her legs were bothering her and she came back to Mwanza. However, she still insisted on walking into the mountains to visit people, scrambling up and down the rocks to huts of people she knew. A bad fall put an end to that and, after she was brought back to the convent, she never went out on mission safaris again.

Sister Hildegarda sat hunched in her wheelchair in chapel with her feet up on a stool. Her old eyes tried desperately to see through cataracts, to read the old German prayers in the big type. Her mouth drooped open often as she took a little cat nap in the presence of her Lord. In sixty-seven years in Africa she had never gone back to Europe. I almost genuflected as I passed in front of her to leave the chapel.

Mwanza is important. There is the breath of a big city there. The shops are full of imports—soap, cosmetics and machines from the States; candy and cotton cloth from England; toys and gimcracks from Japan. In the streets you see the Indians, British, Americans and occasional Arabs done up with wooly turbans. They are the "gypsies" of Africa; they live in closed villages with high walls. Suspicion points to them for kidnappings, shady deals, stealthy safaris at night.

With a population of only about fifteen thousand, Mwanza is still the largest city on the southern end of Lake Victoria. Here, you jump off for the hinterlands. Missioners pack their jeeps full for the long months of rainy season when roads are impassable. Here wealthy sportsmen make up safaris into the Serengeti Plains for wild animal hunting. Here, tour-

ists who are "doing Africa" pick up the darling-est souvenirs. Lake
boats discharge crew and passengers here. Local chieftains gather at
Mwanza. Engineers from the Williamson Diamond Mines, largest in the
world, drop in for a few days' respite and then go back to Shinyanga.
For Mwanza, they tell you, has everything: electricity, telegraph, wire-
less, telephone, an airfield and a water supply. It has a hotel, a good
garage and three banks. Certainly, more than any other town in the entire Lake Province.

We were very conscious of all we left behind in Mwanza as the Opel
chugged along the washboard road which leads north along the Lake.
We were to meet the Sisters from the north on "the road." That's odd,
isn't it? You don't see every car passing on a road. What if a truck
should hide it? What if . . . Nonsense! said the Sisters from the south.
We'll see the car a long way off. It will probably be the only one we
will pass on "the road." What if they come by another road? That
brought a big laugh.

Out here one can easily see how Padre Serra founded the California
missions in a string along Camino Real. The missions make the road
and the road makes the missions. This single road, one hundred and
thirty-four miles between Musoma and Mwanza, is the only road a jeep
or car can navigate in the whole area. Foot paths and small spurs lead
off to a mission or a mine or a cotton ginnery but when one speaks of
"the road" one means this single artery. For miles it plays hide and seek
with the Lake.

Nassa is, of course, on this main road. The mission (which seems to be
all there is to Nassa) surmounts a hill at the end of one of those little
cut-offs. Indeed, we cut off right across the fields, following a foot path
which eventually broadened enough to permit all four wheels to operate
on roadway.

At Nassa, we met a subversive agent—one Father Ganley who did his
best to deflect Maryknoll Sisters, due to come to Nassa, to his mission
at Malili instead. It was fascinating to watch his insidious tactics. Like
a study of crime. He had come as a visitor the night before, extending
the hand of friendship to Father Bayless of the Nassa mission.

When Mother Mary Colman arrived and we started out to look at
the site for the new convent, Father Ganley readied his sniping guns.

"Look at these paths, Mother," he said. "All rough and pebbly. Now,
at Malili, we expect to put in cement paths if we get Sisters."

And the view. "Lake Victoria's all right, Mother. But that's an awful
lot of water to look at all the time. The Sisters might get complexes here.
Malili has a few trees. Oh yes, and lots of wild animals. The Sisters could
have roast rhinoceros every night if they wish."

By this time his host, Father Bayless of the Nassa parish, joined in the game. "Look at those chickens!" he said. "All over the place. You know, Mother, that will be convenient for the Sisters. They can collect their breakfast eggs right on their front porch."

"That's too much work for Sisters, Mother," protested Father Ganley. "You can see that he has no appreciation of the blessing he would have with Sisters. In Malili we have the chickens trained. They come into the kitchen and lay eggs right in the frying pan."

Mother laughed. "You win the prize for tall stories, Father," she said. "But Nassa wins the Sisters."

At Nassa, and again at Tarime later on, we came across the question of building in Africa. Both places were to open in three weeks. Yet Mother was shown several sites to select from and there was desultory talk about what floor plan the houses would follow. Evidently, no one was pressed for time. So Mother said to Sister Margaret Rose, in charge of the work in Africa,

"Sister, we can't let the Sisters go to either place before their house is built."

"Oh, no, Mother."

"And we can't let the girls come before there is an adequate kitchen set up and dormitories, as well as classrooms."

"Of course, Mother."

"But, so far as I can see, nothing has been started yet."

"Well, we have three weeks."

"Three weeks! What is that when you intend to build?"

Sister Margaret Rose laughed easily. "You don't understand Africa, Mother. Out here buildings go up in a week. Father gets some men to come in in the morning and they make mud bricks before evening. Next day, you have your building put up. After that, it's just a matter of whitewash and making partitions and such. Don't worry. We'll be ready."

And they were.

If building is fast, travel is slow. And human weaknesses make it exasperating as well. One learns to keep his temper well in hand. Trailing along a road out there, we were stopped by an elderly Englishman in Bermuda shorts. He stood beside his car on the roadside.

"I say, can you spare a bit of oil?" he said.

Sister started to fuss around in the back of our station wagon but we had no extra oil.

"So sorry to trouble you!" the gentleman exclaimed. "Please don't bother. Someone might be along soon. You see, I had the car in the garage and had all the oil drained. But the boy forgot to put any new oil in."

"How did you get this far?" Sister asked.

"That's it, I shouldn't have. But I never thought to look at the thermometer until it was too late. Now never mind about me, Sisters. Someone will surely come."

We had to go on. But once we got to our destination thirty miles further on, Sister got an extra can of oil and went back in the gathering dusk to see if our friend was still there. Sure enough, he had waited for hours and no one had come.

The ferries slow up traffic considerably in Tanganyika's northwest. As we approached one river, the Sisters groaned that it might mean a four hour delay. The river itself was only about forty feet wide, but the wretched little ferry could take only one car at a time. You waited your turn—that was all. However we found—wonder of wonders!—a bridge of young trees had been constructed. We zipped across in no time.

The ferry across Mara Bay in Lake Victoria is a matter of seven men sitting on boards across a low gutter, pulling on a wire cable with their bare hands. They can take two cars or one bus at a time and the trip back and forth takes about forty-five minutes. If there are four cars lined up ahead of you, you can count on twiddling your thumbs for an hour and a half. There were two buses and three cars ahead of us, as we drove up to the landing place. We could amuse ourselves for three hours as we waited.

The other car which was to share the ferry with us, was a Land Rover midget pick-up truck. All of these people were in it: four girls, an older woman, an African man, two African boys, and three Indian men, one quite old, who restrained his voluminous beard by a hair net. These eleven had gone to Nairobi from Shinyanga, a distance of at least five hundred miles over fantastic roads, and were now returning again. What would make them go through that kind of Purgatory? A wedding in the family. They had been on the way for three days and expected to spend three more before they reached home.

As we waited, they asked to borrow our pump. We unpacked the trunk of our car and lent them the pump. They used it. We put it back and repacked our trunk. "Please, may we borrow a jack?" Unpacking. Finding. Giving. Using. Returning. Repacking. "Maybe we should check the batteries. Have you a hydrometer?"

I would have refused out of sheer exasperation. But Sister Marie William turned on him her nicest smile. Without even a grunt, she got out and unpacked again.

At last the ferry was ready for us. We slid down the muddy shore and wobbled on board. The Land Rover got on too, the passengers enjoying their last bit of fresh air. On the other side, the eleven of them crowded into the dark interior of the little pick-up truck.

You would not believe it, but there are cars that even the natives are ashamed of. We have an ancient Citroen in which Sister Noreen Marie drives three miles to Musoma every day for her religion classes or to do shopping. Its springs are so good that when you sit on the front seat, it goes up and down like a bundle of laundry at the end of a spring scale. Every pebble on the road gives you that air-borne feeling. The paint-job, however, leaves much to be desired. Sister Noreen Marie took a young student to Musoma in it to see a doctor. In the meantime, she did some shopping. When she got out of the store she found the car with apparently nobody in it. Then she found the student hiding under the steering wheel, ashamed to be seen in the venerable Citroen.

Beginnings are joyous, people say. Something new happens every day. "Firsts" are all over the place. Tanganyika is in that stage now. They have just attained independence. They were never a nation before; now they are. They are to open their first school of college level soon. The Peace Corps is to survey roads; they never had good roads before. One feels that he is getting in on the ground floor of history.

You can imagine what a commotion St. Benedict stirred up, when he had the fantastic idea of men living together in community to help themselves and others to follow Christ more closely! No one could see then the blessings which would come to Europe from the monasteries he founded—the books preserved, the fields properly tilled, learning and culture saved from the flood of barbarism.

Similarly, you cannot blame these new Catholics for objecting when their daughters say they wish to become Sisters of the Immaculate Heart. Who ever heard of such a thing? After all, a girl in the family may mean thirty or forty cows in dowry. If she goes off to the convent, where is Papa going to get cows to pay for her brother's bride?

In the novitiate at Makoko, where these Sisters are trained in religious life, we hear and see marvellous tales of the power of God's grace. What these girls will go through to keep a vocation is a powerful lesson. I know I would have crumpled up before such opposition.

The Immaculate Heart Sisters began their training in 1948. When two Maryknoll Sisters arrived at Kowak, they found ten girls waiting for them. One was Ethelida. This is her story:

She was born in a "village," that is, a compound where one man and several wives live in a number of circular mud huts around the corral where they keep their animals at night. The family was up-and-coming; they decided to send one of their girls to school with the White Sisters near Mwanza. Ethelida was about four at the time. When her sister returned home several years later, she heard all about the White Sisters.

"I will be a Sister, too," she said.

It was only a childish idea, people thought. She had never seen one and there seemed little chance that she ever would. But when Ethelida was old enough for marriage, she flatly refused. Beaten, whipped, dragged around and even cajoled, she still said she wanted to be a Sister.

"This is too much of a good thing," Papa decided and turned on the heat. Ethelida ran away to Kowak and asked the priest for refuge. The priest, too, thought the child wanted to get away from persecution at home and the mood would pass. There were a number of women living near the mission; they were widows who would be given out to other men if they stayed in their own tribes. One of these was Marsella who is a whole history in herself. The Kowak priest asked Marsella to take care of Ethelida until she gave up the impossible dream and went back home.

It was longer than Father thought. The girl worked hard around the mission, did her best, never complained, was angelic to Marsella and the other women. Five years passed. Then the White Sisters at Mwanza opened a novitiate for African girls. Joyfully, Ethelida packed her belongings and walked three hundred miles to knock on the convent door.

For a time everything went well. She passed several years as a novice and pronounced her vows. But through some technicality, the congregation did not have a proper foundation in canon law. They were told to disband. This threw Ethelida back to Kowak, no more a Sister than if she had never left it.

By this time, however, the Maryknoll Fathers had taken over the parish. They told the disheartened girl that they intended to have a native sisterhood. If she wanted to wait around a little, Maryknoll Sisters might be coming to get it started. Ethelida waited. She was one of the ten who were there in 1948. During this time, her family woke up to the possibility that they might get her back. Her mother was ingenious; she stood outside the gate and called out for hours on end, "Come home! Come home!" Several suitors came to within a few miles of the convent and sent runners with love letters. They offered so many cows that Papa frothed at the mouth. But Ethelida went quietly on with her far from glamorous work. In 1953, she took the first real step into religious life; she was a postulant. Three years later, she pronounced her first vows. After fifteen years of trying, she was at last a Sister.

A big obstacle for most African girls is the education required. Immaculate Heart candidates must be at least Middle School graduates. Their chief work will be teaching; their community language is English. They must know, besides, Kiswahili and their own tribal dialect. If we were to wait until girls with vocations could get through Middle School, or until Middle School graduates got a vocation, we would wait a long time. So at Makoko, we have a Middle School which is open only to girls who think they want to be Immaculate Heart Sisters. Not all will persevere through the many stages before Profession, but a number will go on to serve God in their own diocese of Musoma.

Wonderful to see the happy spirit in these dark-skinned Sisters! Although so much in the world's estimation separates us from them, I felt at home immediately in their neat little convent at Makoko. They began teasing Mother to leave one of the Maryknoll Sisters with them. "You are so many," they reasoned. "We are just new and have so few Sisters."

"Well," said Mother, "I need all my Sisters but if you want one I can spare Sister Maria del Rey best. How many cows are you ready to pay for her?"

They were disappointed, I could see. They had hoped for a sprightly young Sister. At last they came up with a decision.

"We haven't any cows, Mother, to pay for her. But we have two ducks. Only, we would want you to give one duck back to us for Christmas dinner."

I have been insulted in my time, but never sold so cheap. A ten-cow bride was a princess beside me. Two ducks, and one had to be given back for Christmas dinner! I reminded Mother that a duck is not much use carrying hand-luggage into planes and that she had far too much of it to leave me behind. For I *am* good as a porter. So the deal was off.

Immaculate Heart Sisters already staff one school in the diocese—a Primary School at Nyegina. While we were there, a second convent was opened. This was at Zanaki, one of those spurs off "the road." The parish was out in force, oh-ing and ah-ing at the tidy convent where each Sister had her own small cell. The Bishop was there, so were the pastor, catechist, parishioners, school children and many of the breed known as Innocent Bystanders. It was a red letter day for Zanaki. Also for the Immaculate Heart Sisters, for they will be on their own at Zanaki.

The Bishop drove down in a jeep from Musoma, disappeared into the rectory a moment and reappeared shining in his episcopal dignity. Men of the parish had erected a sort of annex to the church, really just a framework covered with leafy branches to fend off the sun; Zanaki is about 1½ degrees below the equator. Early morning saw the footpaths for miles around, alive with family groups trudging to Zanaki. Africans enjoy a party so much they don't mind spending days to get there. As, for instance, our friends at the ferry who thought nothing of Purgatory for two weeks in a pickup truck to attend a family wedding in Nairobi.

There was a Pontifical Mass and a program and speeches. At the end of it all, Sister Consolata, brand new Superior of a brand new convent of a brand new religious congregation, stood up in her sweet simplicity and thanked everybody of the parish. Her mother was there, a tall thin African woman. Years ago, when there was only one church in all of

North Mara, she had brought her children to Mass over the plains. And now there was her daughter, in the grey cotton robes of an Immaculate Heart Sister, standing up to thank people like her mother. The tall spare woman pulled at her pipe in deep satisfaction.

Every missioner feels the same.

⁅ 4 ⁆ *Lake People*

IF you took equatorial Africa and laid it flat across the United States, putting a thumbtack through Dar es Salaam to peg it to Washington, D.C., you would find that the western coast of Africa would stretch approximately from Helena, Montana, through the Great Salt Lake and down to Phoenix, Arizona.

The country of Tanganyika would cover most of the eastern States. The southern border would be on the line which divides Virginia and Kentucky on the north from North Carolina and Tennessee on the south. The northern border of Tanganyika on the north would come on a diagonal from New York to Saulte Ste. Marie in northern Michigan. Lake Tanganyika on the west would be some place around Chicago, and Detroit would fall upon—and smother—Mwanza, the metropolis of 15,000 on the southern end of Lake Victoria.

The Great Lakes of the United States and of Africa divide the honors of the world between them. At 31,000 square miles Lake Superior is the largest body of fresh water in the world; Lake Victoria is runner-up at 26,000. Lake Huron and Lake Michigan are third and fourth; Lake Tanganyika is fifth. Lake Nyassa and Lake Erie are just about the same size; Lake Ontario is not far behind.

So, in Tanganyika when people talk about "the Great Lakes," they have in mind just about the same size of lakes, at just about the same distance from the coastal cities, as our Great Lakes. If you can imagine that Dar es Salaam with its population of 100,000 is New York around 1785, just after the United States became independent, then perhaps you can imagine what the area around Detroit was like at that time. It would give you some idea of the contrast between Dar es Salaam and the "up-country" section around North Mara and Musoma today, just after Tanganyika has emerged as a nation on its own.

Most of our missions are wedged up in this corner of North Mara and Musoma districts. Just across the border are the famous "White Highlands" of Kenya where in the Mau Mau trouble the Africans expressed their feelings against white settlers.

The eastern coast of Tanganyika has been exposed to civilizations almost as long as there have been civilizations to be exposed to. The monsoons, blowing all winter, brought adventurers from Arabia and India, and blew them back home in the summer. As early as 1000 B.C. traders came from India, Egypt, Arabia, Assyria, and Persia. A Greek merchant found the trade in full swing when he ventured down the coast of Africa around 150 B.C.

The fortified towns they put up in Tanganyika still survive to some extent. The greatest was Kilwa. An Arabian chronicler traces it from about 900 until the Portuguese took it early in the 1500's. During that time, Kilwa built up quite a little empire, subduing other Arabian and even Persian settlements on the coast. It gained a foothold on what is now Somaliland, Southern Rhodesia, Mozambique, and eventually Zanzibar. Chinese traders, too, hitched a ride on the monsoons, and came at least as far south as Malindi. Their trading pieces went further. Chinese coins and pottery dating back to A.D. 713 have been found on the coast. There is a record, too, of a giraffe sent as a gift to the Emperor of China in 1414. Just what the Emperor thought of the giraffe and what the giraffe thought of the Emperor have not been recorded. Two treasures of psychology lost!

For well over 2,500 years, then, Asian traders used Tanganyika as a seemingly inexhaustible mine for gold, ambergris, rhinoceros horn, ivory, tortoise shell and slaves. They brought glass, cloth and metal. They planted coconut and sugar cane.

Around 1500, the Portuguese took Kilwa. Their hold was fast and loose for several centuries, leaving the coast open to raids by Arabs, Turkish pirates, Sultans of other African towns, French slave traders, and even a cannibal tribe, the Zimba, who attacked from the land side. The British too were prowling up and down the coast. The Germans got Tanganyika in 1885 and named it German East Africa. There is a story that the boundary between Kenya and Tanganyika was supposed to run due south of Kilimanjaro, the highest and most beautiful peak in Africa, so that the mountain would belong to Kenya. However, Queen Victoria was grandmother of the Kaiser of Germany and she gave him Kilimanjaro for a birthday present. If the original line had been followed, most of the Maryknoll missions would be in Kenya. After World War I, Tanganyika became a British colony; after World War II, it was a mandate of the United Nations entrusted to Great Britain.

Except for very few reports, one made several centuries before Christ, nothing was known of the interior of what is now Tanganyika until 1850. Germans and Arabians penetrated inland at that time. Just how mixed up they were is shown by the famous "slug map," which shows a huge lake, shaped like a slug, in the center of Africa. It is all the great lakes rolled into one. The map wasn't very accurate but it sparked the Great African Grab. By 1914, England, Germany, Italy, France, Portugal, Spain and Belgium had each its own bailiwick in Africa. Only two small nations were independent—Ethiopia and Liberia.

With this background, it is easy to see how Mohammedanism got a very early start in Africa. Small wonder that most Africans, especially those in towns, wear the red fez of Arabia. Christianity in the interior is less than eighty years old even in Uganda, where Catholic missions began. In the Maryknoll section, less than thirty. The first mission in North Mara was in 1933 when a White Father and Brother set up the cross at Butili. How Christian do you suppose the Germans were thirty years after St. Boniface set foot on the land? Or the Slavs when Cyril and Methodius were there just thirty years? Or the Irish when St. Patrick was getting his first white hairs? Growth is slow but steady. As old Elizabetta said at Kowak, "When I was a new Christian ten years ago there were only three or four bicycles outside of church on Sunday. Now we have bicycle racks for them stretching all across the church front."

Even so, there are many many more bicycles at the "pombe market" on Saturday night. This is a drinking party of county-wide proportions. In the center of any fair-sized town, twenty-five 50-gallon drums of potent liquor are set up in an open square known as the "Kulabu," taken from the English "club." Drinking couples lounge around in doorways, up against telephone poles and street lights, or lie on the ground. The African has served in enough Europeans' clubs to know what happens there. So he goes one better at his kulabu.

They also go us one better in their expressions of joy at Baptism. Out at Rosana one afternoon, the studious quiet was shattered by a mighty shout. Thirty adults and heaven alone knows how many children had passed their examinations for Baptism; also twenty children were to make their First Communion. What better way is there known to man to show how happy he is, than to break branches off the trees, toss them about, shout, sing, dance and leap? Old Konstansia took the lead. She sang out, "We will be baptized. We will be children of God." Everyone repeated this and gave a long drawn out "ay-ay-ay!" up three notes and down three notes. Konstansia carried on: "Father has been good; he has taught us well." Again the repeat and the ay-ay-ay!

The dancing went with it; sometimes a simple hop, kick, slide. Sometimes a high leap and a shake of the shoulders. Many quivered the flesh on their shoulders like the wind ruffling water. The sea of laughing faces, moving bodies and green waving branches gave a feeling of joy you never find anywhere else.

Konstansia chanted a compact history of everything that had happened during the six months her group had studied at the mission. The Sisters did so and so; Federiko's father died but we got him to heaven too. Remember the hard questions Father asked? Yes, and the good reply of Francisco!

The ecstatic catechumens danced by Father's office, stopped at the convent and then went shouting, singing, leaping down the road to Edward the catechist's neat grass-roofed house.

I often thought in Africa of that saint who was being hauled off to prison when he met his deacon, St. Lawrence. The deacon protested, "Where are you going without me? Let me go to prison with you." But the older saint replied, "Your turn is coming. Sterner trials await you."

Stern trials await these new Christians. It isn't easy to be a Christian in an African village, hemmed in on every side by pagan rites. We have four tribes in our section, each one with its own customs and language. And none of them very fond of the other tribes. Mission stations are only a few hours apart, but going from one to another means changing language, dress and custom.

Nyegina is the most southern of these up-country missions. Three miles from Lake Victoria, it is still parched for water. Sister Elizabeth Grace was getting desperate as she saw the stored rain water dwindle to four inches, three inches, two inches in the tank. She has a dispensary at Nyegina. Once the water was gone, she would have to hire a boy to go 1½ miles to a water hole where women wash clothes, ducks swim, cows drink and children bathe. He would carry the water in debbies slung on either side of his donkey. That water would have to be boiled, strained, filtered and cooled before it could be used in the dispensary or even in the convent. Such a prospect would make braver hearts quail. Believe me, her prayers for rain were fervent.

Water is the problem even to villages within a stone's throw of the second biggest lake in the world. When one sees the "tanks" or reservoirs built by the ancient people of Ceylon, and the rice terraces of the Ifugao tribe in the Philippines, it is plain that Africa has a long way to go. A common effort for mutual benefit is a new idea; they are beginning now to make small dams for irrigation. Cooperation on the family level is good, however.

I lay on my downy couch in Nyegina, one midnight, and heard right outside my window the crunching of gravel and the slide of calloused feet. Many feet. Men were talking quietly; women muttering. I got up and looked. Then I slipped on my clothes and went out, for I could see Sister Elizabeth Grace in her nurse's uniform in the crowd.

In the moonlight, a party of about twenty Africans was milling around in our small back yard. They had brought a young woman for treatment.

For ambulance, they had fixed up a contraption—two bicycles roped together with short sticks so as to make a four-wheeled frame. A canvas folding chair was slung between the bicycles and on this was the patient.

Two men lifted her off the chair and laid her on the ground. Sister Elizabeth Grace bent over her. Then she straightened and called, "Gabrielli!" A man detached himself from the shadowy figures crouched by the tree.

"Is she your wife, Gabrielli?" Sister asked.

"No, Seesta. She is my child."

Sister let it pass. Gabrielli is a Christian in dubious standing. He was baptized in danger of death some years ago and has five wives now. Whether this was one of them or just a woman in this village, no one knows. The expression "my child" might mean anything.

Sister went to the convent, got an injection and gave it to the patient. She scolded Gabrielli; this was the second time within three weeks he had brought in a patient at midnight when she had been sick for many days. The woman, with an infection following delivery six days before, needed help long before this. The baby was dead, of course. In this area, eighty percent of the babies die before they are five years old.

Nyegina to Kowak is two or three hours by washboard road. You are out of Sukuma territory and into the Luo grounds. As we approached Kowak, Sister Margaret Rose became strangely exhilarated. Everything began to improve—the air, the mountains, the people, the road, the scenery. Even Mother and I took on a new glow. When we rounded Lolia, the mountain which hides Kowak from the vulgar world's view, "Sister Margarose" (as she is called out here) burst into lyric poetry. Kowak, we gathered, was God's gift to a blighted world, the serenest gem of all Africa's limpid diamonds, the proudest feather in the continent's crown of ostrich plumes.

We did not interrupt. After all, Sister had started our African missions at Kowak thirteen years before. She saw this one small mission station of four Sisters in a school and dispensary grow to eight missions with five schools, four dispensaries, a hospital and a native novitiate. She loved Kowak.

The Luos are "The Strangers." They are not Bantu like the rest of men in Tanganyika, but Nilotic. They spilled over from Kenya and even further north from the Nile regions. The Luo is energetic and intelligent. His tribe is fast rising in the country.

The ancient habit of the Luo is to extract the six lower teeth. "Extract" is not the right word. They are dug out with an ice pick when the child is about ten years old. Very often youngsters come to the dispensary with pus in the sockets. A little girl, playing in the school yard at recess, fell and started bleeding. She almost died before Sister could stop the flow.

The reasons for undergoing all that pain are obvious. The first is that Luos say you cannot pronounce the Luo language correctly with a full set of lower teeth. The second was expressed by a young man in the dispensary with a bad case of infected teeth. "If I go to Kenya and get killed in a fight, how will anyone know I am a Luo unless my teeth are out?"

The convent at Kowak is the usual African type: Pressure lamps, wood stove, candles, bucket for shower, and kerosene iron. The bathtub is purely for ornament at present, but gives promise of running water in the future. Kowak holds a treasure of history. It's a stove left over from the previous century which served gloriously in a mission for the White Fathers years ago. Now retired from active duty, it has yet an honored place in the kitchen. The name of this cast iron stove is MODERN MISTRESS.

Mail comes to the post office at Tarime twenty-five miles away. Any Maryknoll priest, Sister or Brother near Tarime is commissioned to pick up the mail for anybody he is likely to see within the next week.

The roof of our convent is anchored with cement blocks tied to heavy wire. They keep it from wandering off too far in a heavy blow. The kitchen roof blew off last Palm Sunday while everyone was at church. Returning home, Sister James Elizabeth saw a roof in the tall grass and thought to herself, "Somebody must be building a low house over there." Then she saw her own roofless kitchen.

The five Sisters at Kowak don't have much time to worry about such things. They have a clinic, a small hospital and a parish, so to speak, to keep going. The parish work is varied but it all boils down to teaching the people how to lead a Christian life. One of the most powerful means to do this is the Legion of Mary. I stepped over into one of Sister Catherine Cecilia's Legion meetings after Mass one Sunday. To tell the truth, I just followed a number of interesting characters and found them heading toward a mud hut near the church. They ducked inside. So did I.

It was hard, at first, to see. Then I found myself facing three very serious men standing behind a bare table on which were a statue of the Blessed Virgin, the Legion insignia, two candles and flowers in a tin can. The three men dropped to their knees. A noise made me look around. Crowding in the doorway and spreading around the edges of the circular hut came many men and women—about thirty of them in all. They too knelt down on the mud floor and the rosary began.

At the finish, the officers took their places at the table and the rest of us sat down on the low seat which ran like a baseboard around the entire hut. Reports began:

"I went to the village of a lapsed Catholic and talked to him. He will come to Mass next Sunday but does not promise to continue."

"I tried to get my brother to permit his daughter to be a Sister."

Marriage cases usually could not report much success.

Michael, the president, is quite a character. For one thing, he wears red shoelaces in his black shoes. For another, he runs a small "duka" or trading post near the mission. Most dukas are owned by Arabs or Indians. I took a look at the shelves in his store, not more than 10 by 12 ft. in area. He has for sale Epsom salts, chewing gum, shoe polish (where practically nobody wears shoes), dress goods, kangas, ploughshares of iron, knives that could fell a forest giant, candy in tins from England, rubber boots in red and yellow and brand new "rungu." These last are walking sticks and weapons combined. A large knob at the end is lethal. Sister Agnes Jude once saw a man throw a rungu at a snake thirty feet away and smash it right in two.

Michael is also quite a seamstress. He operates the one sewing machine in the area. As president of Kowak's Legion of Mary, he attended a meeting of district officers at Musoma. "On their table," he told Sister Catherine Cecilia, "they had a cloth beneath the statue of Our Lady. We at Kowak can do no less for her. If the Legionnaires buy the cloth, I will run it up free on my sewing machine." Thus does civilization spread!

At Kowak is a small hospital—only a long one-story building of cement block with galvanized iron roof. Several smaller buildings and a few huts are annexes. But it is a beacon of hope for miles around. Sister Marian Jan, a doctor, and three Sister-nurses keep their eyes on twenty or so patients who rejoice in wearing the standard "hospital gown," a bright red kanga. A more cheerful outfit I cannot imagine.

Most of the cheer comes from the obstetrics ward. Twelve beds and twelve bassinets are here. One baby a day is born. Not a spectacular number but when you consider that nearly all the babies live and the mothers are spared complications which could last a long time, then one a day is "nice going" in this sparsely settled country.

"Our emphasis is on an attempt to give some knowledge of hygiene to these mothers: what to eat, how to recognize symptoms of ordinary illnesses, clean habits for themselves and the baby. It's all so elementary to us and yet brand new to them," Sister Marian Jan says. "We have a weekly class for pregnant women and at delivery time they graduate from this to another class held on well-baby clinic days. They seem to like the classes. At least they come."

In spite of the names wished upon them, the babies are content as they lie in their mothers' arms—or on a rag in the corner. Some circumstance of the birth decides the infant's name. Undiak was born when

a hyena howled; Indwi, when a lion was around; Mdege, while an airplane passed overhead. Kungu came into the world during a scourge of
caterpillars; poor little Hittra, during Hitler's rise to power. A little
fellow named Motocaa came by the name because his mother was picked
up on the road and taken to our hospital in the mission's motorcar.
Twins are invariably Apio for "I came first" and Odongo for "I delayed."

On the other side of the hospital are a variety of illnesses—some of
them are practically unknown in the States—chronic malaria, persistent
worm infestations, severe avitaminosis, extensive and long-lasting tropical
ulcers, leprosy and even several cases of African sleeping sickness, once
thought to be eradicated in the Kowak area.

In a separate house is the clinic where seventy to one hundred patients
come every morning. Those from a great distance who need treatment
every day can live in several huts on the mission property. Besides the
Sisters, a fairly good staff has been built up through the years. One
young lad has been trained to wash and care for patients with sores and
cuts; another keeps the records on intravenous injections. The laboratory
technician is a Standard VIII graduate whom the Sisters have trained.

I spent a routine morning in the clinic—routine for everybody but
me. A man came in with his face all but torn off by a leopard; a boy
had been bitten by a snake.

Sister Marian Jan serves as a dentist in a pinch. Brother Damien of
Maryknoll came in from Tarime, twenty-five miles away, with an abscess
and big cavity. Sister did what she could and filled the tooth with
amalgam until he could get to Nairobi for real attention. It was old
amalgam and crumbled. Brother went to Nairobi, saw a dentist and came
home with a filling. However, within a week or so, it fell out. Sister
was in despair. "Our amalgam is just no good, Brother. It's too old,"
she said.

"I'm a provident fellow," said Brother. "I bought some amalgam in
Nairobi. See? I have my filling in my pocket."

One noon, an old woman brought in her grandson, a baby seriously
ill. The abdomen was distended. Preliminary treatment for several hours
relieved the condition a little but it was obvious that the baby needed
hospital care. A messenger went to Musoma Hospital about sixty miles
away to let them know this baby would be coming in the next morning.
The next morning at 8 A.M. a young girl at the mission was sent along
to help carry the old woman's bundles. The Sisters took her to the main
road four miles away, so that she could get a bus to Musoma. The first
two passed; they were too full to stop. The third came along slowly. That
also would not stop but the driver called out to the old woman as he
crawled by, "This bus is breaking down; I can't stop."

At noon, the Sisters went to check on the situation at the roadside. This sort of thing had happened before. The old woman, the girl and the baby were still there in the blazing sun. They brought them back to the clinic, and worked on the baby most of the afternoon. Then they borrowed the Father's jalopy and, wondering how it held together, they drove the little group to Musoma. Luck this time was with them, for they managed to get on the very last trip the ferry made that day.

Just about everybody you see at Kowak has a story. Sister Margaret Rose and I went down to the small houses near the road to visit Marsella. Back in 1948, when the Sisters were brand new in Luo-district, Marsella was a mainstay in language and customs. Anytime they were puzzled, old Marsella could straighten them out.

She was old even then and a firm Christian. In the old days, she was wife of a chief. When he died, she was supposed to marry his brother. He was married already, so she refused. In the ensuing ruckus, Marsella fled to the mission and has been there ever since. Her son Paul came to her some years later; he was taught to read and write. Paul's children are brilliant. In his Cambridge exams after High School, Christiani passed first in all of East Africa. The two girls, Bertha and Gertrudis, are in Middle School now, hoping to be Immaculate Heart Sisters.

Marsella stays in bed most of the time. Her round hut of mud brick is immaculate, although quite dark. Sister Margaret Rose sat on the bed and held Marsella's hand and the two of them talked long in Luo. I perched myself on a stool covered with cowskin and looked around. Then I took a little notebook. A hearty laugh came from the bed. Sister Margaret Rose said,

"Marsella just remarked, 'Look at that clever Wazungu (European)! She can write!' "

"What does she think you are?" I asked.

"Me?" asked Sister. "Marsella forgets that I'm white. To her, I'm just another African like herself."

Which means that Sister has made the grade as a missioner.

At Kowak, they still talk about the night they showed St. Joseph the door. Before the Feast of the Sacred Heart all the Sisters went to church for a Holy Hour at midnight. There was a character around the mission known as Wanga—perhaps a little less than brilliant. Coming home from the Holy Hour Sister Marie William saw everything from the convent piled in a heap outside. She proceeded cautiously inside and there, standing in the bright moonlight, was Wanga dressed in a cloth he had pulled off the table. A brown paper bag was upside down on his head. He folded his arms and viewed her imperiously.

"Get out, Wanga," Sister said in a tone that meant business. "Leave this house."

Wanga was unmoved. "You can't talk to me like that," he said. "I'm St. Joseph." Sister thought quickly.

"St. Joseph," she said nicely, "Blessed Mother is outside and is calling for you."

"Oh, is she?" asked St. Joseph. "Where is she?"

"Right out here," as she led him forth.

Once on the porch, St. Joseph's eye caught the pile of things. "This is my house," said St. Joseph. "You don't take care of the place. I found all this junk in the rooms."

Another day, Sister Agnes Jude and I traveled up a hilly footpath to visit Magdalena. As a concession to my advancing years, she stopped now and then to look back on the panorama of yellowing grass spread behind us. One would think that no human being lived there; grass roofs blended perfectly with the fields. We passed a high hedge of ojuok, a type of euphorbia, which is planted as a sort of fence around private property.

"This was Magdalena's old 'village,'" Sister explained as we passed it. "Her mother-in-law died here last year, so the family had to move away. They built another village further along this path."

There was a small, young hedge around the new village. Even so, we could not see through it, much less step through or over it. We walked almost all around it before we found the opening. Even then, we were not admitted right into the open space. An inner wall of euphorbia made a narrow corridor first. Silvanus and Magdalena want their visitors one by one; that was plain.

In spite of these precautions, it was a friendly place. We emerged into a circle of huts. The largest one was directly opposite the opening; this was Silvanus' and Magdalena's. Another hut was the family dining room; another the kitchen; still another was for Taddeo their son, now a Middle School boy. Ordinarily he boards at his school, some distance away. In the usual village, other wives would occupy huts in the circle.

A little vegetable patch was at one side, with flowers here and there to give color. In the center was the corral for the family cows. At night they are brought in and kept there.

Three women were busy pounding cassava on a pile of stones at one side. None of them was Magdalena. "She has the best stones anywhere around," one of the women told us. "So we bring our cassava over here to pound." They were ready to leave for the day; they left the roots covered with leaves and weighted down with rocks.

"Where did those women come from?" I asked.

"Oh, maybe a couple of miles away in this or that direction," Sister replied waving vaguely. "It's not unlike the old sewing bees at home. They gather at some woman's village and have a good day's gossip.

It doesn't matter if the hostess is present or not. See? Magdalena walked off and left them."

A little girl was sitting on the doorstep of one of the locked and empty huts. She had a small pan in her hand neatly covered with leaves. She showed it to us—meat she was to give to Magdalena.

We had just about given up hope when Magdalena herself came through the opening. She took the meat from the child and crossed the court to greet us, with a wide grin. Like all Luos, her six front teeth were missing from the lower jaw; this made her upper teeth protrude. She hastened to fish out a bright new key from her clothes and unlock the padlock to the main house.

It was a lovely house. Everything simple and in order arranged around a center pole. I had not expected a bed but a big wooden frame occupied almost half the circular room. The weapons were handy. A spear was stuck in the roof, several large knives like machetes were close, and a rungu leaned up against the wall. Many enameled iron basins hung from sisal poles which formed the conical roof. They contained supplies —cassava, dried vegetables, gourds, seeds. Magdalena brought down one; in it were her sewing supplies—needle, thread, patching cloth, etc.

Magdalena has a story, too. Twenty years ago, she was the fourth or fifth wife of a chieftain near Shirati. She wanted to be a Catholic so she ran away. There was a big to-do about the cows for her dowry, but she stuck to her guns. She married Silvanus at the mission. It is a real sorrow to them that they have only one child, Taddeo.

Coming home down the hill we saw two men dragging a woman between them along the mission road. Her screams re-echoed through the countryside. But she did not seem to be protesting, just someone in terrible pain. We reached the mission gate together. When she saw us, the woman fell to the ground and rolled up into a ball. With this, Sister Marian Jan hurried out from the convent. She spoke to the men, standing helplessly by, and they picked up the woman and carried her to the hospital, rolled up just as she was. It was a delivery case. The men had found her some distance down the road and like Good Samaritans had helped her along.

The next morning, I thought I'd look in on this unfortunate woman. In the ward, her bed was empty. I feared she might have died. But no, she was outside with the baby in her arms posing for a picture with Sister Marian Jan, a bundle of smiles. Then she came into the hospital, put the baby in bassinette and went out to wash her clothes, dusty from yesterday's walk. Such is Africa.

Besides the Luo tribesmen at Kowak, often some of the Wasambiti wander into the clinic. These keep pretty much to themselves and we don't know them so well. Their tribal identification is their teeth filed to sharp points. In the clinic the Sisters have had several cases of fighting where the loser's flesh has been all but chewed off by the victor.

Another strange case, a woman, was brought to the hospital by a Sambiti man. She had a tapeworm and intestinal adhesions; surgery was needed. The woman had a 50-50 chance of living. Sister asked a few questions since the woman wanted to be baptized. The chain of interpreters was long—the woman in Kisambiti to the man, the man in Kiswahili to Corneli an assistant, Corneli in Luo to Sister Catherine Cecilia. Sister at first was not quite sure of the answers but she found that this was the conversation.

"Are you married?"

"Yes."

"Who is your husband?"

"The first wife of my village."

"No, no, I mean who paid cows for you?"

"The head woman in my village."

"I mean, what man do you live with?"

"Oh, many! But my husband is the First Wife."

Sister then remembered that she had read of a strange Sambiti custom. If the First Wife wants more children, she pays cows for another woman whom she gives to any man at all. The children are hers.

"Listen," she said to the woman. "You want to be baptized. But if I baptize you, you must have only one man. Which do you choose?"

The patient was silent a moment.

"I choose him," and she indicated the man who had come with her. "He is kind. He brought me here."

Sister turned to the man. "Have you a wife?" she asked.

"I have four."

This looked like a stalemate. "We cannot baptize you," she said to the woman, "unless you promise not to live with any of them."

"How wonderful!" said the poor woman. "How wonderful! I promise with all my heart!"

She was baptized and died the next day.

I don't know what your mental picture is of a Sister who does this sort of thing. It probably has no resemblance to our Sister Catherine Cecilia. She is very young and frail looking, seems to be a dear sweet eighth grader. If you saw her in a bus in Boston, San Francisco, Chicago, or New York, you might think she had no knowledge of the rougher facts of life; her soft voice had only murmured prayers; her mild eyes had seen nothing but kindness. You might be tempted to think, "What a colorless, if not inane, life that child has led!"

But I have walked the African hills with Sister Catherine Cecilia. I saw her get on her motorbike and go off to catechism classes when I was ready only for a cool drink and a soft chair. She took me to several villages where many wives lived. In many there was a good welcome. In others, one in particular, there was only sullen curiosity. Yet in that one she braved the wives, en masse, and did her business with a Catholic girl who had been sold into the menage.

"Elizabetti, I have come for you. Do you want to come with me?"

"Yes, I want."

"Come." And we walked her out of the village.

⊰ 5 ⊱ Queen for a Week

ON to Rosana! Easier said than done. Rosana is on a side road off Tarime, largest town in the North Mara district and the only one with a post office. The latest *Tanganyika Handbook* credits Tarime with 620 Africans, 30 Asians and 10 Europeans. Besides, it is listed as having a dispensary with eight beds, but no garage, no bank, no airfield, and no Catholic church. This last condition has been changed since the book came out. A nice little compound is sprouting around the town's one and only traffic circle. Not a thing is planted in it, but the cement curb is there to show where the side road shoots off. This side road is Tarime's main street.

It was a mistake to stop here; but we did. We had hardly pulled the handbrake when the car was surrounded by people right out of the *National Geographic Magazine*. Brass arm bands made the flesh puffy above and below; short red skirts were the entire dress; anklets and knee bands of brass glinted in the sun. And the ears—they were cut and pierced and inlaid with so much jewelry that they hung down to the shoulders.

But friendly? They were the hand-shaking-est people in the world. Not content with shaking the nearest hand, hundreds of them, it seemed, thrust their arms through the car windows to grab all our hands in fellowship. So many arms came in that most of them were shaking hands with each other across the narrow car. Not that we minded; we had enough to do to keep from being shaken to pieces.

"The best way out of this," I thought, "is to get out of the car and face up to it in the open." A good idea, for as soon as I stood outside and people saw my camera, they suddenly remembered urgent business elsewhere. Thus I learned that the Wakuria people are camera-shy to an amazing degree. I saw three girls, shined up for a day in town, walking down the street toward me and aimed my camera nonchalantly toward them. But just before they walked into focus, a woman called out from the crowd and they ran off the street in panic. It was only in Rosana where the Sisters are well known that anyone would permit it. A woman fears she will never have children once her picture is taken. Even at Rosana, old Birgitta and Victoria had their qualms about it all.

Victoria, although an Mkuria, is addicted to her pipe, one of the creature comforts Luo women like. As the two old women lined up to pose, Birgitta said to Victoria, "Take that pipe out of your mouth. Do you want people to think you're a Luo?"

The Kikuria word for Luo means "slave people." There is little love lost between the tribes.

The distinguishing mark for the Wakuria is the ear. From an early age, the lobe is pulled and twisted until it hangs to the shoulders. The hole is filled at first with bits of cassava, later with wooden plugs, then brass rings go through it. Only grandmothers may wear large brass coils in their ears. Young ladies go through torture when the upper parts of the ear are cut out with a piece of sharpened tin can, and square plugs of ivory are fitted in. Some, not all, of these square pieces indicate that the wearer has been sold to the devil. These are forbidden to Catholic girls, and must be removed when a woman is baptized.

The Wakuria ear is more than an ornament. Local justice recognizes this. Sometimes in a fight the ear, stretched to the thinness of a rubber band, may be broken or even bitten off. Such a case has top priority in the "baraza" or court.

To guard against an accidental break, most men twist the long pieces of skin around their upper ears while working. To break the ear is the worst accident that could happen.

Next to their ears, the Wakuria value their cows. When cattle thieves have come into a village, a most unearthly cry wails through the night. It is taken up from village to village. Every able-bodied man is expected to turn out and catch the thief. Whoever kills him is feted for weeks in his village.

There is a story that a cattle thief one night got into an old man's village. He tied him and his old wife together by a padlock through their ears. He knew that Wakuria would never break their ear lobes. Sure enough. Rather than do this, the old couple let all their cattle go. Only when the thief was far away did they set up a howl to inform the neighbors what was going on.

The Wakuria also love brass. Brass coils on arms and legs indicate wealth. The brass sells at ten shillings (about $1.14) a coil in Tarime. No girl wants to be without some indication that her Papa has a little pocket money. It's a matter of status. And to Papa, a matter of cows. Investment in brass coils today may bring a rich son-in-law.

Beaded collars and belts are another feminine vanity with the Wakuria. Also cow grease, a sort of crude lard, used to shine up their bodies for dances. Nowadays, however, the old cow grease is second best to perfumed oil. Sister Paul Christopher and I went down to a hut to see how one of Sister's patients was coming along. We found a domestic crisis. The young girl of the house was going out to a dance that night. She had just come in from washing in the river and was putting on her beaded belt and the family's dance skirt. Then Mama said, advancing with the gourd of cow fat, "Come here. I want to get you shined up."

"Oh Mother!" the girl pouted. "That horrible stuff! It stinks and the flies come all around and it's just awful. There's some wonderful oil in Tarime. Only two shillings a bottle—not a big bottle but it smells so nice and it lasts a long time. Just a little bit makes you shine beautifully."

But Mama cut up some very odoriferous soap, mixed it with the cow fat and applied it in large doses to the squirming teen-ager. "There now," she urged. "All the bad smell's gone. You look just lovely. Nobody will ever know that you don't have on two-shilling oil."

Teen-agers are not much different in any part of the world. In the Rosana dispensary a girl about thirteen years old was brought in by her father. She had had her ears cut; the piece of tin can had slipped and she had a nasty gash across the back of her head, bleeding profusely. As Sister tended the child her father scolded. "Stop crying. You can just stand the pain. You wanted your ears cut and begged and pleaded. You pushed me into it." When they were ready to go home, Sister said to the man, "I hope you will help your daughter. She has lost a lot of blood." "I'll help her," he conceded. "If she falls, I'll let her rest a while."

It seemed cruel. But this man had given up at least one day's work to bring the girl in for medical care. Then I laughed at a memory. Years ago, I begged my father to let me ride horses. Ten minutes after he gave in and two seconds after I mounted, the horse threw me to the tune of two black eyes and a broken collarbone. The parental explosion that followed was not cruel. It came from relief that my neck was still intact and annoyance with himself for letting me go my silly way. Through my tears I loved him for it.

It seems to be a normal reaction of love. Police say that the first thing parents do to a child who has been lost is to scold him. Even Our Lady chided her Son when she found Him. I had to keep similarities in mind as we watched these very primitive people. Judging from circumstances, it

is so easy to say, "How barbarous!" without weighing the basic ideas un-
derlying the actions.

Every race has its little vanities and women will go through torture to
preserve them. Bunions, callouses, corns and fallen arches are an old
story with us. False teeth, cosmetics and Metrecal keep the cash registers
of the nation merrily ringing. The older the women the gayer they ring.

Old ladies have their foibles in Rosana, too. Victoria, who loves to
putter around the sacristy shining up the candlesticks, often takes a dab
or so of brass polish to give the coils in her ears an extra shine. It's getting
so that brass polish for the sacristy is quite an item in the budget.

Speaking of church, the Sunday Mass was a joy to eye and ear. Men and
women in the bright Wakuria brass toiled up the escarpment (for Rosana
is perched on the edge of the Great Rift Valley) to attend Mass. The
whole church sings the chants in Kiswahili. Sometimes, hearing and seeing the stories of their tribal life, one might be tempted to wonder just
what they understand of the Mass. But to them perhaps, the story of life
sacrificed on the Cross to redeem mankind is more believable than it is to
us. They are so much closer to elemental justice. Their reverence during
the Mass, at any rate, shows that they understand what is going on.

At the Offertory, as the usher went down the aisle, he collected chickens,
fruit, eggs and meat. I was highly edified until Sister James Florence said
to me as we went home after Mass, "I always like to see what comes in the
collection. Now we know what we can borrow from the Fathers."

I spent a day watching Sister Paul Christopher at work in the clinic.
She holds forth under a spreading umbrella tree. Her small white clinic
is as much a haven on the long dusty life-road these people tread, as the
umbrella tree is for the sun-smitten traveler. To us, it is incomprehensible
that people will walk ten miles when they are ill. A night or two under
a tree or in a stranger's hut means very little. A steady stream of patients
arrives each morning. Women whose ears hang to their shoulders, whose
arms bulge above and below tight brass bracelets, whose babies seem to
have no chance to live. Sometimes, they wedge a leafy branch between the
bracelets and their arms, to form a bit of shade for the baby.

Men with dreadful sores; children with worm-filled tummies; boys
trembling with malarial chills; any and all diseases come to the umbrella
tree. There were more than fifty patients sitting along the hedges or spread
out on the grass the day I was there.

Most are pagans. Many wear the square plugs in the upper ear which
indicate devil worship. Some had discarded the arm and leg bands—sold
them, perhaps. The limbs regain their normal size but marks of the rings
remain on the skin.

"These people are so patient," Sister Paul Christopher said as she examined a woman stretched on the table. "This woman has walked nine miles, starting out before dawn, to get here. She has waited several hours under the tree. What's wrong? Malaria, for one thing, malnutrition, worms, bilharzia, and she is two months pregnant. She has had two miscarriages already. I think the malaria is at the bottom of her trouble."

"She seems very young," I said.

"Maybe 16 or 17. The serious business of life starts very early out here."

The next patient tottered in on a walking stick. The old fellow's long ear lobes were looped around his upper ears to get them out of the way.

"What can I do for you, granduncle?" Sister asked.

The old man pulled his animal skin cloak about his stooped shoulders and shuffled up to stare into her face. He blinked almost blind eyes to get Sister into focus.

"Give me the kind of medicine you take," he said with real envy. "You look so healthy!"

Sister laughed and turned to her cupboard.

"What will you give him?" I asked.

"Just a few vitamin pills and some worm medicine to begin with. It's amazing what medicine does out here. The people have so little that they respond quickly to anything."

Your heart goes out to the Wakuria people; they seem involved in pain from the first moment of their lives to the last. And so much of it is self-inflicted. Women, especially, take suffering for granted. In the clinic, I heard a mother say to her two-month-old baby as the youngster howled during a treatment, "Hush up! How do you expect to stand childbirth if you can't stand a little thing like this?" They certainly pay for Eve's transgression.

Both the Wakuria and Wasambiti have circumcision rites for boys and girls. The boys' day fell a week or so before I arrived; the girls' were "done" in a small house down the road from our mission. Some twenty girls were operated on with a razor blade as an introduction to womanhood. To them it had all the glamor of a first pair of high heels. They are brought in procession to and from the hut. I stood by the road and watched several of these processions pass by as the girl was taken back to her village. The first was advertised a long way off by the high screech of whistles. The crowd of thirty or so people came around a bend in the road. Three small boys dressed in withered corn stalks and leaves danced backwards and forwards across the road, now approaching the girl, now backing away from her. The adults in bright brass arm and leg bands danced alongside of her. One man carried a flag (really just a kanga waving from a sisal pole); he and others blew little tin whistles.

And the girl herself? She walked stiff-legged in the center. Opposite me, she stood still and reeled a little. One of the women had an enameled iron

tea pot of water. She poured water over the girl's head and let it run
down her face. The child stood in the center of the road's dust and let the
water trickle over her kinky hair and down her shoulders. Then once
more she took up her painful walk to the hut of her father.

That was a big party. After this, some ten minutes later, came a smaller
group—only about fifteen men and women. One woman blew the whistle
and danced in front. This was just about all the jubilation. The poor
child seemed much younger and smaller.

Opposite our mission the caravan rested on the long pilgrimage home.
The girl stood; she put her arms around her mother's neck and rested
her head on the broad shoulders. But there was no whimpering or crying. This group seemed more in sympathy with their child. Several
women took the girl's hands as they started along the road once more.

Sister Paul Mary and I followed along to the top of a hill. We looked
down on a small village below, probably the home of one man with six
or seven wives. Five flags waved from five huts. People were going back
and forth across the open space; groups sat in the shade of the overhang-
ing grass roofs. I thought of the five mutilated girls within those five huts,
condemned to the hard life of an African woman.

At least, the worst of their agony was over; they were to sit and rest for
about a week and be queen of the village. Served and tended by all, the
girl will never again be so feted. Outside her hut there is laughter and
singing in her honor. People from other villages come and drink millet
beer; her own relatives go to dance and drink in her girl friends' villages.
Wherever a flag waves from a village, a circumcision party is going on.
The little ladies, for all their pain, are proud and happy. They wouldn't
miss it for the world.

We went to a village and happened to attend one of these circumcision
parties. We could hear the drum some distance away. In the open space
surrounded by the huts a one-man orchestra was in full bloom. He had
a stringed instrument with the sound-box covered with zebra hide. His
toes worked a stick with bells. He sang and drooled along with appropriate
noises. Beer was being served in one of the huts; men walked in and reeled
out. Women were not permitted to drink until all the men were finished.
They gathered in front of one hut where the flag was posted; I suppose the
girl was there. They were some distance from us and kept that far away.

However, the men were having a good time. They weaved up and down
to the music, linking arms or doing extemporaneous solos. One old fellow wearing two hats kept up a steady chant, "I'm dancing because this is
a party." He came up to us and asked, "Did you-all use to dance like this
when you were pagans?" Before we could think of a good answer, an
old woman sidled up to him and the two of them went dancing away.

On the sidelines was a truly magnificent figure. Tall and muscular, maybe forty years old, he wore a monkey-fur cape, a necklace of some kind of animal teeth and a circlet of ivory around his upper arm. It must have been a two-inch-wide slice of elephant tusk. He looked with disdain on the proceedings.

Other guests were not so colorful. Behind us was a very prim and proper boy in pressed khaki shorts, white shirt and pullover sweater. And a man in shirt and long pants wore a dilapidated hat once the proud badge of the King's African Rifles—a large affair turned up on one side like the Aussie hats.

The drunken old man and several of his friends came dancing up again. "We'll give you a show," they offered. Then suddenly, a man ran from the rear and pushed the dancers away. "You've danced enough for them. Now get out!" We felt that his "get out" was addressed more to us than to our friends. We turned to go.

The gentleman in monkey fur and ivory came with us. He asked several polite questions. He spoke in Kikuria, of course; the Sisters translated into English. Where are you from? How long are you staying? Then he invited us to a party in his village on Thursday.

"I'm sorry," Mother said, "but we will be going on Tuesday."

"Do stay until Thursday," he pleaded. "You'll miss half your life if you miss my party. I'll have much better beer and I've hired a number of dancing girls." He might have been a multimillionaire inviting us to a week-end on his yacht.

Nevertheless, we left on Tuesday.

To keep the girls from growing up too fast, to give them something more to think about than the glory of their circumcision party, to prepare them for marriage which will produce healthy families, Sister James Florence has started sewing and hygiene classes. "A definite gap exists between the time when our girls finish Primary School at Standard IV and when they get married. Up to a year or so ago, they have just sat around and waited for life to begin," she says. "I started classes in simple sewing, health, reading and writing three afternoons a week for fourteen girls who live within a mile or so."

The classroom is a newly white-washed shed; the blackboard is Contact Paper stuck to the wall; the pictures are calendars and old Christmas cards. Seats were a problem until the girls solved it; they went outside, picked up some boulders and brought them in. They're good, but sometimes Chacha can't resist the temptation to wobble Matiku's rock just when she is writing.

If you are nervous, perhaps you should stay away from Sister's sewing classes. I thought one little girl was chewing something but when Sister asked a question, the child took a razor blade out of her mouth to answer. Sister James Florence is used to it. "Oh, that's nothing," she calmed me.

"Even youngsters in First Grade carry razor blades under their tongues. Sometimes, they stick their tongues out of the slit in the middle. I have never heard of any accidents—nobody has swallowed one nor cut himself. Razor blades are used for everything here—cutting hair, fingernails, corns, callouses and so on. If you asked any girl here what is the most necessary thing for sewing, she would say, 'A razor blade.' "

All through this primitive section of Africa, I had the feeling, "This won't last long." Truly, things done as they were ten years ago are a hundred years out of date. Also things done ten years from now will be a century further advanced. The girls circumcised today will not permit their daughters to go through it. The school boy in prim khaki shorts and white shirt will not be content to live in such a village as the one we saw him in. The girls who ran off the road in Tarime lest I take a picture of them may ten years from now stand on a stage near the crossroads and pose anyway you wish for a shilling a pose.

Already, the great-grandfather of the supermarket is riding the roads of northern Tanganyika. Early Friday mornings an enterprising merchant starts off with a truckload of fresh fruits and vegetables from the lush gardens around Nairobi in Kenya. The shortest route over a fantastic road to Rosana is all of two hundred and twenty-six miles; the truck stops at every mission, government house, mine or ginnery in the area. It goes eighty-six miles further on to Musoma and ends out at Makoko often after nightfall. By that time, the vegetables are wilted and the fruits not at their peak. But they are far better than any available nearby. The meat we don't trust after twelve hours in such a truck, but we are glad to get the green goods.

This Indian will take orders. If you know guests are coming next week, you can ask him to save some lima beans for you, or maybe strawberries. Seeing his tired face as he turned the empty truck to drive through the African night back three hundred miles to Nairobi, I thought of him twenty or thirty years from now when he will own a supermarket chain, a fleet of trucks to provision them and, perhaps, hundreds of acres of farmland. Then people will growl, "Why should he have so much and we so little?" They should remember the truck, the road, the twenty-hour working day and the smile which is bright right down to the last customer.

The amenities are creeping into the district at a fast pace. One of our convents has Afrigas, a bottled propane gas, for hot water heating. This is definitely civilization on the march.

Africans are a little tired of being "colorful." They feel it's another way of saying "underdeveloped" or "backward." Those who have had good education don't like the world to think that every African wears monkey fur and files his teeth. Even in places like Kowak and Rosana, many are ashamed of the old ways. The Luos are getting false teeth to fill the gap in their lower jaws. The Wakuria are cutting off their long ears and sewing them up. Many cases of infection from this come to our clinics.

Anchabina Boke is a round-faced, round-eyed miss at Rosana. Her mother came to Sister James Florence recently and said that Anchabina would be out of class for a few days. "She is old enough to have her ears cut in the upper parts," she explained.

"Oh, I wouldn't do that," Sister argued. "It's not the style any more. That sort of thing is going out fast."

The mother thought it over for a few days. "You're right, Sister. I'm old-fashioned, I guess. We'll let it go for Anchabina although her older sister had it done."

The Africans are sensitive; any difference they feel is a slight. Sister was showing a picture of many nations gathered around the Christ Child's crib. The Chinese wore his saam; the Filipina, her terno; the Japanese, a kimono. But Matatiro pointed to the African boy. "Why doesn't he have clothes? Everybody else does."

On a ferryboat one day a woman we all know greeted Sister Margaret Rose and spent some time talking to her. She had on a very bright kanga and I took a picture of the two as they talked by the railing. A young man came up to me. "You did not ask that woman's permission to take her picture," he said.

"Why, no," I excused myself. "After all, she saw the camera and could have stopped me in a moment. I don't think she minds."

But I stepped up to her and told her, asking permission post facto.

Americans like to see the skyline of New York or a view of the Rockies on travel posters advertising the States; Tanganyikans feel that the harbor at Dar es Salaam, or a shot of Kilimanjaro, best advertise their country. We would not be pleased to see America shown as the country of Tobacco Road and the well-filled spittoon. We can understand the African's feeling.

Nevertheless, the situation poses a touchy problem for the missioner. He hates to see the distinctive things of African civilization thrown away with the "backward" things. That's like throwing the baby out with the bathwater. The dances, the intricate designs, the tremendous verve of Africa—it would be a shame to squeeze these into conventional Western molds.

At Rosana, an incident happened which sums up the situation. A man and woman brought a baby to the dispensary in very bad condition. Sister Paul Christopher took care of it. She could see the child was dying and advised the couple to have it baptized. However, they refused and went away.

The next morning during Mass, when everyone was in church, a plaintive wail came from outside. "Hodi! Ho-o-o-di!" This is an expression like "Hello, may I come in?" When you approach a village and want to rouse someone to open the gate, you call "Hodi!"

No one answered; the door was wide open and anyone could come in if he wanted to. The cry of "Ho-o-o-di" was insistent. After a time, Sister Paul Christopher went out. It was the couple with the baby, now plainly at the last gasp. They did not ask for medicine this time; they asked for Baptism.

The Africans are outside the Church politely calling "Hodi!" Someone must go out and invite them to come in.

It was over. We had come to the end of our line in Tanganyika. There were still eighty-two miles to go to Musoma where a small plane would take us to Nairobi. From there we were due to fly to Bombay.

Long drives may be dull in some places but never in Africa. The jeep becomes a post office with a letter that Marwa wants us to mail in Tarime as we go by. To whom is Marwa writing? The wobbly handwriting on the envelope reads:

Sears Roebuck, Chicago, U.S.A.

Boke has a sackful of corn to be ground at the mill. May she go with us as far as there? It will save a fifteen-mile walk. Jukara wants her scissors ground; will we take them to Musoma? A young man over in Father's house has an alarm clock which doesn't keep perfect time—doesn't keep time at all, to be frank. Can that be left for repairs? Fortunately, this time there was no one sick who should go to the hospital; more than once the jeep has been an ambulance.

We got to Musoma, however, and went out to the airfield where our plane, a four-seater Cessna, was to land. The "airdrome," as the official listing of Musoma's facilities has it, is nothing but a large field and a small shack. It is like all other large fields and small shacks around, except for a grass-free strip down the center and a "stocking" wind indicator flying in the breeze.

It was market-day in Musoma. A stream of people were crossing the field with all the week's garden produce on their heads. I held my breath as the tiny speck in the sky circled, getting bigger and bigger, and finally slid down neatly to earth. The stream of market-bound buyers and sellers stopped for hardly a second as the Cessna sped down the strip, disappeared into the tall grass at the end, and taxied toward us.

Out stepped a compact man, with bronzy skin, bright blue eyes, a slightly rolling gait and many squinting wrinkles. All business, he walked toward us pulling an old envelope and a pencil stub from the pocket of his worn zip-up jacket. By the time he was within speaking distance, he was ready: "Good morning! Who are the passengers? Names, please."

He was Dutch. Indeed, he should have been a gnarled farmer with wooden shoes, smoking a pipe on his peaceful doorstep. But here he was flying a tiny plane over Africa, ready for any assignment from tracking an elephant across the Serengeti Plains, to driving three nuns one hundred and fifty miles to Nairobi.

We were stowed inside the plane as into a compact car with seats and headroom for four not-too-big people. The single engine sputtered and roared. The plane lifted. This is the way to travel! Jets fly too high; you see nothing. Jeeps fill your eyes and nose with dust. But a single-engined plane with wings overhead skimming just below the clouds is perfect for see-it-alls.

The earth looked as if God had just this minute made it and He hadn't had time yet to smooth out the jagged cliffs, to sprinkle greenery around and turn on the rivers. Here and there, miles and miles apart, were villages, looking like craters on the moon. Six or seven huts in a circle, surrounded by thorny hedging, were the commonest type. Others were wheel-shaped, each hut separated from its neighbor by the spokes. Now and then across the wide empty spaces, a herd of cattle broke into a wild gallop out in the middle of nowhere. They must have belonged to someone; how could anybody keep an eye on them?

This is the Great Rift Valley, a gigantic "fault" which cracks the Near East and Africa all the way from Palestine down to Mozambique, Portuguese East Africa, four thousand miles. Back in geologic ages, somebody pulled a strip of carpet out from under Africa and that area just fell down. It accounts for the Sea of Galilee, the Jordan Valley, the Dead Sea, the Gulf of Aden, the Red Sea, and for all of Africa's Great Lakes except Lake Victoria. The section from 1° north to 1° south of the equator is the most spectacular. Cliffs rise thousands of feet on either side. Winds roared up the escarpments as they are called, and gave us a biffing. Wobbling on the air currents, I looked at our pilot. He was bored with it all, holding his hands low on the wheel and looking ahead with the air of a man trundling home to supper and bed.

Suddenly he perked up. We swung over still another sharp cliff and we were—in paradise. Green fields well laid out, substantial houses with tennis courts, swimming pools and planned gardens, acres and acres of white erithium flowers, the largest crop in Kenya. DDT is made from erithium flowers. It was Kenya—most developed, most settled and, according to Tanganyikans, most favored of the triumvirate of East African countries.

Nairobi is a frontier city. Chicago, before Mrs. O'Leary's cow practically rebuilt the city, might have been like it. This is East Africa's jumping-off-place to the world. Jets from Rome, London, Bombay, Aden, Johannesburg, circle her airstrip. Mud-spattered Landrovers lumber through the street, stopping at traffic lights beside limousines and every conceivable type of truck. All sorts of people jostle on the sidewalks—diamond prospectors, Protestant missioners, fair-skinned English schoolgirls, Indian traders and their sari-clad wives, nuns who hold their pocketbooks tight as they stare at school supplies in the bright windows, scientists out to do a study of hog typhoid, government people and airlines people, smart young business women and missioners' wives with straight hair and leathery skins. And Africans! Africans with ultra correct clothes and those with practically none at all. Some with ears full of holes and hanging to their shoulders and some in the smart uniform of policemen or soldiers.

I used to know a girl who made a unique potato salad. It had radishes, pickles, olives, onions, garlic, pimientos, green peppers, bacon, hard boiled eggs, bits of ham, and Heaven-knows-what-else in it. The inventor claimed that no one mouth was big enough to hold a sample of everything; therefore every mouthful tasted different. So it is with Nairobi. No one day standing on a street corner could give you a complete idea of its variety. It would take weeks.

A sample: We went to Ethiopian Airlines where a Mr. Chong, a Chinese, arranged for us two Americans to go from Ceylon to the Philippines, via Siam, using Air India, KLM Dutch Airlines and Scandinavian Airlines. This was done in the British Protectorate of Kenya in Africa.

Of course, we went to Woolworth's, the universal mecca of Sisters. There I watched an Indian buy a hairnet for his beard. Iron grey and very distinguished, he bent his turbanned head over the envelopes of hairnets and carefully chose the color. Then he stood in front of the counter mirror and saw how the net would match his beard. I must admit, it was a wise move; in a high wind, such a beard would be a hazard to vision.

Wild animals are a norm in British East Africa. We saw ostriches, monkeys, giraffe, baboons, zebra, wildebeest, hartebeest, crown birds, two lionesses with six cubs and even the nostrils of a hippopotamus as he snoozed in a river. These are commonplaces for tourists. We enjoyed them but paid little attention. However, it was the wild animals who gave us the nicest farewell to Africa.

As we drove along the macadam highway to Nairobi's airport Father Bordonet jammed on his brakes quickly. A herd of wildebeest sailed over a fence and across the four-lane highway. Traffic on both sides halted in a hurry. Wildebeest are gnus; they run hunched over like the American buffalo.

Wild animals are something of a problem in Nairobi. There is a wire fence around the airport where it borders Nairobi National Park, sanctuary for thousands of animals. The poor beasts are constantly straying in the path of planes—a custom which is good for neither. The problem must have been much the same in the old days of America when buffalo herded across the transcontinental railroad tracks.

There are still frontiers; there are still nations not yet fully jelled. There is still greed and heroic self-denial, leadership and chicanery, heights to be won and troughs to be skirted. And through it all, I could hear the high wail of the African family outside the Rosana church, calling "Hodi!"

CEYLON

From Bombay

INDIA

• Madurai

Adams Bridge

Tuticorin

Trincomalee

Polonnaruwa

to Bangkok

KANDY

COLOMBO

INDIAN

OCEAN

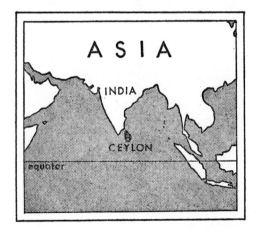

ASIA

INDIA

CEYLON

equator

CEYLON

𝔈 6 𝔈 *Mr. Nervous and the Resplendent Isle*

I FIRST noticed him at Nairobi airport—a tall thin Indian with a sharp nose and prominent eyes that darted to right and left, up and down, anxious to see everything. We were standing in the long lines inevitable to customs, passports, baggage, bank statements, health certificates, and tickets. The airport was crowded with Indians en route, as we were, to Bombay. Schoolboys in bright pink, lavender, or yellow turbans; women in nose-jewels and saris, girls in gold kid slippers; men in drab business suits looking like Bill Hinkson from Peoria—all standing guard over a welter of baggage on the handsome parquet floor.

The tall thin Indian stepped over our baggage and pushed to the head of the line. He thought nothing of easing first his fingers, then his arm and at last his whole body in front of you. International passengers are usually a meek, brow-beaten lot. "This ticket window is closing; please go to another window," usually sends them shoving their hand luggage into another line without protest. "Flight #616 is expected to leave at 1 A.M. instead of 8 P.M." brings nothing more than a sigh as they go to buy a magazine. Customs men leaving one's best party dress a mess of wrinkles get only a mild look of reproach.

But let anyone jam ahead of the lines and the worm turns. I was fascinated to watch this Me-First push through the patient hordes of the rest of us. He seemed so afraid that something was going on he didn't know about, that something was being passed out that he should be getting, that he was being left out or left behind. He wriggled his way to the ticket windows to ask questions, dashed up to the gateman to see if the plane was going soon, shoved to get a place on the waiting room benches only to spring up in a minute and rush over to the bulletin board. A placid, chubby Indian was standing near me. As he caught my eye, he lifted his shoulders and spread his hands with a smile. "What can you do with a man like that?" he asked. I smiled vaguely and went back to minding my own business.

On the plane, as we took our seats, the Nervous One and the Placid One were seatmates. Nervous had the window, Placid sat in the middle and a husky Englishwoman with long legs had the aisle seat. The three were a circus to watch all night.

Nervous was like a live nerve wriggling at the end of dental forceps. He stared out the window, twisted violently to see what the hostess was doing in the galley, wrenched back to the window, stood up to get something from the rack overhead, crouched on the floor to drag out his briefcase, tested the tray which comes out of the seat ahead. If you have ever ridden in Economy Class, you know that economy of motion is essential to happiness. The only good seatmate is a dead seatmate, or at least one sound asleep.

Then Mr. Nervous wanted a magazine. His feet sailed over the two pairs of knees between him and the aisle, and went to the magazine rack in front. Back in his seat again, he remembered that he needed a drink of water. Again, "Pardon me, pardon me!" as his largish feet grazed Placid's nose by an inch.

At Aden in Arabia, he was first out for the free drink at the airport. It was only half drunk when he remembered that his luggage was unguarded on the plane. Zip—out he dashed.

Mother and I walked around the airport a bit. Arabia at 2 A.M.! Well, it might have been Idlewild, or O'Hare, or Hong Kong, or Tokyo. The stars were dimmed by the glow from jeep and gasoline truck headlights, the searchlights swinging around, the lighted airport.

The Air Age has brought forth a new race of men, a vast array of mechanics of all facial molds and colors. They swarm around airfields and minister tenderly to a metal bird that swoops down from outer space to rest a half hour or so on land. As it wobbles to a stop a crowd of men converge to oil it, to stock it, to clean it, to feed it, to check wings or tail or feet. Their jobs are identical whether they are performed in Addis Ababa, Delhi, Manila, the Aleutians or Tahiti. They may scramble onto the wings and walk over the hot metal in bare brown feet, but they cock at the wing flap the same knowing eye that the mechanic gives at Idlewild.

In the pool of brightness around our bird, a familiar figure rushed up the steps, paused a moment at the doorway where the hostess stood, and came down again. We met the Nervous One at the foot of the stairs. "They won't let me in!" he exclaimed. "All my things are in there." He watched each Arabian cleaner as he passed us up or down the stairs. He searched each one, piercing any non-personal bulge with his eyes. But he controlled himself. Except for two more forays up the steps, he waited until we got the green light. Of course, by the time two slow-going nuns entered the plane, Mr. Nervous was feverously checking his belongings around that window seat.

Our last look at him was characteristic. He was bound to be the first off at Bombay. As we sped down the runway he was standing with luggage in hand waiting for the door to open. The rest of us were all seated calmly.

Then Mr. Nervous came crestfallen back to his seat and climbed over the well-worn knees to sit down disheartened. He had not counted on the fumigator. In many Eastern cities, no one is allowed off until a Department of Health man comes through the plane spraying ceiling, floors, seats and passengers with a germ killer. It's one of those little indignities which make international relations in the East interesting. India says, "You came from Africa? My, you must be terribly germ-y!" Ceylon says, "From India? We must spray you!" Siam says, "If you want to enter our fair country, get rid of those Ceylonese germs."

The spraying seemed to take all the spunk out of our friend. This time, he let the Englishwoman in the aisle seat, the chubby Indian beside him, and even us pokey nuns get out before he once more gathered his luggage and deplaned. Poor fellow, he was exhausted after a hard night.

I felt that Mr. Nervous should have had a placard across his shoulders labeled Excessive Nationalism, for he seemed a symbol of it. This may have been his first plane ride; no wonder he was nervous. A good man, no doubt, anxious to gain a living for his family, to give them all the things they had a right to. Eager to take his place in the world. Fearful that he be pushed behind; suspicious of the stranger; determined that the good things of life do not pass him by.

It is all very understandable. Only later will it be plain to him that even with the most powerful nations, life is mostly Give and very little Take. Until small nations do learn it, they can play havoc with the very people who want to help them.

Mr. Nervous was a good introduction to Ceylon.

I could sit all day in the Bombay airport and watch East and West parry, thrust, merge, embrace, divide, tease and torment each other. Buddhist monks, smart turbans, filmy saris and nose-rings, fantastic baggage of wicker and bamboo, beards that would startle even your grandfather—these things are part and parcel of the jet age. I watched a crowd of school-girls in flowing saris, gold kid sandals on bare brown feet, nose-jewels, earrings and caste-marks of gold paper pasted between the eyebrows. Some had flowers braided into their long hair. The girls giggled and cast languid eyes at a group of boys also going home to Madras from high class schools in Bombay.

At one point the girls bustled out of the waiting room. The baggage truck from school had arrived. In they came again with their luggage. I wish you could have seen it—very smart cosmetic cases, millions of tennis racquets and, if you please, well-used track shoes with spikes. These houris from Arabian Nights were track enthusiasts.

Madras. Colombo. And up the mountains to Kandy by car. Practically nobody in Ceylon has an American-sized car. It wouldn't fit the narrow roads and hairpin curves. Kandy, ancient capital of Ceylon and world center of Buddhism, lies seventy-five miles from humid Colombo, directly inland from it and almost straight up.

We really don't live in Kandy but some three miles out of it at Kunda-sale, the smallest of small towns. The address is swanky—Paddiwatte Estate. But an estate in Ceylon is like a hacienda in the Philippines, a finca in Chile, a chamba in Tanganyika or a plantation in the South. In other words, a place for growing some crop for sale. We live in a bungalow on an estate growing cocoa, coconuts, and pepper. In other words, we live in Paradise.

If you want to know what Eden looked like before the Fall, stand outside the little white church of Our Lady of Fatima, as daylight lifts the night mists off river and rice fields. Like everything else near Kandy, the church perches on top of a mountain. After early Mass, the fog of dawn reluctantly leaves the valley down below. The silent huts are still wrapped in quiet. A pointed temple on the opposite mountain gradually clears.

Then you start walking home. Day begins in the small thatched houses. Children run out to take your hand. A woman looks up from her washing at the stream and waves. It is idyllic.

Then you see that the child whose hand lies in yours, is limping. A tropical ulcer has eaten deep into his leg. An estate worker overtakes and hurries past you. Young and very frail in body, she carries a great basket of coconuts on her head. As you get nearer home, the old smell comes back. It is "the lines" where hundreds of estate workers live in one room per family. You can smell "the lines" a long way off.

You know that the snake is still around Eden and Adam has lost none of his taste for apples.

The Sinhalese name for Ceylon is Sri Lanka, translated as Resplendent Isle. The guidebooks call it "a pear-shaped island," and so it is, of course. But the practical man might see in it a smoked ham. The sentimental would say it is a tear dropping from India. The artistic call it a pearl set in blue-green seas. To us, coming from parched Tanganyika, it was an emerald of verdure, one hundred and forty miles wide and two hundred and seventy miles long at the greatest measurements. But all agree that it is just a bit too close to India for comfort. Twenty-two miles separate the Pearl of the East from the teeming land of India. Hungry eyes look over that strait at the fertile valleys and cultivated mountainsides.

The Sinhalese themselves came from the valley of the Ganges five hundred years before Christ. The Tamils arrived later from southern India. In the thousands of years that the two peoples have lived in Ceylon, there has been some intermarriage, but the six million Sinhalese and two million Tamils still remain separate and hostile. The Europeans, chiefly English,

have added a third element. Not so long ago, Ceylon was a country of three
languages. Bus signs, store fronts, billboards, railroad crossings and stations all carried three lines of information. English appeared in our
familiar alphabet; Sinhalese showed its own curly script; Tamil used
straight up-and-down characters. Since 1956, when Ceylon became a
Dominion of the British Commonwealth, the reins have tightened against
minorities. On most signs, the Tamil has been blacked out with a vin-
dictive brush; English still shows on a few signs but the number is
growing fewer. In January, 1961, Sinhalese was proclaimed the only
language to be used. This leaves the Ceylon people isolated with a language known to only six million people in the whole world, a language
unknown also to one-fourth of the people who were born and brought up
in Ceylon.

The Sinhalese script is fascinating—as if a tipsy worm was trying to get
home after a gay evening. Time and time again, I asked the Sisters to read
a billboard showing a languid lady in sari and jewels. It always said something like, "I bank at the First National," or, "Use Dial Soap. I do." What
a shock to find that a line of such beautiful curves means only, "Keep off
the grass!"

The people are beautiful too. Every one of them. Straight noses, dark
eyes, wavy hair, graceful carriage, pearly teeth and soft voices, they have
them all. A photographer goes crazy in this country. Each child is more
exquisite than the last; every mother, even if her sari is tattered and her
nose-jewel tawdry, is a picture of gentle dignity. Going down our road to
the main highway to catch a bus or buy a few peanuts, you are bombarded
with heavenly smiles. Children run out to greet you, putting palms together in front of their faces and shouting "ayubowan!" Mothers come to
the doors, hoping to catch your eye so that they too can put their palms together and call out "ayubowan!" They are the friendliest people in the
world; if you produce a camera, you are mobbed. It's a cooperative project
—picture taking. Ratnapala holds the flash gun; Appuhamy stands guard
over the case; Sirisena hands you the flashbulbs. Everybody else gets into
the act and will stand on his head for an hour if you want to take the
picture that way.

I didn't expect to find much friendliness on Ceylon. After all, we Maryknoll Sisters are foreigners in an intensely nationalistic country. We are
Catholic missioners stationed at the heart of pure Buddhism. But anyone
going down our road would think we were the answer to Ceylon's prayer.
Buddhists, Hindus, Moslems and Catholics all give us the "ayubowan!"
treatment.

Our bungalow is very small; it requires rugged economy of space. Only
after the front door is closed, can Sister Maria Luz spread out her fold-up

cot against it. There is no electricity. Kerosene lamps are the staple light; two pressure lamps are for chapel and reception room. The Sisters' trunks are tables; cupboards are made of packing crates; small fruit boxes are bedside stands. The nicest piece of furniture in the convent is ingenious. It is a bookcase using planks as shelves and uprights of bricks; it looks like something out of *House and Garden* recommended for a hunting lodge. The kitchen has two kerosene burners on which the Sisters perform miracles three times a day. An old (and empty) gin bottle serves as rolling pin and also for grinding pepper right from the vine. An open fireplace of cement heats water for baths and laundry.

Most of the daytime light comes through small skylights let into the roof. They make the cozy house very cheerful on a sunny day. One of these skylights shines on the tabernacle on the altar; it looks like a well-placed floodlight. Several times, leaving the chapel, I felt around on the wall for the electric switch.

Across the road from us is a large cemented area about the size of two tennis courts. All day long in the hot sun the estate workers spread out cocoa beans to dry, in neat squares of Grade One, Grade Two and Grade Three. The workers are Tamils, small of frame, very dark-skinned, bright with earrings, bangles and hair ornaments. A handsome people, they have innate grace as they carry baskets of coconuts on their heads, or swing a heavy brazen jar on their hips.

They are very fond of us, and we of them. The children crowd around our back door every morning and Sister pours into them their vitamins. That's right, pours. The bigger children come up with their mouths open. Sister drops a pill into the mouth and with her other hand pours some water from a high-held bottle to wash it down. The system was devised to keep the pills from being handled by grubby hands, and the water from being drunk from a common glass. The smaller children and babies are vitaminized by a spoonful of liquid poured into the open mouth. Any of the mothers who need it get the same treatment. It's like watching a nestful of little birds get their daily worm. All the children of estate workers are on the morning line-up, plus a dozen or so little chiselers who come from across the paddy fields.

At Kundasale, Maryknoll Sisters have a small maternity hospital and staff a clinic. In thirteen years of medical work on the island they have learned the customs. One is that Tuesdays and Fridays are bad days to take medicine. Also the first day of the month and the "poya" days when the moon is full, find skimpy lines at the dispensary.

In Ceylon they shake the head "Yes" just as we shake it for "No." It's sort of a wobble like a reluctant "No."

"Does it hurt here?"

The shy woman wobbles "yes." If the Sister is new she goes on. "Does it hurt here? Here? Well, where does it hurt?"

"Here!" and they are back to the first place.

We often meet very bad sores in the mouth and all the way down to the stomach, from the habit of chewing betel nuts, spiced with pepper leaves and sprinkled with lime. The people even make a paste of the lime and spread it like peanut butter over the roof of their mouths. You meet betel chewers in many parts of the world, but I never saw such havoc from it except in Ceylon. The blood-red juice squirts out of a million faces in market, streets, plantation "lines" and school yards.

As nurses, one of the hardest things to get used to, oddly enough, is the Buddhist's respect for life. A man who in anger will slice up his enemy, still cannot bring himself to kill a cockroach or a snake in cold blood. Even bedbugs are allowed to live. The most we can get hospital orderlies to do, is to brush them away. One evening, a deadly tick polonga was found near a patient lying on the clean floor. No one would kill it; the orderly gently picked him up on a stick and placed him tenderly outside.

To watch a mahout with his elephant is a lesson in labor management. To watch an elephant with his mahout is a lesson in devoted service. The two form a unit, a happy marriage, a smooth capital and labor combination, a real team of brains and brawn. Of the two, I think the mahout works harder. He rides on the animal's neck where he can whisper sweet nothings into his ear. There is definite "elephant talk"; it eludes grammar and syntax. But each understands the other perfectly.

Every afternoon around three o'clock, the elephants swing down to the river for their daily bath, each with a mahout riding on his neck. In the shallow banks at Katugastota, the animals stretch out full length in the cool water. Now the mahout's work begins. Like a chauffeur polishing up a Cadillac, he goes over every square inch of that elephant (and an elephant has plenty of square inches) with a coconut husk brush. The long skinny tail, the great flaps of ears, all the way down the trunk from forehead to nostril—the mahout scrubs carefully. Then he gives a command. The elephant opens his eyes, flicks his tail, slowly raises his head and oh, so wearily stands up. Then the feet buckle a little and, first thing you know, there is a large displacement of water as His Majesty slides into the water to expose his other side for scrubbing. Perfect contentment. Nirvana.

For his master he will push anything, uproot anything, stand in any sort of pose for tourists and expect nothing in return but a bale of hay. And that daily bath. Without it, he is just not a happy elephant.

In Kandy, elephants are not only work animals but they add style to a procession. Like limousines at a funeral, they measure the importance of the event. We often passed small processions en route to this temple or that, but once we saw a seven-elephant procession bringing the first rice of a nearby village as an offering to the famous Temple of the Tooth in Kandy. Oddly enough, the elephants carried no rice. They just walked along, as gayly decked out as the dancers who twisted and leaped and danced all the way into Kandy. When we saw it, the procession was trudging a dusty road; the dancers were sweaty and played out. Men under an ornamental canopy carried the rice sacks on their heads.

These Kandyan dancers are a race unto themselves. They train from childhood for muscle control which makes possible the fierce leaps that end every dance. We passed a wooden hut on the roadside one day and noticed a small sign in Sinhalese, "Dancing taught here." So we asked the shabby, middle-aged man who answered our knock, if we might watch. He was all smiles. Inside, three or four low benches faced a low stage. The ten-or-so students were furiously climbing into their best costumes, now that an audience had arrived. They ranged from about ten through sixteen years of age. The excitement and chattering were what you would expect of any youngsters that age. They pushed each other out the rear door so as to leave the stage ready for action.

Wham! goes the drum. The gourd rattles take up the rhythm. And in come the children—not children at all but stylized creatures picked off a travel advertisement. Palms spread open, feet at odd angles, the head stiff and knees bent, they did their master proud. Like the father of them all, he sat on the front bench and beamed at them and at us.

Suddenly, I felt that a curtain had fallen. I did not know these children. In fact, they weren't children at all. The jolly little man who was their teacher, so smiling and human a moment ago, he too had stepped into a world beyond my understanding. Something I had never experienced.

Children in Hong Kong, children in Africa, children in the Philippines —I have taught them all. They are different from children in Chicago and San Francisco, but they stay children. Little ones on the island of Yap do the same dances their elders do, but they do them in a childish way. However, these Ceylonese youngsters were hardened performers, dead serious, and almost in a trance. It was such a relief at the end to see them break the pose and scamper off stage.

﴾ 7 ﴿ Coolie Bishop in a Buddhist World

KANDY is the center of Buddhism, not only for the island but for the world. Ceylon, it is estimated, is sixty-five percent Buddhist, twenty percent Hindu, six percent Mohammedan and nine percent Christian. In Kandy, the religion is at its purest, without the furbelows added to it in India, Siam and China. Buddhist leaders of other countries make pilgrimages to Kandy to venerate the Tooth of Buddha, and to study the religion as the monks of the great Temple of the Tooth practice it. From this temple the Great Perahera procession originates; ninety magnificently caparisoned elephants bring the Tooth out among the faithful. There is some dispute about the authenticity of the Tooth since the Portuguese in the sixteenth century took it to Goa and ground it to powder, but tradition says that the particles reunited and came miraculously back to Kandy.

For our pilgrimage Sister Regina Therese and I caught the bus at the corner of our country lane and the "big thoroughfare"—well, anyway, it was a macadam road and wide enough for two cars to pass. On second thought, "caught" is hardly the word to use. The bus was standing in the shade of a big tree, like an old horse with his head between his knees. Wijesena, the driver, was stretched alongside deep in an after-dinner siesta. Sister and I climbed aboard to join the six or seven passengers who sat on the small wooden benches waiting for Fate to nudge Wijesena awake and get the bus moving.

It took more than Fate to accomplish that. Wijesena awoke refreshed, eager to compete once more in Life's Frenzied Battle. He leaped aboard, twitched the ignition key, twitched and twitched again. No result. He shouted something to the passengers. Three or four men got out and started to push. The old bus moved imperceptibly from under the tree's shade out to the road. All of a sudden there was a frightening roar, the motor caught on and we were off to Kandy.

We made up for lost time. Trees, bullock carts, bicycles, small huts and rice paddies flew past the window. Kandy clings to the side of several steep mountains. Even walking has its hazards when a banana peel can hurtle you several hundred feet straight down. But since Sister Regina Therese sat there so placidly, speaking of birds, flowers and Sisters we had known in Hawaii years ago, I commended my quivering soul to God and decided to be just as nonchalant.

Ceylonese have the steadiest nerves I have ever seen. I used to think the

Chinese were the experts at looking Death square in the face and yawning politely as they did it. Both races are good, but there is a difference in their techniques. The Chinese have zest in the danger as if to say, "Oh, boy! I missed the grave by half a second that time. Let's try for a quarter second next time." The Ceylonese on the other hand avoid obliteration as if it didn't exist. There are no wild leaps, no scurrying, no grabbing the child away in the nick of time. There is not even a glance at approaching disaster. Yet, as the bus passes, you see that the filmy sari has stepped aside, the child is not on the road, the man's big brown foot which should be under the wheel now is whole and well. There is a good inch to spare. These people who were so close to eternity may glance at you with a quiet eye, but there is no rebuke nor perturbation in their hearts.

It all adds up. What I said above is true. Obliteration doesn't exist; a Buddhist believes that he is probably doomed to live on this earth in eternity in some form or other. If you are convinced that you will return in another shape, maybe you won't care too much. Any change might be for the better. Only the very holy can break the bonds of existence and attain to blessed non-existence.

The animals too seem to believe this. They wander the streets with ease —not to call it insolence. A gentle cow will not blink even though her eyelashes are singed by the exhaust pipe. Why should she? She was probably one of the ancient Kandyan kings seven hundred years ago.

As we all but made an ink spot out of a miserable dog, I said, "Any animal as flea-bitten and starved as that should be put out of his misery."

"Don't say that," Sister said. "He might be your Uncle Joe."

"Well, if he is my Uncle Joe I think I'd treat him a little better. Cure his mange, feed him something, clear up his fleas."

"Yes, but you don't know. That's the hard part of it. Maybe he's Hitler or Stalin or Jesse James or somebody wicked. No, no, better play it safe, Sister. Let nature take its course."

The famous Temple of the Tooth stands on Kandy's main street, a jumble of low buildings erected, it is said, by Portuguese prisoners some four hundred years ago. This accounts for the squat octagonal tower. The "new wing," not yet completed, was begun thirty years ago. For those who have seen the Buddhist temples of Japan, Korea, China and Siam, this is very unimpressive. There are no red and gold rafters, no solemn sitting Buddhas twenty or thirty feet high, no great halls redolent of incense. "This might be one of the lesser California mission monasteries," I thought.

It was about one o'clock in the afternoon when Sister Regina Therese and I stepped through the low stone door. We confronted a corridor some ten feet wide with a rough stone floor. Nobody was around. We advanced cautiously. Ten seconds later, our fate was sealed.

All I could comprehend at first was a mouth full of red betel juice talking very very fast Sinhalese. Then the rest of him became apparent—rumpled black hair and oddly appealing eyes, the tattered and dirty shirt, the cotton wrap-around skirt that nearly all men wear in Ceylon, and the bare feet beneath it. He was gesturing toward our feet in an agony of apprehension.

"We have to take off our shoes. This is holy ground," Sister translated at last. "He wants to take us around."

To say truth, I was disappointed in the great Temple of the Tooth. Our voluble friend showed us a sitting Buddha in a glass case. A table littered with flower heads was before it—a shabby table with dead and dying flowers. A few feet further down the corridor, there was a smaller Buddha sitting in another glass case, like someone in a smudgy telephone booth. The tables were ugly, the walls were grey stone and whitewash, the floor a dull uneven grey stone. You might find this sort of thing, I thought, in any small Buddhist chapel hidden behind a market stall in Honolulu or in a corner of a farmer's house in China or Japan. Where was the splendor of the great Tooth Temple with its hundreds of monks in the monastery, the ninety elephants of the Perehera festival known all over the world?

Our friend was chatting away in Sinhalese. He pointed out the railing which separates the monks from the people. "If you wish to consult one of the monks," he explained, "you ask at this door to see him. Then he comes out of the monastery and seats himself at this table. You ask your questions and he answers you. This railing is always between you. He never leaves the cloistered area."

He pointed through an open window across the court to what he called the "new wing." The English words stuck out in his rapid Sinhalese. "That building is where the monks have their living quarters," he said.

We went around some more. Suddenly we found ourselves in a large room, like a gymnasium with no equipment. A shabby wooden partition, perhaps twelve feet high, blocked off about half this hall. A dingy door was open in it, and our friend disappeared inside. We would have followed, but a sign, the only one in English, stopped us. NO ADMITTANCE EXCEPT ON BUSINESS. Well, that let us out. We stopped short. It seemed an abrupt end to the grand tour, but we bent over to put on our shoes and leave.

"No, no!" Our betel-juice friend was back, standing in the doorway and waving us on. We pointed to the NO ADMITTANCE sign. Still he waved us to come.

We came. He ushered us into a small room, rather dark. Confronting us were two Buddhist monks arrayed in saffron robes and quite unsmiling. One was tall and well built, maybe forty-five years old, with shaven head, face, eyebrows and even eyelashes. The other was short and rather plump.

He too had shaved head, cheeks, chin and eyebrows, but a goodly growth of hairs sprouted from his ears as if to taunt, "Try to catch us here!"

We were speechless. We had expected another sitting Buddha, not live monks.

"Do you speak English?" I asked the larger monk, feeling like Goldilocks when she woke to find three huffy bears staring down on her.

"No," said the monk and that was all.

By this time, our betel-chewing guide had recovered his breath. He rattled on and Sister Regina Therese translated in tremulous English. It gave me a chance to look around.

A large business-like desk was up against one of the drab walls of long-unpainted wood. The bigger monk may have been working there; the top was littered with papers and a wastebasket beside it had overflowed on the floor. Under the high window on the far side of the room was a bed with a square mosquito net. Beside this was an alarm clock of ancient design with two bells on top. In the other corner was another bed, or rather a cot with rumpled bedclothes. A washstand with pitcher and basin completed the furnishings. This was evidently a combination office and bedroom for these two monks.

I looked at Number One closely. I have seen that sort of face on a New York banker—or managing editor of a newspaper—or a Jesuit superior—or a trust fund administrator when you come asking for a grant. He was looking at me too, and I could see the questions in those very suave, knowing eyes. What are you here for? What's in that bag you carry? Are you a spy, or a bomb setter, or just an innocent tourist?

In the meantime, Sister was translating. "He says that the monks arise at five in the morning and have prayers. Then they expose the Tooth for veneration by the public at 6:30 and again at 9:00 A.M. Many people come at those hours. The Tooth is shut off from view at other times except at 6:00 in the evening when it is again shown to the devout. He says we may not see the Tooth now, but if we wish we may leave flowers outside."

We thanked him for the information. The monks nodded that this was indeed the schedule of hours. We knew well that we need not have been brought into the monastery to be told it. These monks wanted to see what kind of people we were. We were about to bow out when I decided to put those steady eyes and saffron robes on film. I stepped forward and opened the airlines bag I use for a gadget bag.

"Pictures?" I asked.

A dither ensued. The big monk turned to the wall where the washstand was; the little one dashed out of the room.

"Now you've done it!" I thought. "You'll be lucky to get out of this alive." How does one expiate an insolence to the Buddhist Father General?

The rack? Sitting in hot sun? Buried in ants? Washing dishes for life? I started to put the camera away. The guide stopped me.

"They just want to change their clothes for the picture," he explained.

Sure enough! The Number One monk was swinging another bright saffron robe around himself. Monk Number Two soon came in arrayed also in new clothes and a broad smile. They posed like models, anywhere I wanted them. We parted a smiling, urbane, very chummy group.

Looking back on the incident and translating it into the same situation in America, I can see what happened. The political situation was tense against Catholics. The government had said it would take over the management of all private schools; Catholic families were camping in the classrooms to forestall such a move. Then, at noon when few people would be astir in the Temple of the Tooth, greatest of all Buddhist temples in Ceylon, two Catholic Sisters wander in with an airlines bag. What would happen if two Buddhist monks in their saffron robes, carrying a suspicious bundle between them, came into a big city's cathedral, just when a Catholic government—God save the day!—was to take over Buddhist schools? Maybe the pastor would send a sacristan to show them about and try to find out what errand they came on. It was obvious that they would not show us the audience chamber where the famous Tooth was. They were wary of letting us anywhere near that Tooth.

The relief in my heart when the monks joyously posed for pictures must have been nothing to the relief in theirs.

Ceylon is thoroughly Buddhist. When a bus passes the Temple of the Tooth, most of the passengers rise from their seats and bow toward the structure. On a trip to Polonnaruwa, our bus driver stopped to buy a coconut and smash it against a stone before a wayside shrine. If it had not broken, it would have meant bad luck and probably he would have refused to make the trip. On the way home, he bought another coconut to smash in gratitude. What hurt was that each time he borrowed ten cents from us to buy the coconut.

The sacred bo tree is never destroyed. Tradition says that Buddha rested under a bo tree when he had his revelations.

Every bo shoot has enjoyed immunity thereafter. When a new bo tree is discovered, the faithful drape ropes around the branches to indicate that it is sacred, and place votive offerings and lights on the ground in front of it. The bo leaf is round with a long tapering point, rather like the headdress of Siamese or Javanese dancers. Possibly the pointed headdress is derived from the bo.

Buddhism came to Ceylon around 300 B.C., leaping over from India. In the two thousand three hundred years since then, it has been the cornerstone of Ceylon's history. There have been several Temples of the Tooth;

the sacred relic, reputed to be Gautama Buddha's left canine tooth, has been carried from capital to capital as Sinhalese kings have evacuated one town after another. Its present home is by no means the most gorgeous. We had to go to Polonnaruwa for that.

One thing about Ceylon—the people are not parsimonious with their syllables. Particularly in names. Kandy and Colombo are plebian names, corrupted by short-tongued foreigners. The real Sinhalese names are un-rememberable at first and unforgettable later. The effort to master them fixes them indelibly in mind. Sight and sound have but the vaguest connection; Nurawa Eliya is pronounced Nuralya.

A mere babe in arms carries a name which drags along the floor after him. Surely, nobody who loves the child will deprive him of a few syllables when they are free for the asking. I asked a lad what his name was, expecting a handful of syllables but not what I got. "Mawaranuwa Bandu-tanaikara," he said. I tried adding him to my list for the Commemoration of the Living at Mass, but it put me two pages behind the priest in the missal.

Small wonder then that on a map of Ceylon the town names begin in the middle of the island and keep going for an inch or more into the ocean. Polonnaruwa seemed close to Kandy. But I was looking at the end of the word; the dot next to the P was fifty miles away.

Polonnaruwa is a mine of antiquity. Through wild jungles which look as though the hand of man had never touched them, our crowded Volks station wagon ran. If we had had time to hack a way through the tangled vines and undergrowth, we could have stumbled upon many an ancient irrigation canal, many a reservoir and pool. This whole area was once rice fields and gardens. But we were bound for Polonnaruwa, city of the kings of the Resplendent Isle from 1056 until around 1220. Before that, it had been the summer resort of Ceylonese nobles from Anuradhapura. After that period it was and has been a jungle.

Americans, when we think of background and history, follow a familiar line back to Adam. There was George Washington, and before him, Europe. Before Europe was Rome and Greece. Then comes the Old Testament back through David, Moses and Abraham to Adam himself. We may take a side line through Egypt or Assyria or northern Africa, but on the whole the path is well marked. In the house of our family tree, these are the ancestors who hang on the walls.

Wandering through Polonnaruwa gave me a queer uninvited feeling. Like a child who has gone to bed and finds it isn't his mother who is tucking him in at all. Or a guest at the wrong party. Or someone who thinks he is going on a boat ride and finds himself going down a snowy slope with skis on his feet. I felt I had gone into the house of history and found the wrong ancestors hanging on the wall.

For, while our Greece and Rome and Europe were bowling along, other civilizations were erupting elsewhere. The Incas in Peru, the Aztecs in Mexico, the Chinese, Japanese and Ceylonese. Climbing the ancient ruins of Polonnaruwa, one doesn't know whether he should say, "How strange!" or "How familiar!" The human problems are so ordinary; their results so strange. You sit down on remnants of a royal bath and you think, "These were men like us. They had the same human nature to contend with as we do. Their objectives seem to have been about the same. Civic welfare, development of public works, how to make the 'haves' share with the 'have-nots'—the welfare of religion, defense against enemies within and without. Our newspapers could have been published in Polonnaruwa in the year 1156 just by changing a few names and technical terms."

The greatest king was Parakrambuha. (I told you the Ceylonese do not skimp on syllables.) He got his throne without too much trouble. He was nephew of the old king and, from his youth, had shown he was rich in genius as well as everything else. They say he had some Tamil or South Indian blood; certainly he had the energetic approach to problems which the Indians have. On his coronation in 1153 he said, "It is my ambition that no drop of water in my kingdom reach the ocean without having benefited mankind."

This is the origin of the "tanks" of Ceylon. They are really artificial lakes; the one at Polonnaruwa itself covers four thousand acres. The whole thing is so perfectly designed that when British engineers reconstructed the area they could not find better places for the locks and gates than those the ancient Ceylonese builders had used.

The city and cultivated rice paddies and gardens all around it extended for miles and miles. The site of the city thus far excavated, although covering an area four miles long, is only a small cleared patch in the jungle which has grown over the farm lands of old Ceylon.

Palaces with council chambers, sleeping apartments and gardens; monasteries for thousands of monks; theaters and picture galleries; fountains and baths with elaborate underground piping; the original Temple of the Tooth, and many other shrines, are scattered here and there. Just to stand at the doorway of the monastery known as Lamkatilaka (if you can't pronounce that name, try its other one, Jetavanarama) and to gaze at the gigantic Buddha on the far wall, more than fifty-five feet high even without his head, is to realize the mental power of these old Ceylonese who laid brick upon brick here eight hundred years ago.

Most impressive of all is the Galvihara, where four huge figures of Buddha are carved out of solid rock. It is as if you had cut a pound of butter in half, pushed the front part away and carved the statues out of the cut surface. The standing Buddha is twenty-two feet high; the reclining Buddha forty-four feet long, and the sitting Buddhas slightly smaller. After all, the Christ of the Andes is only twenty-six feet high.

Beside these colossal figures carved in the rock is a huge "page" of writing. I asked the Sisters to read it for me. It is, they said, something like what the Rule of St. Augustine is for Catholic religious—a rule of life laying down general directions for community living. It's a good idea to cut it into stone. Our copy of the Rule at Maryknoll is always wearing out; the monks of Polonnaruwa had one that has lasted for eight hundred years.

The trouble is, it outlasted the monks. As I looked, a green lizard skipped across the great foot of Buddha. And among the ruined buildings were little grey monkeys, gathering acorns and scratching themselves, just as their ancestors did in A.D. 1100. Their ancestors' homes are gone long since, but the lizards and monkeys remain. The homes of men are still there, even their Holy Rule, but the men are gone.

Compared to Buddhism's age in Ceylon, the Church is a mere upstart. And Catholics show something of the spunk of the early Christians. Portuguese brought the Faith around 1500. Dutch came around 1650 and Catholics had to go underground for one hundred and fifty years. Yet their numbers grew. The main figure during this time was Father Joseph Vas, a Goan, who came into the country disguised as a Tamil laborer. By skipping away from the police often enough, he managed to live to a ripe old age.

Ceylon's Catholics are invigorating. More than seventy percent of their priests are Ceylonese and four of the six bishops on the island are native. There is a vigor and youth about them that bodes well for the future. Many have studied in Rome, England or the United States; they have a worldly polish as well as solid Catholicity. Sisters too have joyousness and vitality. There are six hundred Ceylonese Good Shepherd Sisters and many from other congregations as well.

They will need, it seems, all the spunk and polish they have. Not long ago, Catholic Sisters who had staffed some of the government hospitals—at the previous government's urgent invitation—were summarily dismissed. The result is awkward for those who invited them to come and a little bit disastrous for the sick.

Schools came next. About two-thirds of all children in school attended Catholic schools. At the same time, the Ceylon *Times* estimated that between 400,000 and 700,000 children had no schools at all. Yet the Catholic schools were taken over or closed down and no new schools were opened. The Catholics put up a stiff fight. Something of their calibre can be seen from this incident.

During the Christmas vacation of 1960–1961, Catholic families took turns occupying their schools on the premise that they had built the schools and financed them, and therefore they could sleep in the classrooms if they wished. This was to prevent the government from using the schools for its own purposes, since it took over the management but not the property of Catholic schools. A young girl from the country was attending High School in Colombo; since things were so unsettled, she decided not to go back to her home town for Christmas but to spend the feast in Colombo. However, her mother wrote:

> My dear daughter,
> As you may have heard, the Catholics of our town are taking turns in occupying the school; each family has a night of the week. It may well be that we will be called upon to suffer for our Faith on the night our family occupies the school. I would not want anyone of my family to be absent on such a glorious night. Come home.

The government gave one of those "or else . . . ." choices. A Catholic school could "go private," which meant that it might open its doors but charge no tuition. It must depend on good-will contributions for support.

As a result, every diocese started a School Fund. Catholics wished each other "A Courageous Christmas!" They sent no Christmas cards, bought no new clothes, ate no Christmas candies, and drank no Good Cheer. Money thus saved was donated to the School Fund. They realized a tidy sum but not enough, of course, to operate all the schools.

The Ceylonese are a deeply spiritual people. Their shrines are under every tree; consciousness of the supernatural shines in their eyes. They know how to manage the world. Some of them manage it superlatively well. But their main interest is in things of the spirit. This is true of Buddhists and Catholics alike. Of all Ceylonese.

I met a remarkable man in Ceylon—remarkable to me, but not so extraordinary as Catholic Ceylonese go. He had just retired as manager of the Government Farm School where he had spent forty years. At last he had time to pray! I found him going from church to church with a beatific smile on his face. At our request he wrote out the plan of his pilgrimage.

TOKEN OF DEEP GRATITUDE TO OUR LORD
What shall I render to God for the things He has rendered to me?
As an esteemed token of my love and gratitude . . . for helping to perform forty years of meritorious government service in the Department of Agriculture with a clean record, I have decided to make a private pilgrimage to forty churches commencing from the Feast of the Purification (February 2), to be completed if possible before Easter Monday (April 3), and to conclude with a Thanksgiving Mass. My wife will accompany me if she can and at the Thanksgiving Mass I wish my whole family to attend and receive Holy Communion.

Then follows a list of prayers to be recited kneeling. The list would fill an hour very easily, as he sprinkled benefactions on millions of people, from the Holy Father and all mankind down to the last soul in Purgatory. Not one escaped his generosity, now that he had time to kneel quietly before God and talk to Him about them all. I wondered how many Catholics in the States had similar retirement plans.

We spent Christmas in Ceylon—the Courageous Christmas. It was all wrapped around with interest in Bishop Regno, who is as saintly in a European way as the retired farm manager is in the Ceylonese way.

He is known as the Coolie Bishop—this small Italian with the ponderous beard and quick laugh. More than fifty years in Ceylon, he first worked with the Tamil laborers on big estates. Stories are rife as to his prowess. He walked more than thirty miles from place to place. He slept and ate in "the lines" with the workers, refusing invitations to stay with the owners. His polished manners and gay humor made him good company for wealthy people but he preferred to stay with his parishioners. Even when he was Bishop of Ceylon's proudest city, he still rode in buses and third-class railroad compartments. He resigned in 1959 in favor of a young Ceylonese and chortles in glee that he can now ride with the common people and not excite comment. He wears no stockings except on state occasions. He insists on being his own sacristan, caring for the altar and vestments himself. He gets his candles made from the stubs of votive candles before the statues in his church. He has no housekeeper because he eats but one meal a day and that is breakfast at the Maryknoll Sisters' convent.

Since we are three miles from Kandy, it is sometimes awkward to get transportation when the Sisters attend school plays or functions in the city. On one occasion, the hostess arranged that the Bishop and the Sisters would return in a car she provided. Bishop Regno, seeing that the car would be crowded, slipped away early and came home by himself. The next morning at his breakfast, Sister Regina Michael ventured to chide him, "You should not have done that. There was plenty of room in the car, Bishop."

The Bishop playfully popped a cashew nut into his mouth. "Don't worry about me," he assured her. "I came home in one of the biggest and most expensive cars in Kandy. Had a professional chauffeur, too. I always give myself the best." Later Sister found out that the most expensive cars in Kandy are the city buses.

On Christmas Eve, the nine of us dressed silently for Midnight Mass and walked down the country lane to Bishop Regno's church. Past the patch of snake gourd where the serpentine squashes glistened with strange brilliance in moonlight. Past a rice paddy; one could almost hear the roots stretching down through the ooze at the bottom. Past a row of huts dark with sleep. Yoganandra's house, and Mari's who always carries her baby brother, Ratnapapala's house, and the champion of them all, Nawaranuwa Bandutanaikara. It was odd not to see them run out into the road to greet us. Poor children, they slept fitfully on the earthen floors inside, unaware that Christ was being born again, not in faraway Palestine but in the white church at the crest of their hill. This afternoon, they had been Sister's Little Helpers setting up the crib in church. Questions galore from them. But we dared not tell them about Jesus' coming tonight. Who knows? Stories get around and soon the stern finger of the law would shout, "Proselytizing!" It's a pretty fix for missioners to be in, but we were in it.

We made the steep climb to the top a bit breathless. After all, when you are trying to pray for everyone you ever knew and all those you wish you could understand, there's not much breath left to push old Brother Ass up a hill.

The church was full and filling fuller. On the pews were Sinhalese, middle class women in filmy saris of most exquisite color and texture; children in dresses and white suits, smart young fellows in shirts and wrap-around cotton skirts; older men with white hair and mustaches contrasting with their dark skins. Squatting, kneeling, sitting on the familiar floor were the Tamil estate workers. Judging from wrinkles, many coats had lain folded in trunks for most of the year. Nose-jewels and bracelets even on the poorest, even on the babies. Many old men wore their hair in a bun at the back and their ears were adorned with rings.

The Bishop was hearing confessions right out in the open with only a screen between him and the penitent. Midnight came, 12:15 and 12:30. Still the confessional line had always three or four. The Bishop peeked around his screen several times and thought he would finish those few, but new ones continually had a bright thought, "I think I'll go to confession!" and joined the line-up.

We didn't mind too much. It was good to sit there jammed together with Sinhalese and Tamils and Europeans, knowing that in our very closeness we formed a solid block of humanity welded by Faith. With that in common, all our differences dwindled to the vanishing point. Each of us had something personal to say to God on this night; yet besides our individual stories there was the common cry for light to see God's Will and strength to follow it.

At Holy Communion time, the whole mass of us surged forward, stepping over the Tamil babies left behind on the floor. The heads were tilted back—heads with turbans or hats or veils, heads with whiskers profuse, or cleanshaven, heads with dark faces or light ones—the tongues came out and the Lord of us all rested on them. Our fusion was nothing to His.

Ceylon Catholics were tense that Christmas on account of what might happen. Think of all the Christmas Masses in countries where it had happened. Our schools were threatened; in so many other lands they were closed. Long closed. Foreign priests and Sisters wondered, "How long before the government cancels all visas?" Think of the nations which have driven out even native priests. There was much to think about, much to pray strength for.

After Midnight Mass, the Bishop went walking. Arrayed in all his episcopal robes, down to the black pumps with red pompons (which I am sure were part of his original outfit when he became Bishop of Kandy years ago), he set out to walk through his unconscious parish. We Sisters followed him: two little altarboys went along for the fun.

It was fun. He left a trail of quips, bright remarks, quick laughter along the silent streets. We went past the dispensary; no lines waiting outside. Past the shops, shuttered and boarded for the night. Past the bus stop on the main road. Past the children's houses, past the growing rice and the snake gourd patch. We were back at our bungalow. The path was outlined by tiny flames from wicks floating in coconut oil in half-shells. An outdoor crib made of brown paper with silhouettes cut from X-ray film glowed before the door. We sang some hymns with the Bishop trailing an octave below. Then we swung into Christmas gaiety over a hearty cup of cocoa and mammoth doughnuts. The Coolie Bishop joined us, displaying a coolie appetite for good things, all the good-er after his long fast.

The talk soon turned to—yes, more Sisters. The same old story; so much to be done, so few to do it. As I feared, Mother put me up for sale. How much? The Bishop offered an elephant. The Ceylon Sisters thought that reasonable. One elephant for another, I suppose. Fortunately, we travel on tourist rates. "What about an elephant in those tourist seats, Mother?" I asked. The subject, thanks be to God, was dropped.

Later, I rather wished I were an elephant in the tourist seat en route to Bangkok. For one thing, with a tough skin I might not have felt the people behind walking up and down my seat back; for another, with a long trunk I might have done something about it. Like squirting water over my head at them. These people behind seemed never to be settled, pushing and poking while they rearranged their hand luggage under, over and around their feet. Then they gave the whole floor space over to baggage and propped their feet up against the chairback. *My* chairback. That got boring, and they tried leaping all over the back, jumping from my waist to my head to my shoulders in gay abandon. I couldn't resist taking a look. They were an Indian couple, newlyweds probably. They were having such a good time billing and cooing, I hadn't the heart to look severe and sat down again.

After a while, as I leaned on the armrest, something touched my elbow,
—touched and stayed pushing forward. I looked down. It was the fair
bride's foot, resting casually halfway into my armrest. It stayed there
for some time; I could observe it well. Besides the bright red nail polish,
each toe had a silver ring on it. The stones, believe it or not, were between the toes. This is real penance.

You often hear about the East rubbing elbows with the West, but
I never thought an Eastern foot with rings on the toes would be rubbing
my Western elbow. But that's what travel does to one.

PHILIPPINES

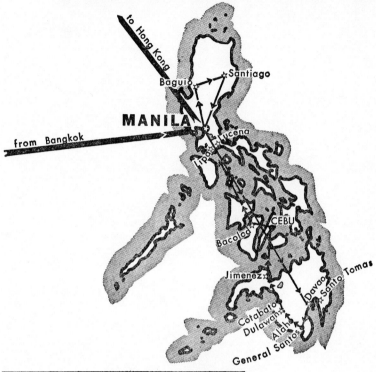

to Hong Kong

Baguio ☆Santiago

MANILA ☆

from Bangkok

Lucena

Tipo

CEBU

Bacolod

Jimenez

Santo Tomas

Davao

Cotabato

Dulawan

Aloha

General Santos

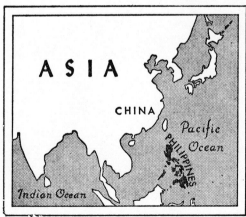

ASIA

CHINA

Pacific Ocean

PHILIPPINES

Indian Ocean

PHILIPPINES

⫷ 8 ⫸ *Sentimental Bus Ride*

SHE'S a lovely lady. Dignified and warmly human. A widow twice over now, fond of both her husbands but subservient to neither. Now that she is alone, she rather enjoys making her own mistakes. They aren't the mistakes her husbands would have made, but what's the use of freedom if you can't make your kind of mistakes? That's the fun of handling your own affairs, isn't it?

She is Manila, a woman of history. Her girlhood was wild and free, playing around with Chinese, Japanese, Malayans and Borneans, who ran in from the neighborhood. She was well educated, had a written language, made pretty things of gold and silver, hammered out bronze and iron tools.

Then, one morning she woke to find herself married to Spain. Not an easy marriage, but she learned to mingle with her husband's family, so unlike the neighbors' children she grew up with. At first she was bewildered in her new setting; often galled by their calm assumption that all she had learned before was stupid. But she picked her way daintily through the European household and looked over the tray of jewels they offered for her adornment. Some she liked and kept; others she appraised and threw away. Of one, she said, "This is for keeps." It was the family pearl.

Even when her second husband, the energetic young American, took possession of her house, she kept that pearl. Sometimes he laughed at her for thinking so much of it; most often he shrugged as if it were a thing not worth bothering about. More than once she went up to the attic, thinking to put it away with the few keepsakes of her first marriage. With the trunk open, she would pause to look at her pearl. And to look again. No, no. Her Faith was not just a recuerdo of Spain; it was part of herself. She closed the trunk again and came downstairs.

It isn't often one sees an old friend with enough years between visits to let you note the changes. Mother and I knew Manila during the heyday years before World War II. We knew her when strangers' boots tramped the streets—when the prisons were full of her sons and the nightclubs were full of the strangers. After the liberation, Mother returned to the States. I stayed on for two years while Manila dug the bodies out of the air raid shelters and pushed the buildings back up. In 1949, I saw her again as she struggled to her feet once more. Now in 1961, we saw Manila flourishing again, strong like new growth from a charred stump.

I went out to make acquaintance with the lady again. I had an idea that there would be changes. Even from the air, flying over the harbor, I could see no Japanese ships on the harbor bottom. Right after the war, an American soldier took us up in a plane and we saw straight through the clear water to the fleet hobnobbing with the fishes down there. In 1947, our ship steered gingerly through a forest of mast heads, all one could see above water of that fleet below. Two years later, the ships had been raised, bailed out and the rusting hulks pulled over to the breakwater just to get them out of the way. Now—well, now nobody remembered them much. When I asked what happened to them I felt like Hannibal asking where his elephants' footprints were in the Alpine snows.

"How would you like an expedition into the dim mists of history?" I asked Sister Paula Cathleen. She eyed me warily.

"How far back?" she wanted to know.

"Twenty years or so."

"Oh," she said, "I'd like that. I teach history, you know."

"Ancient history?" I asked.

"No, medieval and the beginnings of modern history. This will just fit in. Let's go."

We went. At the corner of our country road, we hopped a bus coming from Marikina, bound for Divisoria market in Manila. The buses haven't changed much I noted. Still no room for my knees. Probably the very same bus honked along this street twenty years ago. Speedometer and mileage meter put out of commission; wooden floor unswept, wooden seats the same. The scenery outside was unchanged, only there was more of it. Interminable lengths of small sarisari stores, selling bits of clothing, crackers, canned foods, toys, religious statues, artificial flowers and candy in glass jars. But now the peanuts come in cellophane bags and the flowers are wrapped in plastic to keep the street dust from settling on them.

The city started to grow up around us. A much bigger city. Manila has two and one half million now sprawled out around it like Los Angeles.

Out of the open window (are windows ever closed on Manila buses?) I saw Bilibid prison. Couldn't resist it. Hopped off the bus. Dear old Bilibid! Just around the corner from Santo Tomas University where seven thousand American civilians spent the war years in internment. Old Bilibid! A Sing Sing alumnus could not have been gladder to see the dear old place. Here Father Cummings of Maryknoll and eight hundred of his comrades in arms sweated and starved and slaved. From Bilibid, he boarded the prison ship to Japan and died on the way, having used his last teaspoonful of precious water to baptize a dying soldier who asked him for it. God rest his soul! And God rest the soul of his Japanese guard who kindly let him out one afternoon every two weeks to forage around his friends in Manila asking food and money for disheartened, sick American boys. Hataji his name was—a name that comes often to the lips of those Maryknoll Sisters who knew him. Hataji was killed when Americans liberated our internment camp at Los Banos.

I looked at those squat towers of Bilibid as tourists might view the Colosseum in Rome. Many a martyr died there.

We hailed a jeepney and squeezed into it. For the uninitiated—those benighted folk who have never squeezed into a jeepney—this requires a bit of explanation. The word "jeepney," dear children, is a hybrid derived from "jeep" and "jitney," with all the good qualities of both. It was spawned in postwar years of the Army jeep and will go down in history as the Filipino's gift to the god of Enterprise.

The basic idea is to get a jeep by fair or foul means. Then remove the back seat, build out the rear end to a fabulous length. Then place seats lengthwise so that eight or ten people can sit, squeezed in tight with interlocking knees. This is the basic procedure. From here on, the imagination can free-wheel to creative heights. Paint, chrome trim, jigsaw work, painting on mirrors, dainty curtains, and tinselled shrines— one jeepney can use them all.

Sister Paula Cathleen and I waded out in midstream traffic to where the jeepney driver was courteously waiting for us. The honks behind him meant nothing to this Sir Walter Raleigh. He would spread his Sunday shirt upon the street if it would direct two more customers to him. We crawled into the back seat; Sir Walter lurched forward to get the green light, and we sat down suddenly. Beside me was a middle-aged man with his favorite fighting cock on his lap. The cock was quiet, blinking at each of us with brilliant, stupid eyes. Every now and then Mang Andoy stroked his iridescent tail feathers with the touch of affection.

Our jeepney too had had tender care. Curtains with chenille balls dangled at the windows and framed the back door. Bright paint spangled the ceiling and outside walls. A mirror spread from side to side in front of the driver—not at all content with a single rear-view mirror. In white paint on it was "In God We Trust." A rosary dangled before the windshield. A St. Christopher medal and small statue of Our Lady danced attendance on the dashboard. Anyone who must jerk and push, swerve and leap through Manila traffic twelve hours a day if Mama and the kids are going to have rice tonight, is wise to get the whole of Heaven plugging for him.

The jeepney is old stuff now; in fact, it is going out. City fathers—
who have Cadillacs to ride around in—say it is a hazard to life and limb.
Of course it is! So is mountain climbing, and automobile racing, and bull
fighting. Some people spend lots of money for the thrills a common
"tao" gets from merely crossing Plaza Goiti in Manila. But that's progress
for you. The expensive thrills remain; the cheap ones are condemned.

Remember the millionaires, proud to say they started out in business
as newsboys? Well, try to find a newsboy these days. Hopping on and
off trolley cars, slipping past the traffic cop, selling papers as customers
hang out of bus windows—these are passé sports now. But a sizable
number of boys do a similar job in Manila. In a traffic jam waiting for
the lights to change, a slim lad eased his way through the cars. He was
selling cigarettes, one at a time. It was a step up from the African in the
market who sold one puff at a time. These cigarette boys selling "loosies,"
are the modern newsboys in Manila. Quite a number of them go to our
Maryknoll Free School in the heart of the city. Most have had schooling
for only two years. We offer them a completely free education under
excellent teachers. Maryknoll Free School is reserved for children who
are willing to study hard but who cannot afford a good school. Others
need not apply. One of these lads works in the slaughterhouse from 5
to 11 P.M. Another puts in several hours as "conductor" on a jeepney;
that is, he yells out the destination all the time, keeps an eye out for
customers, helps stow the baggage, and collects the fares.

The teachers get the spirit of Maryknoll Free School. One came first
to offer his spare time; he was a teacher at an exclusive school for American
children only. Next year, he quit that job to teach our poor children
full time. Then he offered to teach algebra from 5 to 6 P.M. to any
child who wants to excel in math. It's amazing, the intellects discovered
in these underprivileged children. One boy went through Grades Two
to Seven in two years; he had missed many years of school in his short
life. He won a scholarship then to the Ateneo, the best school for boys
in the Philippines. Many a rich lad would give his eyeteeth to be accepted there.

Into Quiapo! You must have lived in Manila to appreciate Quiapo.
The cacophony of jeepney horns, the smell of gasoline, the constant
shouting " 'Soria 'Soria," "Malabon, Malabon," "Paco, Paco, Paco," "Pasay, Pasay"—as bus and jeepney conductors try to inveigle passengers
for these various sections of the city—it's a nightmare. A delightful nightmare. I could never be in Manila and not go to Quiapo there to be
strangled by the fumes and deafened by the roar just for old times' sake.

I'm glad I went. Next time I see Manila, law and order will have
taken over Quiapo. They are building a tunnel to ease the traffic situation. That huge plaza before Quiapo church is mostly a big hole. But

still the buses honk and the jeepneys squirm; Mamita with a basket of fruit on her head and a cigarette backwards in her mouth pulls her Pedrito out of the way of oncoming annihilation. Still the devout pour in and out of the old Spanish church, done up anew with aluminum paint and new decorations. Still the venders of drygoods, religious articles and hair ornaments keep calling the passerby.

We too went into the church. Here the Black Christ is venerated. Every Friday at 3 P.M. from time immemorial, the Black Christ of Quiapo has a service; every Good Friday men who will not darken the doors of a church at any other time, fight for the honor of bearing the Black Christ in procession around the plaza. The inside of Quiapo church, once the mecca of enthusiastic unregulated devotion, is succumbing to law and order also. A railing around the shrine makes people come up one at a time to venerate the statue. People still crawl up the middle aisle on their knees but they finish by kneeling at the altar rail before the Blessed Sacrament. Many more were quietly sitting in the pews and praying. A blind beggar at the door was saying his rosary, not calling out as they used to do. We gladly gave him fifty centavos.

Quiapo Market—could it be that law and order had penetrated even to Quiapo Market? Well, not entirely. But it is making headway, even in this citadel of the picturesque. There are no flies—repeat: no flies— around the meat and fish counters. However, baskets of fruit skins and left-overs, bits of wilted radishes and carrots, squashed squashes, and slightly rotten fruit clog the aisles in the good old way, and the floor is wet constantly—if not with dirty water, then with clean water put on to mop up the dirty water.

But the heart of the Filipino market venders is unchanged. It was good to hear them call out, "Mother! You will buy my eggs, Mother!" "See the pechay, Mother. Just picked today!" It was not that they really wanted us to buy. But a bit of conversation with the Sisters going past is good for the soul and, perhaps, for the pocketbook as well. They were so friendly, so pleasant, it was a shame we could not buy out everybody.

A silly incident came to mind as we wandered through the market. When I was new in Manila, Sister David Marie and I came here to do the family marketing. As we bought the last thing, she put the change in her purse and said, "Now we go soak." All the way down the street, I puzzled silently on "go soak." Soak whom? Does she mean we cheat somebody? Maybe it's a whimsical way of saying we will go to a swimming pool. What could be nicer? Or perhaps we soak our feet in a doctor's office. They're so tired. Maybe we go home and take a bath. They were all pleasant thoughts, but just then we turned into a Chinese hardware store. Over the door was the owner's name GO SOK, pronounced with two long O's.

I looked for Go Sok's as we went down Echague. Also for Ah Gong's where once we asked for "dog meat," meaning meat for a dog, and the clerk thought we meant meat of a dog. Echague is a welter of Chinese stores, selling cloth or glassware. Go Sok has a brand new three-story store in a swankier part of town. Plastic has taken over the cloth and glassware stores. Cups and glasses, plates and serving dishes are all of plastic now. The bolts of cheap cloth are mostly synthetics or plastic, too.

And into Santa Cruz. This is the heart of town. Plaza Goiti used to be the meeting place where hawkers and sellers from Quiapo on the east, and the more staid business people of Escolta on the west, met with the intellectuals and government workers who came across Santa Cruz Bridge from the south. Dominating the welter of people, buildings and bridges, is Santa Cruz church. Before the war, you couldn't see the church for the shabby, fly-by-night stalls and small stores set up all around it.

But war smashed the church almost to the ground; fire burnt out the stalls and stores. I remember coming across Santa Cruz Bridge when it was a makeshift affair of planks and pontoons put up by Army engineers. In those days, nobody had any transportation but Army personnel. We Sisters used to stand on street corners surrounded by our bundles, hoping that some private, colonel or general would take pity on us for a few blocks at least. Thus we got home from shopping trips by stages.

During one of these expeditions to replenish our cupboards, Sister David Marie and I went into the ruins of Santa Cruz church to refresh our spirit and to rest our feet. I'll never forget it. The Blessed Sacrament was exposed on the altar, under a galvanized iron roofing. The rest of the church was roofless. We sat on some benches in the bright sunshine or knelt on the old tile floor in those spots not dug up by bombs or shrapnel. The benches were fairly well filled with people who had lost the roofs over their heads, too. They had come to visit with our Lord, now in the same predicament. When we had rested, Sister David Marie and I went out the door to Plaza Goiti and looked down the Escolta, Manila's proudest business street. Three tall buildings had been smashed across the street as if a mighty hand had come down upon them from the rear. Just heaps of rubble. Others thrust jagged walls against the burning sky. This was Manila in 1945.

But not now. Sister Paula Cathleen and I came out of the beautifully rebuilt Santa Cruz Church where the Blessed Sacrament is always enthroned, and looked down an Escolta that far outshines its predecessor. Air-conditioned office buildings, svelte stores, wholesale firms resplendent with neon signs—these line the Escolta. It's a one-way street now. Yes, the Escolta—where traffic used to be a knock-down drag-out struggle where the best man reached the other curb and the second best went to bed!

You have to dip down into side streets to get any Philippine flavor. There you find the little camera stores, where a patient craftsman will spend an hour or more to help you find a screw to fit your tripod and charge you fifty centavos for it. There you find Mama sitting behind the counter with a cigarette in her mouth, the family sewing in her hands and the newest baby in her lap. And you need only to go down a few stairs from the Escolta to see the boat families who live in cascos plying up and down the Pasig River and penetrating the "esteros" or canals through the city. There are few canals left; the sanitation boys have been around. But the Escolta still bridges one in the heart of the city.

Then we took a carromata. Nowadays, the gracious carromata is called "a horse-drawn rig," and traffic regulations forbid such to canter down the main thoroughfares. Before the war no one dared make such a ruling; the "cochero vote" was a potent factor in any election. But in war times the horses were eaten up and the cocheros turned to other work. Now they are almost a relic, even though you find some very handsome carromatas decorously plying the side streets.

We hailed a beauty replete with silvered harness and fancy curtains. The horse was tall for a Filipino horse. Since the shafts in front of the wheels were high to accommodate him, the seat for passengers in the rear tilted back comfortably. Sister Paula Cathleen, for all her youth and long legs, had quite a time climbing over the wheel. These young Sisters are used to scaling nothing higher than a Fifth Avenue bus. Eventually she put one foot on the small iron support and swung herself up over the wheel with help from the cochero above and me below. Joy filled my wicked old soul when I reached the seat with a single graceful step from street to footrest to carromata. "Cluck, cluck" went the cochero and we were off, down Rosario, to Binondo. The wheels were not in alignment; the cart swayed from side to side going over the cobblestones.

Binondo in the bad old days was the Chinese ghetto. Many Chinese people still live in Binondo, in and out its devious alleyways, behind its warehouses and atop its shops. The church at Binondo is still roofless sixteen years after the war. In an over-enthusiastic beginning, a replica of St. Peter's in Rome in bas-relief plaster was put behind the main altar. But money stopped there and the rest of the church has a scrappy tin roof over part of the nave. The back is open to winds and sky. Bright sunshine floods the rear. Here an enterprising family has put up a nipa hut and even planted a papaya tree beside it. It was laundry day when we were there; the clothesline ran from the bars of one ancient church window across the nave to those on the other side. And this inside the church, with the tabernacle in plain view. It was the only church I saw in the Philippines not repaired. A good record, surely, for it is estimated that from 1941 to 1945, churches were demolished or damaged to the value of $75,000,000. The Church also lost 275 priests and religious who died in these years.

I wondered if Our Lord minded this Filipino family who had moved in with Him, putting up their kind of a house in the middle of His kind of a house. They seemed so perfectly at home with Him. Maybe they were very holy people who did all their daily chores "in the sight of the Lord." Maybe they greeted Him from bed in the morning and said "Good night" to Him after a quiet evening sitting on their front steps. And they guarded Him all night. If anybody came over the doorless threshold, or scaled the roofless walls, Our Lord was not alone. His house guests would come to defend Him. When we were there, nobody was around. But doubtless they would be back to spend the night with Him.

Outside Binondo church, we hailed another carromata. Very easy to do. You just say "Psssst!" and the carromata comes. I think either the cochero or his horse is psychic. Maybe both. Sometimes you just think "Psssst!" and you get results. Sister Paula Cathleen had another fit of giggles trying to get into it, but we went off in state in an equipage spangled with silver all over.

Divisoria market. Pots and bamboo sieves and hair ornaments; wooden shoes, ribbons and even false teeth—you can buy anything at Divisoria. We parted with a modicum of money. I bought one onion for five centavos, two bits of ginger for two centavos, a toy turtle made of papier-mâché and a rubber band for ten centavos. Again, we were invited to buy everything we passed. Not a commercial lure at all. They meant, rather, "Come over here, Mother, and talk to me."

Tabora, outside Divisoria, is a street noted for remnants. In the old days, the shops overflowed into the street with baskets of scraps—velvet, satin, cotton, spangles. Pieces left over from slipper straps, tatters no bigger than a few inches, were carefully picked over by dressmakers. They could use just such a scrap for an appliqué flower or leaf. Things are a little different now. I didn't see remnants but good bolts of material, although some of them might have been end-of-the-bolt pieces. The baskets of scraps are no more.

Right here we saw a sad little fellow digging around in a rubbish can, so we gave him a bit of money. He was too dazed to know what was happening. A young fellow nearby kept urging him, "Say thank you!" I only hope the child was not robbed as soon as we left him.

From Tabora we emerged to Azcarraga and took the first jeepney that came along. It was marked Jones Bridge and Pasay. So we honked and hooted, lurched and jolted through Manila's business district again, and over the span named for Jones, an American congressman who fostered Philippine self-government. This brought us to the entrance of Intramuros, the old Spanish walled city, practically wiped out in World War II. Where hundreds of thousands once lived and died in unbelievably crowded houses, now fewer than three thousand are in the makeshift huts thrown up in Intramuros' tall grass. It's an area of warehouses, newspaper offices, and piers. Only a few relics of the past remain. One is St. Augustine Church, the only church left standing in Intramuros after the war. It was in the sacristy of St. Augustine's that Admiral Dewey and the Spanish Governor of the Philippines signed an agreement to turn over the city to the United States in 1898. Toward the end of World War II, thousands of terrified people took refuge in the cellar of one of those solid Spanish buildings while American forces bombarded Intramuros. Hand grenades were thrown in on them. They all died except one Augustinian Brother who stayed seventy-two hours under the pile of corpses. I was there several months later when steam shovels dipped down into that cellar and brought up the bodies. Relatives seeking news of loved ones stayed around to see if they could identify a belt buckle, a shoe, a few artificial teeth, a wallet, a bit of jewelry. If so, then they knew where one more of the family had died.

Our own St. Paul's Hospital was in Intramuros, housed in a building hundreds of years old. The floor boards were two feet wide and four inches thick; the walls were solid masonry six to eight feet thick. Ceilings were twenty feet high; and the rafters were whole trees of wood like iron. Yet there is nothing of St. Paul's Hospital left. It is a field of high grass now behind the magnificently rebuilt Manila Cathedral.

Sister Paula Cathleen and I, on our sentimental bus trip, left Intramuros and walked up Taft Avenue. In the old days, lofty trees lined the broad street; government buildings sat back behind pampered lawns. Farther south were Philippine General Hospital, the University of the Philippines, large private schools for girls and boys, Jai Alai the gambling center. I tell you, Taft Avenue was an address worth having.

It still is. Seeing the buildings all repaired, the street smoothed out again, students, professors, government office workers, smart women bustling by, the picture I had in mind seemed the veriest illusion. For in my mind was the thought that two Maryknoll Sisters and a Filipina friend had crawled across that street on their stomachs. It took them two days and two nights to go one short block and reach safety in Philippine General Hospital in February, 1945. From curb to curb, they lay out flat many times when bullets and shells flew by. And a young girl who had started out with them from one curb, did not reach the other. She was snatched away and never found again.

It struck me that there are no lofty trees in the city any more. They were burned in the last days of struggle. In 1947, there were blackened stumps; in 1949 there were little saplings; and now the trees were fair but not venerable.

Yes, Manila is a city of young trees. Dewey Boulevard, the Luneta, Plaza Lawton, Taft Avenue, all of Ermita and Malate, once filled with solid homes in dark green gardens, look different somehow. Like a woman who has changed her make-up. The features are the same, but the aura is different.

I wonder what it does to the psyche of a city—not to see a tree more than fifteen years old. I know what it did to me to turn into the garden at Assumption College and see once more just a few grand old trees. The bark is blackened from fires, but these few had not died. We went up to them and patted the dark trunks, for these trees had shared our life for more than two years.

More than trees, I wanted to see Mother Rose who had taken thirty-six Maryknoll Sisters under her wing and shielded us as long as she could. Mother Rose of the Assumption Sisters is like her trees—her head high in the sky, her roots deep in Philippine soil. Her habit is deep purple, her head is straight, her heavy brows move up and down to punctuate her sentences, her wit is penetrating, her kindness legendary. She is eighty-nine years old now. Her daughters rise up and call her blessed. In sixty years in Manila, she has educated most of the country's well-placed women and pounded Christian principles into them. Governments also rise up to do her honor. France and the Philippines have pinned medals on her. Last and least of those who love her, we Maryknoll Sisters (who were her houseguests for two years and found we could not wear out her very durable charity) rise up to call down benedictions upon her.

You can't help but enjoy Mother Rose. Little, sprightly, quick in repartee, she sits straight as a ramrod at eighty-nine, yet flexible as a young girl. Sister Paula Cathleen and I sat in a parlor awaiting Mother. She came in with two cold bottles of Coca Cola on a tray. Even without seeing us she knew we would be thirsty. From then on she was her old delightful self.

Sixty years ago, Mother Rose came to a Philippines just lifting its head after the Spanish-American War. The physical damage was not great but the psychological impact was worse. She helped pick up the pieces and glue them into a new shape. Her type of religious superior is best described by the old saying: She has one foot planted firmly on earth and the other as firmly in heaven.

We walked a bit under the old trees in Assumption Garden and talked about them. How they provided dark shade when loyal Filipino friends stealthily brought us food in those days; how they arched over the men and women, British and American, who came to Assumption for refuge in the early days of Japanese occupation; the Christmas feasts and Easter tidbits when Assumption Sisters shared their best with us. They're party to many a secret, those trees.

Then, Sister Paula Cathleen and I took a prosaic old bus and went home to Quezon City over Ayala Bridge. Which means we passed the vast modern Magnolia Ice Cream Company which cools off millions of sweaty Manilans every day. This is at one end of the bridge. San Miguel Brewery is at the other end, equally famous for refreshing people. And in the middle is a stairway leading down to an island in the river, Hospicio San Jose, where for hundreds of years unwanted babies have found a haven. In the old days, the babies were brought by boat and left in a turn at the Hospicio gate, silently, anonymously. Hospicio San Jose— St. Joseph's refuge for the Little Unwanteds.

It was the Rush Hour. In any city this means the hour when nobody can rush. As our crowded bus stopped and started, we took time to hang out the window and see everything. There was Singian Clinic, once a very shabby building and, after the war, the only hospital in working order. And Malacanang Palace, now in its fourth era as Chief Executive mansion. Spanish Grandees, American Governors, Japanese Commanders and now Philippine Presidents have used it for their official residences.

Then we left the city behind and crawled out to the suburbs, those dreary, dusty lines of small shops along Santa Mesa Boulevard. Gradually, people got off. First we could breathe, then we could move. At last there was no one on the bus but Sister Paula Cathleen and me and the woman conductor who slumped in one of the seats. She looked so tired.

"You seem tired," I commented.

"Yes, Mother, I am tired."

"I hope this is your last trip today."

"Oh no, Mother, I must work until 11:00 tonight. I begin at 5:45 in the morning and work until 11:00 at night."

It was true, I found out later. Labor regulations do not apply to those on piece work or on commission. Bus conductors are paid on commission. There is also a law that women workers must have seats. And who can gainsay the claim that there are always plenty of seats in a bus? As in the New York subways, there are plenty of seats but somebody else is sitting in them.

I felt sorry for her. But was it really necessary? She felt it was. She was putting her son through medical college. When he got his MD her life purpose would be over. She could fall under the wheels of the old bus, for all she cared. She would die happy; her son was educated.

Those who delve into such things, tell us that in the Philippines, the Pivotal Institution—that "Idea" around which everything swings—is Education. In the United States, they say, it is Money; with the Chinese, it used to be Family. In East Africa, it is Cows. Among the Japanese, it is probably the Emperor. Up to the time of our bus ride, I was inclined to believe the psychologists had made an error; but the weary bus conductress convinced me that they are right.

There is little time for sentiment in the Philippines today. Everybody is too busy building up the new life. Enterprise is bursting out all over.

Spurred on by government offers of land, homesteaders by the thousands leave the settled places and strike out for new farm lands in the north of Luzon, and in the southern islands. Since 1945, there has been a standing offer that one may get twenty-four hectares per man if he cultivates it for five years. He gets a free patent but cannot sell it for a certain term of years. This has brought many families into new areas. Later, in Mindanao and up in Isabela, we saw how the plan worked out.

Even those who stay in the old farms are planting new crops. Just driving through the coconut groves in Batangas and Quezon provinces, it's a joy to see planted between the rows of coconut trees—corn, papaya, pineapples. Formerly coconut groves were coconut groves and that was that. Canning native fruits has taken quite a hold on the country. Mangos —those big "carabao" mangos, pride of the Philippines—come in cans now. Bangos, the islands' favorite fish, are canned, too.

Heavy industries too are moving in. A steel mill is proposed in Mindanao; the Philippines imports steel worth fifteen million dollars a year. Oil companies have a foothold already. Caltex has had a refinery at Batangas since 1954; begun with almost entirely American personnel, it is manned now by Filipinos except for two Americans. Shell Oil, Standard-Vacuum and a local company called Filoil plan to open refineries. Prospectors hope to find oil on the islands. Near Santiago, Isabela, in northern Luzon, engineers started to drill; they were sure that oil would be found at fourteen thousand feet. But at twelve thousand they struck the hardest rock they had ever met—so hard and so big that they could not get through it nor around it. After six months of expensive effort, they pulled up their stakes and left. But some day, someone will strike oil in the Philippines.

There is much more variety in the occupations, too. Time was when everyone was either a doctor or lawyer. Now chemistry, engineering, foreign service and agriculture are among the favorite college courses. Filipinos are branching out into many fields they never thought of before. An old pupil of mine has made a fortune in chemical supplies; another is a researcher in plastics.

Something new in Manila and the suburbs is modern housing developments. Philippine American Life Insurance Company has built Philam City, where houses are identical with upper middle-class homes in the States. Out in Forbes Park are palatial homes such as you could find in any "upper-bracket suburb." Stultifyingly American. Old time Filipinos, if they made money, built a mansion right where they had always lived. A beautiful home on a squalid street was ordinary. They had no idea of zoning so that the "right people" could be happy that the "wrong people" were kept out. They did not intend to take up with a new set of neighbors, just because they had struck it rich.

To counteract Philam City and Forbes Park, a friend took me out to Bagong Bantay, or "new village," as the Tagalog name implies. This section was set aside to resettle families who had been squatting in Intramuros—people who had come in from the country and, having no place to live, had thrown up a shack in the old Walled City. They have to build their own houses at Bantay but they get the plot of land free.

The "new village" had the old flavor. We visited Marcellina who came up from the island of Samar four years ago. She and her husband looked for work and squatted in Intramuros meanwhile. They were glad to get out of it. "Many bad people live there," Marcellina said. She beckoned me up the bamboo ladder on to her split bamboo floor. "Maupo kayo, Madre!" "Sit down, Mother!" and she cleared off a chair. The house was very poor, of course, but very clean and neat. Probably much better than they had had in Samar. And the ground was not going to waste as a mere residence, either. A marvelous big pig, very clean and white, and struggling vegetables decorated the back yard. Flowers in tin cans were all over the place. The welcome and hospitality—ah, that's Filipino to the core!

Marcellina's husband makes 120 pesos (about $36.00) a month as orderly in a hospital. He has to spend thirty centavos a day in bus fare to and from work; he tried walking but he almost broke down under the four-mile jaunt twice a day. This is the family's only objection to Bagong Bantay.

Marcellina's hut was not hot; in fact, it was cool. The air conditioning was simple—just keep trees around, and let air come in through the woven bamboo walls and up through the split bamboo floor. They captured any breeze that might be moseying around. Out in Forbes Park, people build homes of air-tight concrete and then have to spend more money for air conditioning.

"So! It's old-time Philippines you want!" exclaimed Gilda Fernando. "Come, I'll take you to Miss 1896 herself!"

Gilda could be Mrs. 1961. Small and fair, compact, mother of four children, and housewife with a *House-and-Gardens* home, she is—more important—a writer who can write rings around any other pupil I ever had. Her short stories bring in a tidy bit for the family budget. And she loves her native Philippines.

"Miss 1896" I found was Marcela Cuenca in Bacoor, Cavite, just around the south end of the bay from Manila. We picked up a Mrs. de Guzman who knows Marcela very well. "We are town-mates," she said. If you know the Philippines, that means they are very close indeed.

Marcela, Ladislawa and Pura Cuenca live in a very old house on Bacoor's main street. A plaque in Tagalog marks it.

> THIS HOUSE OF THE MARRIED COUPLE
> JUAN CUENCA AND MARGARITA BAGTAS,
> SERVED AS SEAT OF THE REVOLUTIONARY
> GOVERNMENT FROM JULY 12, 1898, TO
> SEPTEMBER 15, 1898. HERE WERE HELD
> SESSIONS OF THE PARLIAMENT OF THE
> PHILIPPINES UNTIL THE GOVERNMENT
> EVACUATED TO MALOLOS.

We went in, admitted by Pura, a mere stripling of seventy-five. It was one of those magnificently practical old houses, built for coolness and yet for privacy. The door, a mere slit in the wall, opened into a dark cool first floor. There were oddments stored here, a broken chair, an ancient and battered brass urn which may have come from China years and years ago, a cot and mosquito net for the servant girl. First floors here are like the attics at home.

Pura Cuenca was waving us up the broad stairs. "Itaasin ninyo!" (Come upstairs!) she called, begging us to invade her home. Her grey hair was pulled back; she wore a simple peasant woman's blouse and plain wrap-around skirt. But she might have been Queen Elizabeth throwing open Buckingham Palace. We followed up the wide stairway of burnished molave wood, as straight and true as the day it was built, the wood so hard that seventy years have worn no hollows on the treads.

A Filipino home is like a box, with a central staircase leading to a foyer. All the rooms are little more than alcoves of this central space, lighted and aired by sliding windows and doors with panes of sea-shell cut so thin that it looks like frosted glass. On hot days, the windows open so wide that the whole wall seems to drop out.

There was a commotion on the stairway behind us. "Ay!" said Pura, "Marcela is coming." At the bottom—indeed half way up—was Marcela, ninety, leaning for support on a child not more than three years old. But he helped his great-great-great-great-grandaunt carefully up to the last step.

The old lady was duly introduced. She took command at once; Pura somehow melted away. In Spanish and Tagalog, she told us her story.

In the sitting room were six rattan chairs placed stiffly like museum pieces, which they were indeed. "Here," said Marcela touching one with a trembling hand, "Mabini sat." She referred to the paralytic, Apollonario Mabini, reputed to be the brains of the Filipino revolution.

She shuffled into the next room, a small bedroom with a monstrous bed made of carved wood with a canopy to match, fit for a royal pair. "Here," said Marcela, "Mabini slept."

She crossed the hall, blessed herself, dipped in a quasi-genuflection and brought us to the oratory. A statue of Our Lady decked in white satin surmounted a small Spanish altar; she carried the Christ Child, also arrayed in nice clothes and a crown. "Nuestra Senora del Rosario," Marcela announced. And at the left, "La Magdalena." At the right, "San Jose." Finally with another dip of the knees, "Mass was celebrated here."

"Yes, it was," Mrs. de Guzman explained. "The parish priest followed Gregario Aglipay, who founded his schism at that time. Only eight families in Bacoor remained true. The Cuencas were one. So this house was used as the parish church. You see, the Aglipayans held on to the church building."

"When was that?" I asked.

"Oh, around 1900 or so," Gilda answered.

"Ay!" Marcela moaned with all the weight of Cassandra, "It was— then!"

Marcela goes to Mass every morning now, walking about a quarter mile. I wondered that she was able to do it. "Able?" she bridled. "I am unable to live through a day without Holy Communion."

We saw the dining room—huge dark buffet of bygone luxury and simple table with cheap plastic cover. In the kitchen, food is still cooked over depressions in a concrete slab where open fires of twigs and branches burn. I rubbed my hand over the kitchen table; it seemed so clean and smooth. "Done three times a day with sandpaper vine," said Marcela. She pointed out the window to a vine climbing up the wall. Good old sandpaper vine! At Malabon, too, we used to pluck all the steel wool we needed right out the kitchen window. Talk about convenience! All the window sills in the house are done with sandpaper vine and then oiled. "I tell them not to scrape so hard, or they will wear away the window sill," Marcela complained. But there is a good three inches of hard molave wood to sandpaper through. Seventy years of scraping has made no impression on it.

We sat down then in the revolutionaries' conference room with the six huge chairs. Marcela told her story.

Our father was Juan Cuenca—'Mayaman Cuenca' (Richman Cuenca) he was called. Ours and the Angeles were the two wealthiest families in Bacoor. But that was long ago.

I was twenty years old when this house was built in 1892. It was the pride of Cavite. We were in it only four years when revolution broke out. Ay, Good God, so much burning and killing! Everyone running here and there. Cavite Province was the center of it all, for many of the head revolutionaries came from here. Aguinaldo, the chief, came from Kawit, just east of Bacoor. He was exiled to Hong Kong and things quieted for a time. Then came war with America; Aguinaldo came back to Kawit, passing through our town—right outside that window on Calle Real. Pura (she pointed out the door to where Pura was fussing over refreshments for us), Pura was very young then.

We moved to Manila. And hardly were we there when the revolutionaries took this house for their headquarters. The next day, Spanish soldiers marched my father to prison. He must be a revolutionary, they said, or why is his house their headquarters?

My mother and I went from officer to officer. Anybody we knew or had ever heard of. All day, every day, we went from office to office, to army camps and government buildings. At last, we had him freed. Then, we put the younger children to board in Manila schools and we came back to Bacoor, staying in a small house not far from this one.

The Spanish closed in around Bacoor. They were determined to burn this house. I pleaded with the Captain. But he would not listen to me. 'I must burn it,' he insisted. 'Aguinaldo and the others are there.'

I was leaning forward to hear more. Marcela's eyes had glanced upward in supplication to the Spanish captain. They stayed up while tears welled and flowed over on her cheeks. I thought this was just superb acting; the past was so real to her. But her eyes wandered here and there over the ceiling. "Nasira-sira!" she said at last. "Ang aming bahay nasira!" (Broken! All broken! Our house is falling apart.)

It was, too. The light blue plywood ceiling was cracking, parts of it hung in tatters in the corners. Rain water had stained the upper walls. The roof evidently had needed repairs for a long time.

"Broken!" she mourned and pulled out a purplish flowered hankie to wipe her eyes.

I couldn't help it; I knelt beside her and hugged her. What could I do to help? Nothing. The old house would go; Marcela would go; the times they belonged to had gone long ago.

⊰ 9 ⊱ Go North, Young Man, Go North

LUZON is quite an island, as islands go. On the map it looks like a fried clam—a chunk of land with an indeterminate straggle at the end. The big part in the north is about one hundred and twenty-five miles wide and three hundred long; not many people are there. The straggle in the south has most of the people and nearly all the money. There, you can't go more than thirty miles, east or west, without hitting sea water.

Luzon is not the only Philippine island, of course. Seven thousand others jostle each other out there in the far western Pacific, nearly all of them less than a square mile. But Luzon on the north and Mindanao on the south are sizable. Among the world's millions of islands, they both rank among the top twenty. Luzon is about as big as Tennessee, Kentucky, Ohio, or Virginia, and not much smaller than Pennsylvania—really a respectable size.

Northern Luzon has always been more or less undeveloped. It's hard to get at because the mountains make rugged going for trains, cars or buses. Even for horses. In ancient days, as waves of Malayans and Indochinese pushed for a foothold on the island, the original inhabitants retreated into the mountains. That is why you find up there semi-civilized tribes like the Igorots, Benguets, Ifugao and others, and even some in the bow-and-arrow stage like the Negritos in Zambales. At that, the fleeing tribes got the best climate and scenery. The pine-clad mountains are cool while Manila swelters.

As you might know, Americans soon made a resort up there in a town called Baguio. Its origin is said to be this: William Howard Taft, when he was first Civil Governor of the Philippines, found Manila heat enervating. He decided to try to get to Baguio. Not so easy to do, since nothing but trails went through the mountains. Furthermore, Taft was a very large man and the Philippine horses are small. However, he made it all right and informed the State Department, "Am in Baguio. Made the trip on horseback. Feeling fine." The State Department answered (so says the story), "Good! How does the horse feel?"

But the Taft days are long gone. Even before the war, a road wound up the mountains and leaped over canyons. This road rejoiced in the title, the Zigzag Trail. It was a symbol of hope to Americans who lay at night in Manila with their tongues hanging out the window for a breath of air.

"De Zeegzawg," as the Filipinos call it, was for a long time like a draw-bridge for Baguio, the only way to get in or out of it. Then Naguilian Trail was constructed. On these two roads depended the fate of the whole mountain province. The Japanese army had to fight its way up these two trails in 1941; the American army did the same in 1945. Filipino guerrillas hid out in the mountains near Baguio during the war years; Yamashita re-treated to Baguio and surrendered there in 1945. Long after that surrender small detachments of Japanese lived in caves and fought the war out to a bitter end.

It used to be that when one announced, "I'm going to Baguio," he got congratulations and envious looks from everyone. But there was one last struggle before he could relax. Five hours in a train and another two hours in a bus, squeezed in with chickens, vegetables, babies and dogs—and he was quite ready for a rest cure. It was always a day of heat and soot and constant war for one's right to space against the ducks in the rack overhead and the pig nestling at one's feet. I never minded it. In the Second Class coaches, people were always so happy to be getting away from Manila heat. Thrifty folk, they hoped to sell some of these things to help pay for the vacation.

But now, after an hour in a comfy plane, we slid on to a flattened shelf in the mountains and stepped out fresh as daisies into the waiting arms of our Sisters. Planes ply back and forth to Baguio like the subways to Flushing.

To old timers, Baguio is a wee bit of a shock. Our convent used to be far out, beyond the beyond, on the edge of civilization. If you heard a car on the road you knew it was coming up our driveway because there wasn't anything further out. But now the convent is surrounded by modern homes, both modest and affluent. Campo Sioco, a miserable collec-tion of huts at the foot of our hill, used to be the domain of the Igorot King; his palace occupied one corner, not much more solvent than the others. Denizens of Campo Sioco were our friends; they came to Mass in our chapel, sold us vegetables, hung around the backdoor, sent their chil-dren to catechism classes, lent us their ox carts on occasion, and figured largely in our prayers. But the Igorot King sold Campo Sioco to a smart real estate operator and now we have the "Happy Homes Subdivision" at the foot of the hill. Nice split-level homes in pastel colors with streets, driveways, garages, and even street lamps—every one of them dreamed up in *Ladies' Home Journal*.

Houses are everywhere. There's even one set up on high stilts on the mountainside so that nothing of it touches earth but the front doorstep which gingerly reaches out for the road. It's a good idea for discouraging thieves. All you have to do is to pull in your doorstep at night and you're surrounded by a moat of air. Even so, I hardly think you would sleep comfortably; an enemy might saw through one of the stilts and your house would slump twenty or thirty feet to the ground.

But if the Happy Homes Subdivision took over Campo Sioco, what happened to the Campo Siocans? Some took their houses and households down "Dominican Hill" where the good Fathers rent them land for one peso a year. Others, and thousands more like them, retreated to the hillsides still farther out of town. The mountains are covered with a honeycomb of huts belonging to people who came to Baguio to make their fortune and didn't.

Indeed, the boom is on. Most places demolished by bombs are rebuilt, or cleared away and something better built. Now and then through town you see reminders—a set of concrete steps with no house to belong to, or a chimney standing gaunt and alone with fireplaces on its sides to warm rooms no longer there. Our own house looks as it always did. You would never think that in 1945 the roof was more off than on. I remember running around to close the windows during a storm and getting wetter from the holes in the walls than we would have from the windows. Inside, neat squares of new wood show shrapnel holes in floors and partitions have been repaired. You see, it was Japanese headquarters once. From our front windows, they could see the American fleet land at Lingayen Gulf twenty miles away, just as we saw the Japanese land at the same place a few years earlier.

In those days, Igorot men wore a G-string, long hair and, in cold weather, a shirt. American visitors were always properly shocked to see the shirt walking down the road with no trousers below it. Women wore their own tribal dress of plaid hand-woven cloth. They carried a basket on their shoulders supported by a leather head strap. It was heavy. Because ours was the first house they came to, they used to stop at the backdoor trying to sell as much as possible. There would be that much less to carry on to the market. Now, nobody carries vegetables, firewood, bananas and her newest baby in a basket. Oh no, indeed. Market women ride past in jeepneys, and if you want vegetables you can go to the market and they will deal with you there.

Baguio is in full swing of modernization. People once thought of nothing but growing sweet potatoes to get money for clothes or farm implements or a new water buffalo. Now they are tourist-conscious. A young fellow stands in the Baguio market in full Igorot dress with some fanciful additions of his own; he will pose for you for one peso a shot. Even old women in market stalls expect money for posing. And, to give you your money's worth, they will suggest angles to make it more colorful. Igorot wood carving once featured carabaos, nipa huts and native faces. Now it goes in for bloodthirsty warriors carrying human heads on high or women with a human leg ready for the stew pot. The Igorots used to be ashamed of their old head-hunting days, but now they know there is cash in them tha'r hills of shame.

However, it's commercialism in a simple style. If they ever start putting on fake head-hunting parties, or stage a dog-meat canyao at ten dollars a plate, or charge admission to see the shrunken heads at Crystal Cave, then we will know that Walt Disney has moved in. You can still go down the mountain paths and see young boys and old men carving wood or fashioning exquisite things of fine silver wire. And if you bring a chart of religious pictures, they will ring around you and ask questions. "Did you say that God became a man and lived on earth like us? That he did it for our sakes?" Some believe; for others, it's too good to be true. But they all wonder.

Christianity among the Igorots is fairly recent. I remember going on horseback with Sister Fidelis to small hamlets in the woods—places with just a few families here and another few several miles away. There she relied on my strong right arm to hold up the chart while she taught ten-or-so women with their million-or-so babies. In the early 1930's, there were fewer than twenty Catholics. Before 1940 they numbered around three hundred. Now that the second generation is coming along, our chapel is just not big enough to hold everybody and, anyhow, it is better for them to go to Mass in town or in their own localities. But four groups of Legion of Mary workers meet on Sunday mornings in the school rooms at Maryknoll convent. I sat in on several of these meetings. It was a joy to see these sturdy mountain people sit on our kindergarten chairs and discuss, in a very business-like way, the work to be done and who is to do it.

To tell the truth, one morning I was very glad that the machine age had caught up with Baguio. We took a jeepney out to Atab, the smallest of small hamlets along the road to Santo Tomas mountain. Otherwise we would have had to walk it and I am not ambitious like that any more. We supervise a two-room school house out there for some sixty children who would have no schooling at all otherwise. This Atab school is one of the many mission projects supported by our other schools in more settled areas. We found classes going on apace in both sides of the wooden school. Three youngsters to a bench and not much in the way of equipment, but considering that they never speak a word of English otherwise, they read amazingly well.

We started to walk back home, thinking no jeepney would be along for several hours or so. We stopped to catch our breath and to gaze entranced with the view of mountain after mountain straight over to the horizon, each a different shade of purplish blue. Then I heard music, very, very soft, and the accents of a man's voice, and again music like a symphony orchestra. Where could it come from out here in Luzon's mountains?

Then I saw him. A very old man in baggy coat and G-string, squatting on his heels under a tree, his hands around his knees, his eyes looking out across the wonderland of his native heath. His fathers had tramped these mountains, perhaps hunted heads in them, performed pagan worships in their caves. He held his head at an odd angle and there was a strange intensity on his face. Then I saw that he held in his hand a small transistor radio. He was listening to a wonderful voice from a land far away, luring him to a world outside his ken. I thought: "His eyes are on Baguio and he loves it; his ears and his mind are in America. He doesn't understand what he hears but he is fascinated by it. More so than by what he sees. God grant he goes into the radio-hi-fi-TV civilization with his heart still loving the culture and hills of his homeland!"

A jeepney came along unexpectedly. We left the Old Man of the Mountains who has seen things that, as a young man, he would have deemed quite impossible. That a voice, speaking in America, could be heard from a little box in his hand . . . . How ridiculous can one get!

Santiago, Isabela, is one of those Philippine towns you can't see until the dust settles. Which it rarely does. If it isn't a carabao dragging his feet on the road, or a pig rooting around in the pulverized dirt, it's one of those big trailer trucks rolling by loaded with farm tractors and such. The dust is really high around Santiago these days, for carabao and pigs and trucks are making speed up there. So if you want to find Santiago for yourself, put your finger on the dot marked Manila and move it about one hundred and fifty miles due north and slightly east. Your finger is now in the middle of northern Luzon and it's pretty dry. If you want to wet that finger you will have to move it about seventy miles east or west and over high mountains in either direction before you can dip it into the Philippine Sea or the China Sea.

A carabao or a pig making dust? One expects that in a town like Santiago. But a trailer truck! And loaded with those yellow iron monsters? You'd think that everybody in town would be out gawking at it on the roadside. Far from it. The carabaos plod alongside it, still twitching their ears in utter boredom; the little caratela horses don't skitter; the children in their shirts and nothing else hardly look up from playing in the mud. In less than fifteen years, Santiago has become accustomed to many things. All of Isabela Province is waking up.

Mother and I had taken the 8:15 A.M. plane from Baguio. Seen from just under the clouds, the pine-clad mountains were a travel poster. Sharp shadows from the morning sun on the cliffs made a geometric pattern; the shadow of the plane rose and fell up and down mountainsides like a toy on a string.

Too bad all this beauty was wasted on birds for so long!

Then we skimmed over broad flat lands planted in rice, rice and more rice. Forty minutes in all from Baguio we dropped on to the grass airstrip at Cauayan, center of the Cagayan Valley. It is a fabulously fertile valley— before the airplane, a hidden garden hemmed in by the sharp Baguio mountains on the west and the horrendous Sierra Madres on the east. So impassable are they that in pre-aviation days, land passage from the civilized South was impossible. You had to sail all the way around Luzon to Aparri on the north and trickle down south on the Cagayan River. There wasn't much fun raising rice, either, when it had to go by oxcart one hundred and twenty miles north to Aparri and more than seven hundred miles by ship around the western shore to Manila. The plane has put new hope into the Cagayan Valley.

You probably don't know Sister Robert Marie. It's just as well for you that you don't. She can charm the last dollar out of your pocket. Worse still, she can make you work to the bone and love doing it. There are just two automobiles in the whole town of Santiago (pop. 37,000), yet she managed to borrow one and to persuade Dominador, the owner, to drive it to the airport to meet us. He was smiling as he did it, too.

To Santiago, it was fifty miles over a dusty road dignified by the title Provincial Road and honored with a red line on the road map. We must have left that road very clean behind us because we certainly picked up all the loose dirt as we went along.

Outside of the dusting, it was a wonderful ride between two mountain ranges. Flat land devoted to rice fields spread over to the west where Baguio nestled among pine-clad beauties. On the east rose the Sierra Madres, a formidable wall between this fertile Cagayan Valley and the Pacific Ocean. So formidable, indeed, that the entire eastern coast of Luzon—three hundred miles from north to south—is cut off from the rest of the world. There are no good harbors. In all those three hundred miles of mountains there is but one horrible road which even the road map admits is third class, and one trail. These are one hundred miles apart.

Some of the places in the Sierra Madres have not been explored. A race of wild men, aboriginal pygmies, live in mountain hideouts and make periodic raids on the outskirts of our little Santiago. Even the Ifugaos, classified as semi-civilized, are surprisingly naive. Virginia, an Ifugao girl, came to work in Santiago. She was stupified when she saw a hose. "You turn this thing at one end and water comes out of the other end?" she marvelled. She was to wash clothes, so she picked up the basket and asked, "Where is the river in this town?" The idea of water coming to her, rather than of her going to the water, was soul-shaking.

As we bowled over the road, Dominador was quite talkative in the front seat. At first we talked too, but every time we opened our mouths, the soil of Isabela Province rushed in. We learned to grunt "yes" or "no" and let conversation go at that. On the edge of town, Dominador stopped. He

This bell once clanged from a railroad locomotive in the United States, but it serves the little thatched church right well.

TANGANYIKA

Form IV students (12th Grade) take the fearsome Cambridge examinations in stride.

LEFT. African Sister does a neat job on the sewing machine as Mother Mary Colman watches.

BELOW. I thought Fideli (RIGHT) would be dead, but found her ready to pose with her new baby.

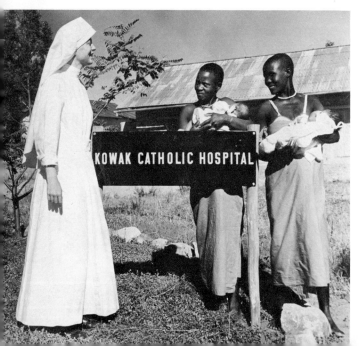

KOWAK CATHOLIC HOSPITAL

African school girls get into a friendly hassle with the referee.

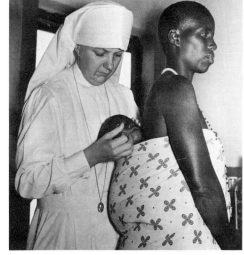

RIGHT. Maternity work in clinics and hospitals is most important.

BELOW. No lack for good biology specimens in Tanganyika!

Emmanuel's family show me their western clothes *and* kangas.

RIGHT. Two Morogoro students arrive for the new school year carrying baggage the easy way.

LOWER RIGHT. A wooden comb makes mama beautiful.

BELOW. The Sultana Bernadette and Princess Dolores show papa's monkey-fur regalia to Sister Martin Corde, an American Negro Sister.

Mother looks at a monastery sitting on the shore of the lake in the center of Kandy.

CEYLON

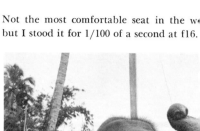
Not the most comfortable seat in the w[orld,]
but I stood it for 1/100 of a second at f16.

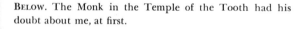
Wrap-around skirts are tucked up when men are working.

BELOW. The Monk in the Temple of the Tooth had his doubt about me, at first.

BELOW. The vitamin pill is dropped in and a swallo[w of] water follows.

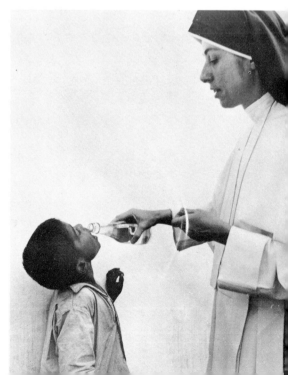

The school bus at Pakil is a "banca" which ferries across Laguna de Baye.

PHILIPPINES

Homesteaders at Sto. Tomas, Mindanao, take pride in their crude church.

Progress has invaded Dulawan by way of street signs and Coca-Cola.

Lucena is set in coconut country. Sister Godfrey plays Pied Piper.

The street vendor at Lipa wants five pesos; I got the mat for four.

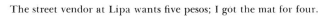

Neighbors in Ceylon

Small patient in the Philip

The student in Tanganyika

Sister on Taiwan

Big Sister in Hong Kong

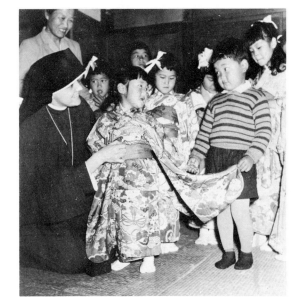

Neat little Miss in Japan

Nurses in Korea

Jauan child with papaya

HONG KONG

Any way you look at it, Hong Kong is crowded. These fishing boats are homes as well.

What land there is, is well used. Cottage type units are in front; 7-story "daai-ha" behind and tinderbox shacks left rear.

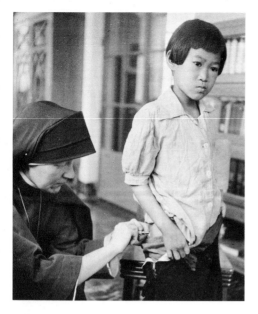

This is Peach Blossom. She died four days later.

RIGHT. I tried to win her with the toy drum, but she much preferred to get her scrap paper tied up.

BELOW. Home is where you take off your shoes.

New clothes (ABOVE) and a sack of rice (BELOW LEFT) bring the faintest of smiles to the faces of refugee children, but . . .

Students at Blue Pool Road enjoy a 'tween-classes session with Sister Maryam.

Where to hang the laundry is Hong Kong's biggest problem. These people put their bamboo poles from roof to roof.

wanted to clean up; nine hundred boys and girls of Our Lady of La Salette School would be on parade to greet us. So he opened the back door, shoveled out the brown dust and picked off the back seat three shriveled Sisters, dried to a crisp. At that stage, we could have been put into an ordinary envelope and sent through the mails for 4¢ First Class. It would have saved money on plane fares, but we never thought of it.

Dominador poured us each a drink of water from a thermos jug; like mashed potatoes you buy in boxes, we swelled out to normal. A good thing, for the nine hundred were upon us, complete with band, uniforms and flags. As the car advanced through town, first one wheel and then another dipped into the holes in the street. We maintained equilibrium and smiled graciously, feeling not unlike bronco busters in slow motion.

These youngsters range from kindergarten straight through Junior College. Good schools in "the province" are one answer to the Philippines' social and political problems as well as the religious ones. The emphasis has always been on Manila; the capital of course would have cultural advantages. But in ten provincial towns in the Philippines there are schools, mostly High Schools, staffed by Maryknoll Sisters. In some, we work with men's religious orders—Columbans, Oblates, La Salette and Maryknoll Fathers. Others are "on our own," which means that we are responsible for operating them. But all of them are dedicated to the job ahead—to build up an intelligent body of Catholic citizens in every part of the Philippines.

Up until 1945 or so, the Cagayan Valley lay fallow, a potential bread basket isolated from the mouths that could empty it. The government offered free land to anyone who would settle and cultivate it. Homesteaders are coming in now, picking their property and setting to work. Population has almost doubled in the past twelve years, growing from a quarter-million to a half-million in Isabela Province alone. The Sisters say that hardly any of the older children in school were born in Santiago.

As in any pioneer town, rumors of great developments are rife. The Manila Railroad is to be extended all the way to Aparri. Planes will come every day rather than twice a week as now. Airfields are to be opened; even Santiago will have one.

Well, I can believe it. I spent five minutes in Santiago doing nothing more ambitious than looking out my window on to the provincial road. First came a cart filled with jute sacks for rice. The carabao picked up his feet and put them down again at the same speed and in the same way he has done for centuries. A man rode on his back because there was no room on the cart. He was sleeping soundly as he jogged along, his head bent low and the GI helmet, probably picked up from some battlefield further south, almost bobbed off at every step. Then a horse strung with fancy harness and bits of silver ornament trotted by with a highly ornate caretela.

Behind him was a rider with wooden saddle and rope harness. He left in the dust the plodding carabao. Suddenly from behind came a loud noise, a grinding of gears and, in a perfect billow of dust, a huge Coca-Cola truck overtook all of them. He was in a hurry. Why not? The 7-Up truck had made deliveries in the town market half an hour ago; the Pepsi-Cola man was hard behind him. Whoever got to the vendors first will sell drinks to the carabao man, the caretela driver and the horseback rider when they arrive thirsty at the market. No longer in provincial towns do we see the man who used to dispense "tuba," a fermented coconut drink, from a section of bamboo slung over his shoulder. Who wants lukewarm tuba when the market has slot machines full of ice cold drinks? Such is progress!

Yet there is not prosperity nor even sufficiency in Santiago. The harvest dictates whether Juanito goes to school this year or not. Often the Sisters carry them along without tuition. Many a child, they say, goes home at noon for lunch, finds nothing on the table and comes back early for afternoon classes. And no complaint. We came across several women threshing rice with their feet—green rice which is hard to thresh. "Why don't you wait until it's dry?" Sister asked.

"We can't wait; we need it for dinner today," they replied cheerfully.

And yet it need not be so bad. The whole economy of the area is in one basket—a rice basket. Between rice harvests, the ground lies fallow.

"Why don't you plant some vegetables?" the Sisters ask.

"But we don't like vegetables," is the answer. Not as bad an answer as it seems. If they don't like vegetables, others don't either and there isn't much sale for unpopular items. The answer is, of course, education as to food values. A long hard road, but one that leads to many good things for body and soul.

We have been in Santiago only about five years. In five years, a lot of water flows down the Cagayan Valley. Changes, as in any pioneering country, occur overnight. Tales of the Sisters' early days at La Salette sound fantastic now as you see the young boys and girls change classes, carry books for the teachers, raise their hands to answer in class, act as students do all over the world.

Sister Aquinata tells the tale that soon after school opened in 1956, she asked why Pedro was absent. "He is in jail today, Sister," his classmates volunteered. "He was fighting and used his knife."

After class, Sister went to the jail to comfort the prisoner. Pedro was properly contrite. He promised to study in jail and catch up to the class. "I am a La Salette boy," he said. "I can never forget that!"

As Sister turned to go, a ruckus started in the adjoining cell. The prisoners came to the bars and called, "We too are your boys, Sister! You will come to visit us!" Sure enough, during the day others had landed behind bars.

But things have tamed down in town since then. Almost nobody fights with knives—at least in the school yard. The jail must look elsewhere for tenants. La Salette isn't quite up to the expression, "Oh, we don't do that sort of thing at St. Xavier's." But it's getting there.

In the country districts feuds die hard. Revenge doesn't hesitate to strike at a hated man through the things he loves, rather than directly at him. For instance, Macario and Alberto were in Sister Patrice's class at La Salette. Macario's father worked for Alberto's father and both boys knew there was no love lost between the men. Alberto's father was known to be a hard overseer. However, the two boys were the best of friends. They went home deep into the mountains for the Christmas vacation.

One evening Alberto heard Macario whistling outside. It was a signal to meet. "I'm going out bird-hunting with Macario," he told his older brother.

Three days later, they found Alberto's body in the woods. An arm had been hacked off; a rope was around his throat; the boy had been tortured horribly before the bolo went through his heart. No one is absolutely sure, but suspicion rests on Macario's father.

When Macario whistled, did he know he was luring Alberto to his death? Sister Patrice cannot believe it but men in town have no doubt about it. "Sure, he did!" they say. "He may have been under pressure from his father, but he did it knowingly." Certainly Macario is a changed boy since that Christmas vacation. Whether it is a guilty conscience, or sorrow for his friend, or fear of reprisals, who can tell? He is quiet, almost sullen, and he keeps his secret to himself.

Sister Patrice has a talent for counseling boys. I remember her in Hawaii where we taught in a school near the docks. There Sister spent her after-class hours talking cold turkey either to boys liable to get into trouble or to their mothers after they had gotten into trouble. In Santiago she told me the story of Pablo. This young lad wants to be a priest but the road before him looks mighty difficult.

He graduated from High School as valedictorian. Then, almost immediately his family acquired a farm away out in the mountains, surrounded by the Ifugao tribe. Pablo started gathering the young fellows about him to teach them the Faith. When I was in Santiago, he had ten young men and boys who wanted to be baptized. Pablo's new area is so far from town that he has to walk three days and then take a bus for a peso. (You can get an awful lot of bus mileage for a peso in the Philippines.)

Pablo, being new at teaching religion, wasn't sure that his converts knew enough about their Faith. He made the trip in to Santiago to consult Father about it. Father sent him over to Sister Patrice. One of these prospective Catholics, Pablo reported, is a young man who has already killed three people.

"Three people!" Sister Patrice gasped with her hand up to her cheek. "What on earth did he kill them for?"

"When he went to ask his girl to marry him," Pablo explained, "he wants to show her how brave he is. Also, his father will not even talk about marriage until the young fellow has killed a man and put the head on a post in the girl's front yard. So, this boy thinks he will do the thing up brown and put three heads on posts while he is at it."

"Whom did he kill? Were they enemies?"

"Oh no, Sister," Pablo was very patient with her. "He is not killing them because he does not like them. But he needs the heads. He went down to the river and saw a man fishing, so he went up and got his head. It is the same for the others."

"But Pablo—he must have known that was wrong."

"Sister, I am unable to convince him that murder is wrong. Maybe you will do better. He says that it is the custom of his people; it just shows that a man is very brave. Besides that, he is a very good man. He knows his prayers very well and answers best to the questions."

"But there's more to it than that, Pablo!"

"Very well, I will bring them all in here next Saturday. You can examine them all then, Sister. Maybe I did not teach them right in everything."

Too bad—I had to leave Santiago before that Saturday.

But in spite of things like that, Isabela is still a pioneering neighborly place at heart. We were to leave by plane from Cauayan but reservations were a bit shaky. There is no telephone in Santiago that really functions; we decided to take our chances on being bumped. Still and all, it's no fun to drive fifty agonized miles to Cauayan just to learn there is no room for you on the plane. We put the affair into the angels' hands; after all, they have used the airlanes for a good long time.

The day before zero-hour, Felicita in Grade Five said to Sister Robert Marie: "The airlines agent at Cauayan says there is room for you on Thursday's plane."

"Oh? How do you know? Did you see the agent?"

"No. Our truck driver told me." Felicita hops a truck each morning to come to school.

"How did your truck driver know?"

"Well, a friend of his was passing the Cauayan airport and the radio man ran out of his cabin and asked him to tell our truck driver so that he could get word to you."

It beats the old Pony Express. The chain of command, so to speak, seemed a bit involved, but Felicita had the right information.

"The plane's up in Tuguegararao." The radio man smiled when we appeared at the door of his cabin. "The pilot will have his lunch and then he's coming down here for you."

Manila greeted us with scare headlines:

CITY IN ICY GRIP
SIBERIAN BLASTS SWEEP AREA
MERCURY PLUNGES TO LOW 60's

Which proves, it's all in the point of view!

⅍ 10 ⅀ Go South, Young Fellows, Go South

EVEN as a child, Florencia Castinila was the Dainty Miss. Like one of those fragile orchids her mother often sent us from her collection. I used to look down the rows of school desks at the youngest Castinila with her luminous dark eyes, her long braids, her ultrafeminine way and say, "Please, life, be easy on her."

After the war she met Andres and fell in love. Born in New York but brought up in the Philippines, he had graduated in accountancy from one of the big Manila schools and took a job with Caltex. In 1945 he joined the United States Army and spent a year in Japan. Here he saw the intensive farming Japanese excel in. It fired him with enthusiasm. His own family had coconut plantations in Zamboanga, but the young man burned to hack out his own fields from the jungle. So he spent another year at Louisiana State University studying agriculture, especially rice growing. Armed thus with all the book knowledge he could acquire on the subject, he returned to the Philippines and went down to Mindanao to get a place to begin.

Mindanao, even more than northern Luzon, has attracted homesteaders. Eighty percent of the land area is still undeveloped. Five years working a farm gives title to it. Andres enlisted his cousin Diosdado into the enterprise. They rolled up their sleeves and went to work. Just about in the dead center of Mindanao, an island as big as Indiana, they found what they were looking for—land good for rice. Andres invested his money in a tractor, thresher, harrow, plough and harvester. Modern science must have modern tools to work with.

He put down his stakes and started to build what they always called "House #1" in expectation of Florencia's coming. It never had time to grow up to be a house. He had the four posts in, the roof on and two walls in place. But a high wind demolished House #1 overnight. Nothing daunted, Eulogio built House #2. Then he went to Manila to be married.

"What a wedding!" Florencia told me.

I had just graduated from college; our families had known each other for years. After the Nuptial Mass, the Breakfast, the Reception, the pictures and good wishes, we ran for the boat which would take us to Cebu, half way to Mindanao.

During the week's honeymoon in Cebu, we bought a hundred Hamberg chicks. For two days and three nights on the boat to Cagayan de Oro, the cheeps and chirps of chicks came from under the bed in our cabin. They were my chicks, Andres said. I loved every one of them.

Cagayan de Oro is not a big town—not to us coming from Manila. But it has ships and stores and now even planes. It's the jumping-off place for the interior. A good road, rambling for two hundred and sixty-five miles, leads from Cagayan de Oro on the north to Davao on the south.

Of course, we took the bus. Three or four wooden seats were up front; the rear was filled with our wedding presents and household things and somebody else's carabao. We were to go seventy-five miles to Valencia and from there we would strike out into the hinterland. The bus trip should have taken less than two hours but one of the passengers asked the driver to wait until he had finished his dinner. And the driver thought he would do a little gambling while he waited. So we all waited until the driver had made up his losses.

We passed the Del Monte pineapple plantation at Maluko, twenty-five miles from Cagayan de Oro. A marvelous road. And they call this roughing it! I thought. Then we passed through Malaybalay; the road was not so marvelous. And on to Valencia. It's very, very small; has a market day only once a week. Everybody knew everybody; they had all come from small towns in the Visayan islands. Many were from the same town. My ritzy Manila bride's outfit seemed so out of place down here.

Diosdado had brought the tractor out from the farm. We piled our household things in the trailer and I sat on top. Andres and Diosdado manned the tractor and off we went over the fields seven miles to our palatial estate at Maapag. Don't ask me why they named it that; to say truth, there really wasn't anything to name.

It was delightful climate, a high plain like Baguio. Mountains surrounded it on every side. Often from the top of our heap in the trailer I could see nothing; the cogan grass was so high. 'It shows how fertile the soil is,' Andres called back to me.

At last he called, 'There is the house!'

'Where?' I strained my eyes in every direction.

'There! There!' he shouted. But I could see nothing until we were right in front of it.

He wanted to carry me over the threshold. But I took one look at the bamboo steps and declined. They were too narrow and shaky; I had no desire to start off my pioneer life with a broken leg and/or a broken husband.

It was a nice nipa house with two bedrooms, a split bamboo floor and a thatched roof. A Coleman lamp hung from the center beam, gave a good light. Andres and Diosdado had made the furniture from crates, and very well, too. That night, going to bed, I found that the window was just a hole; there was no way to close it. Also the door had no lock. 'Just twist the wire around those two nails,' Andres advised. In the middle of the night I heard a strange noise, waked, and saw two big eyes looking in the window. I screamed. 'Oh, it's just an owl,' Andres said, annoyed. I got a blanket, brushed the owl off the window sill where he perched, and covered the window. I did that every night thereafter. It was my first rejection of nature in the raw.

Next morning there were bright sun spots over everything. The roof was full of holes. I remembered Andres' letters where he had said, 'I never clean; the rain comes and washes the floor for me.' Sunshine filtering through was cheering, but rain was another thing. We were glad of it though, for soon the brook overflowed into our well and polluted the water. We gathered the rain from the roof, then, boiled it and drank it even though it was an unpalatable brown.

I had so much to learn! How to make a fire, for instance. I cooked on a table covered with galvanized iron, and three stones made a tripod for my pots. But I could not get that fire started. I puffed and puffed; I was covered with soot. But I learned. I learned.

It was worse killing a chicken. Diosdado said, 'I've seen them holding it by the neck.' So we did until it died. Then we could not eat it; the blood was coagulated in the meat. So I wrote to Mama in Manila. 'How do you kill a chicken?' She answered, 'Take it by the neck but don't hold too tight. Step on the wings. Hold knife in right hand and cut through neck.' So simple when you know how. But the nearest post office was at Valencia; I walked five hours to mail that letter, and walked five hours back.

The primeval forest was just thirty feet from our house. So many lovely birds and flowers delighted me. Monkeys and wild pigs were there too and they were naughty. Often in the morning we woke up to see that monkeys had eaten our vegetables and wild pigs had rooted up what was left. But revenge is sweet; the wild pigs we caught had very tasty meat.

As I said, the chicks were mine to keep. The breed mixed with the wild chickens from the forest. In a way it was good, for they were sturdier, but the meat grew tough. The eggs were good. I never did have good luck with the Hamberg chicks; some died, some were run over by the tractor. When the last one fell into the well, I cried.

We were not so isolated as you might think. About four miles away were a couple, the Maretas, who were working on the Areneta experimental farm. They lived on a hill and we could see their light at night. Now and then the Manobo tribes would be around; they are nomads, burning the land one year, sticking seeds into it, and moving on the next year. But our nearest neighbors were Visayans at Laligan about three miles away. They were a comfort to me; there were many things I could have learned from them if I had made friends sooner. But I do not speak Visayan dialect. I visited there often. In the dry season it was easy to ford the river but during the rains I went on a log thrown across. Once, as I walked, I saw a snake on the underside. Green. I backed off and went home. And once Andres was bathing in the river and had to shoot a crocodile.

Poor Andres! He worked so hard. He and Diosdado ploughed day and night to get it all done before the rains.

One day he slaughtered our pig. He dumped seventy-five pounds of fresh pork into my lap. 'It's all yours, honey,' he said. What would I do! No refrigerator. And I didn't know how to smoke it. By that time I hated salt pork. I wept over that pig. I was exhausted.

I was sick, too. The next day we started for the hospital before dawn. We had hired a carabao and sled from the Visayans. I lay on the sled with a burning fever, five hours to Valencia. There we got a truck to take us to Malaybalay and arrived in the late afternoon. The driver went straight to the hospital rather than letting us off at the bus station. I was so grateful to him. The doctor said it was due to bad water, salt pork, and everything else.

After a week I felt stronger. 'Let's go to Valencia,' I said, 'and get a house. Then you will be closer to the farm, and I will be closer to a doctor.' So we did. This was House #3. It was a rickety thing, infested with lizards and chicken lice. But I must confess, we had a good time in that house. The neighbor's chickens used to peck holes in our sacks of rice which we kept under the house. I lowered a noose made of string from between the floor bamboos above. I caught one over the head and we had chicken that night.

We had lots of fun. We bought an old phonograph you wind by hand. Andres and I danced and danced, just to feel the house sway. One night as we slept, it swayed more than we wanted. Earthquake? No, it was only a carabao rubbing himself against the front steps.

We soon found that I was pregnant. And I wanted water chestnuts in the worst way. We call them 'apulid.' Andres asked Diosdado to go seventy-seven miles to Cagayan de Oro and get some. He came back empty handed. 'Say, what are those apulid?' he asked. 'I asked every hardware store in town for them.'

I went back to Manila to have my baby and returned when my little Enrico was a month old. My husband had built House #4 by then, about a mile from Valencia. I had Dr. Benjamin Spock's book on babies. It became our bible; we read it page by page. Enrico must have read it too for he did everything Dr. Spock said he would do.

But things were going badly. I caught malaria and weighed only ninety-three pounds although I am 5'6" in height. The farm was plagued by either floods or drought, maya birds, locusts or rats. The tractor could not be used in the mud and our modern equipment was not made for carabao.

My malaria recurred again and again. Eventually we went to Cagayan de Oro, and Andres became personnel manager for the Del Monte pine-

apple plantation. Then we sold our rights to the land and came back
to Manila.

Our Visayan friends are still there. They prove our conclusions about
the Maapag valley for homesteading. It's very good for farmers with
carabao, but not for modern machines. And since one man with a carabao
cannot till a large area, many farmers are needed. You can't start any
big farming operation—at least not with rice. The area would be wonderful for ranching, though.

Homesteading is quite the thing in the Philippines. What were heart-
breaks for Florencia are part of daily living for most homesteaders. They
are born farm folk. They have spent their lives tilling small farms for
landlords. The prospect of land to own is like an invitation back to the
Garden of Eden.

Mindanao is the Land of Promise. Settlers are going down there by
droves; it is estimated that five hundred new settlers arrive in Davao
every month. The whole area has a Wild West feeling, a "Howdy, neighbor, where'd you come from?" attitude, an Oklahoma land-rush air. This
is, definitely, the time to get in on the ground floor in Davao.

Before World War II, the Japanese knew a good thing when they saw
it and started much of the agriculture of Davao. The government offered
this land, formerly owned by Japanese, to veterans and homesteaders.
Now that the fever has caught on, frontiersmen have gone way beyond
the Japanese lands out into the virgin hillsides.

In the late 1930's, Jesuits in Manila were urging their students: "Go
south, young fellows, go south." It was a fantastic idea, then. In the
late 1940's it was a rumble; in the 1950's it was a rush. The Church is
swimming along desperately just keeping her head above swirling waters.
Bishop Clovis Thibault of the Quebec Foreign Missioners came as a
lone priest in pre-war days to take over a parish of almost 8,000 square
miles. He hid in the hills during the war years, emerged to go on with
his work afterwards, and then found himself bishop of the place in 1954.
He now has almost a million people under his episcopal wing with five
hundred new families coming in every month. Two years ago, there were
only six hundred and fifty thousand. You can see why bishops' hair
grows grey and worry wrinkles come into their benign faces.

We plunged into Davao's enthusiasm at an early hour. 8:30 A.M., to
be exact. We had left the Hub of the Universe (Manila, not Boston,
out here) at 6:15 A.M. and arrived at the Fringe of the Forest Primeval
two hours later on a non-stop flight. For pioneering, this beats the
covered wagon by a couple of months. Only, in the Philippines covered
wagons would be of little use to pioneers. The real ones come in boats,
large and small, from the Visayan islands.

Those who are a bit hazy on Philippine geography should know that the Philippines consist of three parts: 1, Luzon, a big island in the north, where Manila is; 2, Mindanao, a big one in the south, where the pioneers are; and 3, the Visayas, many small islands between the two big ones, where the pioneers come from. All the Philippines stretch a thousand miles north and south; the distance from Manila to Davao is more than six hundred watery miles.

There is a hearty enthusiasm about Davao. They can do a welcome up brown. Even from the plane, we could see a hubbub at the airport, just a quonset hut on a grassy strip. The middle of the commotion was a man walking around with a sign such as pickets carry during a strike. It was readable as we got off. In foot-high letters it said:

WELCOME TO OUR DEAR
MOTHER MARY COLMAN!

The mob was a pleasing welter of men and children and women and Sisters and Maryknoll Fathers all trying to be the first to pin a huge bouquet on Mother's very small person. Mother usually out-shrinks the shrinking violet. However she went through it with a smile. She did not quaver even when the sign was roped to the front of a car and she rode in state around town, trailed by loyal cohorts.

We headed for the Apo Hotel for a reception. Mt. Apo is the highest mountain in the Philippines; it dominates Davao just as Illimani lords it over La Paz in Bolivia. The Apo View Hotel is just going up. Indeed, we had to step over soft cement, wooden horses, and workmen to get into the front entrance. But already, it is passé; a much bigger hotel will start building soon.

The reception was brief, but everybody had a chance to say "Hello! Glad you came!" One of these was a young college student who knew what the books say about speech making. He started off:

"Reverend Fadders" (with a low bow to the priests)

"Revered Mudder and Seestahs" (bowing to us) and with a big wide generous gesture taking in the whole room,

"Distinguished Everybody!"

Mark my words, someday that lad will be Senator from Davao.

But our missions are not in Davao. We went twenty jiggly miles to the north to Panabo. It's a good example of a boom town.

Twelve years ago, the Panabo district had a population of 13,000. It had 47,000 two years ago, and 60,000 this year. The parish was opened in July, 1959. Down here, a new parish opens every year. Even that is far from taking adequate care of the people; the old parishes are growing too fast. Just comparing figures in the 1959 *Catholic Directory* with those for 1961, we see things like this: Lupon parish grew from 20,000 to 37,000; Magugpo from 30,000 to 62,000; Nabunturan from 25,000 to 35,000; Mati from 13,000 to 22,000. All within two years.

Of course, everything is very new. Our convent is the upstairs of a school building. Two classrooms take care of First and Second Year High School. Houses, schools, churches, offices are going up like mad. The classrooms for Third and Fourth Year High we hope will be finished in time to start the new year.

Sister Ramona Maria is an itinerant dentist down here, so to speak. She got a dental chair and a foot-treadle drill from Army surplus—possibly Civil War surplus—and set them up in the school office. She takes care of the children's teeth with most of the school peering into the window and down the victim's throat. There's never a whimper out of any of them; that's for sure! Sister is the only dentist in town but she cannot stay long in any place. She packs up her equipment and takes it to our other schools on Mindanao.

I met Judge Luis Consolacion at Panabo. A graduate of the Law College at the University of the Philippines, he came in 1950 as a very young man and set up a law office. Now, in his early thirties, he is a power in the community, and one of Panabo's most enthusiastic citizens.

"The place is bursting out all over!" he said. "And not just with settlers but with good substantial businesses. The Dalisay Corporation down here is making bamboo plywood for a luxury market in Europe. Dalisay also has a corn mill in Panabo. Corporations like Tadeco, Dapco, Merco, Minda, Diokno, Napro and many others used to raise abaca (Manila hemp), but after that was almost wiped out by the mosaic pest, they turned to coconut, coffee, corn and rice. They're clamoring now for an irrigation system and, mark my words, they'll get one before long. Things happen fast down here. Some companies were able to control the mosaic infestation; as a result they lead the Province in producing hemp.

"As for transportation! Why, these companies have built beautiful roads all through Davao Province. The Inigo and Alcantaro lumber people have thus helped our small farmers immensely. I remember that whenever we went to Esperanza seven or eight years ago, we had to cross the river six times in thirty miles. And there were no bridges. Now we cross it only twice. A logging company opened out there and couldn't stand that sort of nonsense. We have two navigable rivers too, the Lasang and the Bincungan. The Davao-Agusan Highway passes right through Panabo. We're twenty miles from Davao, which is just right. It makes our town an ideal place for residence. You can partake of the fresh air of a rural life as well as the hubbub of the city.

"Sometimes settlers come down and can't make a go of it. Or they need outside jobs until they can get on their feet. Well, we have them.

The logging industry employs hundreds of laborers who would otherwise be a drag on society. We hardly ever see a 'one day, one eat' gang loitering around the market place.

"Although we used to be just a barrio of Tagum, Panabo was made a municipality in 1949. Only a Fifth Class Municipality, but in ten years we climbed up to First Class. Now, some of our barrios like Malativas want to become separate municipalities on their own."

Judge Consolacion shifted to the edge of his chair, afire with his favorite subject. "Why, Panabo has vast fertile lands and coastal swamps covered with fishponds. We have marvelous forest products—hard woods and soft. Our potentialities are enormous. Best of all, our citizens are industrious and public spirited, the best people on earth. A man comes down here destitute. Within five years he is a landed proprietor. Not much land and it's rugged living at first, but his life is his own and that's what he came for. I'm telling you this town will be one of the most prosperous cities in Davao Province. Maybe in all the Philippines. Perhaps in all the world. Expect big things of Panabo."

I do. The Panaboans are on to public relations techniques. Getting advertisers to finance the job, they put out a printed sheet extolling the advantages of their town. You would think they had enough new inhabitants, but they want the whole world to know how wonderful is life in Panabo. It ends thus: "Panabo grows not only economically and politically but also spiritually. Although a regular parish was not established as soon as we became a municipality in 1949, the Catholic community banded themselves together and organized the Panabo Catholic League. Through the untiring and persistent efforts of this association, led by Silvestre L. Gavins, president, a church, school and convent were constructed. On August 3, 1955, this town became a real parish."

Of course, any church constructed in 1955 would be utterly inadequate in a few years. Father Leo McCarthy, when he came in 1959, found his congregation hanging on to the chandeliers. Only there were no chandeliers to hang on to. No need for them because there is no electric power in Panabo, yet. But it's coming. Oh my yes, mark my words, it's coming. The logging companies have generators; we'll soon have electricity right in our homes!

"You've heard of buying meat 'on the hoof,'" says Father McCarthy. "Well, out here we buy a new church while it's still in the forest. You keep your eyes open as you go along the road looking for good trees. Then you choose one. After that you go to the owner and say, 'Look here, you can't put money in the collection basket because you need your money right now to develop your business. Why not put that tree into the basket instead?' So he gives you the tree.

"I have my eye on a kalantas tree for the new church. It's twelve feet in diameter and the fins go up thirty feet. We can make all our pews out of that. The owner has given me the tree; now I have to persuade somebody else to build a scaffolding thirty feet high and steady enough to be a firm foundation for sawyers."

In the meantime, Panabo's church has a shell of concrete. The floor is of rough concrete. "We expect to put in tiles, later, when we can afford it." There are no windows to open or close. "We've ordered the glass, though." The roof is single thickness of galvanized iron. "Some day we'll have a ceiling." No pews, of course. "Wait till we get that kalantas tree sawed up." The essentials are there—an altar and a pulpit.

Yet in Panabo we had a Solemn High Mass. We knelt on shaky old prie-dieus; the priests had workmen's benches in the sanctuary, and Panabo's high school students sang the Mass just as if they had not learned it only a week ago. A plethora of altar boys roamed the sanctuary trying to find enough employment to justify their being there. Two took the cruets, one clutched the bell, one got the censer and it took two to hold the Communion plate. Others found supervisory jobs. Father McCarthy wanted to make a good showing for Mother; he confessed later that he had mustered out his entire altar boy troops in her honor. They wore all sorts of cassocks and cinctures with a charming variety of hemlines. Some wore sneakers, some chinelas, some bare feet and many had borrowed daddy's one and only pair of shoes.

It was beautiful to see the priests at Mass. Still more so, to look beyond the lovely vestments, the ceremonial gestures, the ancient chants and still older words. At the bottom of all, there were three pairs of muddy boots. These boots had sloshed through rain and jolted in jeeps to get to Panabo for the solemn High Mass for Mother. Three priests at one time in the same place? In Mindanao that takes travel. Each of these priests had to come in from his own parish.

Part of the parish is the Davao Penal Colony. Panabo's Public Relations sheet has this to say of the local jail: "It looks more like a civilian community than a penitentiary. Here one can find a botanical garden, a wide, well-kept park and playground, a Catholic church, secondary and elementary schools and a social hall. The residential lots are very well planned and laid out. When one goes outside the 'poblacion' he sees big plantations of abaca, ramis, coffee and kenaff, as well as irrigated rice fields covering 500 hectares (about 1,250 acres). It is said that this institution supports itself."

This seems correct. The idea is that prisoners from all parts of the Philippines can work out their sentences here, learning agriculture. They may bring their families down, build small homes, work farms allotted to them and, when their sentences run out, the land is theirs. In the case of life sentence, the land goes to the widow and the children. It's an old idea; wasn't that the way Australia and Georgia were started? There are few restrictions at the Penal Colony—no walls, and only a small corps of guards. As you drive on the public road through the colony, the prisoners wave and smile at you as any group of free men would.

It was raining—not to say pouring—that day. We went on to Santo Tomas as the heavens wept. This is the domain of Father Walter Maxcy, who should have a book all to himself. But first, his parish!

In 1955, Santo Tomas did not even exist. The place was virgin forest. Population: zero. Six years later, population: five thousand. And ten thousand more in the parish.

More than a thousand children are in the Elementary School; there is no high school for them. Father Maxcy is sawing wood and mixing concrete like mad to get one built. The beams are hewn right there from logs brought from the forest practically in his back yard. The wood is so hard, it is termite-proof; no termite is going to bruise his little nose trying to get through that stuff.

When it is finished, it will be the only building in town that is not a shack. Father lives in a shack and the church is two shacks holding each other up. It has a mud floor, a tin roof and twenty ancient pews. Father's shack is falling to pieces, leaking like a sieve, overrun with rats, with no stove, no icebox, no windows. He gets his meals from the sari-sari store at the corner. "I used to buy food and keep it here," he explained, "but the rats ate most of it. Now I let them eat it at the store and I buy what's left. At least I don't have to pay for their meals as well as my own."

For a long time, Father slept on the floor. He is chaplain at the Davao Penal Colony. One day, when prisoners were bringing something for the new school, they saw how he was sleeping. So they ran out and stole a bed for him. Well, maybe they didn't steal it but they won't tell where they got it.

The hero of these yarns is a debonair young priest, very much of the Bing Crosby type. For ten years he did heroic work in New York, doing everything possible to interest people in the missions.

"People would do anything in the world for Father Maxcy," one woman told me. "If he had asked me to stand on Times Square and hold out a tin cup for Maryknoll, I would have done it gladly. One time he called me up and said, 'Would you want to go to Maryknoll tomorrow? You may have to ride on the fenders, but if you want to go you can.' I went to the Maryknoll Fathers' House on 39th Street the next day. The whole front room was crowded with people. They were from all parts of the city, even from Philadelphia. Not one of us knew any other. But we were all friends of Father Maxcy, and when he came he had mustered enough cars to take us all to Maryknoll, just to see the place where the Church's frontiersmen are trained."

Father Maxcy, with his charm and wit, could live a very easy life in New York, but here he is in Santo Tomas, Mindanao, fighting with rain and rats and a population which swells every time you breathe. He says about his shack, "I'll have to move from here, someday. But when I do I'll do it with regret. This is the kind of house the people are used to. They feel they can come in here to see me without feeling strange. I love it."

As one of the priests said, "The Church in Mindanao is in the nail and hammer stage, not yet graduated to the brick and mortar stage. Every parish is building a church, a rectory, a school or a convent, or all four together. A portable sawmill is set up in one parish and moved to the next as soon as the job is finished. It's like the family car; you have to sign up for it and take your turn."

Although a priest may have to be builder, plumber, educator, tree-collector or anything else on occasion, his first job is to say Mass and administer the sacraments. We were looking over some logs that Father McCarthy expected to make into cabinets for his sacristy, when a very thin elderly man came up to us. "Father, my wife is dying. Will you come with the Sacrament?"

Sister Rhoda and I went along in the back seat of the parish jeep. There were three up front: Father, the man, and the Lord of Heaven and Earth. The man pointed the way up a side road and we stopped before a small nipa house, such as you see in any town on any Philippine island. Quite a crowd had collected around it. For these pioneers often live in towns and go out to their farms during the day.

The family led us up the bamboo steps; the daughter-in-law and grand-children stepped aside, hushed and awed. Old Macaria lay on the floor in the front room on a rice-straw mat, clean and cool. As Father came up the steps, she tried to stretch her arms out to greet Our Lord. She was very thin, very weak. Father knelt down to hear her whispered confession; he placed the Sacred Host on her tongue. She swallowed gratefully and lay for a long time quiet. The family prayed with her. Then we talked to them for a while. They had been in Panabo for four years and were doing quite well. Expected to do even better next year. Good, solid, hardworking people who expect only a sufficiency from life. Then we drove home.

As we entered the church, a young couple had been waiting for Father. Baptism for the baby, please. The little thing was decked out in a cheap pink dress, very prudently left open in the back. Husband and wife were so proud. They had a farm some miles out; they had left Samar on their wedding night and this was their first child. As they left the church in the late afternoon, they caught a bus going their way. There would be a few miles' walk into the jungle afterwards, but what was that when little Eulalia, their very own flesh and blood, had been made a Child of God that day?

5 A.M. in Panabo—and life gets under way for the day. The cries of men hitching their carabaos to sleds, of women getting fires alight, of children yawning into consciousness. Above and throughout these sounds is the steady crunch of the town pump as everyone works the handle to get the first pail of water for the day. The long, slow pulls of a man, the short jerks of a child. It's a never-ending task, from the dawn of human life to its close, to get water.

The day could be translated into our own terms when America was settled, be it in 1621 or 1961. It's great to be in at beginnings!

⚡ 11 ⚡ *The Sons of the Prophet Are Children of Adam*

"ARE you going by bunny or kangaroo?" is a common question in the Philippines. Local planes go bunny-hopping; expresses leap like kangaroos. Having leaped by kangaroo from Manila to Davao, we now went bunny-hopping around Mindanao.

Cotabato is one hundred and sixty miles west of Davao as the crow flies. But crows take no passengers, so we went one hundred and twenty miles by Philippine Air Lines to Dadiangas; and on to Alah, another sixty miles; and so to Cotabato one hundred miles further. I was glad. We traversed the length and breadth of Cotabato Province. *The Phil-Asian Atlas* claims that this province alone could feed every Filipino man, woman or child for years to come. Indeed the Philippines need not fear a population explosion; if developed, it is said the country could feed one hundred times as many people as are there now. Small wonder, then, that the province has leaped in thirteen years from less than half a million to 1,168,000; this is sixty-five percent gain as against forty-two percent for the country as a whole.

Yet we Maryknoll Sisters are not in this rapidly expanding part. For the new influx is of Christian Filipinos mostly from the Visayas. We are at Dulawan, recently renamed Datu Piang, a settlement ninety-five percent Mohammedan, and forty miles southeast of Cotabato City. The town used to be on the main road from Cotabato to Davao across the island, but the new road bypasses our town. The ferry isn't used; the old road is not maintained any longer. Our population of nineteen thousand stays where it is.

Just how Mohammedans got into the Catholic Philippines is sometimes asked. The answer is easy. They were there first. The original inhabitants of Mindanao were slightly Hindu in their cast of thought. Even now their mythology has many Hindu touches. Around 1380, Makdum arrived in Sulu from Malacca; not long afterwards, Rajah Baginda came from Sumatra. These two converted Sulu and from there Mohammedanism became strong in Mindanao and spread northwards. If the Spanish had not come when they did in 1565, all the islands would have been under the crescent. Even Manila was a Mohammedan settlement when Governor Legaspi arrived to set up his office there in 1571.

At last, after three hundred years, Governor Claveria got three steamboats and went against Jolo, the citadel of Mohammed. They were the first steam vessels ever seen in the Philippines. These did the trick although not at once. Governor Urbiztondo had to bring out the same steamboats and reconquer the Sulus seven years later. Within ten years, with eighteen steamboats bought from England, the Spanish chased the Moro raiders up their rivers faster than the wind could blow their vintas. The final blow fell in 1876 when Governor Malcampo finished the job and broke Mindanao up into Provinces and Sub-Provinces. After three centuries of trying, Spain enjoyed the victory only twenty years when she lost the whole Philippines to the United States. Americans had a good deal of trouble down that way, too, before things smoothed out. The Mohammedans are still violently anti-Christian.

It is odd, then, that Datu Piang, chief of Dulawan, approached the Bishop Gerard Mongeau, O.M.I., of Cotabato and asked that the Church staff the high school in his town. He was really up against it. For some years, the boys had threatened the teachers with bloody vengeance if they did not pass tests, and even pulled knives against them in the classrooms. One year, the staff resigned en masse. In 1954, three Maryknoll Sisters arrived to take over that school. It wasn't easy and it didn't happen in one day, but eventually the school straightened out. Now, one hundred and ninety-three boys and girls are enrolled, half of them Mohammedan. This shows the growing confidence of local parents. It is all the more remarkable since a new school, advertising "a complete Moslem education," opened the year before.

All of this led to a trenchant remark by the Datu. "You Sisters seem to be very well liked in this town," he said. "You have been here five years and haven't been killed yet."

The whole feeling here is quite different from any Philippine town I ever knew. The people show little friendliness to us, and little among themselves. They go up and down the street without greetings. They don't stand together in neighborly groups on corners or in doorways. They don't even talk together while walking. You can't help but miss the children running up to you, the happy smiles of women, the wave of a hand from men.

However, some citizens of Dulawan are cut on the old pattern. A horde of small fry live around the convent. "Live" is the correct word. They sit on the back steps, peer into the windows, lie in wait for any Sister stepping outside. Then they rush forward and each of her ten fingers is commandeered by one grubby hand. In a settlement behind the market, too, the Sisters have loyal friends. So there is some improvement. When the Sisters first came to Dulawan . . . well, it's better now.

There is no electricity in Dulawan. Seeing fluorescent bulbs in the convent, I had hopes. But it seems that a wealthy woman has the electricity franchise in town. Three years ago part of her generator broke down. She refused to have it repaired until outstanding bills were paid. So we do without electricity.

Transistor radios are common enough. One hears them from dawn to dusk. Bishop Mongeau and his Oblates of Mary Immaculate have established twenty-five high schools throughout Cotabato Province. Each year a week of field days brings the athletic teams of all these high schools to Cotabato for baseball, basketball, softball, tennis, track and other sports. Our Notre Dame de Dulawan school has never won much of anything, but the interest is intense. We followed our team's progress by radio, either our own or the neighbors'. You can walk to the market and pick up the scores along the way, first from one tienda (or small store) and then from the next. In between you learn all about the superlative properties of Fletcher's Castoria and Tide Detergent.

But lest you think the townspeople very American in their ways, the girl in our kitchen used laundry starch in apple pie. And one of the boys in school is named Maseen-gun; he was born during the war when machine guns were popping. Many boys in school have burnt patches on their arms. When they were five or six, their grandfathers put small balls of cotton on the inside of the arm from the wrist to the elbow. Then the balls were set aflame. The child proves he is of worthy stuff if he lets them burn out without shaking them off.

Here again, we met Sister Ramona Maria, the dentist. There is no dentist among the Moros. One went through dentistry school but failed to pass the Board examinations. A dentist "from outside" has set up shop in Cotabato City, but that is forty miles away. The Moros do have four doctors and fifty lawyers. The plethora of lawyers is due to the fact that, not so long ago, they elected a Representative for the Legislature in Manila. This man was not a lawyer and felt he was held in small esteem by other Representatives. From that time on, any family aspiring to politics puts its boy through law school first. Dentistry can wait. The local blacksmith is willing to chisel a hole in your front tooth and fit into it a gold heart or key or Ace of Spades.

Sister had come from the school in Panabo. She can flatten down her collapsible dental chair into a package no bigger than the rest of the baggage one sees loaded on top of buses in Mindanao. As she goes from one school to another, all she has to do is to buy a ticket and catch the next bus at the corner.

If Sister's equipment is rudimentary, her knowledge and skill are not. When she has a Mohammedan datu on the chair (for she takes in emergencies), she sometimes must practically stand on his chest to ease out a molar. But she does it with consummate art. She has been not only a tooth-saver but a life-saver for many a poor country child.

"There was a little boy, only seven years old," she told me. "He had a tumor beside his back tooth as big as that." She pointed to the top of a medicine bottle on her shelf. "He couldn't even close his mouth. I took out the tooth and the tumor and saved him from possible cancer. Another boy, thirteen, had a cancer on the roof of his mouth and a girl I found with a tumor under her tongue. Of course, they went to the hospital in Cotabato, when I insisted."

I spent a half-hour in chapel one morning in most distracted prayer. The windows face on the main street. Only when I resolved to pray especially for everybody who passed, was I able to reconcile piety with curiosity. First, a carabao came along ponderously, pulling his sled and his owner on top of it. Next came a man swinging a piece of meat from a rattan string. Horrors, he's turning in here! Is this our dinner? Then an old man in a wide straw hat walked hand in hand with a small boy, no more than three years old, who wore a "copia"—the white cap of one who has been to Mecca. The copia is the white "overseas" cap we associate with pictures of Nehru; the women wear a white scarf called a kagi, loosely draped around the head. The old man and boy were slow; from behind came a billow of dust as the bus roared by. It was close, but the old man pulled the child to him and they were safe. From the market, a woman with a basket of fish on her hip approached. Behind her was the ice-cream man pushing his wagon and ringing the bell. Heading for school recess, no doubt. The woman with the fish put her basket on the ground, rearranged her off-center topknot of hair and pinned it together again. She fixed her skirt; that is, pulled out the single cylinder of cloth far too wide for her, wrapped it around her hips and pulled the excess into a knot at her waist. That done, she picked up the fish and went on. A goat and several kids got my next prayers. Then, a smartly dressed woman, maybe a newcomer to Dulawan, with high heels and Western clothes. For lack of beneficiaries, I prayed for the pig rooting along the roadside. A jingle of bells and a tricycle-cab rolled by with two passengers. None of these people had spoken to any other.

By this time, the children who swarm around the convent had found me sitting in chapel. They took up watch as youngsters do at the Monkey House in the Bronx Zoo. I could not understand their language, but the general tone was uncomplimentary. So I decided to change occupations and type a while on the other side of the house.

But they found me. I typed in the limelight of twenty children's riveted attention. We communicated by gesture only and got along quite well. The typewriter was more fun even than I. We have no glass windows in the house—just screening across the window frames. They imitated my fingers on the keys, listened for the carriage bell, put in a new sheet of paper, turned to a new leaf. The typewriter was the strangest table ornament they had ever seen; I was the oddest character ever dropped from Mars. We were great friends before long.

"I have to take care of a woman behind the market," Sister Patricia Marie put her head in at the door. "Do you want to come?"

Sister Patricia Marie is from Philadelphia. I lived ten years with her at Malabon near Manila, when we two formed half the convent of four Sisters. We went through the war together sharing the same bowl of lugao, so to speak, and even at one time possessing a pair of red leather shoes between us. There was little we did not know about one another. We used to play duets together. If you can play duets with a person and turn the last page still on speaking terms with her, you have a beautiful friendship. Sister is a teacher; she does not pretend to be a nurse, but she has some simple remedies which help cuts, boils and so on.

So we set out, surrounded by the children who were thrilled to see me leave the typewriter and come out into the open. We passed a house distinguished from the others by a red car parked in front. "That's the ex-mayor's house," Sister said. "He has thirty-eight wives and that red car. That makes him very opulent indeed. We could run our school just for his children, they are so many. It's impossible to keep track of who is whose full-sister or step-sister."

We turned a corner and came on to the riverfront. The Rio Grande flows by Dulawan en route to Cotabato City where it empties into the ocean. It's a magnificent river, yet the boating on it seemed very small. Outboard motorboats were parked alongside dug-out canoes. Geese strutted up and down the riverside. Stores, warehouses, small piers seemed very busy indeed. We got no hearty greeting from passers-by but every now and then boys or girls of high school age invited us into their family's stores and the parents came forward politely. We tried to rent a boat for half an hour or so; the boatmen seemed loath to do so, but eventually one man agreed. Once everything was settled, he could not have been nicer. We paddled down the river a way, viewing Dulawan's riverfront. Many people were hurrying into a large but shabby tin-covered building vaguely resembling a temple. It was the Mohammedan mosque. "Our school lets out at 10:30 on Friday mornings, to give the children time to bathe and dress for religious services at the mosque. Between 12 and 1 o'clock on Fridays, no traffic may pass it. It will soon be noon; that's why all the people are hurrying in, now. We can pass it in this canoe, but cars or outboard motorboats are taboo."

We got out of the boat and proceeded market-wards. Halfway down the street we met a man draped in a towel around his neck, shaved on one side of his face and gummy with lather on the other.

"What's the matter, Akas?" Sister asked.

"I was getting shaved there," he pointed toward the market, "in the shop of Dadtum, the barber. He had just started on me when a fellow came in wearing brass knuckles and he hit Dadtum all over his face. Then a lot of men gathered round and they took Dadtum and the other man off to the mayor's house. But in the meantime, here I am not shaved yet."

There was nothing we could do about that. We went on to the market. Nobody there, of course. From 10 A.M. onwards, a village market is an empty field strewn with the well-picked garbage that nobody can sell. We passed through it, then over a foul creek and onto a ledge of land barely above water. Here were eight or ten nipa huts, ready to fall down any minute. Sister got a tremendous welcome here. She went into one house after another, treating women lying on the floors, breathing all day the fetid air of ground moistened by garbage rills from the market. There was a case of mumps in a shaky house set in filthy goo. An old woman was dying in a very small house no larger than five feet square. On the porch of another, a young woman lay on the floor too languid to sit up, burning with fever. Sister gets gifts of money at times to be spent "for charity." With these she buys vitamin pills, antibiotics, ointments, antiseptics, etc. She has been able several times, too, to send severe cases to the hospital. We met one woman who could not welcome us enough to her small home. "She had a large tumor," Sister told me. "I sent her to the hospital; it was removed; and now she is a well woman. In gratitude, her husband and oldest son appeared at our back door one afternoon and said they would guarantee to keep our basketball court in good condition. They do, too. Every week or so they come to give it a trim and a conditioning."

Even in this wretched place, however, many women had gold stars, keys, Aces of Spades inset in their teeth, and not a few wore twenty dollar gold pieces fastened on to safety pins and worn as brooches. "Why don't you get that converted into pesos?" I asked one of them. "You could get many things you need, then."

She smiled sweetly and turned away. I don't think she even recognized it as negotiable currency. Probably it had been in the family for years as an ornament. My suggestion would be equivalent to saying, "Why don't you hock your wedding ring?"

We went back over the deserted market to Main Street. A young girl from school stopped us, said a few words to Sister and passed on.

"She was Queen Killed To The Last Rat in our school," said Sister Patricia Marie.

"Queen what?" said I.

"Queen Killed To The Last Rat," she reaffirmed. "Rats are such a pest here that the Bureau of Health instigated a contest in the schools to collect rat tails. They were to keep them in salt solution and bring their collection to the municipio once a week. Pinadtaya earned her title the hard way. Dear knows how many rat tails she produced to be crowned Queen Killed To The Last Rat. But she made it."

At this point we met Dadtum, the barber, coming back from the mayor's house. The marks of his recent assault were obvious, a swollen lip, closed eye and blood on his shirt. He was one of the few Christians in the town although just how Christian he was, I don't know. However, he stopped to tell us that his assailant was now in jail.

The sound of gongs, struck lightly, wafted on the dusty air. We soon saw the cause. Brass cylinders, some of them two feet across and ten inches deep, hung from the rafters of a porch facing the street. Smaller gongs sat in a wooden rack in gradated sizes. Three small children went from one to another tapping them with well-worn sticks topped with balls of leather. It was like a fairy concert.

"That reminds me," said Sister. "We have to get home. Some of our high schools girls and their mothers are coming to give a concert on the gongs this afternoon. There's just one place I want to go first."

We stopped at a small house down a side street. "Tarhata!" Sister called at the window. A smiling woman appeared. "Francisca," Sister went on and gave her a message.

"Why did you call her Tarhata outside the house, and yet Francisca when you were talking to her?" I asked.

"She's a Christian woman sold to a Mohammedan in payment for a debt," Sister explained. "She's known as Tarhata here although her husband is quite good and lets her practice her religion fairly well."

Back home, we found preparations for the concert well under way. A board had been nailed to the basketball standard. The huge gongs called Ahgang were tied with rattan to this. These aren't made in Cotabato

Province; they come from Lanao to the north. Slightly smaller gongs, called Gandingan, hung on racks about five feet high. The small ones, Kalintang, rested in a lower rack where one operator could sit down and reach all of them, as a xylophone is played.

Such a concert is a cooperative effort. Four girls took their places between the great Ahgangs and the smaller Gandingan. In each hand they held a stick topped by a ball of rubber bands looped and twisted together. Another girl, Maruha, who wore the kagi veil to signify that she had made her pilgrimage to Mecca, sat at the Kalintang. She was the star performer. At the last minute a young man walked over with an umbrella over his head. He took his post between two big gongs. "Who is he?" I asked.

"He really doesn't belong to this team," Sister said. "He has conjunctivitis of the eyes and came only for some medicine at the convent. He's a good player and the girls asked him to help."

For more than two hours they played. For rhythm and variation in volume I have never heard the like. In spite of the umbrella, the young man kept several gongs going rapidly. Sometimes he fixed the umbrella handle under his chin so that both hands could play. We stood in the hot sun or sat on the school steps. A goodly crowd gathered. The girls were much shyer with us than Christian girls would have been, but for all that, there was a pleasant feeling throughout. At the end, they hired several tricycle-taxis, loaded the gongs into them and went off having given us a concert indeed.

Maruha, the star performer, stayed behind a few minutes. She made the pilgrimage to Mecca when she was nine years old; it will place her in honor all her life. Her white kagi was of filmy stuff, intricately embroidered in white. She was so pretty, so graceful, so poised and dignified, I felt honored to have seen her and heard her play.

Mohammedanism is not a gentle religion as Buddhism is. It seems to have violent penances and violent orgies. The Sisters tell of a boy in class who studied very hard for an examination. "If I pass my father has promised me I can have two wives on graduation," he told them.

For one month a year, the fasting is extreme. From sunrise to sunset, they eat nothing. They do not even swallow their spittle.

"Running amok" has become fairly rare due to the red tape one must go through before indulging in this old Mohammedan sport. Indeed, much of the fun has been eliminated but enough remains to make it highly exhilarating—to spectators at least.

It used to be that any market day or holiday when the streets were filled with business men or merry makers, you might spot a hungry looking fellow in red pants wandering through the crowd. He would be carrying over his shoulder or under his arm an "upo"—a gourd maybe two feet

long and five or six inches across. Then, all of a sudden, he'd give a fiend-
ish scream, whip a bolo out of the upo (which was only a scabbard to hide
the weapon) and start slashing around him. Arms, legs, heads, ears—anything at all might sail through the air for the next five minutes or so until
somebody with a longer bolo and a steadier eye had dispatched the
"amok."

The custom comes from the pious idea that anyone who kills a Christian
rides a white horse to heaven. The chances are that if you kill a dozen
people, one of them is bound to have Christian tendencies.

But now, as I said, red tape complicates the process. In Dulawan, when
a man feels like going amok, he has to go through quite a process. To begin with he says to himself, "I will run amok. I probably won't live much
longer anyhow and I would like to go out fighting. Also, it would be good
to arrive in heaven on a white horse, no?"

He makes a vow. He must report this vow to the datu, the police and
the pandita (the priest). This takes much of the zest out of the enterprise.
It spoils the element of surprise. However, the Sisters say that most comply
with this regulation. The datu is held responsible for any murders going
on unless he has informed the police. He wishes to make this religious act
as safe as possible.

The amok then goes on a nine-day fast, eating nothing from sunrise to
sunset, and then only a very spare meal. On the appointed day, he shaves
his head and puts on red pants. Next he hollows out the upo and conceals
his bolo in it. Then he strolls casually down the street to the market place.
Everybody knows the signs, of course. When they see him they should
start going home, but often they stay around just to see the fun. The
marked man saunters nonchalantly until people are off guard or until a
Christian shows his face. Then he screams and runs amok until he is cor-
nered and killed by the police. He stands to gain eternally even if he has
no Christian scalps to show. He can always report to Mohammed, "I
tried."

Fighting is inbred. The schoolyard is often an arena. When the Sister
comes along the boys protest, "Only in fun, Sister, only in fun!" But after
class or beyond the schoolyard, the fight goes on. Sister Patricia Marie
knows how to handle them. She separated two gladiators and took a kris
(a wavy-bladed dagger) from one and a hooked blade from the other.

"What are you fighting about?" she demanded.

"When we were cutting the grass yesterday," Abdul said at last, "Akmad
came very close to me. He almost cut my pants."

"Did you mean to cut his pants? Answer me, Akmad."

"No, but now I do," lunging forward.

Sister settled the feud. "Abdul, you will shake hands with Akmad; then
you will shake hands with me. Akmad, you will shake hands with Abdul

and then with me. There! Nothing can break that pact. We are all friends together." It sounds silly, but it worked.

Dulawan is a fascinating town; the spiritual potentials are enormous. Most of these people have such good qualities, if they could be turned from destructive uses. It will take day-by-day, week-by-week education. It's the hammer, hammer, hammer drives the nail home.

So we took the bus back to Cotabato for another series of bunny hops in Mindanao. In some future age, Maryknoll Sisters may learn that bus schedules in mission lands are "such stuff as dreams are made on." This generation has not yet learned it. The bus was to stop at our door at 11:00 A.M. At 11:00, we were ready. At 12:00 the bus arrived; we piled on, three to a small seat. The bus looked full to our untutored eyes. For an hour afterwards, we roamed up this street and down that, picking up passengers. We passed our own door three times—maybe more, because we could see nothing over the solid block of suffering humanity wedged in the aisle and between the seats. Men standing in the aisle hunched over the fortunates in the seats; baggage was tied on top; chickens stored in the steerage compartment between the wheels. The driver himself was only one of eight men jammed in the front seat. When he was sure of a profitable trip, he steamed out of town.

The road was fair, all of coral rock. It seemed the only solid land between swamps aglow with pink lotus and beautiful white birds, cranes of all sizes, some also dark grey with white markings. The people were used to all this beauty; they did not bother to look. The seat before us held a sick woman who rested her head on her husband's shoulder. He was very attentive. A boy got tired standing and sat down on the aisle floor. Many of the men wore copias of white velvet, plastic or cotton cloth, proud of having fulfilled the obligation of the true son of Mohammed— to visit Mecca at least once in his lifetime. How human they all were! Love between man and woman, weariness of a long journey, pride in the badge of honor. Though they are sons of Mohammed and we are Spouses of Christ, there can be no doubt that we are all children of Adam.

≼ 12 ≽ Sunday Morning in the Plaza

IF Panabo's youthful Chamber of Commerce can ever decide just where the entrance to their fair city is—that is, if they can fix upon a spot which will not be swallowed into the middle of town in a few months—they should erect a bamboo arch with the words, "Welcome to

THE FUTURE." And the Moros in Dulawan could well put up a road sign, "You are entering ANOTHER WORLD ENTIRELY." So Jimenez, our next stop, should advertise, "Come, enjoy THE PAST."

Mindanao is an odd-shaped island. You can think of it as a face with a receding chin, blowing out a billow of steam on a frosty morning. (Welcome thought—a frosty morning on Mindanao!) The billow is the fascinating Zamboanga peninsula. Where the breath issues from pursed lips it is very narrow but it soon broadens out. Right at this isthmus, where Panguit Bay on the north almost meets Illana Bay on the south, is the metropolis for this area, Ozamis City. It is a very up-and-coming city indeed. A new city gymnasium was just dedicated, built for 107,000 pesos; a new city hall is going up, to cost 500,000 pesos. Some 175,000 pesos will go to lengthening the wharves, and a supermarket is on the way which will cost 500,000 pesos. Ozamis City and environs have some excellent roads, most through self-help endeavors. Those who dream dreams of Mindanao's future, talk of cutting a canal through the eight miles between Panguit Bay and Illana Bay. This will save ships the trouble of going all around Zamboanga peninsula.

Few on Mindanao do not dream dreams. A hereditary ailment, it seems. When Governor Claveria and his three trusty steamboats waged war on the Moro raiders, perhaps some of his men saw the possibilities in this inviting coastland. In the next fifteen years or so, quite a few settlements had sprung up at Ozamis City and the land around. Jimenez is a little town about twenty miles north. Now and then a visiting Augustinian, Padre Jimenez, came out from the city to say Mass and administer the sacraments; in gratitude, the town was named for him.

But things never took root until the Man of the Hour arrived. This was Padre Roque Azcona, who was the first resident pastor. He took his job seriously. The town of three thousand people then lay on the seashore near the Palilau River, subject to floods. Father Azcona planned a new town, a bit inland. He said, "Let's use the lowland for rice fields. We will irrigate it properly and build dikes." And so it was done and now is. Then he viewed the thick forest inland. "Let's build the city of Jimenez here," he decided. "We will have wide streets, ample trees, and a broad avenue from the plaza which will take the eye straight down to the sea." So it was planned and so it is now. "We will have a reservoir and water system for drainage and for irrigation," was next. "And now we are ready to build our church, parish office, rectory and school. And we lay out a cemetery." All these things were done; they remain to this day in full operation. A fifty-mile road along the western shore of Iligan Bay is still the main highway. That was one of Padre Azcona's projects.

Then he set to work on the people. He got them to plant coconut, rice, corn, coffee and cacao on a big scale. He encouraged them to get into the abaca trade. He also kept a watchful eye on who was marrying whom and thus built up some of the First Families of the area. The Hynson family is one; the Bernad is another; the Ozamis is a third. They have all made great contributions to the land here.

The original Hynson came from England to America and settled on the Eastern Shore of Maryland in 1630. He became a landed proprietor in St. Mary and Charles Counties. The Maryland Historical Association has his family tree. His descendant, Thomas Hynson, came to the Philippines on an unfortunate whaling ship which left him in Cagayan de Oro. The only other white man there was the redoubtable Father Roque Azcona; later, when Father Azcona was sent to open the new parish of Jimenez, he invited Thomas Hynson and his family to come along.

Father Azcona wrote letters back to his home in Spain; his words threw a glow around Mindanao. His brother, Manuel, decided to emigrate and try his hand at pioneering. Father Azcona had a likely young bride picked out for his brother but she died before he came. Manuel then sought the hand of Basilia, Thomas Hynson's daughter, the most eligible maiden in Jimenez. This was in 1870. Consuelo Azcona, their child, married Anselmo Bernad, the son of Ramon Bernad who had emigrated from Spain in 1860.

Mr. and Mrs. Anselmo Bernad, with the blood of pioneers flowing in their veins and pride of Spain setting their shoulders square, were head and front of Catholic resistance to the Aglipayan schism which split the Philippines from top to bottom in the early 1900's. Anselmo was Governor of his province for many years. When Spanish priests left the islands after the Spanish-American War, all of Mindanao was left without a priest for twenty years. Jimenez itself had none for thirty years. But even a large city such as Ozamis was bereft. During that time Bishop Hendricks of Cebu found himself, an American, ecclesiastical head of all the Visayan Islands, hundreds of them, and of half of Mindanao as well. He came to visit Ozamis City, then called Misamis. As his boat drew near to shore, the forlorn band of Catholics, headed by Anselmo and Consuela Bernad, knelt on the sands to receive their Bishop. The Bernads offered him hospitality. At dinner, the house was mobbed by Aglipayans shouting, "Death to the Bishop!" "Down with Hendricks and Rome!" Lest he bring harm to the entire family, Bishop Hendricks left for the parish convento, then in ruins. Anselmo stuck with him; he too moved into the convento for the duration of the visit. The Municipal Council of Misamis formally passed a resolution approving the mob and took the trouble to present a copy of it to the Bishop.

Later a Jesuit priest, much beloved even yet, Father Gabriel Font, had just about half of Mindanao as his parish. They say he used to marry people in the bus as he went along. From 1921 until 1927, he lived on the road going from town to town in a desperate attempt to be twins or triplets. The Bernads' son, Miguel, was his traveling altar boy. Now he is a Jesuit priest himself, a mine of information on the history and temperament of Misamis.

The Bernads' daughter was Concepcion, who married Dr. Bomediano, grandson of Romualdo Bomediano, an artist imported from Bohol to paint the church. He made it one of the most elegant, spacious churches in all the provinces. And if you think that is small praise, you should see some of the tremendous buildings put up by Spanish friars far from the centers of culture. This one in Jimenez had a magnificent organ from Spain and a bell tower with a chiming clock. I, myself, taught school beside a village church which would put to shame half the churches in American cities; it might make even Grand Central Terminal blush a little.

Dr. Bomediano was acting Governor of Misamis Occidental during World War II. He and Concepcion hid out in the mountains near Mt. Malindang. "The town was occupied by Japanese," he told me, "but nobody was in it." He is now with Philcoa, a government organization responsible for the quality of copra shipped out of the country. Copra is still first on the Philippine export list. It was slipping due to poor methods of drying, but Philcoa is trying to keep the quality high.

Concepcion Bernad de Bomediano is a very simple, straightforward woman. I met her in her pharmacy on Jimenez Main Street. We shook hands over the counter. Then she left the store to the care of a girl and we went upstairs to their comfortable but modest apartment. She spoke of her childhood in Jimenez. "In the early days, there was always a raid going on, it seemed to me. The Moros slipped across Iligan Bay from Lanao by night and took crops, women and children. They sold them. My grandfather bought three children who had been stolen from other islands. They did not know where they came from. One of these lived with my mother until she died at a very advanced age. She had kinky hair so she may have been a Negrito from as far north as Zambales on Luzon.

"During the Aglipayan days, when for thirty years there was no resident priest in Jimenez, eight families remained loyal. We used to go to church regularly every Sunday even though there would be no Mass. The head of the Catholic Action group opened the door for us and closed it again after us. He held the keys. This was very important; the Aglipayans had to build their own church. In many towns the Catholics had no church; the Aglipayans had taken over the parish."

You cannot go far in Mindanao without coming across another remarkable family, the Ozamis. The father came to our little town of Jimenez in 1890 or so, as purchasing agent for Tabacalera, a Spanish tobacco firm.

He settled down, married a Fortich (another name to conjure with in these parts) and had one boy and nine girls. The boy became Senator Jose Ozamis; during World War II he fought bravely as a guerilla and was executed for it. To honor him, Ozamis City adopted his name; formerly it was Misamis City.

The girls all manifested that undying energy which is the stock in trade of well-born Filipinas. Remedios Ozamis married Senator Fortich at the beginning of World War II. When they were hiding in the hills during the war years, he was mortally wounded by Moros. As he lay dying, Remedios reminded God that her husband had made nine First Friday Communions and that He had promised that none such would die without the sacraments. Out of nowhere a priest came just in time to hear his confession and to bless him. After the war, Remedios filled out her husband's term as Senator. She is now head of the National Rural Rehabilitation Agency responsible for the government's homesteading projects. She lives out in pioneer land at Malaybalay where my friend Florencia passed going out to her honeymoon nipa hut in the wilderness. With her booming voice and mannish ways, Remedios sees a job to be done and does it. Her father, so tradition says, used to call her "My little typhoon."

Nieves, her sister, went to Manila and allied herself with the Roces family, publishers of the *Manila Times*. She writes for the newspaper and is in printer's ink up to her elbows. Paulita went to Cebu where she built up a restaurant, The Bee Hive; she has a thriving catering service, too. Consuelo is unmarried and keeps up the old home. Quiet, she is a power for good in every Jimenez civic and church project.

Carmen has the business head. Her father chose her for the job. She operates haciendas of coconut, rice and corn in Jimenez; a cattle ranch in Bukidnon and a pineapple farm there as well; lumber and coffee estates in Cebu. She has a large interest in Toledo Copper Mines in Cebu. The Visayan Electric Company is another of her pet projects and, just to keep her hands full, she manages the Shell Oil depot at Jimenez. Outside of those trifles, she has nothing to do. She has no telephone, of course, but uses a lot of telegrams. Like other big business executives, Carmen is always looking for talent. She picked up a poor boy named Cruz Lagura, sent him to school in Cebu for automotive engineering, and put him in charge of all the tractors, trucks and jeeps used in her various enterprises. He is also her personal chauffeur, driving her Buick which no one else is allowed to touch. Carmen does not use it much; she prefers to walk. Nearly every morning finds her walking up Main Street to early Mass. The car is as much ours as hers, judging from the use of it.

The important families of this town, which is just emerging from the chop-the-trees-down stage of pioneering, stand in contrast to those of another section of the world. At first glance, one might suppose conditions would be similar in Jimenez and in the middle of Bolivia. Both are isolated sections of the great Spanish empire, established long after the sun had set on its colonial glory. Pioneers to Jimenez came over the sea; those in Bolivia's jungle lands paddled down the rivers and portaged the rapids. Both are hot countries; pioneers in both were surrounded by hostile neighbors, the Indians in Bolivia, the Moros in Jimenez.

While in Bolivia, I stayed several days in the deserted Suarez mansion, far grander than anything in Jimenez, a palace built in the humid jungle of South America's Green Hell. The fancy English plumbing had rusted beyond use; mould hung in festoons on the damask wall papers; the inlaid hardwood floors were half in and half out. The once handsome bathtub had been torn from its pipes, hauled outside and, upside down, served as a shelter for chickens when it rained—which was always. In the early 1900's, Nicolas Suarez built up a tremendous rubber empire. His wife, Judita, grew her own sugar cane, crushed it and boiled the juice. I saw the vats she used, in a small clearing in the jungle. Nicolas and Judita are buried beside the mighty river which carried them from civilization to this primitive rubber kingdom. But their children, educated in Europe, live in foreign countries and have little interest in the land their father worked so hard to conquer.

The Ozamis family is not unusual in the Philippines. Every province can point to families who came early, settled down and formed the bedrock of the place. Very often two such families intermarry until you cannot tell them apart. Our own Sister Concepcion comes from two of the most powerful families in Batangas Province, the Kalaw-Katigbaks. The intricacies of the business-social-political life therein would baffle a mastermind to unravel. She has cousins and in-laws in every field of life. Yet Sister Concepcion, like all her family, is a very simple forthright person who washes dishes and teaches catechism to youngsters with the same zest as she stands before a college class and expounds nuclear physics. Master of all trades and jack at none—that's Sister Concepcion.

It is Sister's job, among others, to collect the tuition fees at St. John the Baptist School in Jimenez. Let it be understood from the beginning that this school is strictly nonprofit. Strictly. To pay living wages to lay teachers (and we have nineteen on the staff) so that they can teach children whose parents do not have a living wage themselves—this requires a good squeeze on every penny. The school pays out much more than it takes in on fees. Bazaars and benefits fill the gaping holes in the economy. This instability would make any bursar turn green at the edges but Sister Concepcion knows that in her books, cold arithmetic meets generosity at home and abroad, and melts at the impact.

One Sunday morning, a slight man came to the convent steps to parley with Sister Concepcion. His statistics are unassuming: Lives at Carmen, twelve miles up into Mt. Malindang. Has eight children. Four now in our high school. Has little money. Sells farm produce in market.

Such is Ceferino Lumantas. Like many others, his children live in town for the week, walk home on Saturdays, wash their school uniforms, get supplies and come back Monday morning. The road is often so muddy that it takes devotion above and beyond the call of duty to get home. At first, only one Lumantas child lived in Jimenez during the week. He could stay in any house and be welcome. But as more came each year, Ceferino decided to build a nipa hut for them in town. An ambitious project? He thought so too. He came to Sister Maura Shaun with his heart in his mouth. Would she lend him about ten dollars to build a house? This paid for the nipa; Ceferino and his boys did the work. Now, after seven years, the nipa hut had collapsed in the night. The Lumantas clan planned a more solid wooden house. So—well, he might be behindhand with his bill for a while.

In Carmen, there are few practicing Catholics. It's too hard for them to attend Mass and they have grown indifferent. But the Lumantas tribe are different. They were the first children from Carmen to go to high school. Also the only ones to receive First Holy Communion. They prepared for it at Jimenez, but Father went out to Carmen to celebrate the Mass and made a real barrio fiesta on the Great Day.

Ceferino Lumantas spoke quite a while with Sister Concepcion. In a quiet dignified way, he asked her to carry his account along for a time. She said, of course she would. Then she offered him a meal before he started back to Carmen. He said he really didn't need it, thank you. The slight man with waning hair and just the beginning of a stoop turned down the steps and set his face toward Carmen, twelve miles into Mt. Malintang.

St. John the Baptist School is housed in the old rectory. Built nearly one hundred years ago, the posts and beams are hardwood logs. One can easily see the tree in them. Today, they would cost a fortune but they probably had to be cut down anyway to clear the land in 1870. Floors are wide planks of polished wood—narra, molave and Philippine mahogany. These things make interior decorators drool. Walls are of Spanish plaster fortified with bamboo. In some rooms, windows of shell tilt out to open the whole side wall. The rooms were huge. I say "were" because they aren't so any more. For instance, we cut the reception room up into three classrooms.

Jimenez boasts of a telephone, a wind-up affair connecting convent, rectory and school. It was a walkie-talkie during the war but has retired to spend its old age in the service of Holy Mother Church. "It's fun to fool with it," says Sister John Francis. "There's always the chance that it might work this time."

Electricity is on from 6 P.M. to 6 A.M. As the priest comes on the altar for Mass, all the lights go off. During Mass, the sun comes up shining through the back windows and lighting up the gold-leaf altar. Just at the consecration, it leaps clear of the horizon and blazes in glory. The priest disappears in the splendor that fills the sanctuary. Then sunlight catches the white host elevated for all the world to adore. And after that, the golden chalice and the golden sun return gleam for gleam. It's magnificent! You can't tell me old Fray Roque Azcona didn't have it in mind when he built that church.

Something else he had in mind. When the priest turns around for the last blessing, he lifts his hand over the whole town. From the altar steps, his gaze goes out the great front door, across the plaza and down that wide main street, straight and true to the sea several miles away, shining in the new day's sun. He blesses all his parishioners, some of them holy, some of them not; some rich and some poor; some clear-minded and energetic, some hazy and slow; some always in church, others who darken its doors once standing up and twice lying down. For they stand up for their weddings but take Baptism and the funeral prayers recumbent. Whoever they are, whatever they do, they are the padres' spiritual children. Irish Columban Fathers have the parish now. These two Irishmen, when they turn around at the altar, bless fifteen thousand people in a parish they cannot possibly cover adequately. In the United States, there is one priest for every seven hundred Catholics; in Jimenez—quite a well established mission in the Philippines—there is one for every seven thousand five hundred.

Our school has seven hundred pupils—six hundred and ninety-nine to be exact. About forty percent are grade school youngsters; forty-five percent are in high school and fifteen percent take a junior college course. It's the only good school in the province, except for one in Ozamis City. We aim to keep the standards high. This is our purpose—to establish good schools in the Philippine hinterlands.

The best way to savor Jimenez is to spend Sunday morning on the plaza. You might as well; everybody else does. The old trees spread a grateful shade. Families lounge in the shadows. Carabao snooze in the coolness and dream of heaven where all yokes are sweet and burdens light. Goats nibble the grass. Horses exchange gossip about themselves and their masters. A cow, hungry for salt, licks the coral imbedded in the church wall. The chickens strut around. One corner of the plaza is a basketball court; another is laid out for volleyball. Some older men bat a rattan ball around with their ankles. It's the ancient Filipino game of sipa. Market women rest on the knobby roots of the great trees. A young colt rolls from side to side on the ground, kicking his hoofs in the air. There's plenty of room for everyone. Come and enjoy it!

On the edges of the plaza, two-wheeled carts called tartanillas jingle past, the little horses bright with metal ornaments. Small refreshment stands, not too avid to do business, offer bananas roasted over low charcoal fires, or corn on a spit, or babinka which look like steam-rollered pancakes, or vicious colored ices. The sellers of these delights are in Sunday morning mood, too. Neighbors for many years, they comment on everybody going by and speculate on the day's business. When you take a picture, they call out, "Take mine, too, Sister!" and explode in merry uproar when you do. "Show my face in America!" the victim implores as you leave.

Then the Angelus rings out from the great church tower. Everyone stops dead. A few very silent minutes. Then we go home. Sunday morning in Jimenez plaza is over.

Four bunny hops over water brought us to Bacolod on Negros via Dipolog, Dumaguete and Cebu, each on a different island. Negros is the "sugar island." We have a hospital about thirty miles north of Bacolod, barely discernible over the waving tassel tops of sugar cane. Sugar lined the road and stretched far far away to the horizon—some of it just planted, some blossoming, some six to eight feet tall and some harvested. America's troubles with Cuba gave a great boost to Philippine sugar and Negros was making the most of it. The workers were at it continuously, sometimes far into the night, but the common laborer got little increase in wages. He is paid by the day, and that doesn't mean an eight-hour working day.

Planting, harrowing, fertilizing are piece work and paid for by the hectare. The whole family works together, yet often all of them get only about ₱1.50 ($.50) a day. The children cannot afford either the time or the money to go to school. However, harvesting pays ₱2.30 a day; only men can work at this.

In such a setting, we staff St. Joseph's Hospital for the Victorias Milling Company, a sugar refinery. Quite definitely, the company tries to operate along lines of social justice. The minimum wage is ₱4.80 a day plus "fringe benefits." One of these fringes is a boys' technical school operated by the Salesian Fathers. Formerly, only sons of employees could attend, but the school is so good that now the doors are open to boys from many towns and provinces. Besides the academic studies, they learn mechanics, tailoring, electro-mechanics and/or cabinet making. Since 1958, junior college courses in engineering and industrial education have been added. Thus teachers for large or small factories are trained here.

The popularity of technical schools in the Philippines is another post-war development. It used to be that education was only for the professions; what was the use of educating a lad if he was not to be a doctor, lawyer, dentist or pharmacist? Don Bosco Technical Schools are now thriving institutions spotted over the Philippines in Laguna, Rizal, Pampanga and Negros.

Our hospital is another "fringe." When they need care, any employee and his family may occupy one of the one hundred and twenty-five beds at St. Joseph's. If I were there, I would be tempted to fake something if I could get away with it. Nice clean bed, cool breezes blowing through the ward, and tender loving care from Sisters who serve God by serving me. Sounds nice. Mighty nice. Some have tried it. Not many, but a few have got away with it. A young fellow, when I was there, celebrated a solid year of tender, loving care at St. Joseph's. Not employed by the company in any way, he was drunk one night and crawled under a sugar-cane car to sleep. The train started and the boy was badly injured. While it was his own fault, crooked lawyers might claim that the train personnel had not checked sufficiently. Many of the accident cases come from the company railroad which hauls cane from fields to mill, and out again to ships in the harbor.

Signs are everywhere in English and Visayan: "The company is not responsible for accidents to unauthorized riders." Yet when you are poor, and you want to get some place, and you can't pay bus fare, and it's a long hot walk, and right there is a sugar-loaded train going where you want to go, ... well, most people hop on for a free ride. That's how it was with the unfortunate Dominguez family, Juan, Crisostoma and nine-year-old Asuncion. They were going to Victorias. Usually they slipped off just before crossing a bridge where company guards might see them. But they were slow this time. Then all three jumped quickly. Crisostoma missed her footing and was killed outright. Asuncion was dragged seventy-five feet; Juan leaped clear and then ran after his mangled child. The child had two broken arms, a broken clavicle and a head so crushed that gray matter was oozing through.

Of course, the train stopped. Of course, the company ambulances brought the child to us. Of course, we took care of her until she died. Of course, the company paid for everything on the case even though nobody in the family was employed either in the mill or on the haciendas. The point I am making is that social justice works two ways or, if you want a sub-title to that, companies have to absorb a little injustice sometimes, too. And, thanks be to God, they do it graciously.

A "kangaroo" took us to Manila, three hundred watery miles away. Manila, as you may have guessed from what has been said before, is an old shoe to Mother and me. Very comfortable. Just ten miles north, on the shores of Manila Bay, is a venerable old church with lopped-off towers. They were shot off, so tradition says, when Admiral Dewey steamed into Manila Bay in 1898. Some wooden towers take their place but they do not match the building. Beside this church—indeed, attached to it—is an old Spanish "convento" which was the first Maryknoll school in the Philippines. Today it is vastly expanded and with twelve hundred pupils is one of our largest schools. This is St. James Academy at Malabon, Rizal.

It was the same with other provincial schools. They have struck down roots and spread. At Lucena, Quezon Province, Maryknoll Academy vastly overflowed the original building and is now jamming the extensions added in the past few years. In Lipa, Batangas, a new girls' high school is crowded and the old boys' high school is so old that it cannot long endure the tramp of manly feet. Every evening, the Sisters pray that it will fall down during the night; every morning, they pray that it will hold up until classes are over. In Pakil, Laguna, the Maryknoll Fathers' High School could use more space easily. At Pako in Manila, the waiting line forms at the right; please go to the end of the line. While out in Quezon City, Maryknoll College has sixteen hundred pupils from kindergarten straight through college. The trouble is, you have to register a child as soon as she's born to secure a desk and a place at the blackboard for her.

One of the great joys of growing old (besides having people run to pick up your suitcase—which I am still waiting for) is that you can sit back in your wheelchair and think on your rugged youth. Then all the hard moments smile right back at you. The little numbskull you pounded arithmetic into is running a nuclear laboratory; the girl who couldn't care less if she never saw the inside of a church again, is a Carmelite nun. You used to be on yard duty, watching the kiddies as they ate lunch on the front steps; the gleaming new cafeteria seats five hundred. You, who had books lining the staircase and set in shelves straight up to the ceiling, can rejoice with the new librarian as she reigns in a hushed citadel of learning. And Francisco—why, he's a living saint beloved by God and man! Which Francisco? That Francisco, the one you prayed calluses on your knees for.

What's more, they crowd around their aged teacher and tell her she had a hand in it. You may not put full faith into that but it folds around your soul like a blanket on a cold night. It's good to feel that somebody might think it's true.

So it was with Mother and, to a lesser degree, with me when we came back to Maryknoll College, now on a spacious campus in Quezon City on the outskirts of Manila. Mother spent much of her youth smiling bravely to parents, creditors, fellow teachers and inspectors from the Board of Education. Her gallant spirit failed not, though the roof leaked and the yard boy may have run off with the funds saved for a new micro-scope. Twenty years ago Maryknoll College moved from one rented build-ing to another. All too often, the end of a school year saw Mother packing her blackboards, charts, dictionaries, textbooks, globes, science equipment, chalk and erasers, to start up again in another new location.

Now she stood at the window and watched twelve handsome buses un-load children at the front door, family cars disgorging youngsters, groups of classmates running up the front path. She walked over to the new dormitory for college students where girls from all parts of the country mingle while they learn the intricate art of injecting knowledge into children. She, who had produced Shakespeare in a little garage, stood on the stage of the beautiful auditorium, gazed up into the catwalks and fingered the heavy curtains. She stood a long time there with her hand on the curtains. I couldn't see her eyes; my own were a bit misted.

Just the atmosphere around the college is erudite. Even the mosquitoes are intelligent. Maybe that comes from drinking so much Ph.D. blood from the Sisters. I used to be a match for any mosquito. All one had to do was to butter a plate very thickly, then swing it around in the air, and all the insects would stick to it. But I spent a night matching wits with these college-educated mosquitoes and came out the small end of the horn.

A mosquito net is a godsend. It ranks next to the wheel as Man's Greatest Invention. That is, if mosquitoes play fair and stay on their side. These slick boys, however, hide in your hair or under your pajama collar and come along in with you. For hours that night we batted it out. Then the cold war started. I wrapped up completely, leaving only a small section of one cheek exposed as bait. A hand was raised ready to swat the first paratrooper to land on it. Do you think they bit? No, indeed. They re-tired to a corner of the net and played pinochle until I tired of this waiting game and threw the covers off into the sweltering night. By next morning I was bled white and they were stupefied with gorging. It was rare revenge to roll them in the net and squash every one. If they had stuck to mind over matter, they would be happy intelligent mosquitoes today.

All ye who teach, take courage! Fear not; your children remember you. Malabon spread a red carpet all the way down Main Street and over the bridge. (No, no, not literally.) The town has grown from the days when Manila Bay gently lapped the Municipio and the cemetery wall, and rolled under the bamboo stilts of a few houses along the shore. There is a Malabon Chamber of Commerce and a Malabon Women's Civic Club. Land has been filled in to make a shipyard where six good-sized vessels for deep-sea fishing were building at once. The row of tiendas, or small shops across the street, is replaced by a bank with Greek-columned portico. Trucks, buses, jeepneys outrun and outshout the horse-drawn caretelas on our street and—horrors!—a traffic cop is stationed on our corner, so important has it become. How metropolitan can one get?

And the old students! Just as, during the war, they had swarmed around bringing rice and meat and fruits when they, themselves, had all too little, so now they came bearing gifts. They came to talk. "Maring" took us around town to see the old places. Many are teachers, some are social workers, others have forged ahead into new businesses. Liberato deals in chemicals; Ramon is a doctor; Sebastian is in the Bureau of Commerce. Gilda writes short stories for newspapers; Flaviana operates a fleet of fishing vessels; Paz is Dean of Women at the University of the East. Carmen specialized in Home Economics and is going around the country giving lectures on nutrition and how to make the most of native fruits and vegetables. Dominador went on with his hobby of photography and now all the movie stars and society women come to his air-conditioned studio.

Best of all were the teachers—Rufina, Belen, Purificacion, Lucia, Illuminada, far too many to list. For years they have poured their best into the children of Malabon. God bless them for it!

I could start now and sing a panegyric in praise of the Filipina, but it's not necessary. The Book of Proverbs has done it already. "She brings her bread from afar; she rises in the night and feeds her household; she considers a field and buys it; she shall not fear for her house in the cold of snow; she has made fine linen and sold it and delivered a girdle to the Canaanite." These things the Filipina has done from time immemorial. Her business acumen has earned itself a place in the language; "ang may-bahay" (she who owns the house) is the common term for a wife in Tagalog. And none of it interferes with her primary work of wife and mother. High-born or low, she was the Emancipated Woman long before Susan B. Anthony went on the stump for the rest of us.

The modern Filipina has everything. She dresses daintily; she dances superbly, especially her own native dances; she speaks English well; she is good at mathematics, tea drinking, piano playing, running a household and driving a good bargain. On top of all that, she has, like every good superior, a sense of self sacrifice. Let me tell you about Gregoria in Pakil, a country town on the shores of Laguna de Bay, the largest lake in the Philippines.

She is young and pretty with a trim figure, an oval face and a silky mane of long black hair sometimes hanging down her back, sometimes knotted into a business-like pug. She has never gone beyond sixth grade but her manners are nice, her clothes attractive. Working for an American family, she earns her family's living. She keeps her marketing accounts up well and, an avid disciple of Fanny Farmer, she shows intelligence in managing a kitchen. The biggest part of her salary goes to her mother for the family needs; some goes to help her younger brother and sister pay tuition; they work for the rest themselves. The family is giving one priest to the Church; "Goring" helps pay his expenses. She would like to continue school. At times she says, "I used to be good in arithmetic," in a wistful way. She knows now that she will probably never go back to study, but she is so convinced of the value of education that she will put off her own marriage until her younger sister and brother are through.

Such is the Filipina.

HONG KONG

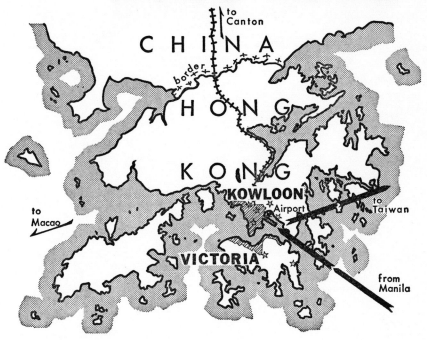

☆ Maryknoll Works

HONG KONG

◄ 13 ► A Portly Old Gentleman
in Cutaway Coat

How odd! Prowling the streets of Hong Kong! Quite a portly gentleman, too, and most respectable looking. I saw him poking his cane into open drains to get them unclogged. He counted the huts around a public water tap. He stood on street corners and noted the fatness or skinniness of the babies on their mothers' backs. In his cutaway coat and morning trousers, he went before me down the crowded alleyways in Hong Kong where men dangle baskets at the ends of a shoulder pole and women push baby buggies, full of almost anything but babies. "Fat foreign devil, stand aside," they say with scant respect for his ruddy face and snow-white mustache. And he does. He squeezes himself by the side wall. When they have passed, he continues gently but firmly to inspect the fruit on stands in that alleyway.

I've seen the old gentleman in the back of classrooms, counting the children at the desks. Sometimes, he takes one on his knees, feels the skinny little arms and stuffs the child's pockets with vitamin pills and food tickets. He sidles up to the clinic desk and peers over the nurse's shoulder as she takes down information and hands out medicines. He tiptoes into the storeroom and counts the bandages, the pills, the antibiotics. Then, as often as not, he clucks sympathetically and writes out an order for more. Late at night he tiptoes through hospital wards, feeling the quality of the sheets and pushing the hair away from sweaty brows.

Who is this odd fellow? He is GOVERNMENT spelled with capital letters in Hong Kong, or Good Old Guv'ment to his co-workers. I first met him in 1947 when I tried to spend two weeks in Hong Kong. Guv'ment told me then, with obvious reluctance, that I might come into the colony (1) if I had a place to sleep other than the streets, (2) if my friends would feed me and (3) if I wouldn't stay long. "You see," he explained, "the war has uprooted a lot of people and we are very crowded. Later we hope to have room. Sorry to be so inhospitable but—ahem—you see the situation." Yes, yes, I saw it. One million six hundred thousand people in forty square miles. Several years later, I came back. The situation was no better, but Guv'ment did not question me.

Now the situation is twice as bad. We found Hong Kong in the throes of census-taking. Three million one hundred thousand at least stood up to be counted. How many others preferred to be unidentified is a moot point. Some say another half-million. This is no shock to the old gentleman now, but it was when he first realized how many Chinese from Red China had parked on his doorstep.

Along about 1952, Good Old Guv'ment stepped outside his cricket field possibly to pick up a lost ball. But he met an odd sight which made him forget the ball entirely; he hasn't looked for it since. A pillar of smoke was twisting up from a mountainside opposite his playing field. And from the base of the smoke, swarms of black things were fleeing. Were they beetles? Or ants? Guv'ment fished out his pocket binoculars and took a good look. My word! My goodness me! They were human beings—ragged, hunched over, carrying what they could, hurrying along small children. Bless us! Their shacks are burning, thought Guv'ment. Where will they go?

Through the hours of that night he worried. He had seen armies such as this before. Had seen crowds pushing out of Red China. Had seen line-ups before relief doors. Had heard—and smelled—the tenement houses for years. Every now and then, it seemed, something had happened in China to which large numbers of Chinese objected, and they had poured into Hong Kong. They hung around a while and moved away —either to foreign shores or, if another upheaval at home put their party on top, back into China again.

Hong Kong was used to taking a deep breath, squeezing them all in for a time and then breathing out in comfort in a few years. The Communist scares in the twenties, Japanese forays in the thirties, World War II in the forties—during these times the colony's population swelled to one and one half million and deflated down to five hundred thousand. They would sleep in the streets or build crazy shacks on the hills, pester the life out of decent people with their begging—and then move away.

But Guv'ment tossed and turned that night in 1952. He wasn't so sure this was just another temporary swelling. For a long time, now, reports had floated across his desk: Thousands over the border every week. Squatters filling the valleys and pushing away up the mountains. Soup lines beseiged. Seven hundred huts go up in flames. Woman found dead; cause, starvation. The fact was plain. This crowd was not moving away.

"Looks like I'm stuck with them," he commented in the dark to where he hoped his guardian angel was. "Well, nothing to do, I suppose, but to roll up my sleeves and take care of them."

"That's a good idea, Guv'ment," said his angel wryly. "Now I'll let you get some sleep."

"But things are so different in England, you know," Guv'ment muttered. The angel smiled and tucked him in.

"You're here on Her Majesty's Service, my boy. And England expects every man to do his duty."

Old Guv'ment made no reply. He turned over, sighed mightily and dropped off to innocent slumber.

He was early at his desk the next morning. Carefully, he cleared the papers off, laying them on far tables. Then, on his empty desk top, he made plans to help those ant-like people. He had done a little already, in 1948 and again in 1951, to get squatters to move out into the country. But most of them did not want to move so far from possible jobs.

There were many missionaries and volunteer workers already at work. He enlisted their aid, let them go ahead with their projects and gave them a boost with money and authority. Then he got into the game himself. This solution of Hong Kong's refugee problem makes the world take off its hat to Good Old Guv'ment.

The first thing to tackle was—space. Kai Tak Airport, for instance, had always been famous for being hard to get at. Pilots had to land and take off on a dime. The only way to get in or get out was through a narrow valley between mountains. Planes swooped through this valley, made a sharp right turn and dropped like a ripe coconut on to a field hemmed in by mountains and often covered with fog. Once aground, they had to stop fast or they kept right on dropping, this time into the harbor. Jets certainly needed more elbow room. Seven years ago, less than 5,000 passengers landed at Kai Tak; last year, 186,000 stepped off planes there.

But Kai Tak airstrip has been stretched out into the harbor. Good Old Guv'ment knocked a couple of mountains into the sea and built a jetty out to accommodate the big birds. Coming from the Philippines, Mother and I came down over the sea and slid on to the airstrip as gently as an ocean liner edging into a pier.

It was a good introduction to Hong Kong where they make a specialty of pushing mountains into the sea. "Space! More space! Give me room!" is the cry from those three million people jammed on the island of Hong Kong and the strip of mainland known as Kowloon, an area of forty square miles. The New Territories, some three hundred and seventy six square miles, hold less than one-sixth of the population on its farms.

In Hong Kong, Guv'ment decided, land is not found; it must be made. He makes it by pushing mountains around, lopping off their tops, taking a slice or two from the sides, hollowing out a niche and half-burying a twenty story building into it. There is a new building downtown where you can go into the front door at street level, take an elevator to the seventeenth floor and go out the back door also at street level. Places far from the waterfront, wildernesses before, are apartment beehives now. Apartments run up fifteen and twenty stories high. We have a new school on Blue Pool Road, "away out of town" three years ago; today, the Sisters have a hard time to keep the neighbors from prying into our fifth-floor convent. A new building is going up right behind our Kowloon school. I said to Sister Clement who has rolled up thirty years in Hong Kong, "Too bad. That new building will spoil your view." "Not at all," said Sister Clement. "We never had any view. A mountain used to be there."

One has no trouble disposing of mud in Hong Kong. When you dig your foundation or shear off your hill, Good Old Guv'ment is right behind you to collect all the mud you don't want and drop it into the sea. He sneaks around Fido when he buries a bone to catch the mud he scratches up. He's that avid for land. All the mud from the foundations of our Maryknoll School's new building was hustled right over to Kai Tak to build up that airstrip jetty. So much land has been thrown into Hong Kong Harbor that the ferry trip from Kowloon to Hong Kong is cut from fifteen to seven minutes. A bridge across the harbor has often been projected; it will be possible to walk across, perhaps, before the bridge is built.

It's the Space Age in Hong Kong. Everyone is space conscious. More than one school is built with movable walls which slide away to make a church for Sunday mornings. School desks for the week fold down to make kneeling benches.

Laundry seems to be Hong Kong's great outdoor sport. Rags are out drying on every bush and tree. Washlines and bamboo poles canopy the streets; the resettlement blocks, huge buildings of one-room dwellings, look like the Royal Navy out with all flags flying. Because the city is one mountain jostling another, retaining walls are everywhere. Bamboo poles are stuck into the drainage holes in these walls and each pole is strung with somebody's wash. Often when poles stick out over half the road, buses, taxis, cars and pedestrians go single file on the other half with no complaint. Everyone knows that laundry is important.

It all boils down to Government facing up to the situation. They're here. They need help. What can we do? And still refugees flee from Red China, slipping into Hong Kong, it is estimated, at the rate of one hundred a day.

Most of these go directly to the heart of the colony, the cities of Victoria and Kowloon which hem in the harbor. A better chance for jobs is there. As a result, in twelve square miles, more than two and one-half million people live to a density of four thousand per acre. This means that if they all lay down at once, there wouldn't be room for them if each person used a space six by two feet. Some would have to stand up. Obviously housing must be in stories. The early types of relief housing were "cottages" to replace the shacks which clung to mountainsides. But there isn't enough land for everyone to have his own front door. Cottages take care of only two hundred per acre. Thus the "Resettlement Estates."

That word, "estate"! Webster says of it: "Individually owned piece of land containing a residence. It is usually large and maintained by great wealth." In Ceylon, it means a plantation for growing a cash crop. In Hong Kong, it means a seven-story concrete building, H-shaped. The two long sides of the H consist of sixty-two one-room dwellings connected by the balcony outside. In the central bar of the H are common toilets, washing tubs, showers, etc.

Each room, some ten by twelve feet, must house four to five adults; each child under ten counts as half an adult. Thus a father, mother and six youngsters under ten may rent a room. But if Grandpa and Aunt Susie and her baby come to live with them, they cannot get another room because the group counts only seven and a half. They need eight for two rooms. During the years Government has experimented with different-sized rooms, and has different regulations and different rents. The ten-by-twelve rooms, however, are typical.

Rent is $14 HK a month or about $2.42 US. If you can afford electricity, that is 53¢ US extra; water is 17¢ US a month. These charges, small as they are, loom large in a family budget that starts off—if Papa has a steady job—with $20.87 US a month, the usual salary for coolie work. Small wonder that Mama and the children make plastic flowers, knit socks and mittens, paste up cellophane bags, embroider handkerchiefs or make rattan things. If ever you went calling on a family on its "estate" you would be hard put to it to find room on the floor to place your feet. I have often thought, "They must sleep like birds—perched on things."

At Wan Tai Sin there are twenty-five such housing blocks already built; eight more are on the way up. Some 71,000 people live on "the estate."

Elsewhere thirty or forty such blocks, each with a population in the thousands, comprise one "estate." They don't have street numbers or names for they are built one behind the other up a hillside with only stairs or footpaths connecting them. One lives in Block A or Block B and, when the alphabet runs out, in Block AA to Block ZZ.

Nevertheless, every woman has a permanent wave; wrist watches are common; and the blocks are alive with aerials for something they call "Rediffusion," a type of radio service. The company installs the receivers and you get music and talk from 7 A.M. until midnight. Price? The first month $2.55 US; the second month $1.73, and the succeeding months only 85¢. Why anybody would bother to pay it is beyond me. In our convents near the "estates," we miss nothing that is broadcast, don't pay a cent, nor even have to give the receiver houseroom.

Here I met Precious Peach Blossom, eight years old, with solemn eyes and a Dutch haircut. Eight years old, with a little sister and brother, and a mother who ran off with somebody else two years ago. Eight years old, and housekeeper for their father who painted ships when there were ships to be painted and tramped the streets when there were not.

Peach Blossom cooked the food when they had any, wiped little sister's runny nose, carried little brother on her back when she went for water from the common taps where sixty-two families on her floor filled their tin cans. She took time out two hours a day to walk to Maryknoll Boys' and Girls' Club. Here Sister Marie Thomas guided her dirty hand over the paper for writing and figuring, put the tattered book before her solemn eyes and tried to bring a smile to play around the sober little mouth. Peach Blossom, like so many other ragamuffins in Hong Kong, learned to read and write, but never mastered the smile.

Small wonder. The inside of her cheek, her teeth and gums were a putrid mass of infection. One day she came to "the club," as such schools are called, with her right cheek so puffed that she talked out of the corner of her mouth. Sister Marie Thomas pronounced "Mumps!" and took her to Sister Maria Fidelis, a doctor. Sister took one look into her mouth and shuddered. The teeth had decayed straight through to the roots; the whole mouth was a shambles.

Peach Blossom winced as the medicine rolled over those ugly sores but gave no whimper. A bottle of milk went down fast, but we saw the grimy hand stow all the cookies in her pocket. "For Sai Lo," she said.

"Little brother can have others," Sister insisted. "You take those."

"No, for my sister," she countered.

"You eat those," Sister insisted. "You'll get something else for your sister."

She was sick all over from the infection. Definitely green around the mouth. We hired a taxi and took her home to the Daai Ha (Big House, as the Chinese call the resettlement blocks). The father is a good father; certainly the children cling around his legs when he stands and climb on his lap when he sits down. But he is no housekeeper. Peach Blossom had done her best. She had no strength to clean the room, wash the clothes and the children. Enough if she could get fuel and water to cook the rice.

We put Peach Blossom to bed. Very simple; we just laid her on the rags in the corner. Then we asked the woman next door to look in now and then until the father got home. At the end of the week, we thought the infection would be down and she could go to a dentist.

That was Wednesday. Next day, before we could bring her clean bedding and a replenishment of food, the whole family came to see us. Peach Blossom was greener than ever. She sat on the table in our convent while Sister Maria Fidelis explored her mouth, too apathetic even to wince now. Another bottle of milk, another penicillin injection in the lean buttock and she turned to go home.

But not this time. Sister talked to her father. Then she phoned Kowloon Hospital, imploring space. This is another of Good Old Guv'ment's projects.

On Friday, the chart at the foot of her bed said, "Acute leukemia." Sunday she had a blood transfusion. Tuesday she hemorrhaged.

"Do you want to be baptized?" Sister whispered.

"Chungi" (I want) was the last word she spoke on earth.

When I get to Heaven, one of the first things I'm going to do is to get Peach Blossom to laugh for me. Believe me, it will be worth waiting for.

Roughly one-third of Hong Kong's three million people are under fifteen years of age. What about schools? Back in 1954 Government put on far-sighted glasses and made a plan. "In the next seven years, beginning in 1955, we will provide at least 215,000 more places in primary schools." With one year to go, the Board of Education can report, "We are well ahead of schedule with 262,000 created already and 91,000 in the making before April, 1962."

This means, in plain English, that a newly-built school has been opened every seven days for the past five years. This does not include schools opened in adapted premises or extensions to existing schools. Every primary school has one group studying in the morning and another in the afternoon with ten minutes or so between to let them get in and get out. You can also see little muffins trailing home from school around nine o'clock at night. A good start in life for night watchmen, nurses on night duty, airplane pilots, cloistered Sisters who pray at midnight, burglars and second-story men, as well as young husbands with cantankerous babies. However, as the Board notes, "We do not accept evening schools as a permanent state of affairs. We want our schools in the evenings for adult education."

Then, there are the "clubs" such as Peach Blossom attended. They give twelve thousand children a bit of reading, writing, figuring and handiwork. Eighty thousand others have no chance at all. One sees many small boys on construction jobs helping plasterers, bricklayers, carpenters. "They are apprentices," a foreman told me.

"We thought at first that the refugees would use Hong Kong as a jumping-off place for greener pastures elsewhere," Dr. Douglas J. S. Crozier, Director of Education throughout this period, told me. "But in 1954 we decided they were here to stay. At least, until the children grew up. So we drew our plan and we kept to it. Even bettered it by some 138,000 places in primary schools.

"That was an effort, to be sure, but it was easy compared to what lies ahead of us. Secondary schools are the rub, now. Only one child in seven is able to go on after primary years. I'd like to see that cut down to one in four, at least. The cost of secondary schools is overwhelming to our poor little budget. I don't know how we are going to be able to do it. But we shall!" Ah! That's the sort of thing Old Guv'ment likes to hear.

Plans like those take care only of normal children. The old gentleman hasn't forgotten the others. "We have very much at heart the need to expand our meager facilities for handicapped youngsters. Also, adult education is a 'must' to help those who missed out on schooling entirely.

"In all these plans and their fulfillment, Government has leaned heavily—and let me say gratefully—on religious and welfare organizations. We have three teacher-training institutions turning out 1,700 teachers a year, but even so we could not have staffed the primary schools, let alone the secondary schools which need teachers of higher qualifications."

In the Resettlement Estates, schools are either Ground Floor or Roof Top. Nobody lives on the bottom floor of a block; that is reserved for stores, or a clinic, day nursery, noodle factory, or some other welfare project. Quite often it is a school with eighteen classrooms, each used twice a day. Eighteen teachers and one principal work in the mornings; a similar crew mans the ship of learning for the afternoon. The whole project is under a general director. Maryknoll Sisters are responsible for four such schools, and we conduct three Boys' and Girls' Clubs as well.

Sister Famula's school is in the Ground Floor of Block U at Kun Tong. I don't envy her the job. It's a brand new Block. She will have on her hands twelve First Grades of forty to forty-five children each. Eventually the school will iron out to six "streams" of six grades—that is, thirty-six classes in eighteen rooms used morning and afternoon. But right now, she has five hundred First Graders to lead upward and onward to wisdom. Try it sometime on a dull afternoon!

I was there for the registration. First come, first served. Long before dawn, the line formed. Many a mother did without a day's work to make sure her child got a place in that school. This meant, probably, that they did without food that day, too. Jade Flower stood in line for hours to register her little sister. That done, Sister Famula said, in Chinese of course, "What about you? Aren't you studying?" "Oh no," said Jade Flower in a very matter-of-fact tone. "I have to work."

Many times a mother asked, "How much is the tuition?" And when Sister said, "87¢ a month," she turned away. This is a government school; we merely run it. Fees are set and we cannot make exceptions. But, if I know Sister Famula, she will dig up 87¢ from somebody's pocket.

Anyone who yearns to live dangerously can do it by putting a sign in his front window: "School Here. Registrations Tomorrow." He will find himself torn limb from limb the next morning by eager pupils and their mamas. We had a near riot at Maryknoll Convent School during a two-day registration for Grade One and a few seats in Grades Two and Three. Well, they had to call out the police with tear gas bombs. You might think somebody was giving out gold bricks or guaranteed Sweepstakes tickets.

The mob surged around Waterloo Road and Boundary streets. Some stayed all night; others came at 3 A.M. and found the place jammed. By 9 A.M., street and schoolyard were in a state of riot. More than thirty policemen and women descended on the mob, sorted them out, put them in line and stood guard with billy sticks poised for action. Some of these people were able to pay handsomely for their darlings' education. They brought the darlings and anybody who might have influence—like the second cousin of a former Maryknoll pupil. Well-dressed women stood in line for hours or shuffled forward under the eye of the police while amahs and chauffeurs brought them mid-morning tea or a bit of lunch. It was something!

And what was the result? Thirteen hundred were registered. They could come back, take an examination (for First Grade!) and in the end only three hundred and twenty would be accepted. Our schools are good—let me not deny it—but they aren't *that* good!

One feature of the Hong Kong school system was a bit too rugged for a peace-loving soul like me. That was the annual Music Festival. It had all the sweetness of a bullfight and the festive spirit of a knock-down, drag-out prize ring. The idea behind it is good. All the little girls and boys, according to their grade in music, practice a certain piece all year long. Then a prominent musician is invited to come from England and hear them all play that piece. He decides which one plays it the best.

When the big night comes, Eddie Tze and Phyllis Lee and Reggie Wong and fifty or sixty others appear before the dread judge. Like the hangman's noose, a lone piano fills the stage. The Great Man sits in the audience surrounded by a table full of papers and the dread instrument, a small bell. Eddie mounts the scaffold; the Great Man tinkles the bell; Eddie plunges into THE PIECE OF THE YEAR, let us say Chopin's Etude, Op. 25 #9, G flat Major. Eddie finishes. He wobbles off the platform. Winifred Wu takes his place on the piano bench. The Great Man tinkles. Winnie plunges into Chopin's Etude, Op. 25 #9, G flat Major. Winnie finishes. She all but collapses over the keyboard but gathers strength to leave, passing Phyllis Wing on her way up. And so it goes. After forty-five renditions of that Etude, you are either stiff stark staring mad or you subside into imbecility muttering "Shut it off. Please, please, shut it off." But the deadly bell tinkles once again and little Reggie has taken the plunge. Even if he weren't there, I think the piano, like the old fire horse it is, would start right in.

The last contestant has returned to his place in the hall, wading through blood, sweat and tears. His own sweat and tears but Chopin's blood. A hush falls over the house.

The Great Man fumbles with his papers, coughs into the microphone and begins the judging. Jacqueline Ko was heavy with the left hand. Dorothea Chui used the pedal a mite too much but her grace notes were effective. Phyllis Yung's trills earned a full fifteen percent but her left hand was six percent harsher than her right. Jacqueline Ko and Reggie Wong are exactly even; her tone was warmer, but Reggie's staccato was better. In the end Winnie Wu with ninety-three percent wins the British Council Trophy because she maintained the legato so well. Runners-up are Pamela Chong with ninety-one percent and Eddie Tze with ninety percent. The other youngsters can go home and have a good nervous breakdown all to themselves.

This preoccupation with marks springs from what Dr. Crozier pointed out. Only one child in seven will be able to go on to Secondary School. His chance depends on examinations, just as gruelling as this Music Festival. We do our best to have the children take these hurdles in stride, but more than one ten-year-old has had hysterics over examinations. It's not only impoverished children who suffer from school shortages; those who can afford to pay find themselves left out because there simply aren't enough school desks to go around. Little Sybil Ching may pass Sixth Grade with fairly good marks, but she cannot go on to Secondary School. In Hong Kong's patter, she had "passed" but not "placed."

Good Old Guv'ment has asked us to do other odd jobs for the refugees. A new hospital has just opened near the Kun Tong Estate. Only sixty beds, it is nevertheless a large project; the out-patient clinic carries most of the burden. This is one of the poorest places in Hong Kong. People there cannot afford to spend time in bed; they much prefer to come back and forth every day. The hospital, right in the middle of them, is the only medical help for some distance around.

In Kun Tong, too, we have an apartment convent. It was still in the plaster and steam-fitting stage when I saw it. Only two rooms and a kitchenette, it was to hold four Sisters. They walk down five floors to Mass in the morning; up five floors to breakfast; down five floors to the school or clinic or catechetical center for the morning's work. Up five floors for lunch; down again for the afternoon; up again for supper and, please God, to stay the night, unless there are evening sodality meetings or such goings on.

And at Wan Tai Sin a day nursery for two hundred toddlers. It's a pilot project; Government wants to see how it goes and then make others like it, if possible. The youngsters get practically three meals a day and are there from 8 A.M. until 6 P.M. It costs 50¢ HK a day (about 9¢ US) but the mother would have spent that much for baby's food anyway. This Wan Tai Sin Community Center is a three-ring circus of good works all day long. Just a glance at the daily bulletin board leaves one gasping. Tailoring classes, folk dancing, Chinese shadow boxing, ping pong tournaments, a movie, baseball practice, classes in Mandarin language, a Fathers' Club party, instruction for deaf mutes, literacy classes for adults, flute band practice, hygiene and home-making classes for mothers, and a group to practice Yoga, the meditate-while-you-stand-on-your-head religion. A library with ten thousand books is also going full-steam ahead every day.

And who are the people who play basketball on the courts, read in the library, leave their children in the day nursery, or go to the Fathers' Club party? All sorts of people. The ragpickers, for instance.

We went out to see our neighbors in that interesting occupation. A ragpicker works hard and gets little. Mama, Papa and the whole family scavenge the town for cloth of any kind—old jute bags, torn pieces thrown into trash barrels, stuff soiled with unmentionables and, if Providence is kind that day, perhaps something lifted from a clothesline when the owner was looking elsewhere. This is one reason why Chinese women prefer a bamboo pole to a rope line. They put the pole through both sleeves of a shirt or through one leg of pants and put it out the window on wire racks saying, "There, steal that, if you can!"

The ragpickers have only begun their job when they get the rags. They hustle them home, wash them after a fashion and spread them out to dry. Often they need space for spreading so they pre-empt the public road. I don't know how often we pushed over to the wrong side of the road because our side was covered with rags out drying. Once dry, they are carefully stacked and soaked in paste. Then dried again. Use? Well, shoe factories stiffen the tops of cloth shoes with them. Collars in women's saams are stiff, too.

It seems a sad end for cloth that once (who knows?) was the seat of an upholstered chair or a brocaded tablecloth in the Governor's house. The ceaseless work, work, work of the Chinese goes on endlessly. Not even a piece of cloth can retire from active duty.

Sad stories in Hong Kong are a dime a dozen. They become all the sadder when you realize that these people were not always poor. Many were teachers, government workers, army men, merchants who had a little more than their envious neighbors. Ah Keng was typical. I met her behind a cafeteria counter at Blue Pool Road.

Born in Vietnam, she married at seventeen and went to live in China, rather well fixed in life. When Communism spread, the family started to move toward Hong Kong but were caught in a small town near the border. Several years ago, Ah Keng managed to slip over the border;

her husband, son and daughter stayed behind. It is far more difficult for a man to get out. Ah Keng has steady work and saves almost every cent she makes. Every couple of months she gets a permit from Hong Kong to go to the border, and another to get her into China. Then she takes to the family anything she can.

On her latest visit, Ah Keng reports that her husband broke his arm working on a reservoir. It healed indifferently and he cannot lift heavy things. So he is a Class 2 worker. His work is to grind oyster shells so as to make lime for construction works. He really doesn't know what his salary is. He works on the "merit system," as they call it. At the end of a month, the paymaster gives him $3.00 or $4.00 HK (between 55 and 70¢ US) and says, "This is what is left of your salary after food, light, rent, etc. have been deducted." He must take the man's word for it.

He is allowed, each month, thirteen catties of rice (about seventeen pounds), less than a pound of sugar, and two ounces of oil, a black oil nobody can stomach. But he never sees it all at once; it is served up to him and other workers at the rate of five ounces a day. Men and boys get this ration; women and girls get four ounces a day. Boiled vegetables come with it. Not fried, nor steamed, nor flavored in any way. To a Chinese, boiled vegetables are the last stage of destitution. The workers also get one set of clothes a year.

Ah Keng wants to take food and clothing to them but she finds that customs men at the border commandeer any large supply. So she takes only small amounts. At that famous border, Hong Kong Chinese and Communist Chinese match wits. It used to be that Hong Kong people could take in clothing for their relatives. Then the customs men commandeered extra clothes. So the Hong Kong people began to wear many layers of clothes across the border and shed them when they saw their relatives. To counter this trick, the customs men counted the layers of clothes on each person crossing the border and insisted that he wear the same number of layers going out. Not to be outwitted, the Hong Kong Chinese now wear many layers of new clothing across the border and come out in layers of rags. They have changed clothes with their relatives. Just what the next move in this game will be is anybody's guess.

Ah Keng is trying to get her little girl out of China. She has no hope that the husband and son will escape. Others in the same situation have resorted to this trick. They kidnap a child in Hong Kong of the same age and sex as the child they hope to get out of China. Then one fine day, they go across the border with the kidnapped child, leave the poor waif there to fend for himself, and come out with their own child. Many cases have occurred in refugee areas where our Sisters are working. People will do anything to get their families together in Hong Kong.

"Virtuous Dragon" let us know just how people on the other side of the border feel about Catholic doctrine they cannot openly proclaim. This virtuous dragon is a young man twenty-two years old—only twelve when Sister Ignatia was forced out of China. She had instructed his family for Baptism. Now he is an office worker in the Communist government. Every now and then he manages to get a letter over the border to let Sister know how things are going.

'Dear Sister Wheat,' he writes. (Sister's name in Chinese, 'Muk,' means 'wheat.')

'I hope you are well. Sister, the education you gave us—we always feel peaceful with. My mother has gotten to Hong-Kong; I hope you will see her for she is lonely by herself. I and my sister and brother believe your education with our whole hearts. Your great help to us, we will remember forever.

Wish you long life and good health!

Virtuous Dragon.'

Typhoon warnings were posted in the city, as I landed at Ho Man Tin one day. Gusts of wind tore around the small cottages near the road and shacks which mounted up to the mountain top. Some are canvas lean-tos; some cardboard shanties; some piano crates or refrigerator boxes; others are caves dug into the clay hillside; the palatial residences are of real, genuine wood, dug up from heaven-knows-where. Rain came and went in torrents or in dribbles. Nevertheless the lines were full. Women pulled rubberized sheets over the babies on their backs and crowded up on the porch of the clinic. As many as possible jammed inside. At the school, 1,080 children were in the classrooms, unable to go outside to play during recess. But not one had missed school that day. No indeed, Chinese children never get prizes for perfect attendance records; their policy is, if the school building is standing, I ought to be in it.

The biggest crowd, however, was in front of The House Of A Million Noodles. You'd never look twice at the place ordinarily. It's just one of the huts which line Nairn Road. In more respectable Kowloon City, the Road is a street of middle-class apartment houses. But it slinks behind a market and emerges as the main street of Ho Man Tin. A stiff climb up the mountain is slowed by the traffic pouring down from side paths, tumbling down from the shacks on the hillsides.

Twisting among the water carriers, the school children, the men and women carrying laden shoulder poles and the toddlers wobbling down the street, you might very easily miss The House Of A Million Noodles. But then you have to leave the sidewalk and go into the street, for the sidewalk is massed thick with people. They all face the same direction— toward the inconspicuous door. Everyone holds a bucket or basket or shopping bag. Some old, some young, some women, some children, some gossiping, some too quiet. These are the people who love that House Of A Million Noodles.

Outside is a sign, Catholic Relief Services, a branch of National Catholic Welfare Conference in Washington. The door swings open and Number One in the line steps up with her bag opened. Sister Moira picks up a large tin can of still-wet noodles and dumps it into the shopping bag. A smile passes over the woman's face. "Thank you!" she says and runs home.

This noodle deal is the brightest idea in relief work. It used to be that when good flour was sent to the Chinese for relief, it was practically useless, for refugees had no ovens for baking. Then Monsignor Romaniello, in charge of the distribution, harking back to a childhood of spaghetti, thought of making the flour into noodles, something the Chinese can't get enough of. Now, in eight noodle factories, wheat flour, corn flour, milk powder, vitamins and Multi-Purpose Food are combined into the tasty noodle. It slips down very easily. I tried a plateful myself. It does.

At Ho Man Tin, Sister Moira supervises the making of 8,900 pounds of noodles every day. That much is given out every day, too. In fine weather they are dried, but in rain there is nothing to be done but give them out wet. They are usually cooked and eaten that day, anyhow. Every one of 6,250 families in the area gets six pounds every two weeks. In a year, 1,068,000 pounds of noodles are used. Even in typhoon weather the line-up for noodles always jams the sidewalk.

Back at our convent, we found a woman with her little ones dripping and cold on the doorstep. Her house had blown down, she said. Of course, we admitted her. By early afternoon, the lower floor was full. Some Sisters from the center house in Kowloon came over to help us move furniture around and make room upstairs. By 10:00 P.M. some five hundred women and children were sheltered in the convent and four hundred and fifty more were to spend the night in the Primary School up the hill.

As they poured in Sister Moira said to each one, "You know, there's no room to sleep." But they all said, "We don't mind, Sister. We just want to be in a safe place." They either stood up or sat upright all night. But the little ones had a place to sleep—each step of the two flights up was a crib for the night.

No electricity or phone service, of course, that night. In the wee sma' hours, a woman started the pangs of childbirth. It would not be an easy birth. How to get her to a hospital! Luckily, a private car was passing the front door and Sister hailed it. The poor woman was having a hard time. The shock of her collapsed house, the terror of trying to get the children to safety, the dread of returning the next day and probably finding all the family possessions smashed under the debris—it all added up to a most difficult delivery and the baby died.

However, that night, five other mothers were sturdier. I never saw so many babies born in one night! They sat happily on the floor with their newborns until we could get things organized a bit. Then we had benches put together to make five beds in a separate room.

Next morning, of course, with the typhoon going off, the families were out in the wet putting their shacks together again. For several days, we had two thousand rolls made up out of relief flour and gave them out. It would take time to get cooking pots again. In a week, however, the typhoon was not even a memory.

If Jonah had been a Hong Kong refugee, he would have spent a very comfortable three days in the whale's belly. I can just see him irritating the poor beast to boiling pitch, cooking his tin can of noodles over a heated artery, and cutting himself a good slice of tasty whalemeat from the inside to put a little flavor into the pot.

${\rm \textbf{14}}$ *Pigs' House, Dogs' House and Firecracker Factory*

ONCE, in those dear dead days now blissfully beyond recall, I was a heedless youngster in a parochial school beside the Pennsylvania Railroad. I don't know if the school was there first and, some foul night, the railroad sneaked up and parked behind it. Or whether some sadistic mind, knowing full well that four railroad tracks lurked behind the fence, planned to torture generations of innocent children and hundreds of angelic nuns. However it came about, the school and the railroad were cheek by jowl all during my youth.

We got used to it; even learned to profit by it. Classes stopped automatically when a locomotive rounded the bend; often it gave us a chance for a furtive peep at the book before we had to answer. The pastor, too—for the church was alongside—stopped in the pulpit, took time to clear his throat and rearrange his thoughts.

Whether the Sisters of Charity got used to it, I can't say. It would take heroic virtue to make spiritual profit out of the sight of one's nightie, newly washed and out on the line, being sprayed with soot from an overly busy railroad. But they bore it with equanimity if not with joy. Their white collars, sleeves and head pieces were always spotless; they thanked a merciful Providence that the rest of their clothes were black.

Old Sacred Heart School in Pittsburgh, Pa., now long dead, haunted me in Hong Kong. History repeats itself. Our Kowloon school stands vis-à-vis a range of mountains. Between the school and the mountains—

right in that valley—the world's airlines swoop to rest at Kai Tak Air-field, not ten minutes away. The jets scream, the engines roar, the landing gear trundles out. They come so close, the Sisters say, they can read newspaper headlines in the passengers' laps. I don't go so far as that, but certainly the swoosh from the jets slammed my bedroom door shut more than once. And soot sprinkles our plates in the refectory. Soot from Thailand, Burma, Manila and Ceylon tastes no better than soot from the Pennsylvania Railroad did.

It's one of the things you get used to. When the Tokyo Express or the Canton Local bears down so that sound waves crumple the roof, the Sisters don't notice it any more. And they drive through Hong Kong and see the ludicrous signs without even a smile. Over an expensive store front was:

LE FAT
LADIES' GIRDLES

And on a side street:

JOSEPH NO SQUEAK
SHOE REPAIR

A billboard speaks in bold letters of a medicine "perfect for everything from pimples to cholera."

Traffic signs have the British flare:

DEAD SLOW—for "stop."
DIVERSION—for "detour."
DUAL CARRIAGEWAY—for "four-lane highway."

Drivers get a homily for character-building now and then:

BETTER DRIVERS GET INTO THEIR CORRECT LANE
IN GOOD TIME TO REACH THEIR DESTINATIONS.

or   BETTER DRIVERS GLANCE IN THEIR REAR-VIEW
MIRRORS AND SIGNAL THEIR INTENTIONS.

The buses are long-winded, too:

PLEASE REFRAIN FROM TALKING TO THE DRIVER.
IT IS LIABLE TO ENDANGER PUBLIC SAFETY.

Best of all is the British version of Hail Hail the Gang's all Here!

Cheerio, cheerio,
The multitude has assembled!
Why should we concern ourselves?
Why should we concern ourselves?
Cheerio, cheerio, the multitude has assembled!
Why should we concern ourselves at the present
moment?

Hong Kong, to put it into British understatement, is "quite nice, you know; very nice indeed." The harbor is as lovely as God made it and as picturesque as the Chinese have made it and as dignified as the English have made it! The water is so clear and green one can read the labels on beer cans at the bottom. Views are unparalleled from the Peak; roads magnificent throughout the colony; food not to be equalled in Chinese restaurants. It is the City of Split Skirts, the City of Streets of Steps, the town cut in two by the harbor so that every day hundreds of thousands cross from Victoria to Kowloon or vice versa on ferries.

In Hong Kong is the Street of Ten Thousand Fragrances. You think it is a perfume factory? Oh no. The fragrance comes from fish and pickled cabbage and glazed ducks and salted pig's snout and kerosene lamps. The street starts in a most inconspicuous manner, between two shops opposite Block A of the Tai Hang Estate. It is wide enough only for foot traffic, but here is where two Maryknoll Sisters live and work. Of the ten thousand fragrances, they say the first nine thousand are hardest to get used to. Here live Sister Margaret Marie and Sister Doretta, both Americans, but one a Chinese born in San Francisco, the other an Irishman of the Brooklyn Irish.

We took a walk around the area. Past the tattered canvas awning propped up on four corners by poles, where mahjong goes on day and night. Past the outdoor barber shop. Past the house where seven families live, each in a tiny room. Past the woman selling pickled turnips and Chinese worm medicine. Out on the main street where a fish store displays a six-foot eel. An old woman with bandages over her eye—a recent cataract operation—bows and invites us into her one room of the daai-ha. Magnificent use of space! Her son, daughter-in-law, and their children live here with her. Inventory is simple. One double-decker bed; one cot; one single burner for kerosene; dishes stored below this, a bowl for each inhabitant; boxes under the bed neatly stacked. A girl, ten, sat on the cot sewing up the fingers of knitted gloves. She earns 7½¢ US for each dozen pair. The color—black. And she works under the single fluorescent bulb in the room. Just 7½¢ for sewing one hundred and twenty fingers on black gloves. Think of that the next time you buy a bargain pair.

Then up the hill surmounted by the new Police Headquarters which dominates the whole region. The Sisters don't come up here often. Crowds gathered. The children gawked; the grown-ups talked together.

"Who are they? Men or women?"

"Men, silly! Look at their big feet."

They soon made friends with us. Then a woman called from the edge, "Is there a Catholic Church around here? I'm new; I was looking for one." We walked slowly along and half the crowd followed. A woman edged up to Sister Margaret Marie.

"My son is in America," she said. "Fall River, Massachusetts. He sent me this." It was $4.00 taped to a Christmas card. "What should I do with it?"

"You can get $25.00 HK for it," Sister said. "That ought to pay some bills."

The woman did not believe her. "Ah, no," she sighed. "It is only a souvenir."

"You're crazy!" Sister said with vehemence. "Here you are starving and you hang on to an expensive souvenir? Don't be silly." She took it and changed it for her.

"It's unbelievable, just unbelievable," the old woman muttered to herself going off.

Sister Doretta waved her hand to the mountainside, scrofulous with huts and shanties. In the dusk, small pin-points of light began to appear. "No electricity. All kerosene oil lamps," Sister said. "People up there are in dread of fire. And yet, in a way, hoping for it. As fire victims, they could get White Cards from the government, and thus be eligible for a room in the Estate."

On to church for Good Friday services. To our way of thinking, these people live Calvary every day of their lives. Flies, heat, physical pain— they walk a bitter path like Our Lord's, even to being pushed out of their own city to die on the doorstep of China. Perhaps that is why they love Him so much when they come to know Him.

Crowds surged up to venerate the cross spread on the floor before the high altar. They jammed the aisles until a Chinese priest called over the microphone like a traffic cop. I knelt in a front pew watching the faces of those who knelt and kissed the cross. So many women with sleeping babies tied to their backs came forward. As Mama bent over to the cross, the baby's head bobbed forward as if to ratify the act. There was an old woman beside me saying the rosary. I tiptoed out after a half hour; I don't think she even knew I had gone, so intense was her meditation. On that Street of Ten Thousand Fragrances, many a holy soul adds a special fragrance of her own.

Bathed in the Paschal moon, we walked home past the mahjong table, now under a pressure lamp. Searchlights at the four corners of each daai-ha lit the path after a fashion. Moonlight was kind to the shacks. Children played in the evening coolness. The church glistened in the bright air. A Maryknoll Father talked to his parishioners. It was Tai Hang Tung, home, sweet home, to thousands.

Things are better out in "the country." Chai Wan used to be a fishing village on Hong Kong Island. Government pushed some mountains into the little harbor for fishing boats and built on it several Resettlement Blocks. The squatters in huts reaching to the sky will have to move down into the Estate.

No place in Hong Kong is level, but Chai Wan really stands on its ear. Steps are the usual streets. Sister Rose Bernadette and I had just come down a most impressive set of steps when we met, at the bottom, a woman carrying an older woman on her back. She had just trudged up a hilly street from the government clinic. Now she eased the old lady down so that her feet touched the ground but the younger woman bore most of the weight. She wanted a breather before she began carrying the older woman up the steps to their home.

"She's my mother," she explained. "She has a bad heart, so I carried her to the clinic this morning."

"And where do you live?" Sister asked.

The woman twisted her head back and pointed far up. "Near the top," she said. "Nice and quiet—when you get there. But it won't be long now. Government says we have to move to one of those." Her hand gestured to the seven-story blocks where three thousand people pushed and squirmed, slept, ate and washed together.

She wasted no sympathy on herself. She bent over, pulled her mother's arms tight around her neck, hitched the old lady's legs around her waist and started to mount to her aerie near the sky.

"Three hundred and twelve steps to the top," Sister said. "I counted them once."

And that means, we figured, that our friend carried her mother up the equivalent of fifteen floors in a walk-up apartment.

Sister Maria Teresa took me to the prison. She goes every Sunday morning, so that, now, old offenders welcome her as an enjoyable part of prison life. The three hundred inmates are divided among three small enclosures downstairs and "the big room" upstairs. Below are the infirmary where often two patients share a bed, the "new place" where new arrivals are kept until they have been checked for disease and cleaned up, and the Good Behavior Quarters. These are palatial dwellings in Chinese eyes. Each woman has a small private room painted bright blue, a bed, chair and table. If she needs it, she has a crib for the baby or small child. But we went upstairs to "the big room."

Sister Maria Teresa is Chinese, with Catholic ancestors who stretch back five generations. She knows her Faith and she knows her Chinese people perfectly. "Cho San! (Good morning!)" she called out. Immediately about two hundred women in coarse but clean white saams surged toward her. They got as close as the iron bars would permit, climbing up on the double-decker beds or sitting on chairs or the floor nearby. There were six or seven pairs of legs swinging from each upper deck.

Most of these women were caught selling heroin. One can understand. Here is a woman working like a horse—indeed, doing a horse's work—and getting less than $1.00 HK or 17¢ US a day. At the same time, she is worrying about the children in the shack at home for she cannot stay with them. Then, along comes the chance to sell heroin and make $30.00 a day without even leaving her shack. All she has to do is to keep quiet about it.

The women listened with riveted attention. One seemed very young—just a teen-age girl with bangs over her eyes and a full pony-tail. Another had a worn face. While her eyes stayed on Sister, her lips and cheeks constantly caressed the baby sitting on her folded-up legs. A wild-haired creature sat alone on the upper deck of a bed far off. Her cheeks were gaunt; her eyes encircled with darkness; her mouth half open. Her gaze never left Sister Maria Teresa. How much of the good tidings fell into her mind? Two others on a distant bed were very busy indeed. They were plucking eyebrows and pinching blackheads for each other. It wasn't long before they, too, edged their way over to the crowd.

Sister Maria Teresa will never see sixty again, but she has the vigor of twenty young Sisters. She asked me to go down to Macao to see "the pigs' house," that is, a former pig-breeding place where she and Sisters Patricia, Beatrice, Corazon and assorted others had maintained an orphanage for five hundred boys during World War II.

Macao is forty miles from Hong Kong. A Portuguese colony, it is just a tiny peninsula on the coast of China. It advertises itself as "The Monte Carlo of the East with round-the-clock gambling." Boats ply back and forth, making the three-hour trip several times a day.

On the way down, Sister Maria Teresa sat on deck and told me about the old days in Hong Kong and Canton.

> My Aunt Mary, oh, she was the one! In the old days, you know, not so many Chinese were Catholic. People didn't know how to take us. My family lived in a big old ancestral home in Canton. A new family moved opposite us and when they learned we were Catholic, they put up a mirror and a rooster on their house, so as to send the bad luck right back to us.
>
> But to get back to Aunt Mary. She didn't want to marry and yet there were very few Sisters in China. And all we Chinese are matchmakers. So my grandfather said,
>
> 'All right, you don't want to marry. But I'll not have you sitting around doing nothing. If you don't marry, you will have to spend your life working for the Church.'
>
> 'Just exactly what I want to do!' Aunt Mary returned.
>
> So grandfather gave a big party. Invited all the friends and relatives. There Aunt Mary made the announcement.
>
> 'I don't want to marry.'

Then she vowed her virginity to the Blessed Mother and combed up her hair. This combing up the hair was the sign she was a consecrated virgin. And she worked for the Church. Oh, how she worked! She knew all the dialects—Mandarin, Cantonese, Swatonese, all of them. For thirty years she worked in Canton. Then my mother died and left six of us. I was the youngest, just born. In fact I killed my mother. Aunt Mary came to take care of us. Then we all moved to Hong Kong with her. My father remarried but we all preferred to stay with Aunt Mary.

In Hong Kong, Aunt Mary kept on with her work for the Church. When she was eighty-six, while the Japanese occupied Hong Kong, a bomb exploded behind our house. She wasn't touched, but the fright killed her. Oh, Aunt Mary! We loved her. The Goddess of Mercy's motto could be hers, 'No son, no daughter. I sit in the lotus flower of purity.'

Sister Maria Teresa's uncle, Quincy Wong, was adopted by an Englishman and studied in England. He returned to Hong Kong and became chief detective for the city. One famous murder he solved in a typically Chinese way. The culprit had been free for more than a year. So Quincy Wong put on a pilgrim's disguise and haunted the Chinese temples. He knew the Chinese habit of praying out loud. One day he saw an old woman praying in a small temple off the street. "Thanks very much," she told the gods, "my son has not been caught yet." Quincy Wong followed her home and arrested her son.

Macao is a bit of old Portugal, crossbred with China. Pink, green and yellow houses line the harbor and are embedded in luscious dark gardens. Hong Kong thinks it intolerably slow; Macao thinks Hong Kong is intolerably fast. We by-passed the old churches, the cozy restaurants, the conducted tours, the hotels where floor after floor is devoted to gambling, and made our way out near the border to "the pigs' house."

It's a pigs' house once again. The odor told us that long before we saw the high brick walls built solidly around an entire block, enclosing a center court where the pigs roamed at will. Sties for the sows lined the wall on the inside. In this place, four Sisters kept five hundred boys picked off the streets of Macao during World War II.

You see, as it is now, the colony was a place of refuge. Thousands— millions—poured into Macao, colony of neutral Portugal. They died on the streets and children were left to survive as best they could. Eventually the government took over this pigs' house for boys. Girls went to "the dogs' house," a kennel for racing greyhounds, sadly defunct in those war years. A firecracker factory across the street was taken as a sort of Poor Farm for those picked up in the streets starving.

Sister Maria Teresa talked a blue streak walking around the pigs' house.

Such a time! Such a time! Five hundred boys and only a pig pen for them. Oh my, the dirt! We clean and clean and still the bedbugs are awful. Father, mother, grandmother bedbugs!

And no meat for the boys! We caught sparrows. The boys were good at it. They had done it on the streets. Then a Chinese woman married to a Portuguese soldier—she called him Number Five Foreign Devil—came to us. 'The only way to raise money,' she said, 'is to raise pigs. I'll show you how.' So she gave us four pigs of her next litter. Showed us how to feed them, take care of them when they're sick, and keep them clean. Oh, my goodness! You know Sister Patricia. Nothing but clean, clean, clean around her. Our pigs were so clean we could eat off the floor. Sister Corazon, our doctor, gave the best obstetrical care to the mother pigs. One time when fifteen piglets were born, she gave some to a mother dog to nurse.

Government gave us a plot next door and we went in for farming. Had chickens, ducks, goats and rabbits. I had twenty mother rabbits. My heavens, multiply so fast! Every forty days more rabbits. But it's good. We had meat for the children and could sell for what we needed. And turkeys. Thirty of them. Saved for Christmas dinner. One got very sick. 'I know what's wrong with him!' and Sister Patricia took a knife, cut the craw of that turkey, pulled out something he ate and sewed him together with plain thread. He had a special pen that night but was okay in the morning.

Very hard to get soap. I was in the market one day.

'What you want, Sister?' said a market woman.

'Soap,' I said. 'We're desperate for soap.'

'You're foolish to try to get soap these days. Try these.' She showed me leaves from a spiky plant. I bought them—fifty leaves for three cents. We pounded them with a stone and soaked them for an hour. All soft and soapy. The string inside makes rope or you can use it to scrub tables with. Excellent! We never used soap again.

No fuel. All these boys to cook for and nothing to burn. We sent the boys out to get grass. But they spent their time fooling in the mountains. So we said, 'The boy who brings lots of grass, eats much; he who brings less, eats less.' It worked! I weighed each boy's grass when it came in.

We were outside the pigs' house by then. All of a sudden Sister put her hands to her face. "That was the place!" she said. "Oh my, the poor boy! One of ours, Chung Lu, was a big boy when he came to us, sixteen years old. Had been on his own too long. Always going out over the wall at night and often stealing something from the house when he did so. He'd be gone three days at a time. Well, we didn't run a prison, so we tried to get him to stay through kindness. One day he was missing, and the next and the next. Also some of the boys' spoons and some rice. After a week, the other boys complained of a bad smell in the tall bamboo which arched over the wall at one point. We thought it might be a rat or a dog. But it was Chung Lu. He must have fallen off the wall. And there were the spoons. The only way I knew him—I recognized the coat I had patched for him. Poor boy, poor boy! I pray for him often."

"Many people in Macao were very good to us. We got help from kind ladies, and government gave us rice. Many boys had eye troubles. Sister Corazon, our doctor, took care of our boys but she needed an eye specialist. Small wonder! Boys three to eighteen years, all eating very bad or not at all. A doctor, specialist in eyes, said to her, 'Sister, I cannot come by day but I will come by night.' So good! Often 10:30 at night, the doctor came after his busy day and treated our boys."

We went around the corner. "Ay ya!" shouted a hearty woman from her doorstep. She all but smothered Sister Maria Teresa. She was Wu Tai Kao, the woman who had helped them to raise pigs. Such a reunion! One would think it was the Battle of the Century; there is no language that can equal the Chinese in sounding like a fight no matter what is being said.

We went toward the border where Red China begins. In Hong Kong, there is a wide expanse of No Man's Land where no one is permitted to wander. But in Macao, only a few hundred feet of road separates the two countries. Sentries—those smart, black policemen from Angola, resplendent in red fezzes and brass buckles, stopped us. A funeral procession was passing. The leader showed a pass; the sentry nodded. All the tintinnabulation of a Chinese funeral paraded by—the sedan chair bearing a large picture of the deceased; the tree-hewn coffin on the shoulders of eight men; another chair with the ancestral tablets of the deceased; and finally the mourners with white bands around their heads. They coolie-trotted by. We watched them down the block and through the gate. Another Chinese was going back home dead.

TAIWAN

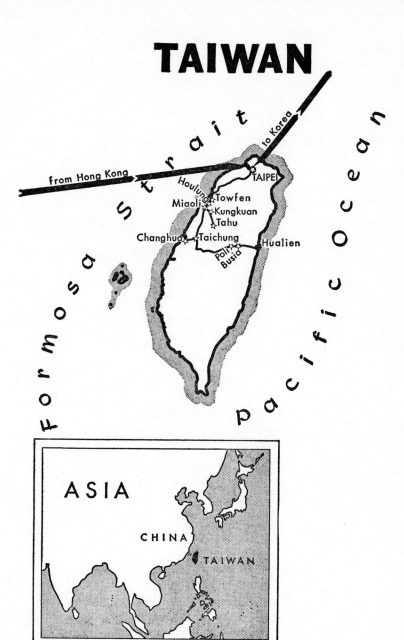

from Hong Kong

Formosa Strait

to Korea

Pacific Ocean

Houlung
Miaoli
Towfen
Kungkuan
Tahu
Changhua
Taichung
Poli
Busia
Hualien
TAIPEI

ASIA

CHINA

TAIWAN

TAIWAN

⫷ 15 ⫸ Nylons, Plastic and House-Cleaning Day

TAIWAN is really hard to figure out. Like Saturday night's soup which has something of all the week in it, Taiwan is a potpourri of all Asia with a dash of western influence to pep it up.

The aborigines are Malayan. In their dances and clothes, they remind one of the semi-civilized tribes of the Philippines—the Igorots and Benguets. The "Taiwanese," mostly Hoklo-speaking, came from China hundreds of years ago and consider themselves a nation distinct. The Japanese occupied the island for fifty years and left traces; also, they brought many westernized ways with them. So much so, that Taiwanese think they are speaking Japanese when they say "towelu" for towel; "trucku" for truck; "tomahto" for tomato; and "isucreemu" for ice cream. The last migrants into the island are the "Mainland Chinese," a million strong, who poured over the China Sea ten years ago. Small wonder Taiwan has less elbowroom than all of Asia—even Japan. Only Holland and Belgium keep the human family in closer quarters. Connecticut and Vermont combined have about the same area with less than one-fourth the people.

However, the aborigines are pushed up into the mountains where their corn and sweet potato fields are so steep that they say at a funeral, "Poor fellow, he fell off his field!" The Taiwanese cultivate the river beds with rice and vegetables. This leaves room in the cities for the mainland Chinese. Taiwanese look at them in the same kindly light as the Southerners did the post-Civil-War carpetbaggers.

Such a welter of languages! Spellings and pronunciations are anybody's fair game. There are so many right ways in Taiwan that any one of them is the wrong way to millions. Each city and town has a Mandarin name, a Taiwanese name, an old Japanese name and, in the mountains, an aborigine name. In the Miaoli area, a Hakka name as well. This makes letter writing or travel a fascinating sport. Even the name of the island is vastly under dispute. You can whip up a bloody battle by calling it Formosa. Protagonists for Taiwan or Free China see red.

The Old and New are so mixed up, East and West so confused, that one hardly knows just where he is in time or space. A woman working in the fields pours fertilizer from buckets on her shoulder pole; as she waves to you the sun glints on her wrist watch and she smiles through her lipstick.

You ride in a bus on good roads in the lowlands and note many urns in the rice fields—large pottery vases about three feet high. They hold the bones of someone's parents. After several years in the ground, the bones are placed in such an urn. The idea is that the spirit will protect the fields he used to work. Later, when the gods give a propitious time and place for burial, they will be put into the ground.

As in Japan, personal cleanliness is such a fetish that Clean-the-Teeth sinks in private homes may be six feet long and elaborately tiled. The Wash-the-Body room is always large, too, and well appointed with buckets, soap dishes, towels and maybe even a showerhead. Bedbugs are unknown, the Sisters say, but cockroaches are immense and plentiful. Clothes are usually clean; women get on the bus with pretty dresses, nicely fitted. Yet the sanitation problem is staggering. Sewage flows through the streets in open ditches; fields smell to Heaven for vengeance. Hookworms, tapeworms and round worms flourish and their tribe increases daily.

According to ancient tradition, dog meat is considered a spring tonic; around March and April the number of people advertising for lost dogs is alarming. In shops, it is sold as "Fragrant Meat." Every now and then, there is a scare in the newspapers about something far worse. *The China Post* issued a warning against eating sausages; they have been found in local shops made of rat meat.

The rat meat items ran for several days. Then, as a service to readers, *The China Post* gave instructions on how to tell good sausage from the other. I quote:

> You can tell by the taste. Rat sausage tastes better and has a stronger flavor. But it is hard to chew. Pork sausage can easily be ground by a set of good teeth.
>
> The prevalence of such sausage in the shops has sent the demand for sausage plunging. Our reporter interviewed many owners of meat shops. 'It's so terrible,' complained one, 'that I had to exhaust all my eloquence before I could persuade a customer to buy my sausage.'
>
> Sugar cane farmers of central and southern Taiwan get $5.oo NT per catty (1⅓ pounds) for dead and dying rats. Rat population exceeds human population according to agricultural experts. After sugar-cane farmers apply rat poison, great numbers of huge rats can be picked up in the fields.

In spite of odds, the Nationalist Government seems to have plunged ahead with plans to make Taiwan a going concern. One of the things it can be proudest of is the East-West Highway ($11,000,000!). It cuts across the island where formerly only coastal roads ran north and south. Over the years, headline readers got a quickie on the story:

WORK BEGINS ON EAST-WEST HIGHWAY

LANDSLIDES DELAY WORK ON EAST-WEST HIGHWAY

FUNDS NOT AVAILABLE TO CONTINUE EAST-WEST HIGHWAY

And finally:

EAST-WEST HIGHWAY NEARS COMPLETION
TICKETS AVAILABLE NOW FOR TRAVEL ON HIGHWAY
WHEN COMPLETED
BEST TO TAKE FOOD AND CLOTHING FOR SEVERAL DAYS
DUE TO POSSIBLE LANDSLIDES.

DIGNITARIES PLAN CEREMONY FOR OPENING
EAST-WEST HIGHWAY

CEREMONY POSTPONED DUE TO LANDSLIDES ON HIGHWAY

At last:

GOVERNOR CUTS RIBBON TO OPEN EAST-WEST HIGHWAY

and next day:

THOSE WHO BOUGHT TICKETS FOR EAST-WEST HIGHWAY
MAY HAVE THEIR MONEY REFUNDED BY APPLYING AT
GOVERNMENT OFFICE. LANDSLIDES, WASHOUTS TO REPAIR.

Penetrating to the interior, I went over most of this famous highway. We could see what they meant; the maximum speed is posted at 16 miles an hour. In several places we took to the riverbed. What was meant to be the road swarmed with young soldiers pressed into duty as highway repairmen. There were no cranes, bulldozers, steam shovels, that we could see. If a pile of dirt was to be taken from there and put here, it went in wicker baskets at the end of a shoulder pole. Stones were lifted one by one; cement was stirred up in little masses and shoveled between stones to make retaining walls. But there were no footings or foundations for these walls. When the next floods come and eat away the dirt at the bottom, the whole wall will crack again and fall away. Already the river-bed was strewn with huge pieces of former retaining walls. One bridge has been built three times within as many years.

Most are suspension bridges for single-lane traffic, so named because they keep you in suspense. You should see a bus go across one. The road-bed sags under the weight like a Beauty Rest mattress in motion, and the whole bridge gives a wiggle of delight when the bus leaves it.

Taiwan is a land of contrasts, indeed. Up in the mountains, I found
Obin. She was an aborigine woman squatting at the door of her mud hut.
Even from a distance I could see her tattooed face—a bluish streak which
spread from mouth and chin right out to her ears like a five-o'clock
shadow. She watched my coming without emotion; her attention was
elsewhere. Her hair was "pahmanetto"; that is, it had a permanent wave,
or rather, a permanent frizz. Eye has not seen, nor imagination conceived,
the country wherein the "pahmanetto" is unknown. Obin was listening to
a hi-fi playing in the mud hut behind her. Schubert's Unfinished Symphony, I recognized it. No connoisseur could have enjoyed it more than
Obin; whether she enjoyed the music or just the thrill of owning a hi-fi,
I couldn't say.

Obin, as a woman, has a fairly happy berth in this world. In Taiwan,
as elsewhere, women make news. *The China Post,* handed out in the plane
as we neared Taipei from Hong Kong, gave an idea of what to expect of
Free China's women. I read that the wife of the mayor of Taipei beat up
one of her husband's administrative assistants because he took the mayor
out on a spree. Evidently the country is ripe for women's rights, for the
mayor's chauffeur's wife next attained fame by "getting hold of another
chauffeur and biting his neck." Then she "dashed to the victim's home
to scratch the face of his wife." So often, man-bites-woman is not news; it
is good to know that woman-bites-man is.

I suppose the ladies feel that something must be done to relieve the
boredom. The government forbids mahjong as gambling. Technically,
the whole country is at war. For that reason, all official buildings are
painted grey. Pill boxes and air raid shelters bristle in rice fields and almost on every corner. Women are supposed to wear subdued colors. Students in middle school, at an age when most girls are experimenting with
all sorts of feminine foibles, are constrained to wear khaki blouses and
black shapeless skirts. Their hair is bobbed and dragged back from the
face by ancient bobby pins. What can one do to relieve the tedium?

In a humble way, I too struck a blow for women's rights. Often, with
other women, we stood in the hot sun patiently waiting in line for a bus.
Being first (and the Taiwanese queue up for a bus) there might be the
ghost of a chance to get a seat. As soon as the bus arrived, a crowd of men
would give up loafing in the shade, swarm forward and knock us women
out of their way to get in first.

We were first in line one hot day in Kungkuan when the bus finally
careened around the corner. It stopped right in front of me. Out of nowhere, a horde of men pressed forward. I let an old man get away with it.
Then a young fellow, no more than twenty, pushed ahead, thrusting his
ticket into the conductress' hand as she stood by the door. This was once
too often. With a firm but ladylike gesture, I planted my hand on his

chest. This stopped him. Then I took his ticket from the conductress' hand and gave it back to him. In a voice of Infinite Disdain, I said, "Pardon me, Sir," at the same time applying pressure on his chest.

He was stunned. Silent. I mounted the steps and entered that bus like Queen Elizabeth entering Parliament. The poor boy didn't know what hit him. Several others of my Downtrodden Sex made hay while the sun shone and slipped in. Luckily, he was a young man with a sense of humor. He came to with a laugh. Halfway to Miaoli, as we bowled along the highway, I saw him across the bus; he smiled in good humor at me.

As elsewhere in Asia, one runs across many mementos of the Japanese Empire, not only in roads and buildings, but in the people's outlook. In fifty years, 1895–1945, the energetic Japanese did much. Telephone and telegraph service is good; mail is prompt and safe, delivered by postmen in natty green uniforms who ride a bicycle to your door. They are so conscientious about Special Delivery letters that they wake you in the middle of the night to thrust them into your hand with a polite bow. Trains run on time and are clean; buses careen down the roads wherever there is road enough to go on; the bicycle flourishes as the family carry-all. Papa operates it, mama sits behind with two children and the baby has a special wicker basket in front where he can grab the handlebars and pretend he is running the whole works.

Irrigation is marvelous. One never sees the old Chinese methods—a boy or woman foot-pedaling water into rice fields, or two women swinging a bucket between them. No indeed. The ditches are straight, the water flows freely, the sluices open and close, and the rice gets water without wearing out human beings in the process.

Every scrap of land is cultivated. The riverbeds are a maze of vegetable gardens. Farmers move in as soon as the floods have gone. "So long as the river isn't using the space, let us use it," they say. Sometimes, the river reclaims it in a hurry and takes the farm along with it, but those are the chances when one borrows the river's bed.

The Nationalist regime carries on with these agricultural improvements. Faced with the densest population in Asia, Taiwan "redistributed" its land in 1950. Anyone owning untilled land had to give it up. This put much of it into the hands of independent farmers. The irrigation system was enlarged. As a result, northern Taiwan produces two crops of rice a year and southern Taiwan, three.

National Spring House-Cleaning Day is another breath of Old Japan wafting around its former colony. We were in Changhua, April 9th, on this Great Day. For several days before, roads and streets were clogged with tatamis, cupboards, tables, chairs, straw rugs, blankets, all airing in the bright sunshine. Women and men were armed with brush and soap; table tops and kitchen things were scrubbed. On the day itself, inspectors came around to see each house. They pasted a report card on the door lintel for all the neighborhood to see. A guest coming to see you takes warning. If your lintel has a blue card (very, very Sub-Standard), he stays a short time and eats nothing. If the card is white, the house has passed but is not commended. Everyone strives for the pink card of a Superb Housewife. How happily she beams as the guest commends her; how she smiles as passers-by note the gay color! Besides inspection, every house is DDT'd twice a year.

Taiwan is a land of bicycles. It's a poor man indeed who cannot pile his family on a bicycle for a family outing. For ricepaddy travel, the bicycle has all other transportation beaten to a frazzle, for the dikes between paddies are around eighteen inches wide. The Sisters are all experts. They sail down the lanes with umbrella, catechetical charts, books and woman companion balanced nicely. Of course some of them are young, not far from the "Look, Maw! No hands!" stage of life. But I remembered with bitterness the last time I rode a bicycle twelve years ago. Trying to show off, I ended up as a tragic humiliation at the Bishop's feet. Never again! Now, I'd as soon try to steer a rocket around the moon. But more than one Sister keeps her trusty bicycle at the foot of her bed in the dormitory at night.

Plastic has taken Taiwan by storm. The pedicab men wear a sheet of plastic for a raincoat; little fans come wrapped in plastic; purses are woven of plastic strips; the oxen have bridles of gay plastic—green, yellow, purple, pink. Even the water buffalo have bright plastic nose-rings. Women use plastic clotheslines; school youngsters have plastic pencil cases; toddlers wear plastic shoes. Plastic garden hose is used all over the country instead of pipes. Our convent in Kungkuan has no water piped into it. Instead, the Sisters arranged to chisel in on the water supply of the man across the street. He has a green garden hose hanging near his faucet; then it swings over the street taped to a bamboo pole, and runs around our house to the back window. When Sister wants some water, she calls across the street and our neighbor connects the hose to his faucet. We can watch the water coming through the translucent hose over the heads of street traffic. In another convent all the pipes are outside the house. This is not so bad but, to turn on the shower, you have to put your dripping hand outside the window to manipulate the faucet. Yet in both these places, natural gas is piped in abundance, cheap and dependable.

Taiwan is comparatively a land of plenty. Next to Japan, the standard of living is highest in Asia. Workers seem happy and content in spite of the long hours they work and the pittance they receive. Their working conditions would make a social worker shudder; safety precautions just don't exist. We visited a glass factory in Miaoli making thermos bottles.

It was a most hit-and-miss affair. I came out aged by thirty years. Young boys wandered around a built-up earthen platform swinging long pipes at the end of which were red hot bubbles of glass. Now and then they blew through the pipes and made the glass balloons bigger. They waved them here and there, missing each other (and me) by a hair, sauntering up and down the platform as if out for a summer evening stroll in the park. Then at just the right second, they were at the edge of the platform, gave a final puff and plunged the glass bubble into a contraption of iron operated by a little girl not more than ten years old. She shut the mold on the red hot glass and threw on it a dipper full of water from the bucket beside her. Another thermos bottle was made. The ground was so hot it burned through my shoes and bits of broken glass were all over, yet everyone in that factory was laughing, joking, friendly and content at work.

At a weaving mill amid the deafening noise of machines, the girls smiled and waved happily, in spite of their standing twelve hours a day on an earthen floor.

At a silk stocking factory—a shack no bigger than fifteen feet by fifteen feet—fourteen girls and women, working as many knitting machines, laughed and talked under a single fluorescent light hung from the low rafters. Here, too, a social reformer would have fainted dead away at working conditions. A galvanized iron roof warded off rain, sunshine, falling caterpillars and leaves, as well as inquisitive spiders. It also held in every ounce of heat and every scrap of air breathed out by those fourteen women. The earthen floor was damp and uneven. The "powder room" smelled out in the back. Ideas of the 40-hour work week, the coffee break, social security, old-age benefits, were as far from their thinking as the formula for atomic fission. Yet Madison Avenue workers probably have more ulcers than these girls. A spirit of cooperation and even gaiety hung around the factory. It was a family affair with a few neighbors thrown in. The Boss-Lady went from machine to machine, stepping over the workers and their babies in a helpful way. When they saw us at the doorway, a great shout of welcome went up. Not a single stitch was dropped and the knitting never slackened, yet they let us know we were welcome indeed.

With pride, Boss-Lady showed us the finished products—filmy nylon stockings shaped, folded and wrapped in cellophane stamped MADE IN JAPAN.

"Made in Japan?" I protested. "They're made right here in Taiwan." Boss-Lady smiled. "The stockings are, but it's the cellophane wrapper that's marked MADE IN JAPAN." It was, too. People here will pay more for what they think are Japanese products.

Workers are happy, no doubt about it. They ride to work; bicycle racks in factory yards are full. Old missioners comparing Taiwan with mainland China will tell you, "Nobody is hungry on Taiwan; they wear good clothes; they eat meat usually once a day. On the mainland, they were lucky to get meat once a month."

The children show the results of a good diet. Two fairly poor families near our Miaoli convent have each twelve children, all of them living and healthy-looking.

Taiwan is intensely religious. Temples adorn every street corner; small shrines dot the roads; each field has a corner cut off and offered to the gods. Every house I went into had a shrine—pagan or Christian—facing the front entrance. Temples are swept and kept clean. The smell of joss permeates the air; you can wander in and find worshippers "bai-bai-ing" —putting their hands together in front and then tapping their elbows, begging for the gods to help them over some rocky spot in life.

Small superstitions flourish and grow fat, inherited from the past or made up on the spot. At parties for children we never give out four pieces of candy. "Never tell a patient to take four pills, nor to take one pill every four hours, nor four times a day," a Taiwanese doctor told Sister Antonia Maria when she hung out her medical shingle on the clinic at Changhua. "Give out three or five pills; otherwise the patient will think you want to kill him outright." Four is unlucky for them, just as thirteen is for us enlightened Westerners. Hospitals and hotels have no fourth floor as we have no thirteenth floor. This little quirk of Taiwanese human nature came from Japan. In Japanese, the word "shi" means "four" and also "death." Any combination of four—14, 40, 44, etc.—using the syllable "shi" is under suspicion. Nobody marries on the fourth of the month; nobody serves four cookies; a hospital—horrors!—would never have four patients in a ward.

Up in the mountains, we come across not-so-harmless religions. The Duck Egg Fast religion for example, so called because they do not eat duck eggs on certain days. It's a secret society condemned by the government and suspected of being Communist. One of its major objectives seems to be to throw a monkey wrench into the Church. A group of aborigines, for instance, will be studying Catholic doctrine. Along come the Duck Egg people and say, "Horrible things happen to Catholics when they die. The priests cut off your head and turn it around, and pull out your eyes and send them to America for medicine. Then they wrench your legs up and tie you into a knot and cut your heart and liver out. They won't let you be buried in your clothes, either." Well! Nobody wants to be treated like that, for sure. Even when old Catholics who have seen many Catholic funerals tell them it's not true, the poor aborigines are shaking in their boots.

Taiwan is a land of hostesses. Every train, every bus, no matter how lowly, has a young girl as hostess, decked out in an airlines hostess uniform, somewhat shabby perhaps, but neat and clean. On the trains—diesel-powered!—running from Taipei to the south, you are smothered with courtesy. The hostess comes around proffering magazines and newspapers, English or Chinese. Every hour or so she hands out small towels soaked in perfumed water so that you can refresh your sooty face and hands. Around noon, she asks if you want a box lunch; how about buying some cookies or salted watermelon seeds? Nobody goes through the train bawling out his wares. This is a personal sales pitch.

Another functionary, as soon as the wheels make their first turn, goes up and down the aisle pouring hot tea into a glass set conveniently into the wall beside you. He replenishes it often, pouring out the cold and pouring in the hot. The bell-hop appears with broom and dustpan, sweeping up candy wrappers, cigarette stubs, bits of paper, and grains of rice which may have fallen from box lunches.

On buses they do not coddle the passengers like this, but the girls are very efficient. They pick up the tickets, help children up the steps and squeeze in the last sardine very graciously.

I watched one of these girl conductors on a fairly long trip. Between stops, she slumped on the hard little seat near the door she can call her own. It snaps up against the wall when she is not on it; when she is, it bars the door. Her "pahmanetto" was just about grown out; her natty coat was ragged; the shoulder-strap purse they all wear to carry money and tickets, was only a canvas bag frayed and worn. She seemed just a child half-asleep on the jolting, racking bus; her head almost snapped off several times when we went over rough boulders. But she is envied by many others. These bus women are the "career girls" of Taiwan. They have two weeks' training and get good money.

And stones! I never saw so many. Rounded stones tumbling down from mountain heights, rolled along by floods and left behind in dry riverbeds. Ox carts go to the riverbeds and men fill them to the top with these stones. Hundreds, millions of ox carts have gone to the riverbeds for hundreds and thousands of years, yet there are billions of stones left. You see them used everywhere. They make the foundations of houses, they build up rice paddy dikes, they line the irrigation canals. They make up roads, huge retaining walls, railroad embankments, bridge supports and stepping stones across the wide shallow rivers. Piled up like cannon balls, they give a Stonehenge look to the fields. But they really take a toll of your patience when they are made into cobblestone streets. After an hour or two on such a street, your ankles wobble even on a polished floor.

Ah yes, if you want to live dangerously, come to Taiwan! If you like the chances to be less than 50–50 that you will die in your bed, come to Taiwan. The country is prepared for war; soldiers swarm everywhere.

Air-raid shelters ornament every street corner—not only in Taipei but in
the provincial cities, too. And if the Communists don't get you, the traffic
will.

Ah yes, you who scorn security, come to Taiwan! Life starts out reck-
lessly. I have seen a premature baby in a cooking pot over a slow fire, as
an incubator. At one month, baby's hair was to be cut—shaved off clean.
What do they use? An inch-thick spike filed down to a chisel-like blade.
To see that going over the baby's soft skull can give a nurse delirium
tremens. When the child gets to be any age at all, his fingernails and
toenails are trimmed with hedgeclippers. He goes to kindergarten in a
little cart pulled by a man on a bicycle, out in a welter of buses, trucks,
oxen, and private cars all skimming past each other. And he spends the
rest of his life sidestepping army jeeps and trucks, bicycles, and "iron-
cows," little tractor-like affairs with two small wheels in front designed
to go through a cultivated field. Worst of all are the three-wheeled trucks
made in Japan, with only one wheel in front. They tip drunkenly as they
swing in and out to get ahead. But why bother about it all? Taiwanese
can expect to live to the ripe age of fifty-five; most other orientals have a
life expectancy of about thirty-five! Come to Taiwan! You have twenty
more exciting years to live!

⦃ 16 ⦄ A Lot for Seven Cents

THE pastor is pope in his own parish. So when the Pope
of Towfen, Father James McCormick by name, not only told us we ought
to see Chinese Opera but said he would pay our way, we gave in with
very little struggle.

He backed his invitation with good reasons. "You will never know good
costumes," he told Sister Paulita, "until you see the Chinese theater. You
think the Three Kings in your Christmas show are gorgeous? You should
see the merest servant boy on the Chinese stage. As for you," and his finger
pointed at me, "if you want to know the theater Shakespeare wrote for,
you will have to see Chinese Opera."

He was talking to three Already Convinced. Sister Luella had a good
reason, too; she would chaperone the two of us. The advertisements outside the theater were horrendous enough to send whole legions of devils
cowering back to Hell, but Father paid his $3.00 NT (about 7½¢ US)
for each of us without a murmur.

The show was well started by the time we found a bench in the dark and sat down. But no matter. It had been going on for hours and would last a good many more. Four hours was our quota, but then we tried to follow the plot. That's a mistake; it tires one out.

"It's like a soap opera," Father explained. "A company of actors comes for eight or ten days and keeps the story going that long. There are several episodes every night like the old Perils of Pauline. They get one going strong and stop in the middle of it. The suckers come back next night, of course, and get involved in another episode."

It was all in Hoklo dialect, although Towfen is a Hakka-speaking town. But language had little to do with understanding the action. Any words from the stage were purely incidental to the clatter of cymbals, whine of music, murmur of audience getting soda pop or water ices, and so on.

So far as I could make out, there was the Good Guy and the Bad Guy. In this case, two brothers. The Bad Guy wanted to get the Good Guy's wife and also discredit him in their Aged Father's eyes, so as to nip on to the inheritance as well. The Good Guy's wife was somewhat averse to this but the Bad Guy's wife was all for it. The two ladies got into a friendly bit of hair-pulling over the situation and for this a servant reported them to the Mandarin in Red.

We now got into the realm of officialdom. The Bad Guy bribed the Red Mandarin so that the Aged Father was beaten with bamboo sticks and the Good Guy toted off to Jail. The Good Guy's wife then appeared with incense sticks in her hair, weeping into the long sleeves of her gown. The incense sticks denote that she was going to Peiping to appeal to the Emperor. On the way, however, she met a really high Mandarin in a natty green outfit with roses in his hat. This Green Mandarin persuaded the lady not to go to the Emperor. In righteous indignation, horrible to behold, he swore to punish the wicked Red Mandarin. Sad to relate, no sooner did he meet the villain than he accepted hush money. The last we heard of the Good Guy and his wife was this Green Evildoer saying "Off with his head!" about him, and "Lock her up!" about her.

There was a Do-Gooder around at the time, identified by a white flowing band around her topknot. She got to the Green Snake in the Grass as he sat in the Emperor's court and upbraided him. From that point on, the plot was a shambles. The Emperor's sister was in love with somebody condemned to death. The Emperor commuted the sentence to a dukedom; both Green and Red Mandarins got into it somehow. A girl wearing a long grey beard and a hat like a Patriarch of the Malabar Rite floated on and off. The spirits took a hand with firecrackers going off; the stage darkened several times while the character who happened to be on stage at the time took a flyer at the end of a wire, sailing up into the air. The spirit of the Do-Gooder's mother came on stage trying to bring order out of chaos. She failed. Several battles ensued; men and women brandished spears, clubs, bolos and swords, did some neat footwork and weapon-twirling and turned somersaults and cartwheels to indicate bloody carnage all over the stage. When things got too hot for anyone, he stood on a stool at the side of the stage to indicate that he was invisible. Minor characters were busy between stints on stage, shooing off the youngsters of various ages who wandered onstage in their underwear or without it. They were children of the actors coming on with innocent prattle to talk to mama or papa. One never knew when a character came on whether he was there to help the plot along or merely to collect a child for baby-sitting offstage.

The musicians were in undershirts at the side of the stage with a whole jazz-band around each one. He would pick up a cornet, or ancient Chinese zither, or an affair like a triangle, or cymbal, drum, trombone or bass violin (but minus the violin part), interchanging them a hundred times in one piece. The smartest trick of all merited a salvo of applause but passed unnoted. The small son of a musician came up to his father demanding a nickel for a bottle of pop. The harried musician reached into his pocket and got the nickel, and kept his zither going with the other hand.

Soda pop played a large part in this show. The back curtain and valance were of deepest black decorated with brilliant gold Chinese characters. In the center was a circle with rays.

"What do they say?" I asked.

"Oh, the characters? They say 'Drink our new soda pop, the Sun-Moon Drink. Made by the makers of Black Pine, the best in Taiwan!' It's an ad. Black Pine paid for the curtain so they could use it for advertising. The circle in the center is their bottle cap."

I could see what Father meant about Shakespeare. The show was continuous. When one scene ended, the curtain with the golden bottle cap fell and more actors ran out in front to carry on with another scene. Nobody talked long; nobody stayed on stage long. The rule was, "Dash in, say your piece and go." Everybody in the house knew how the thing was going to end; they had come to see how well the actors did it. The stage manager came on and off, putting on a chair in time for the Bad Guy to hide behind it, or for the Good Guy's wife to faint into it. Nobody minded him; like a good head waiter, he went unnoticed.

This gives little idea of what it was like. As Father divined when he had to pay seven cents each for our seats, this was a highly successful company. The actors wore the most flamboyant satins and sequins. Their faces were painted dead white with red cheeks and eyelids. They had built up their noses with putty so they stood out like Chinese War Gods' noses. Servants walked with big steps; the rich people minced. All officials wore stiff belts, far too big for them, like hula hoops around their knees. Pompons, flowers, gauzy wings lifted the hats right off the heads. And sequins dazzled the whole stage. "I'm ashamed of my Mass vestments, now," Father said. "I'll have to get something more colorful if my Catholics are to be impressed with the solemnity of the Mass."

These acting troupes spring up and die down quickly. In a village when the rice crop is poor, somebody says, "Let's put on shows for a living." They get a fellow who can read to dish up a play, to coach them and make the business contacts. They rehearse for a couple of weeks, rent the costumes and set out. If successful, the troupe stays together until a main actor dies or the manager runs off with the money. If not, they disband and go back to peanut-growing to live. It's mostly a family affair; nobody has sharply defined roles. If one of the men goes on a strike for more pay, or takes the day off, one of the women can put on his costume and beard and play the part just as well. Who's going to mind if the Green Mandarin speaks in a squeaky voice? Shakespeare's audiences never did. By the time that happens, the customers have paid their seven cents and who cares? "Did you notice two men at the box office?" Father asked. "One represented the actors; the other was for the theater. They both checked on the girl who sold the tickets."

Father McCormick is a whole show in himself. He started out in life in Pennsylvania, was ordained at Maryknoll, and came to the Chinese thirty years ago. Twenty years were on the mainland working with Bishop Francis X. Ford who died in a Communist prison, and ten years on Taiwan with the same Hakka-speaking people, now re-established in and around Miaoli.

Bishop Ford, says Father McCormick, always believed that the Hakka were one of the lost tribes of Israel. It sounds fantastic, but the very name Hakka, "guest," indicates that they are strangers from afar. They may have come from beyond the Gobi Desert with Genghis Khan. Many words in Hakka are like the Turkish which, itself, has some Syro-Chaldean in it. Hakka people, too, have many Jewish characteristics; they love education and will sacrifice anything to get their children through school. They are excellent business men and go to foreign parts to set up commercial contacts. On the island of Mauritius, for instance, nearly all the Chinese are Hakkas. Also they have larger noses than most Chinese.

Father McCormick got to know many of the old French missioners in his early days in China. One was known as "Find-the-Water Priest" and now villages for miles around come to Father McCormick, asking him to find a likely place to dig a well. The trick—if you can call it a trick—is very simple; Father doesn't know how it works, but it does. He takes a Y-shaped branch of live wood, preferably willow, and pulls it as tight as he can, stretching the arms apart and holding the stem downwards.

When he is over water, the stick will turn in spite of anything he can do. Villagers say then that Father is consulting the wind and water spirits. It gives a good opening for teaching Catholic doctrine.

He has done well at that too. Seven years ago, there was one Catholic in Towfen; today, there are two thousand. This is the story pretty much all over the island. So many Chinese-speaking priests and religious were expelled from the mainland, that Taiwan enjoyed a boom in personnel. In eight years, the number of priests went from one hundred and sixty-three to more than six hundred. They found a receptive people. Whereas in China of the old days the average priest made around twenty converts a year, in Taiwan the average is thirty-four.

Everyone on Taiwan worships Ti Kong, the grandfather of all the gods. It is not too difficult, the Sisters say, to transfer this veneration to the One True God. Small wonder then that the twenty thousand Catholics of 1953 find themselves engulfed in the present Catholic population of two hundred thousand. Not many among a population of ten million, but we're getting there!

Father McCormick has another claim to fame. When he was a high school lad at The Venard, Maryknoll preparatory seminary near Scranton, Pa., a certain young teacher from Wilkesbarre, Pa., decided to be a Maryknoll Sister and came with bag and baggage to start her training at The Venard, too. The McCormick lad carried her trunk up to the attic in that dear old farm house which was our convent. Now he, as pastor (not to say Pope) of Towfen, welcomed Mother Mary Colman to his territory.

He did it up brown. He routed out his parish band replete with high hats and gold braid and had them at the bus station when we came in. Our bus was early, but they hastily gathered their instruments and gave a royal blast of welcome. Then they formed a line in front of the parish's 1948 Hudson (Father calls it a Huddleson), struck up "Seeing Nelly Home," and we were off down Main Street. There's a bit of P. T. Barnum in every good missioner!

Maybe it's not so much Barnum as the precious gift of enthusiasm. Missioners need it. Bishop James E. Walsh, whose enthusiasm for God has brought him to a Communist prison in Shanghai, once wrote: "A missioner is sent to a place where he is not wanted; to sell a pearl which, although of great price, is not recognized; to a people who are determined not to accept it even as a gift."

Sister Luella and Sister Paulita, who sell the Pearl in Towfen, are seasoned. They add up some twenty-five years with Hakka-speaking Chinese. Both were expelled—with fireworks—from Red China; both were marched through towns in disgrace. Sister Paulita witnessed the trial of Father Au, her pastor, since then a martyr for the Faith in Communist work camps. She was liberally plastered with mud and garbage en route.

But it hasn't dampened her enthusiasm either for the Faith or for the Chinese.

The Sisters live in a small house like every other house in town. At the parish center they are all things to all men; since nobody in the parish has been Catholic for more than eight years, everyone has a lot to learn. An "old Catholic" here counts six or seven years in the Faith.

Next day we were off to Houlung, half an hour down the coast. Here in the evening we heard Mass in the Village of the Eight-Cornered Forest —figure that one out! It is situated at the mouth of Eyebrow River. Eight or ten fishing families call it home. We walked down the country road in pitch black; Sister Paul Therese had a feeble flashlight in her hand but it shed no light on the mud-puddle situation. Even so, I don't think we missed any. Nobody was around. Small wonder—they were all in one large courtyard looking at Father Murphy's slide-talk on doctrine. He threw the image on a sheet tacked up against the brick house. When Adam and Eve appeared on the sheet a sea breeze ruffled it. The snake coiled and slithered; Adam and Eve shuddered and tried to edge away.

Since I know the story of Adam and Eve fairly well, I left the group and went around the house to the sea. A wisp of a moon had come up giving just enough light to glint the waves a bit and to show the nets drying on racks on the beach. Missioners feel a kinship with fishermen; the reason is obvious.

Back at the house we found the whole family preparing for evening Mass. We went under the doorway strung with papers left over from New Year, and passed the large pagan shrine just opposite the entrance. The grandmother and some of her sons are pagans here. They are hospitable but, of course, they aren't going to pull down their pagan shrine for us. In another room one of the men was setting up for Mass. He cleared off a table, hung up a drape with a crucifix attached to it and unrolled two scrolls to hang on the wall. A single electric bulb with a cord looped over the rafters to the main plug, glared over the makeshift altar.

It was a large room with earthen floor and brick walls. A single window, no more than two by three feet, was shut so tightly I don't think it had been opened in years. The inside of the tile roof was lined with bamboo slats. These and the sturdy rafters made a sort of storage place. I looked above me as I semi-squatted on a low bamboo stool six inches or so from the floor; oars, large pieces of driftwood, old sails, parts of nets for use as patches, some floats tied together—they all hung from or lay upon the rafters.

Father, when he came in, took off his motorcycle helmet and put it carefully on the nearest rafter. This annoyed an old lady of the house. As the oldest Catholic there, she appointed herself hostess and worked hard at the job. "Now Father," she said, bringing her 4'10" up to Father's elbow and tugging at his sleeve. "Don't be putting your helmet there. You'll forget about it and go off without it. Reach it down for me and I'll put it away right." She toddled off with the helmet and where did she put it? She hung it over an ancestor tablet on the pagan shrine next door.

There were soldiers there from an army camp nearby; there were fishermen, too, and boys and children of the house. They sat on wooden horses, on small bamboo stools like mine and on their own heels. The old pagan grandmother-matriarch took a stool and held the youngest in her arms. She was not going to miss any goings-on in that house. Some of the daughters-in-law sidled in or out, until the doorways became so jammed they were caught either in or out and had to stay that way.

Father vested and bent over the table. Mass began. A cloud of Taiwanese chant lifted from that motley group. Soldiers and fishermen, most of them not yet baptized, poured out the Mass prayers. It was so stuffy, so crowded, the smell of hard-working bodies was so thick in the air, it seemed as though we were underground in ancient Rome while one of the apostles celebrated exactly the same Mass. "Do this in commemoration of Me." The words quivered in the dank room.

Tahu is a forty-minute ride up into the mountains. It's a forty minutes close to eternity. The bus ducks through twelve natural rock arches, some of them deep enough to be tunnels. When you see a truck piled high with hay or scrap paper or sacks of rice or bamboo poles—when you see such a truck whizzing into one of these short tunnels, you hold your breath for the workman you know is sleeping on top of the load. More than one poor fellow has been scraped off and smashed on the road.

Sister Magdalena and Sister Rita Clare live in a tiny Japanese house in Tahu, surrounded by a dog, two cats, many plants and more mountains than you can count. Tahu's commercial reason for being is a silkworm factory where millions of the beasties eat their way to an early death in a silken shroud.

The silkworm starts life as one of many little black dots on a card, filed in a deep freeze at five degrees below zero. Everything is tidy. The eggs are arranged in circles all laid by one moth whose file number is imprinted on the card. There are thirty-two eggs from each moth in one circle. We saw a messy card on which several worms had been permitted to lay eggs any old way they wanted to. Most disreputable exhibition of unrestrained instinct!

On each 8½ x 11-inch file card, exactly sixteen thousand eggs adhered. The efficient administrator took several from the shelves in a walk-in freeze compartment. A single card of silkworm eggs, he estimated, would produce twenty kilos (forty-four pounds) of silk thread.

People who want to give the worms a happy home life for a while can buy a card or so of eggs and take them home. Three thousand worms, one woman told me as we watched her, can yield $1,000 NT (about $25.00 US) in about a month. But what a month it is! As another woman expressed it, "I used to keep silkworms but I don't have that many arms and legs any more."

Six times a day the wicker trayfuls of worms need attention. They must have fresh mulberry leaves; they must be transferred, one by one, from a dirty tray to a clean one; the brown paper underneath must be changed. The thing most to be avoided is wetness. Mulberry leaves must be picked after the dew has dried around 10:00 A.M. Then they should be cooled off down in the cellar or in some cave. At the factory, humidity is checked every hour of the day.

They eat voraciously; you can almost see them grow. Six days and six nights they eat, eat, eat. On the seventh day they rest and shed their little skins for new clothes. Within a month they are as big as your little finger. At last they stop eating and begin work. The mere thought of work blanches them; from a pale green they turn oyster white. They come to the edge of the tray and stretch their necks over the rim, searching some good place to go to sleep in. The haggard worm-tender pops each drowsy worm into a little hole in a straw mat and leaves him to weave his own shroud. Round and round and round he goes, up and over his head, down and under his tail. At the end he has spun out eight hundred yards of filament, so fine that the eye can hardly see it. Yet, later when the cocoon is bobbing around in nigh-boiling water, the sensitive fingers of girls can feel the slender filament. They lift five or six strands on to a bobbin twirling above and the patient work of the pampered worm is all unwound.

One of the neatest tricks I ever saw was that of a woman who trained silkworms to weave fans for her. When one of her little pets began to be sleepy, she made a frame of bamboo sticks spread fan-wise. Then she put the sleepy one between the sticks and moved him up and down until he had covered the spaces with his fine silk. The befuddled worm ended up with not even a shroud to cover his naked self. He died in the open.

Four thousand years ago, Lui Tzu in China discovered the voracious worm and the magnificent thread he spun. He learned how to feed the monster, keep him clean and dry, and let him spin out his shroud in comfort. Old Lui Tzu no doubt chuckled to think that the cocoon would cover not only the worm's lowly torso but the great ladies of all the world.

With Sister Marion Cordis, once from Chicago, I went out to Happiness Village, not far from Miaoli city. It had been a rainy morning, but the sun cleared in time for the regular Tuesday afternoon catechism class. After the bus let us off, we had quite a walk single file across the rice paddies. Any boys or girls aspiring to Maryknoll would do well to practice on railroad tracks or, even better, on a picket fence. We headed for a nest of houses set on an island surrounded by watery fields.

"How good is your heart!" The greeting came from Lai Mo, in the rice field. She was on hands and knees in the mud, pushing up the goo around each rice plant's roots. Only in Taiwan have I seen people work on hands and knees, dragging their feet through the mud. The idea is, they say, that you can do three rows at a time. In other countries, they work the mud with their feet, one row at a time. More than any other factor, this work habit accounts for the infestation of hookworm. But Lai Mo was not thinking of hookworm as she straightened and came toward us. "Don't start without me!" she called. "I have to change my clothes but I'll be there."

She had plenty of time. The other women, too, had thought we weren't coming, due to the rains. As we walked on to solid ground, they swarmed around, setting out chairs in the "big room," putting the table against the wall, clearing up the baby's things and the baby as well from the cement floor. Sister stood on a chair to hang the catechetical chart right in front of the unkempt pagan shrine facing the main door. It did not seem to be used much. A picture of the Sacred Heart occupied another wall and an oil painting of a Chinese woman, matriarch of the family, still another. Near this was something that haunted my dreams for months. A wall clock had been installed. A girl's face, lifted from some calendar or candy box, smiled from the bottom section. The eyes were cut out and they were pasted on the pendulum behind. At every tick of the clock, the eyes moved back and forth, back and forth. I tell you, after three hours of this, you are ready to jump into the fields and pull the rice plants up over you.

In all, eight women and their numerous progeny sat on the wicker chairs while Sister and the catechist talked. Men of the family helped with the setting-up and leaned in at the doorways to listen. When it came time to read the charts, one of them who had more learning than others pronounced the words slowly and distinctly.

All these people were so straightforward and direct. Their questions pertained to the basics: rice fields, money, sex, worship, ancestors and children. Like Lai Mo, just in from field work, most of their toes were caked with mud. Some had wooden shoes, but most were barefoot. A few wore Chinese saams, many had western dress, and nearly all had "pahmanetto." They had everything they needed—security, family, solid background. The seed was falling on good ground.

⟨ 17 ⟩ *Bound Feet and an Unbound Mind*

MOLIN's eyes are keen, even though wrinkles distort the blue tattoo over her chin and cheeks. Molin's teeth are strong in spite of the receding gums. For Molin is only in her forties; aborigine women look much older than they are. Molin's memory is accurate on her tribe's doings. And I was a stranger in Busia. She longed to acquaint me with the fine points of history there.

I listened to Molin tell of her father, chief of Sakura, a hamlet of good size not far from Busia, which is the end of the line for most buses. On a winding road, Busia is sixty miles from the coast and, since Taiwan is only eighty miles wide, it is just about dead center in the island. As with most primitive peoples, one village wars against another. It was so with Sakura.

When I was small, Molin said, it was always a gay evening when the men returned from head hunting. They would put the heads in the center of the village and prepare a feast. We children who served the wine always were told to serve the heads first. This was to accustom us to the sight of a severed head so we would not be afraid of them.

My mother never knew her father. When she was two days old, her father said to her mother, 'You gave birth two days ago and you will be resting today. I also will not work today. I will go hunting, instead.' However, he never came back. Probably someone from another village was out hunting, too.

The Japanese were masters of the island; we knew that. But for the most part, they let us fight out our little squabbles by ourselves. Perhaps our chief enemies were people from Mastoban. About thirty years ago things came to a head. There was a Mastoban woman married to the Japanese chief of police here in Busia. Many Japanese officials negotiated for an aborigine wife in order to keep their heads on their shoulders. The government recognized this and took care of the wives and children. When the father went back to Japan, his wife was supported and the children educated. This Mastoban woman was so cared for.

At the same time, a woman from my tribe at Sakura had also married a Japanese. He was only a common policeman and the marriage was not arranged for by the government. When the policeman went back to Japan, the Sakura woman was left to fend for herself. This was too much for my tribe to take, especially since the Mastoban woman's husband, as chief of police, had jurisdiction over our village, Sakura.

So my father and others planned vengeance. There was to be a children's

201

athletic meet at Busia, a general picnic day for all the families as the
Japanese like it. Men from Sakura had knives under their belts. When
we all stood for the National Anthem—that was the signal. They lashed
out right and left. They went into every house in Busia and killed every
last Japanese in the place. Then we all ran down to our villages to await
reprisals; we knew they would come. They came, and in far greater number
than we thought. Not only Mastoban people, but tribesmen from Losan
and Taocho joined up against us. The Japanese too were to send troops
after us. When we heard that, we knew the goose was cooked. We could
fight our own, but the Japanese would be too much for us.

At first, we thought there would be no escape; enemies were all around
us. We were all to die. My mother then said, 'Well, if we are to die, let
us sing first.' She had a lovely voice and sang the songs of our tribe for
half an hour. Just then, someone rushed in to say we could escape. My
father and brother would not go. 'We will commit suicide,' they said.
'We are responsible for the tribe. You and the children go.' So my mother
took us out into the forest. Thus, we lived.

Did you see the stone memorial tablet at the entrance to town? That
was put up in memory of the massacre. The reading on it is new. In the
old days it said 'In memory of the brave Japanese officials who died at the
hands of aborigine terrorists.' Now it says, 'In memory of the aborigines
cruelly massacred by the Japanese.' The Japanese paid for it and now it
commemorates us!

Molin laughed. How she laughed! She bent over double on the skimpy
folding chair we have in our doctrine-teaching room. Other women in
the class joined her. Molin's hand reached over and patted the hand of
Omrad next to her. They were great friends. Later Sister Louise Marie
said to me,

"Do you know who Omrad is? She's the daughter of the Mastoban
woman who married the Japanese chief of police. At first she and Molin
weren't so friendly, although both wanted to become Christians. We had
a little heart-to-heart talk with each. After all, Christians shouldn't be
looking daggers at each other over the catechism books. They're great
friends now."

Busia is a very, very small town. It's the jumping-off place for Aborigine
Territories, something like our Indian reservations in the States. The
census takers credit it with a population of three hundred but they must
have come on a good day. The number goes up or down according to the
arrival or departure of army camps working on the road, lumbering
parties, aborigine families come to town for a while and traders going
in or out the Aborigine Territories.

The whole town consists of two blocks of Wild West store fronts. Our
convent hides behind the Golden Prosperity Lumber Company office. The
church is a store front between the bus depot and the Thousand Happi-

nesses Rice Store. The sign on the outside proclaims not the virtues of
Three Excellences Dried Ginger or the Singer Sewing Machine, but the
fact that the Lord of Heaven Religion has invaded Busia. In spite of
such boasts, the church is extremely poor, with fifteen or so benches arranged to face the rear wall. This wall slides back to reveal the sanctuary
for Mass and closes during the day to make a small doctrine room. A
stairway at the left leads up to Father's quarters above.

Busia's Public Works Department is one old man who sweeps the entire
town at 5 A.M. each morning. The Sisters call him Ojii San (Honorable
Grandfather). He's always there bowing and smiling as they walk down
the deserted street to Mass each morning.

Sister Louise Marie is a doctor, a Japanese. Older people are delighted
that she can talk to them in the language they learned in school. In spite
of the massacre of 1930, the Japanese were respected in Taiwan and put
through many good measures. Sister Marie Bernadette is a nurse from
Hawaii and is of Japanese extraction. The two Sisters operate a clinic
in another store front on Main Street. Up to September, 1959, there had
never been a resident doctor in Busia. There is no hookworm up here
because there are no rice fields. Sweet potatoes, corn and millet are the
staples. "Everybody has roundworms and tapeworms," Sister Louise
Marie says. "Also T.B."

These aborigines take to Catholic doctrine like ducks to water. They
don't have many superstitions. So free are they of ancestor worship that
they don't even know where their parents are buried. The custom is to
bury the body without a coffin and place no marker on the spot. Our task
now is to get them to show respect for the dead and to remember them
in prayer.

Rugged women, these missioners! At Busia, as elsewhere, the day started
at 5 A.M. We met in the combination refectory, community room and
parlor to say Prime, first stint of the Divine Office for the day. The cat
met us there, already curled up in front of the small shrine to Our Lady.
As we recited the ancient psalms, kitty rose, yawned, stretched herself
and lay down with a sigh right on my feet. I let her stay; Busia's mountain
air is chilly.

Then down the street to the store-front church. Half an hour on the
benches talking to God, Who lives so unknown in this frontier town.
Father Knotek clumped down the wooden stairs from his upstairs rectory,
and we left for Mass in Sakura. We climbed into the jeep and were off,
without breaking the silence. The time before Mass is sacred to all religious; we don't chatter then.

The mountain road clings to the cliff like a frightened child. At one
spot there is a bridge built up of bamboos tied together with rattan, and
planks placed on top. The bamboos look rotted at the base. Father passed

this up, preferring to go the long way around the mountain curve. But even with four-wheel drive, we had trouble in the mud.

Nearing Sakura, Father Knotek leaned his full one hundred and sixty pounds on the horn. "What's the idea?" I shouted to Sister Louise Marie. "There's no traffic on this road."

"He's waking the people up for Mass," Sister called back. "We don't have a church bell in Sakura."

Sure enough. As we came closer to the church, men and women emerged from the cabins with a good-natured yawn and waved to the jeep flying past on the road.

We opened the church and Father went to the confessional. A line soon formed. Outside, a bugle tuned up. The sun had not yet topped the eastern mountains. Sakura, deep in the valley, gets no early nor late sunshine. But the sky was luminous and the boy bent backwards to give full blast to his music. It was Silent Night blazing away. Soon a trombone joined him as an older man put forth his early morning vigor. They swung into an Ave Maria which must have pierced Heaven itself.

Again I had to speak. "Why play music now?" I asked. "And why so loud?"

Sister Marie Bernadette smiled patiently. "In Sakura everything is loud," she said. "They have to play loud so that people won't hear the confessions going on. They're usually loud, too."

By this time the church was fairly full. Father began the Mass. It's always a High Mass in Sakura; the people like to sing. They have good voices if you accept their definition of a good voice. "She sings good!" means that you can hear her a long way off. The Mass of the Angels, that tried-and-true sturdy of every parish choir, rocked the mountain chapel. On less solid ground it would have started a landslide.

And home to breakfast. As we got near that wisp of a bamboo bridge, Father hunched his shoulders and called out, "Pray!" as we went flying over it. When we resumed breathing, Sister said, "You never did that before, Father."

"I know," he shot back with a sigh of relief, "but that road is so muddy. I figured if the bridge has stayed up for several months now, it just might be good enough to stay up today, too."

Busia mission has ten outstations, most of them within the Aborigine Territory. Police stations dot The Road (there is only one) and travelers must check through these points as they go along. Eleven miles and four heart attacks from Busia is a sort of platform, eight thousand feet above sea level. It's a level spot achieved by cutting the very top from a mountain. On all sides the ground slopes straight down. I felt I stood on top of a giant orange-squeezer. A bus, once a day, makes the passage over the mountain road, a service just a month old. On the first bus rode the mayor, school principal, postmaster and Catholic priest; it was a gala affair. Up to that time, aborigines had had to walk miles into town.

As we stood looking at valleys and mountains on every side, the Sisters pointed out towns where they go for several weeks at a time to prepare people for Baptism or First Holy Communion.

"There's Mastoban," and they pointed straight down into a deep valley. "It's five thousand feet down. You have to come up here and then slide down the five thousand feet. There's no road to take on the level."

"How do you get back?" I asked.

"It's a six-hour climb, but we make it. And over there," sweeping widely to mountains lost in the mists, "is Father Stratham's parish." They pointed out the vague location of many other towns, but the entrance to all of them seemed to be a long slide downhill and a stiff climb for several thousand feet, up.

Let me say it again—rugged women, these missioners!

Poli is fifteen treacherous miles downhill from Busia. Father insisted on taking us in his jeep, saying it wouldn't cost a cent since he could coast all the way. And besides, he was fairly sure of getting a good dinner out of it once he delivered us at the Poli convent. These Maryknoll Fathers are brilliant men.

On the way the Sisters gave me the sightseer's tour.

"Isn't this the place where Father Bauduin went over the bridge that wasn't there?" asked one of them. "You see, he was in a jeep just as we are now. It was quite dark. The bridge had broken but there was no sign or anything, of course. Fortunately, it had broken on the other side, so Father just rollercoasted down to the riverbed. It was dry; that was lucky too."

"And I think it was here that Father Carbin lost his motorcycle," chipped in the other. "He made the mistake of looking at the scenery and missed a curve in the road. He was lucky, too, for he saw where he was heading in time to jump off the motorcycle. It went over the edge and plunged down several hundred feet."

How deep-rooted is the desire to contemplate God! Away out here on this mountain road—indeed, long before there was a road—is the Monastery of the Awakened Soul where for centuries Buddhist monks have lived. It's a great pilgrimage place for all of Taiwan.

We found Poli in the throes of a wedding slated for the next morning at one of the outstations.

"I have to go out this afternoon and fit the bridal gown," Sister John Maureen said. So we went together.

"This is a hurry-up wedding," she explained as we walked through town to the bus station. "The bridegroom's grandmother died yesterday.

The young couple have to get married before she's buried. Once the old lady is put underground, there must be no festivity for one hundred days. That will land us into the rice-planting season and nobody can take time out for a wedding then. So they pushed the date up a month.

"A friend of mine sent me her bridal gown for such occasions. It makes the sacrament more solemn; we keep it on hand to lend around to brides. I only hope it fits, for we have so little time to do anything on it. We ought to clean up the church a bit too for tomorrow."

I knew I was elected for the cleaning; my prowess as a seamstress is limited.

I have wedged into some mighty crowded buses in my day, but never into the jam which filled this small bus out to Lai De Na (Village Within the Forest). As the last person squeezed in I found myself clutching my camera bag with one hand and grasping the bar along the ceiling with the other. A basket of cabbages knocked my knees inward behind and twenty people's feet pushed my toes in front. Just before me was a woman in worse straits than I. She had a baby several months old on her back and a child around two in her arms.

The women who were lucky enough to have seats offered to take the two-year-old on their laps, but he bawled lustily whenever it was tried. So the women took my bag on their laps and with my free arm I tried to help the woman's thin arm to hold that cantankerous child. The baby on her back, feeling neglected, put himself in the limelight by pulling his mother's hair and tugging at her ears. This was no fun, so he flung his head back and stared into my face. Good! He gurgled and put up one grimy hand to paw all over my face. Then he stuffed his fingers into my mouth. This was exciting! Baby reached up quickly and jerked my glasses. They were firmly anchored, thanks be to God and the religious habit.

Meanwhile the bus swayed from side to side, slid over tremulous bridges and grazed water-soaked rice fields. We passed many people waving for us to stop but the driver called out, "Get the four o'clock bus. We're full!" Believe me, when a driver in Taiwan says the bus is full, it is!

The bride-to-be was thrilled with the dress. She would have had to rent a gown otherwise. It fitted perfectly, except for the length. Her mother and assorted aunts and cousins set to work. They stood her on a bench and with mouthfuls of pins turned up the hem.

I went over to the chapel only a few doors away and swept the floor. Father comes out here once a week to say Mass. The bride's sister and brother came along to help. Christianity is so new in this village that there had never been a wedding in chapel before. The bride's family had been baptized only six months before; the groom's a year earlier.

Next to the chapel was the groom's house. Here the body of the grandmother lay. She had died a pagan, although she was a very kindly woman.

Her son, the groom's father, took us to see the huge coffin. It was sealed with bright blue plastic tape, three inches wide. A plate of rice was offered to the matriarch's spirit and joss burned steadily. Outside the house, tables were spread for the old lady's funeral scheduled for late the next morning, after the wedding. A sort of shabby canvas was draped over bamboo poles to shield guests from the sun. The groom's father had his hands full. Besides preparing for his mother's funeral, he was busy about his son's wedding. A carpenter, he was working on saw horses making wall boards when we came. "These are for my son's matrimonial room," he said. Then he showed us the special place in the house reserved for the new couple, a part screened off from the general large room of the house.

We hired a "haya," to attend the wedding next morning. "Haya" is pronounced as Bostonians pronounce "hire," and that's what it means, a "hired car," an English word transmitted through Japanese into Taiwanese. You soon find that haya drivers are not being especially polite when they leap from their seats to open all doors as soon as the car stops. It's a necessity; there is no hardware that works to open doors or windows in these cars. Ancient jalopies, turned in for ten dollars or so in the States, are shipped over to Taiwan to serve as taxis. The upholstery is in ribbons, the springs long dead, the windows cracked or missing, the paint no more. But they are elegant equipages in Taiwan.

Four of us Sisters, plus dusters, brooms, several vases and flowers for the altar, drove out in the haya. It was no more than one hundred feet from the bride's house to the chapel, but Sister offered the bridal couple the use of the haya to drive to their wedding. They were delighted. The bride stepped into it as Cinderella mounted her pumpkin coach, and at the end of the short ride she emerged glowing with pride.

It was the very first Catholic wedding anybody in that chapel had seen. The men sat on one side; the women on the other. Kerosene lamps lit the scene since there is no electricity in town. Before the Mass, the catechist coached the people on what to do. Then he became altar boy for the Mass. Once he flew down the aisle in surplice and stole to bring a chair from the confessional so that Father could sit down during the Gloria. He surely earned his salary that day. For him, too, it was a culmination of many months of work. With the first couple united in the Sacrament of Matrimony, he knew this group of converts started on the way to becoming a parish of stable Catholics.

From Poli to Changhua is not long in mileage, but several centuries in time. For Changhua is the "Dispensing Culture Place"; it has much more of old China about it. At Changhua I met Lim Sui Sam, a great lady.

She is utterly dignified even when sitting on the cross bar of a bicycle with her bound feet sticking straight out into traffic. Thus she rides to

Mass on Sundays, with her daughter Margaret Theresa pedaling. Bound feet make it impossible for her to walk from their house in the country. Lim Sui Sam makes a procession out of what could be a humiliating experience. I think the angels go before the mother and daughter, like motorcycle police, clearing a way for them in Taiwan's hectic roadlife.

The great lady was born seventy years ago at Lu Kong (Deer Harbor), a rich town of artisans, specialists in idols and temple gods. The town is noted for carving and gold leaf work. At five years of age, little Lim Sui Sam stretched out her feet and they were bound tight in long bands which twisted the toes under the instep. Her feet hurt, of course, and she grew up hobbling on bound feet as a well-born Chinese lady should, but all the poorer girls in town envied her.

She married well. It's on record that her husband rode a horse. Certainly his family owned most of the land around Changhua. He rode the horse to supervise his vast estates. They had six sons and a daughter. Most of them did well. The eldest son is a Government official, the second is a doctor. The third died of his intensive studies; his memory is sacred in this scholarly family. The fourth son keeps the rice fields; the fifth is the black sheep; his wife left town and he disintegrated. The sixth is in the Department of Fisheries.

The daughter too promised well. She was good in school and outstanding in athletics, which the Japanese regime emphasized. But one day she threw her hip out of joint. She became twisted and it was agony to walk. They consulted many Chinese doctors, but nothing could be done. On top of that misfortune, the father died. Then, the Chinese Nationalists took over the island and declared the Land Distribution of 1950. In the shuffle, the family lost most of their property.

Still they lived in the big ancestral home with three wide wings of stone and a beautiful moon gate at the entrance. Across this gate was the family motto, "The money and goods we own must be used for all mankind." Lim Sui Sam regretted her losses no doubt, but she did not pine over them. She was well loved in the neighborhood. A strict Buddhist, she ate no meat nor animal products—butter, cheese, milk, etc. "She lived on vegetables," everyone told us.

The crooked daughter, Jade Flower, went to Sister Antonia Maria's clinic about six years ago. Sister was able to put her hip back into the socket correctly. She walked, she leaped, she rode a bicycle! She invited all the Sisters out to her home and spread a picnic for them. She was then, and still is, manager for the entire estate, overseeing the workers, collecting rents and so on. Lim Sui Sam was the soul of Chinese hospitality to the strangely-garbed American women, guests of her daughter.

Jade Flower became interested in the Faith. A few others in that town thought they would like to study, too. Lim Sui Sam offered a room in her big house as a doctrine hall. Then the fun began. People started stoning the house. They said to Jade Flower, "Who are you, a young person and only a woman, to introduce a new religion into our village?" The persecution never fazed either of them. We withdrew after a few months lest they suffer more on our account. Jade Flower went on and was baptized Margaret Theresa in 1959. Her mother found it hard to give up her beautiful Buddhist shrine, treasured for so many years. But a year later, she too was baptized. They never fail to appear on Sundays for Mass; the crippled girl pedals her dignified mother along the crowded streets to church.

If ever we put out a compilation of Valiant Women, Sister Antonia Maria is going to be near the top of the list. Anyone who has seen the places where she has put in her twenty-three years in China and Taiwan, would start canonization proceedings. As a medical doctor, I suppose she has seen more "interesting diseases" and cured more "impossible cases" than a hundred practitioners in her native Massachusetts.

Jade Flower is only one of hundreds she can tell about. And yet it has all been done in little makeshift buildings, enlarged with lean-tos and, on occasion, expanding to under the nearest tree. Over twenty years I have seen her in Kweilin, Hong Kong and several places in Taiwan. The pattern of "Do the best you can with what you have," has never failed.

On a Saturday in Changhua, we saw her at work in the amalgamation of lean-tos she used as a clinic for a waiting line of about one hundred and fifty patients a day. She is working on a hookworm project, the scourge of this region. The parasite enters the body when the farmer is crawling on hands and knees in his rice field. As a graduate of Mt. Holyoke College, Sister was awarded the Mary P. Dole Fellowship to work on the project. She can study the pest well and perhaps will be able to help remove this one single factor which accounts for so much of Taiwan's physical troubles.

On Sunday, Sister's new clinic was dedicated. Not quite finished, of course (nothing is ever perfectly ready for us!), the new clinic rises amid rice paddies. Sister Antonia Maria beamed all afternoon, "This is the laboratory; this is the treatment room. People await their turn here, protected from wind and rain. My examining room is here; this will be a consultation room. Over here is the X-ray room, ready for when we get the X-ray." Marvelous, wonderful, top-notch!

On Monday I visited her in her glory. She seemed a bit saddened. "I'm lonesome," she admitted. "I'm so far away from the people." She is so used to working with the patients breathing down her neck, that she can't appreciate peace and quiet yet.

Another valiant soul in Taiwan is Brother Albert. For forty years, his good strong buildings have delighted eye and body in China and now in

Taiwan. Probably, the Communists in Red China today are rubbing their hands together in glee when they take over another of Brother Albert's mission buildings.

Brother Albert's modus operandi is simple. He builds himself a little hermitage and stays with the job day and night. Every shovelful of sand, every bolt and screw is put in right, or it comes out again. Vital statistics are simple: born and brought up in Switzerland, he came to America, entered Maryknoll in 1917 and came out to China in 1921. Now and then he visits his family in Switzerland but he has not been back to the States in twenty years.

In his small room at Pou Tau he has his drawing board at the end of his bed and plans for new buildings are thumbtacked onto it. When we saw him, his left arm was still paralyzed from a stroke six months before. He kept muttering "Patience!" because it fell helpless at his side as he sat on his bed.

"It won't even hold my papers down," he complained to Sister Antonia Maria.

"Never mind, Brother," she told him. "Remember how you were when this first happened." He grumbled but had to admit that life had come back to his legs and no doubt the arm would come along in time, too.

But so much to do, so many churches to be built, so many rectories, clinics, schools, converts! With the Church "bustin' out all over," it was hard for Brother to keep to one room with only a drawing board to vent his creative genius on.

The four thousand miles of the Taichung Prefecture (jam-packed with mountains) had, in 1951, only three priests and four thousand Catholics. Dominicans from Fukien had done magnificent pioneering work here, but many places were visited only once a year. Now, ten years later, Maryknoll has fifty-five priests and three brothers at work. The four thousand have expanded to twenty eight thousand. Besides us from Maryknoll other Sisters have pitched in. Providence Sisters from St. Mary-of-the-Woods in Indiana came here and rented a house. In ten years they had Providence English College with three hundred and seventy five students from all over the island in a three-year college course. The set-up is impressive, with dormitories, classroom buildings, auditorium, convent and a brand new library of substantial stone. At work in the Prefecture are Taiwanese Sisters, too, and Mandarin-speaking Sisters, refugees from Mukden, Manchuria. Also, a new community drawn from the locality who are being trained by Mercy Sisters from Hungary. And away out in the rice fields, is a Chinese house where live the Little Brothers of St. John the Baptist, a contemplative order founded in China by Father Vincent Lebbe of blessed memory. Recently, the Holy Father sent them a candle as "the most austere religious order on the island of

Taiwan." But austerities certainly don't deter avid postulants. The Little Brothers have growing pains all over.

Everywhere in Taiwan there is a sense of urgency, a "Let's live while we can" point of view. Taipei especially seemed a city not sure of tomorrow. It's a drab place, definitely a capital-in-exile, with neither the ancient beauty of China nor the bright commercialism of Japan. It's a city hanging in the balance. Something's bound to happen sooner or later to change its status. If the Reds leave mainland China, the capital will shift back there; if the Reds take over Taiwan, Taipei will be an outpost of China again. Every day in Taipei, I was reminded of Manila during the three long years of Japanese occupation in World War II when the question palpitated in the very air: Are the Americans coming back or aren't they?

While Free China waits for the answer, children are growing up. Our work in Taipei is with university students; certainly some are brilliant. For Sister Ann Mary teaches English in both the National Taiwan University and the Taiwan Normal University. Both of these have highest ratings. In 1961, for instance, thirty thousand high school graduates took examinations to fill some ten thousand University freshman places. Of these, the fifteen hundred best will be permitted to attend National Taiwan; the high school graduate has one chance in two hundred of "placing" at this great university where eight thousand students are enrolled. A small percentage of the rest will go to Taiwan Normal. About one-fourth of these crack troops of Free China's intelligentsia are women.

Campuses are in the city behind high walls, but they are not the rolling green lawns we imagine. Instead, as befits the most densely populated country in Asia, the lawns have yielded to vegetable gardens and miniature rice fields. Experimental agriculture is a most popular course at the University. Classrooms are shabby for the most part; halls are unswept; windows bleak and bleary. But the education the students get seems to be top-notch. And, after all, that's what they come for. Perhaps as a reaction to Communism, perhaps as a flash of enlightenment, perhaps as both and for other reasons as well, University students account for more than half the conversions to Catholicism in Taiwan. There are well over one thousand members of the Catholic Students Association at these two great universities.

Certainly, there are no rah-rah boys on campus. Life is too serious for them and for their country. All they have to do to get settled down to the stern business of life is to walk outside that high wall. There they will see immense bulletin boards on which the city's newspapers are posted under glass for all the world to see. The headlines there are guaranteed to make any Chinese young man resolve with grim determination to do his best to make Free China stay free.

KOREA

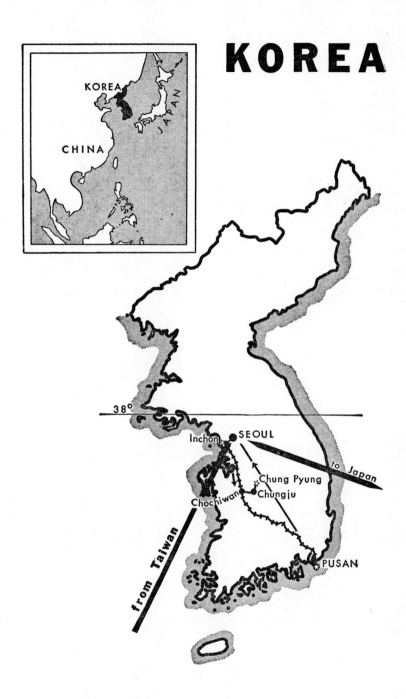

KOREA

⊰ 18 ⊱   *Elizabeth, Eulalia, Ephrem*
and Assorted Others

THERE may be, somewhere, a person who can stay untouched by the Korean people. If there is, I don't want to meet him. No, not ever.

The Land of Morning Calm has been anything but calm for the past sixty years. And there is more of mourning there than of morning. Sometimes it must seem to Koreans that black night has closed in. Their little peninsula has been conquered, exploited, mowed down by tougher neighbors and occupied by whoever feels like sitting on it. The African proverb says: When elephants fight, it is the grass that suffers. Korea has furnished the grass for a good many years now. But according to a Chinese proverb: Have patience—grass soon becomes milk.

Koreans have learned patience. Rice fields, bare mountains, donkeys and carts, men in white and women in dainty pastel colors—you can't imagine anything more peaceful. Barley grows in shaggy rows; rice seedlings spread like velvet; wheat waves in greenness. Far in the distance, barren hills rim the skyline and new thatch on village roofs dots the slopes. Orchards are in bloom—apples and pears. Here and there children in gay colors spread over the fields on school picnics. Pink, yellow, lavender and light green, the women's dresses and parasols contrast nicely with the white gowns of men, walking along the roads, or treading the narrow rice paddies. The farmer trails his ox, with the good earth breaking before the plow as the sea parts before a ship. Work is slow, not to say prehistoric. To repair a rice paddy dike, three men man one shovel; #1 pushes on the handle, #2 and #3 pull strings attached to the shovel blade to lift the dirt and toss it on top of the dike.

It's hard to believe that thirty-three thousand American boys died here less than ten years ago. The countryside tells you nothing. But talk to those three men at the shovel; chat with the man with the ox; stop for a moment the dainty-colored Korean woman who hurries along the road with a jug on her head. Each has a sad story to tell.

Maryknoll Sisters in Korea staff two dispensaries—one in a country

215

town, Chong Pyong in central Korea; the other at Pusan, the big port city at the south. Country or city, the work is endless.

You should see the line-up on the roadway in front of the small one-story brick clinic at Chong Pyong any day of the week and Sundays as well. The favorite ambulance is a flat platform slung between two bicycle wheels. The patient lies on the floor; somebody in the family pushes it. They jolt along the roads for miles. Three or four very sick people on such carts are always waiting in the line, besides the mothers carrying babies, and young children or old people who can't afford a cart. At least a hundred patients every morning. What hurts is that they can't all be cared for. Some must turn away to return tomorrow. It is Sister Ann Patricia's heart-breaking job to select those who need care most.

Sister Maria Corazon, M.D., is an old hand at relieving misery. A Filipina with flashing smile and quick dark eyes, she hails from the broad plateaus of northern Luzon. She set her heart on being a doctor and made her way through the University of the Philippines in Manila. Then she decided to be a Maryknoll Sister as well. So she came to the States. For twenty-three years now, those quick, experienced eyes have been sizing up the ravages of disease as one after another miserable patient comes to her examining table. In interior China, in Hong Kong, in Macao and now in Korea, she has seen more war-victims than one would care to think about. Not the battle casualties, but the innocent bystanders. I stood beside her at Chong Pyong as she examined a bundle of rags which enclosed a six-month-old baby. The mother had died; Pok Dong, aged twelve, brought his baby brother to the clinic practically every day. For a wastrel of less than ten pounds at five months, Kyo Chul wasn't doing so badly now. Sister Maria Corazon looked over his tiny frame and nodded her congratulations to Pok Dong. "Very good," she commented. "You've done well. Now that the worst is over"—and she started picking little grey lice off the bundle of rags as she said this—"you'll have to start cleaning him up. That's the next job; he gets a bath in good hot water with plenty of soap, today. Sister will give you the soap together with the milk feedings. See you tomorrow!" Pok Dong squared his shoulders and almost saluted. He picked up his charge and left with a big job to do.

Chong Pyong is really in the country! The people are what the books call "unspoiled." We saw that one day when we went out to a village in Father Coffey's "sort-of" station wagon—meaning that it is really a panel truck with two wooden benches to accommodate passengers. (Accommodate isn't quite the right word, either.) Three of us Sisters were on one bench talking about old friends and old times as Sisters always do; we couldn't see the passing countryside, anyway. Then we stopped and Father came around to open the door in the back. Old Il Ok was walking to town and Father had offered her a ride. Il Ok was overjoyed. She had never ridden in a car, let alone a handsome truck. She stood a little hesitant at the back door; then, like any polite Korean, she stepped out of her shoes and entered the compartment with us. It looked like a house to her. Only six miles later did she glance out over the driver's shoulder and realize that she was moving. A cry of anguish brought us all to a halt. "My shoes!" she moaned. We turned back, of course, and there were her shoes right in the middle of the road where she had stepped out of them.

In talking about medical work, one is apt to slip into a morass of statistics—numbers, cases, types of disease, laboratory tests, home visits. My mother once complained as she lay in a hospital bed with a pin through her knee and her leg up to the ceiling in traction, "In this place I am only a compound fracture of the tibia." Because the physical need is so urgent, the broad humanities sometimes have to take a back seat. In mission clinics such as Maryknoll Sisters have in so many parts of the world, there is little danger of over-specialization. We must all be, more or less, general practitioners using the latest techniques often with improvised equipment. It makes for the simple direct approach; it makes for a concept of the whole person.

Apropos of this, in Chong Pyong, I helped a queen die like a queen. Queen Elizabeth she was, too. Sister Edith Marie took me sliding down the clay hills and over the slippery rice paddy paths to where Elizabeth was panting on the vestibule of heaven.

"Marita came this morning before Mass to say that Elizabeth had died during the night," she called over her shoulder. "But just when I had made arrangements for the funeral she came back to say that Elizabeth wasn't really dead yet. So I don't know what shape we will find her in."

The afternoon sun slanted into my eyes; I had all I could do to keep up with the fleet-footed nurse. I said nothing in reply but thought, "Ten to one she's dead by now."

Sister thought so too at first when we opened the paper-thin door of the mud brick room, barely five feet high, which had been built on to Bernadette's hut. It was one of ten or twelve houses clustering on a patch of dry land set in the middle of flooded rice fields. Elizabeth's black tousled hair was up against one wall; her feet against the opposite wall. That's how tiny the room was. The old women and children—the only ones left in the village on such a good working day—crowded around that small lean-to. Sister touched the waxy cheek, lifted her eyelids, parted her lips and felt under the quilt for her heart.

"She's still breathing," she said, "but the medicine Bernadette gave her this morning is still in her mouth. She can't last long."

She called her, "Elizabeth, Elizabeth! It's the Sunyo. Your friends are here." But she could not make connections. The hands, with black rims around the nails, hard and chapped, were stiff.

As Sister Edith Marie worked at cleaning her patient, she told me the Queen's story. Just before Christmas, 1960, Elizabeth came to the clinic at Chong Pyong, walking four miles from Mugi Village (Beyond Comparison Town). Sister Corazon diagnosed cancer of the uterus. She came several times for treatment; then, the last time, she asked for Baptism. Although she was a second wife, she was obviously a terminal case and her husband knew it. Baptism was given and she went away very happy indeed.

She walked home that evening to Beyond Comparison Town. She knocked at the door of her home. The husband and wife #1 had had a conference; they realized that Elizabeth would be a burden from then on. So they told her to get going and stay gone. It was late December at the 37th parallel—such as southern Missouri—but she slept that night under a tree.

Next morning she had a showdown. "I'll take my two daughters," she said. They were ten and eleven, children of her first husband, killed in the Korean War. They were freely given her.

"I'll take my things, too," she said.

"What things?"

"My extra skirt, the white rayon one. My two towels. My winter jacket. My comforter. My chopsticks and spoons." She tore around the room grabbing them up as she spoke. There were more than twenty pairs of chopsticks and many long-handled spoons. In past days of glory, Elizabeth had operated a tea shop. A nice one, too.

The two girls helped her stow the stuff into a compact bundle. She lifted it on her head and walked out. Straight to an orphanage. "I'm dying," she told the superintendent. "Take my children." She would not stay herself.

Where to go? In Chong Pyong, the homeless always go to the railroad station. At night they let you spread your quilt on the floor. Elizabeth selected a corner and set up housekeeping. During the day, she went out begging food. But she became steadily weaker, hemorrhaging constantly.

Then she struck up a friendship with Pyong Il. He was just a tramp himself, but he had a shack down against the railroad embankment. Pyong Il took Elizabeth off to his shack one day when she was too weak to get up. He was goodhearted. He kept her for a month, and one day he carried her on his back to our clinic. That's how we had contact with her after a space of three months or so since her last visit.

Sister Edith took her on as a patient for house calls. Elizabeth then earned her title of Queen; she craved the nice things she had had once; how she hated drabness! Sister always brought food as well as medicine, and fed her lying there on the quilt unable even to sit up. Once she brought some rice. Elizabeth took a spoonful. Then she put up her hand protesting at a second spoonful.

"Who cooked that rice?" the Queen asked.

"Why? What's wrong with it?"

"Did you American Sisters cook that rice?"

"No, it was a Korean woman. One of the Catholic women of the parish did it for you."

Elizabeth sighed. "Ah, she should know better! She didn't put enough salt into it."

The old tramp, Pyong Il, was kind, even self-sacrificing. But his language was rough, his manners uncouth. Eventually, Elizabeth's frayed nerves added too much suffering to her worn-out frame. One day, Sister Edith Marie found her face set and her body rigid. "I can't stay here," she stated. "He doesn't understand. I must have a woman take care of me."

Sister Edith Marie went house hunting. It isn't easy in any country to find someone willing to take in a dying woman who needs a lot of care. But Bernadette, a widow, agreed.

"You may find things hard there," Sister told the Queen. "Bernadette is a good woman and kind. But she is not educated as you are. Sometimes she may say things that seem rough to you."

"Oh, I don't mind now," Elizabeth said. "I've lived two lives. I've been rich and now I'm so poor." Silence for a time.

"Sister?"

"Yes, Elizabeth?"

"I'll try, Sister. I'll try to be patient at last."

Father Coffey brought Elizabeth in his jeep—as far as the jeep could go. Then a man carried her across the rice fields. Sister followed with the quilt, the bundle and the box of chopsticks and spoons.

Bernadette had three children and a house. She did her best to earn the small money she got for taking care of Elizabeth. But Christian charity urged her to do more. Her house had only two rooms; she gave the tiny one to Elizabeth, and she and the three children crowded into the other. Every day at crack of dawn, she went out to work in the fields. Before she did, she fixed up Elizabeth, to make her comfortable for the day. Marita, her oldest, stayed close by all day to be of help should the patient call.

So! This seemed the end. I knelt just outside that small door. The neighbors knelt too; the children crouched quietly. We said a rosary in Korean. I confess my mind was not on it. I was thinking of the people, all over the world, dying at that moment while friends said the rosary in French, Spanish, Quechua, Kiswahili, Italian, Tagalog, Hakka and Hoklo, Dutch, Finnish, and the rarer Equimaux dialects. Elizabeth was not the only one edging close to those eternal gates. I hoped that our Korean rosary would spread over the world and help them all; that their rosaries would ease Elizabeth's way. The Church mothers them all.

There was just the slightest breath as we finished. Sister bent over. Yes, she had gone. Sister rose and took a small black lacquer box from the bare shelf over Elizabeth's head. In it were her identification papers and a snapshot. Two little girls.

"Her children," Sister said. "That was her only regret these last few days. Yesterday she said, 'They will never know if their mother is alive or dead.' I promised to tell them."

She opened her nurse's bag to put the papers in.

"Oh, I forgot!" She took out a huge pear. "Marita, do you want to have this for yourself and your brothers?" Marita needed no second invitation.

"I always bring Elizabeth a pear," Sister explained. "She liked them so. She told me why, once. It's because they're expensive. A queen to the end, she was."

We left the village, passed over the spiderweb of dikes over the rice paddies, waved good-bye to the women and children and began scrambling up the rocky path to Chong Pyong mission. The Queen is dead; the Queen lives forever!

And, just to show you that tragedy and comedy stalk around together like twins in Korea, as elsewhere, it was that night I met Eulalia. You see, Queen of the Martyrs parish in Chong Pyong put on a program to welcome the "No. 1 Sunyo," meaning Mother Mary Colman. But even if someone lesser had come or even if nobody had come, we would have had a program. Eulalia was ripe for one.

The first hint that this was to be a really big affair, however, was this: Jacobe, the parish handy man, repaired the steps to the parish hall. That is, he tacked a board under the sagging second step and even went so far as to put a brand new board over the third step which has been missing for months—ever since the night last winter when somebody in town needed fuel for his stove more than the parish needed that third step.

The next hint was that the performers put on their lipstick around 4 in the afternoon, even though curtain time was set for 7:30 Korean time, which isn't at all what American watches register. This meant that the performers ate no Evening Rice lest the lipstick be smeared.

At 7:30—when will we ever learn?—we Sisters made an entry and found things in turmoil. So we backed out again and stayed looking at the remains of the sunset until we got the high sign to re-enter. The parish hall was once the church. The rough floor boards have been smoothed by wear. Wicker chairs were set out for the Fathers and Sisters and the Honorable Catechist. On the right was Ladies' Row; on the left the Gentlemen's line-up. They all sat on their heels. The children toddled back and forth filling in the middle with a shifting population. One took a flying leap to Mother's lap and stayed there for the evening.

The Honorable Catechist stood up in his stocking feet and read a long scroll, unrolling it as he went along until it fell like broad ticker tape in a heap beside him. Then he bowed, rolled it all up again and presented it to Mother. A girl in lovely Korean dress brought a bouquet to present to Mother. She shook her head several times to make her long black braid twitch from side to side.

"She seems proud of that pigtail," I commented.

"She ought to be!" said Sister Corazon. "She rented it for this occasion. See? She has braided her own short hair into it to keep it secure."

Preliminaries over, the performance began. The curtain had an odd design. Then I recognized it. The whole thing was made of flour sacks sewed together. The writing was upside down:

USE NO HOOKS
THE UNITED STATES OF AMERICA
DONATED BY THE PEOPLE OF
BREAD FLOUR
ENRICHED BLEACHED

Suddenly a small boy ran across the room pulling the curtain aside. The stage stood revealed and we were off. Drills and dances, duets and solos. A shabby young man sang about How Bends the Willow; a robust girl bent our ears back with O Susanna, Don't You Cry translated into Korean. Every now and then Sister murmured, pointing out some moppet, "That's Eulalia's grandchild." After the fifteenth grandchild had jerked a quick bow and run off stage, I asked,

"For Heaven's sake, who's Eulalia?"

"She's that old lady in the fur-lined jacket, clapping her hands like mad over there. She's dying to be asked to perform herself."

Sure enough, she was asked to sing a song with Dolorosa, about her own age. Much giggling, much coaxing, far too much protest to fool anybody. Then she permitted herself to be lifted to her feet and the two old ladies stood up to perform.

Dolorosa was no match for Eulalia. She sang mildly, but not the same song nor the same key as Eulalia. She began to feel outdone and snickered. Then she succumbed to the giggles entirely and sat down. Eulalia carried on alone. During the song, she felt the impulse to do a wee bit of dance. That went over well; she took on new and daring steps. They too got applause and Eulalia was off for the evening. Once she crumpled and started to retire to her place among the women on the floor, but the intoxication of a multitude's approval roused her to her feet again. A high pitched song, made up on the spur of the moment, went with the dance. How she ever had breath enough to do both is beyond me. Only when the boy raced across the room with the curtain, shutting her off from the admiring public, did she subside.

I glanced at the line-up of men watching this old woman and enjoying her so. Not in any sneering fashion, but to applaud a good job well done. There was Anton, a soldier home for a few days from patrolling North Korea at the 38th Parallel. And Joseph, the clinic's Laboratory Technician, better educated by far than most of Chong Pyong. And a lad who calls himself in new-found English, "College John," because he is the only young fellow in town who ever went to college. He came up to Mother and introduced himself in English. "Good evening, Mother. I am College John. I would like to strike up with you a Long-Lasting Friendship. It is a Beautiful Evening; do you not think so?"

The Honorable Catechist, very dignified in spotless light grey coat and pantaloons, restrained himself to very moderate applause during the performances. But at the program's end, he advanced to the middle of the room, laid aside his high horsehair hat denoting the scholar, and led the assembled multitude in a rousing Banzai! in triplicate for Mother.

And then, there was Ephrem. In his late 70's, pretty far gone with tuberculosis, he came to the clinic from quite a distant town about a year ago. He was well-educated and keen of mind. "Why do you do these things for us? Why don't you stay in the Beautiful Country, America?" he asked. Of course he got a catechism to read and several books. "Thank you! Thank you!" and off he went.

A year later he came back. I saw him on the bench, an old scholar with quiet dignity, a radiant face and short cropped white hair. No, he didn't want any medicine. Not even an aspirin. He wanted to go to Confession, that was all. He had read—practically memorized—the little book. He loved this God of Mercy Who was so anxious to forgive his past misdeeds. And now that he felt stronger, he came to be forgiven. He had written down the prayer before Confession on a small piece of paper and there he sat memorizing the words as nervous and excited as a child.

Sister Carol has stopped by to visit Ephrem since then. His family is just as friendly; even the dog accepted her without a yelp. Most unusual in Korean dogs. Ephrem is all apostolic fire. He tried to coax his wife to go out and preach this new doctrine to their neighbors, but she, a shy old woman without a tooth in her head, is not the St. Paul her husband is. "I won't live long," says Ephrem, "but I hope to live long enough to bring my whole village to the God of Love. Then I can rest in peace."

It was delicious in Chong Pyong. Nevertheless, we were always conscious that when three guests step in the front door of a compact convent, three little mission Sisters must set up beds in the doghouse or under the stairs.

But they seem to have a good time doing it. There's no protest from any of them, saints that they are, not even at the fantastic methods they must use to take a bath. Someday, when I need a Ph.D. to tack behind my name, I'll write a masterly thesis on "Baths of the World, and How They Are Taken." Chong Pyong has, in a space no bigger than the bottom of a good-sized bathtub, a wood burning stove and a pile of fuel beside it, a fifty-gallon oil drum filled with cold water, a crock about three feet high embedded in cement with a fire roaring under it, a shower curtain, several dippers, assorted hooks for hanging clothes and a bench. There is just room left for a very slender bather.

We liked to see smiling faces at our departure, so Mother or I managed to do something at each mission to make the parting easier. If not positively joyful. In Ceylon I broke one of their two kerosene lamps; in Hong Kong, Mother dropped twenty or so dress hangers on the floor at 2 A.M. In Africa, it was beet juice spilled on the tablecloth. The Sisters saw us off with radiant faces. I forget just what we did at Chong Pyong but the jubilation at the railroad station was unforgettable. It must have been something pretty terrible to make them so happy to see us off.

The one-hundred-fifty-mile trip south to Pusan was eventful too. It started out mildly enough, with the train slipping through terrain that rivaled a travel poster. All of a sudden from the seat behind us came shouts, yells, slaps, grunts and scuffling. A fight. And a good one too between two men. Thief! Blackguard! Robber! Villain! He stole my money! Liar! and that most awful of insults, Turtle! There was no slugging with fists. Rather, each tried—successfully—to slap the other's face.

By the time I looked around, the Complainant had the Defendant by his very handsome necktie. He clutched the poor fellow around the neck pulling the tie tighter and tighter. Trainmen hurried down the aisle. Tch! Tch! Such goings on! This sort of thing happened in Third Class coaches, but never in Second.

They soon had them separated. They hustled the Accused into a small space at the end of the coach where the switch boxes and other paraphernalia were installed. While the car reverberated with shouts from Money Loser, I could see that the trainmen had the Suspect pretty well pulled apart, searching him. He did look like a City Slicker—young, impeccably dressed, with wavy hair and Injured Innocence all over his face. However, nothing was found on him. They took away his identification card without which no Korean travels abroad, just to insure his staying aboard for further investigation.

Then the man who seemed to be the chief trainman came over to Sister Augusta with the identification card, written on one side in Korean and the other in English. It was odd, indeed. The Korean side identified him as Kim Chyong; the English one as J. K. Chung. The head trainman straightened in puzzlement. As he did, I saw his armband giving his official position. On it was written in English letters: J A N I T O R.

While the Janitor was still scratching his head, the Prisoner-at-the-Bar had hopped off the train and was gone. "What will he do without an Identification Card?" I asked. "Don't worry. He probably has six others he can use," Sister said.

The incident started a little conversation between the Janitor and Sister Augusta. It began with the usual question:

"How old are you?" said the Janitor.

"Why don't you guess?" Sister countered.

He thought a while. "I would say, 35."

"Thank you very much indeed!" Sister bowed.

"I am 35 and my wife is 32."

"Yes?"

"We have three sons and a girl."

"Very good indeed. I congratulate you both." The preliminaries over, he got down to business.

"Were you brought up to be a nun, as our Buddhist nuns are, or did you choose the life yourself?"

Sister sighed. She has been through this so often she has a stock reply. "Sit down and I'll tell you all about it." They were off for a half-hour's Korean conversation. It ended with his handing her his business card and asking if he might bring his 32-year-old wife to visit the 35-year-old Sunyo. Sister Augusta, who bade farewell to 35 some years ago, graciously acceded.

I don't know if they ever arrived, for as soon as we landed in Pusan, we were embroiled in so many different activities all going on in the same compound, that a 100-megaton bomb could have gone off at one end of it and I would never have been the wiser. The compound itself stands practically upright against a hillside. Any rocks or stones started from the top make a fine splash as they hit the muddy street at the base. As do any children, peddlers, garbage cans, small carts, bicycles with or without riders and shacks with or without inhabitants that get a push to start them downhill.

The only access to this hill is Harmony Alley. At the bottom it is nearly ten feet wide but it slims to about six inches away up in the heights above the city. I know. Sister Dolores and I followed Harmony Alley to its logical conclusion—standing on a ledge of thin air overlooking Pusan's magnificent harbor. Our Maryknoll Sisters' Clinic was directly below. One false step and we would have landed on our own dinner table, through the roof.

My room faced Harmony Alley. Looking out the window was a study in Korean types. I could see myself an International Scientist looking through my microscope at a laboratory slide of Korea's blood stream. I should have come away with something very profound about the fundamental psychology of the Korean people, but I found every last one of them an individual. To tell the truth, I have a hunch that the fundamental Korean isn't much different from the fundamental anything else.

My window faced the mid-section of a Z-curve on Harmony Alley, and since the whole street is really a roller-coaster slide, people came around the upper bend as if catapulted into view. They half ran, half slid down the mid-section and twirled out of sight where the alley took a sharp left turn directly under my window. Going up was another matter. This was a steady climb. If heavily burdened—and they all were—a rest beneath my window was a "must."

It was around 8 A.M. The first to come around the upper bend was an old man in battered Korean horsehair hat, tied under his chin. He edged his way along, afraid of slipping and starting a terrifying roll to the street below. Children with school bags fastened between their shoulder blades ran past him. Several men in western clothes hurried by. A woman with a bundle on her head, a bunch of green vegetables on top of that, a baby on her back and a toddler by the hand, came by more cautiously. The whole cargo twisted as she turned slowly to watch the old man. He had gone to the side to peer into the deep gutter by the side of Harmony Alley. All night long the rain water had rushed down these gutters from the hill above. The woman spoke. It might have been, "Looking for something, Grandpa?" But he did not answer. She shrugged as best she could, burdened as she was, and went on.

Still huffy, she passed a tinker with his box of stockings, neckties, old bottles, used clothing, odd bits of candy, a few combs, etc., staggering up the hill to make what sales he could in the huts which clung by their eyebrows to the hill above. He is not above trading wares. A good tin can, some wire, a used but usable electric bulb, or an empty bottle preferably with the label intact was legal tender. Oh, why the label intact? So he can fill it with water or something and sell it for the genuine article, to be sure. The tinker, as all tinkers in Korea do, was clinking together a crude pair of scissors to advertize his wares, just as the Good Humor man tinkles his bell, or the junkman of my youth used to string old bells on his cart. The tinker paid no heed to the old man in white coat and pantaloons peering into the gutter. He trudged to the upper bend and disappeared, seeking the Golden Fields of Commercial Enterprise up yonder.

A young soldier in dapper khaki almost barged into him as he shot around the bend. Behind him was a "jiggy man," a stocky fellow with the A-frame on his back loaded with small branches. Not a heavy load, but horrendous in size. He would sell it all in the market below. Several girls in billowing velvet skirts and pastel jackets hurried past him. They had slept the night before probably on a ragged rice straw mat in a shack of old lumber and tin; they had cleaned those pretty white teeth this morning over a brass basin outside their front door and tossed the water over the cliff where it would land on our roof. If we were lucky, that is. Yesterday, they had carried baby brother strapped to their backs, and tomorrow they would be beasts of burden cooking over open fires and scrubbing sooty crocks beside the river. But today—God bless them!— they were young girls off for a day in the town below, dainty, sweet and gay. Their laughter was delicious to hear.

Halfway down that mid-section of the Z-curve, they stepped aside to let two men who had drunk not wisely but too well, stagger past them. They were on the verge of that condition Sister Augusta means when she says "they feel no pain." Arms entwined, the chums held each other up. They had spent what was left of the night huddled against our clinic wall. But the first patients arriving with the dawn had started them on the long climb home to bed and probably a good excoriation from the wife.

There's a shack built up against our wall, right under my window. The family is poor and has no place to go, so we let them stay. As the two drunks weaved past, the woman in this shack emerged with a basin of soiled clothes. She went back in and brought out a bucket of water. Plainly, she was all set for laundry day. She saw the two ex-revelers, put her hands on her hips, called something to them to which they paid not the slightest heed, bit her lip and went back into her shack. The two pals saw the old man poking in the gutter and staggered over to chat with him.

A fairly well-dressed workman now shot around the upper bend and started down the street at a run. He pelted along. Suddenly, he saw the bucket of water beside the soiled clothes and pulled up short. He glanced back. The inebriates had their backs to him. The old man did not raise his eyes from that gutter. Suddenly, the well-dressed man knelt on the street before the bucket of water, leaned over and took a long drink as a horse drinks. He rose hurriedly, glanced at the three again, and dashed off wiping his mouth with his sleeve. Why he did it, I don't know. Perhaps, he figured that every drop of water in his home had to be hauled step by step up that hill, and here was a bucketful of it unguarded. How could he answer on Judgment Day if he had not at least made some use of it?

The woman came out again with her laundry bats—short, heavy clubs. She began the endless job of beating her husband's white coat clean. She wet it, soaped it, placed the sodden mass on some stones nearby and beat the living daylights out of it. Her own clothes could be grimy, but her husband's coat—ah, that was different!

The two happy gentlemen gave up such an unprofitable conversationalist as the old man, and left him to continue his gutter inspection. Suddenly the old fellow went down on his knees and reached down into the drain. Farther and farther he bent into it. Head and shoulders disappeared entirely. One leg kicked wildly and I thought he was head first in the muck. But no, he slowly emerged. First the shoulders, then the head, then the arms, finally the hands. What did he hold in them? It was squarish and flat and small, maybe ten inches by three inches. He tottered in triumph across the road and placed it on a small pile there, something I had not noticed before. His prize was a piece of wood, part of a carton. Use? Well, dried out, it could be coated with Japanese lacquer as part of a piece of a little box or a drawer, or a Korean inlaid screen. Or he might sell it for a patch over a knothole in somebody's hut. At the very least, it would bring something as firewood. The old man placed his treasure tenderly on the pile. He toddled back to the gutter and peered once again. Wily old boy. He knew that last night's rain would wash many things down hill. Finders keepers; losers weepers.

But the real reason why I watched Harmony Alley was not to spy on opportunists like Grandpa. Around the lower bend, just beside the woman who was beating her husband's coat to dazzling whiteness, were the lines of patients for the Maryknoll Sisters' clinic.

⪤ 19 ⪥ No Time for Tears

AFTER plunging downhill for more than a mile, Harmony Alley meets Tae Dong Street as a flood washes up against a slow freight train. People coming down more leisurely slopes are on their way to market. The market itself strings along up Tae Dong Street for a ways— a few peanut stands, a couple of casual sellers of cotton cloth laid out on a tarpaulin or displayed against our grey stone retaining wall. Perhaps, a wheeled bookstall parked for the morning where the gay comic book covers can attract children.

There is selling advantage to this juncture of Harmony Alley and Tae Dong Street. Here congregate the people who hope to get into the Maryknoll Sisters' clinic. There are hundreds every day. No one is there merely for a sore toe; everyone needs care and has probably needed it for a long time. More than one lies on the street; many are propped up against the wall; so very many hold sick children. At that time of the year tuberculous meningitis raged while I was there. Harmony Alley was filled with the querulous wailing of unconscious children held tight in someone's arms, or sprawled on a blanket of some sort on the street. Harmony Alley at this point is paved with misery.

The gate opens at 8 o'clock. The children are carried in, the wives with sick husbands and the husbands with sick wives lean on each other's shoulders, the tarpaulins are picked up from the street and four-cornered through the gate. Then the waiting benches are full, the floors are crowded, and the daily task of relieving as many as possible begins.

We have four Sister-doctors in Pusan and several Korean doctors are employed full-time. Fifteen Sister-nurses and many Korean nurses, laboratory technicians, pharmacists, aides, physiotherapists are everywhere, both Sisters and lay. The difficulty is space. I took a prowl around the treatment room, perhaps 30' by 40', in one of the "temporary buildings" which have lasted ten years.

In the corner are four tables. On one was a man, a heart case, brought in a blanket by his two brothers and wife. Sister Ann Veronica, a doctor, was examining him. On another, a girl, ten years old, with chills. Trembling shakes the blanket. Jaw set, teeth rigid, color greenish. Her mother, small and frail, had carried her two miles to the clinic. She sat beside the table, waiting. On the third table, a boy three years old with severe malnutrition. Skin darkened and peeling; is getting dextrose piped into his thighs from a bottle hung from the rafters. On the other half of this table is a baby with bandaged head. He has tuberculous meningitis. Unconscious for more than a week. His young mother stands staring down on him with the saddest face. I brought a stool for her but she would not sit down. On the last table is a terribly thin man, thirty-four, with malnutrition and terminal T.B. In a coma, he was brought by his brother and a friend; his old mother is hovering around. He has two children; his wife is working to support them all.

Nearby is a little girl getting a spinal tap. Wailing and fussy, poor child. Probably another meningitis case. Her father holds her tight so that Sister Gilmary can work on her spine. Behind a little screen are two men sitting on a bench with tubes in their abdomens, while fluid flows into a bucket between them. Calm and studious, they are reading magazines and newspapers. Next is a boy, maybe three years old, paralyzed from the waist down. He came in with sores all over his buttocks and legs; the flesh has broken down because he sits all day in one position while his mother is out working. During the winter, his feet were frozen. His mother is a good, hardworking soul; she brings him in every day for the bandages to be changed. Yet the Sisters cannot get her to understand that the boy's position should be shifted from time to time.

In the center of the room is the injection table. Here four nurses are on duty all the time giving one injection after another. Mothers get the little ones ready exposing their buttocks and coming up all prepared for the shot. As you can imagine, much yelling and squalling come from here. What took my eye was a boy about ten trying to get his little sister (six or so) ready. He tried to hold her and get her undraped at the same time. She screamed, wriggled, pushed and kicked. Big Brother was most business-like; he grabbed her by the neck and tried to get her over his knee. She went limp and sprawled on the floor. He put a knee on her shoulders and tugged at her clothes. She held on firmly. I watched it for a while, unwilling to get into what was evidently a family affair. The nurse stood by with injection needle poised. They were both getting exhausted, so I took a hand. I lifted the Conscientious Objector over my knee and held her firm. Brother did the job and the nurse moved in with the needle. In three seconds it was all over. By the fourth second, brother and sister were going out the door hand in hand, big smiles on both of them. All's well that ends well.

One of the most ingenious people here is Sister Maura Therese with her Flaw-da accent. She is in charge of the Physiotherapy Room, if you want to dignify her tidy little hut with the name. You'd be amazed at what she can do with an old corset. I visited a man with tuberculous meningitis away up in the crags behind our clinic. He lay on a blanket and pad on the floor and he wore a lady's corset. Some months ago, sleepwalking, he stepped off his front path and fell eighteen feet straight down. Friends took down the door of his hut and carried him on the door to us. At first, they thought his back was broken but the X-ray said no. Sister Maura Therese adapted the corset, which had come in a mission shipment, into an excellent support for him.

She uses plaster of Paris, of course, and surgical bandage, but also a welter of junk sent by well-meaning people in the States. "We got a lot of belts one time—thin ones and thick ones," she said. "Some were made of dress materials, some of leather, plastic, metal—just about everything. They made the best straps and buckles yo-all can imagine. Then one time, we got some really beautiful shoelaces. I use them for the corset laces because they're so much stronger."

Many physiotherapy patients are old timers. Coming for years and years. Children who have had T.B. of the bone when they were very small. Sister makes a wax mould of the child and fits the braces to it. She likes to use wax because she can scrape the wax down as the hump on shoulders grows less and less every month. What a joy to whittle down that hump! One girl came in completely bent over; her hips would not straighten. Week by week, month by month, the cast pulled down those legs until now there's just a bit of a bend at the hips. She can't stand straight yet, but give it another year and she'll be almost normal.

World Medical Relief in Detroit sent some colored plastic. Sister makes gay casts, soaking an undershirt in it and fitting it to the little body. The children in braces love their bright green, yellow and blue outfits. Help comes also from United States Overseas Mission; while I was there, I helped unpack and store away a large shipment of INH, Pas and strep-tomycin and X-ray film. And through the years, Catholic Relief Services has been the mainstay. Besides medicine and supplies—even a mobile clinic outfitted—a steady stream of clothes, toys, money and encourage-ment comes from their projects, such as the Thanksgiving Clothing Col-lection, the Laetare Sunday and Bishops' Fund. God bless them all! We can use every button of the clothes, every pill, every inch of adhesive tape, every last word of "We're 100% behind you" encouragement.

No patients on Sunday. That's the rule. But how is one to enforce it? Our Lord Himself said something about getting an ass out of a pit. True, there are not the crowds swarming over the compound, but emergencies are always cared for. One Sunday morning I passed a lone boy, perhaps eight years old, sitting on those benches beside a bundle of old blankets. Not doing anything. Just sitting and watching everybody going by. I wondered why he was there. Maybe waiting for somebody in the treat-ment room. I went in to see what was going on.

A man gasped and groaned on one of the treatment tables. Wife, brothers, and friends had carried him in on a blanket, shifting and stumbling, pulling and dragging him down the impossible paths. "Heart attack," said Sister Ann Veronica. "Probably won't pull out of it."

On the next table was a two-months baby with empyema. Sister Gilmary had a huge syringe poked into the tiny baby's chest. Ever so gently, she was extracting pus from the pleura while the young mother held the baby immobile. "In the States," Sister said, "we'd never work with this sized syringe on such a small baby, but it just might do the job here. We have nothing smaller."

I turned to go. A stifled sob came from a dark corner. A woman was there with her head turned against the drab wooden wall. Her hair was disheveled, her clothes ragged and dirty, her bare toes twisted under the bench. I went over to her and sat beside her, holding her shoulders close. I could say nothing in Korean. In a few minutes the sobs stopped; she took my hankie to mop her face.

Sister Maura Therese told her story. "She came here two days ago with a baby, two years old. It wasn't her child, she told us. Her husband had another wife and told this woman to take care of the other wife's child. She did. But, day before yesterday she was putting the baby on her back, trying to tie the sashes around him, when he slipped off. He fell on his head. She brought him here unconscious. We did our best for him. She brought him yesterday too, still unconscious. And this morning, she was at the door around 6 A.M., frantic because the baby had died.

"She's afraid to go home, she says. Her husband will accuse her of killing the baby because it is not her own."

The woman was calm now. She stood, bowed ceremoniously to Sister. "Thank you for your trouble to unworthy me." Then she went outside, picked up the tragic bundle on the bench, took the boy's hand and went home to take her beating.

This is just one instance of troubles from carrying a baby on one's back. They are tied so tightly that, especially in winter, they sometimes smother. Or circulation in the legs is interfered with. More than once a woman has come in with a dead baby on her back, not knowing it has been dead for hours. Sister Gilmary wages war against the custom, "Above all, don't carry a sick baby that way. You can't see him," she tells the women.

But when one sees women going uphill to their homes—what else can they do with their babies? Bundles in their hands, a five-gallon can of water on their heads—where else is baby to go?

We have a sort of Death House (or is it a Life House?) here at the clinic. Anyone not likely to get well meets Sister Maria Agnes or Suzanna Chong and hears the Glad Tidings. You can talk right out to these people; they are used to the idea of death. They know it is stalking them. "Do you wish to be baptized?" they are asked. Some say yes, some say no.

One morning I baptized Jean, a woman dying of malnutrition and heart disease. When I finished, she broke into tears. She had been begging her food in the streets. Her ankles were swollen from the heart condition; her face and arms from the malnutrition. I brought her into a tiny room and, over a small flame, cooked a cupful of cereal. It was packed with nutriment —high protein and glucose and everything I could think of. It tasted good to me. Jean was brought into the room and sat patiently on a stool while I made up this treat. I gave her the bowl with a spoon, thinking she would take it eagerly. Instead, she very daintily took several small spoonfuls and gently pushed the rest away. She explained in Korean that because I had gone to the trouble of cooking it for her, she had tasted of it, but she could not eat more. "It sticks right here," she pointed to her throat. She was too sick to eat.

"Maybe you can eat it tonight, or at least some of it," Sister Joan Celine, the nurse with her, suggested.

Jean looked at the dishful. "Yes, I will try tonight, thank you." I put the gruel into an empty tin can and she bent over to receive it in polite fashion. She bowed again and went away, shuffling on those swollen feet. I looked after her a long time; I don't know when I have been so "cut down to size." It was she doing me the kindness, as she waited so patiently for me to stop fussing with that cereal. It was she

who was gracious and kind enough to take a little of it, so that I would
not be disappointed. She put up with me because she knew I loved her.
St. Vincent de Paul's cryptic statement rang in my ears; the idea is: The
poor will never forgive us the bread that we give them unless it is given
with love. I am glad I loved; how it would have hurt her if no love
were sprinkled on that bowl!

Jean, I found out later, did not die. The Sisters were able to get her
into a hospital for her heart condition. Six months later she came back
to visit, looking one hundred percent better and well on the way to
permanent recovery. I never had the heart to ask her if she ate that
cereal or gave it away to the first hungry child she met. I know she didn't
throw it away.

All is not stark tragedy in Korea. Even poor women seem able to
have one beautiful dress stowed away for grand occasions. In the market
are gay toys of plastic candy, stronger in color than flavor, small plastic
bags with colored water to drink, live goldfish in water done up also
in plastic bags, and bright cellophane envelopes of peanuts. Down by
the wharves you see fish for sale on small stands; the women behind
laugh and talk among themselves with grand good humor. Each of them,
no doubt, has a sad story but none of them inflicts her sorrow on others.

The Maryknoll Sisters' clinic has been with these people through
thick and thin. For five years, while war raged all around and immediately afterwards, the crowds outside the gate on Harmony Alley numbered two thousand and more every day. It was, newspapers said, "the
longest charity line in the world." In those days, everyone of the two
thousand was a whole five-alarm fire in himself. Things have eased a
bit. The clinic is able to do some long-term planning. The emphasis
now is on stamping out tuberculosis. Patients are isolated in so far as is
possible in a one-room hut. The family learns how to avoid infection
and how to care for the patient. If necessary, money is given to support
the family until the patient is well. House visits check up on conditions.
Every afternoon Sister Dolores scrambles up the most impossible mountains and ducks into the lowest doorways on this little job.

"Our Gang" is a living reminder of the two-thousand-a-day years. Koreans were never known to abandon their children before, but in the
frenzy of war and destitution, many left babies on the clinic steps.
Timmie was found wrapped in newspaper on Christmas day; his paralyzed legs are much improved and he gets around very well on crutches.
Bundo, who did not smile for two years after he was taken in, is a bundle
of smiles now. He serves Mass every morning standing on tiptoe to get
the Missal, tripping over his cassock en route to the other side, and making
a great to-do about the cruets. Clara, Teresa and Augusta—they are the
happiest, homiest, nicest children you can imagine.

Engrossing as it is, medical work is not all the activity here. As I said, a three-ring circus goes on practically every day of the week; the thirty Sisters involved turn their hands to any good work you can think of. There are nine small houses dotting the hillside from the main clinic building near the street, up umpty-ump steps to Regina Coeli dormitory, which scrapes the sky with its roof.

I investigated a light in a window one evening and stepped into a Credit Union meeting in full session. This was the first ever organized in Korea. Sister Gabriella, who has been in Korea off and on since 1926, started it a little over a year ago among the clinic's employees. There must be some unifying bond among the members—either all in the same business, or the same family, or the same neighborhood. In this case, they all work for the clinic in some capacity, from a doctor down to the clean-up boy. There was great jubilation the night I broke in among them. It was First Anniversary night, and a dividend of twelve percent was declared. It could have been more, but Sister Gabriella cautioned them against wild dividending. What it amounts to is this: the members are their own bankers and collect their own twelve percent. For the Indians of Bolivia and Peru, for Philippine farmers, for any class ridden by money lenders, the Credit Union offers a way to borrow money on short term loans and to invest what little savings they have profitably.

Not long afterwards, Sister Gabriella took me to a newly organized Credit Union—all members of the same parish. We set out around 8 P.M. All Pusan's electricity was off that night; the streets were black. You felt, rather than saw, people moving up and down the street. Every now and then a car tore down the hill with lights blazing. We caught one of these, a taxi. It was a converted jeep, a very neat job. We swerved through the crowds. It was like a Hitchcock movie; where were all those people going in the black night? Why were there small candy and peanut stands out there in the dark? What was the use of those tiny wicks floating in oil? It was as if God had suddenly turned off the sun in the middle of a busy market day.

Our jeep left the main street and started to bound up a hillside. Head-lights showed shacks on either side. Then we stopped. Sister Gabriella got out and paid the man. "This is it," she said.

"What's it?" I countered. "There isn't even a shack here."

"Exactly." She was imperturbable. "There was a church here; they pulled it down to rebuild. The meeting must be some place on this site." With misgivings, I saw the jeep headlights go bouncing back down the hill. If people were meeting on this site, they were mighty quiet and dark about it. Amalgamated Hush-Hush Men, Local #6, maybe.

Sister had a flashlight. Don't misunderstand me. It was one of those fountain-pen affairs you use to find the key hole when you come in late.

All of a sudden there were no crowds. Only a dark hillside plowed up like a battleground the night after the fight. Sister Gabriella started down. Steps, loose stones, muddy spots, a bit of wall. "Now, let me see, where was the basement? Probably here. No, maybe over there. Let's see farther down. . . ." A man loomed out of the dark. "Do you know where the Credit Union meeting of Cho Ryang parish is being held?" asked Sister Gabriella. "A hundred to one," I thought, "that he never heard of Cho Ryang parish, much less the Credit Union."

I was wrong. The hundred-to-one shot came in! "Sure!" said the man, "it's over there," pointing vaguely far away. "I'll take you." And we were off. Through alleys, along paths, out on the main street for a while. Past houses and shacks and shops and fields. Up steep streets and down through gullies. Once we passed a huge crowd standing around a dim light in the middle. As we passed behind them I wondered what they were looking at—a snake charmer? A medicine show? An accident? A street fight? Our Angel Raphael ran on ahead; we pressed in hot pursuit. Up and up, several times over a vegetable patch and once, it seemed to me, straight through somebody's cellar, in one door and out the other side. We called out to him; we shouted out protests. "Never mind! We don't want to go to the meeting anyway!" But Raphael kept just in sight but not near enough to hear us.

Suddenly he stopped at the head of broad steps and let us pant up to him. He was before an impressive iron gate and heavy stone wall reminiscent of a Japanese War Lord's feudal castle. "This is it!" he said. We were stunned. "Oh no," said Sister Gabriella, "you must be wrong. This house was the American Embassy the last time I saw it." But she talked to thin air; the Angel Raphael had disappeared.

Sister sighed. "There are lights here, anyway," she said. "Let's go in and ask somebody to call a taxi for us. We'll go home." We opened the iron gate and trudged up the driveway. All of a sudden, the front door flung open and men and women ran out to meet us. The Angel Raphael was right; this was the parish Credit Union meeting. It seems the house had been bought by the Bishop and lent to this parish until their church was built. We felt like two Tobiases coming home after seven years' wandering.

About thirty-five men and thirty women sat on the tatami flooring. Mostly poor or middle class. Taxi men who owned their own cabs, small store owners, dressmakers, office employees, construction laborers, those with a market stall of some sort. Members must have a steady income. Nobody, for instance, like a jiggy man who depends on chance employment. The members sat before a purple curtain pulled before the Blessed Sacrament in this improvised church-meeting hall. One could see the sanctuary lamp flickering behind, almost as if Our Lord Himself took part in the meeting. Leading the proceedings was a man in grey coat, baggy white pantaloons tied around the ankle with grey bands to match his coat. Tortoise-shell glasses and a stringy beard made him look like a very substantial citizen indeed. He talked much and well; good natured laughter greeted his sallies. Evidently, they wanted him to be president and he pleaded other commitments. They won, in the end, of course.

A tea kettle with a cup over the spout passed around freely from the men's to the women's side. The women spoke some, not much, but they seemed to be making their own business decisions. Unity and good fellowship prevailed through the room. A really democratic meeting.

"We'll call a taxi for you," the pastor said afterwards, leading us into his scholarly living room and winding up the telephone to get Central. I wondered how a taxi could get up those steps in the street. "Must be some other way for a car to get here," I thought. Then the taxi was at the door. We got in and bumped down each step carefully to the main street below. Home to bed. I spent the night dreaming of Raphael and Tobias, and the old Mack Sennett comedies where Model T Fords scaled any height and braved any stairways their zany drivers set them at.

The clinic heals the body; the Credit Union spares the pocketbook. Man has a soul and mind as well. On a Sunday morning, the nine houses turn into classrooms and some sit outside as well. Sister Suzanne Marie has literacy classes for women. The Korean alphabet devised five hundred years ago has twenty-four strictly phonetic characters. Once these are bedded down in the mind, the student can puzzle out anything written. It used to be that time was spent to teach religion by rote to illiterates. But now two birds fall to one stone; the woman learns to read and can teach herself the catechism. She is enabled also to delve much deeper into religion on her own.

Their alphabet makes it so easy to read that Korea is eighty percent literate. Compulsory education laws prevail but the schools are so crowded it is often impossible to get in. Magazines and newspapers, books and pamphlets are in great demand.

Religion classes are in session all over the place. Pupils perch on the examining tables, sit in the laboratory, kneel on the tatami floor, crowd the sewing room, fill the medicine distributing room, and jam into the pharmacy. More than two hundred are distributed here and there every Sunday morning. Some have known the Sisters for years before they inquire into Catholicism; others get the grace on their first visit.

This is just a small part of the surge toward the Church in modern Korea. In nine years Catholics have tripled in number, from 166,000 in 1953 to 500,000 in 1961. Among Korea's population of 23,000,000 this is not impressive, but it shows progress.

I went with Sister Andre out to a leper colony where she has classes every Thursday. We went out past railroad yards, vegetable patches, rice fields, and army depots. Beyond the blue harbor to the high green hills where you can look across Korea Strait and see Japan one hundred miles away. Sister Andre is a cheerful little person, very business-like, very young looking in spite of thirty years off and on in Korea. She handles baggage lists, shipments of medicine, ticklish customs officials, and obdurate porters much of the time, but her joy is to watch the Faith grow in the eyes of pagan women who have never known the God of Love.

That's just what she does at Five-Six Islands, the leper colony. The name comes from the odd fact that at low tide there are six islands visible; at high tide, only five. A run-down quonset hut surmounts the highest hill in the colony. This is the quasi-church and instruction hall. Sister rang the bell in the bell tower such as it is, and the pupils arrived —maybe thirty women with their babies and children. They sat on the floor and Sister began. These people were not horrible yet. Most were in the stage where they have lost their eyebrows and the women had painted eyebrows on their very attractive faces. A few had watery eyes; others had the beginnings of "crab hands." Some noses had begun to fall back. But they were all friendly and happy. Babies born in the colony are not separated from their parents. The babies were passed from one lap to another until only Sherlock Holmes could have told which baby belonged to whom.

Director of all these multifarious works at the Maryknoll Sisters' clinic is Sister Augusta, who is a book all to herself. She was nurse in Meadville, Pa., when, as they say, she "ended it all," took the veil, said good-bye to the world, hied herself to a nunnery—in other words, she entered Maryknoll. Her life since then shows how well she has succeeded in escaping reality. In 1934, she went to Kaying, deep in the interior of China where she spent fourteen years tramping rice fields, talking to Chinese women and teaching them. The Japanese swarmed all over South China but they never bothered the Kaying district. Then she went to the Philippines to help care for sugar cane workers on Negros Island. Five months later she was sent to Korea and arrived just in time for the Korean War to begin. The army evacuated her with the other Maryknoll Sisters in Korea at the time, and she spent nine months in Japan straining at the leash, trying to get back to Korea where people were suffering so much. She did get back. She's been back for ten years now, a one-woman army for good if ever there was one.

Sister Augusta is "involved," as the psychiatrists say, with everyone at the clinic—patients, Sisters, Korean lay assistants and all their kith and kin. I came across her one day at her desk.

"Worried?" I asked. "Why?"

"It's Cheng Lucia," she said.

It seems Cheng Lucia is having a hard time getting a husband. It's not that she isn't pretty for she is, with a longish oval face. And she's capable, a clever office worker. Well educated, able to read English as well as Korean. Good family, too. What's wrong, then? Well, Lucia was born in 1942, the Year of the Horse. That's the whole sad story and her long face reminds people of it.

The year you were born in means a lot in Korea, as all over the Orient. Following the Chinese custom, the years are named in twelve-year cycles. The year of the Tiger is followed in turn by the years of the Rabbit, Dragon, Snake, Horse, Sheep, Monkey, Chicken, Dog, Pig, Rat, and Cow. Then the Tiger takes over again. Years of the Tiger are 1962, 1950, 1938 and so on back.

The Horse is strong, masculine. His is a lucky year for boys, though not for girls. But in winter he can get no food, so those born in Horse years have hard luck in winter. Now, a tiger can eat a horse as well as all other animals on the list. So a boy born in Tiger years is lucky indeed. But a girl? No indeed. She will never, never get married. When the two families get together to talk things over, negotiations fall through. Who wants a Tiger girl to marry a Rabbit boy? Or a Sheep boy? Who wants a Tiger girl in the house, anyway?

A Pig and Rat combination is very good; they're natural buddies. A Cow and Cock wedding will work out well; the cock gets to work in the morning and rests in the afternoon. If Lucia had waited a few weeks she would have been born in a Sheep year. That would have been a wise move for her. Everybody wants a Sheep daughter-in-law—gentle, uncomplaining, soft. The Rabbit can't get food in the day; he must scurry around for it at night. Nobody wants a Rabbit marrying into the family. As for me, I was born in the Year of the Monkey—ambitious, cunning, undependable, tricky. Well! Who wants me? It's a sobering thought. Worse, I'm a twin. There were two monkeys in our house, growing up.

Sister Augusta, as well as everybody else on the compound, awaits Der Tag—that is, Moving Day, when their clinic evacuates its small houses and moves up the hill to the new hospital. I went up there myself to see the finishing touches put on and to see at work "the world's gentlest and daintiest construction man," as one writer put it. Sister William Marie, in other words.

The stories on her are legion. Told in her own very precise and gentle diction, they are priceless. Not many girls, especially not Margaret Villhard of St. Louis, think when they enter a convent that they will be overseeing cement mixing, knocking out walls to accommodate boilers, trading steel rods for crushed gravel. Especially not half-way around the world where construction work is still done to a large extent by pick, shovel and shoulder pole. Yet Sister William Marie graduated in Building Construction Technology, went to the Philippines to erect Maryknoll College, and then came to Korea to supervise the construction of a 165-bed hospital high on the hills of Pusan.

Her business associates are Army men, either Americans or Koreans. One of the lasting benedictions left by our Army was a series of hospitals operated by voluntary agencies of one type or another—Baptist, Presbyterian, Seventh Day Adventist and others. The Army supplied materials; the agency bore the costs of construction and equipment.

Sister's cement is famous. "She pours the best cement in Korea," is commonly heard. One time a young Korean officer working with Army engineers in putting up a building came to see Sister at her desk in the little construction shack. He needed help to understand the English of the plans and technical details. But he took a good look at the then half-finished building. Back on his job, he called his workers together. "Tomorrow," he told them, "we're going over to Maryknoll Hospital and learn a lot. We will have to make many changes. For I am determined that no woman in Korea is going to pour better cement than the Korean Army. Ours is going to be as good."

Sister used to sell the cement bags. They are very valuable. Often, more than one group would compete for them. One morning a group of Koreans came wanting to buy sacks.

"How much?" Sister asked.

They offered 50 huan a bag. She knew the market sold them for 60 to 65 huan each.

"I'm sorry," she said. "55 huan is my price."

They shrugged and went out. Hardly were they gone when another group came in. They offered 55 huan without a murmur. Sister was just ready to close the sale when in came Group #1 again. They saw how things stood and offered 56 huan. "No," Sister said in that precise way. "You had your chance. I will sell to these men for 55 huan."

They argued. "You have so many cement bags to sell. Why not sell some to us and some to them?"

Such a commotion ensued! Such yelling, such fist shaking! Now, if there is one thing Sister William Marie cannot abide, it's yelling and fist shaking. "Now listen," she said to them all. "You have to thrash this thing out, I know. But you must fight like gentlemen. Decide yourselves on a price, and I will sell some to #1 and some to #2. But please discuss the thing like gentlemen."

They were contrite. "Of course!" they murmured. Forthwith they all took off their hats and held them against their chests. This is the posture of a gentleman. They then fell to yelling just as loud, hurling all sorts of hard names, screaming imprecations. But with their hats against their chests, they were fighting like gentlemen. In the end, she sold two-thirds of the bags to Group #2, one-third to Group #1. All for 55 huan.

We were standing by an unfinished doorway as she told me this story. Sister rubbed her hand over the raw building. "Isn't it beautiful?" she asked. "This is real architectural cement. I love it."

She paused a little, just savoring that cement.

"I've found it true in Korea and also in the Philippines: the men want to be held to a high standard of work. At first, they were so used to mixing up some sand and blowing a little cement into it, that I had to show them what proportions were best. I had to mix it and put it into place myself. Then I had to check continuously. Not that they wanted to do things wrong, but they were so used to the old way.

"After a wall was up, I'd come around and tap each block—mostly with my Profession ring. Just knocking it against the block. It should have a good solid sound to show that it is really set. The men stood around and watched my face. At first they thought me just odd, but soon one or two would take up nails and help me tap the blocks, learning the right sound. If my face was pained they were so cute! 'You're not happy over this. Not happy?' Several times they put me out of the room while they took out the hollow-sounding blocks to reset them. All they need is someone to praise good work and be sorry about bad work. Just like people the world over."

Construction work has infinite detail. Especially a hospital. In a large quonset serving as warehouse, I was Alice in Wonderland aghast at the variety of stuff—sterilized water, steel window frames, shovels, motors for the refrigerating plants, student chairs for nurses' classes, an iron lung, door knobs, flour sacking to insulate steam pipes, garbage cans stacked up, an X-ray machine in house-sized crates, screws, nails and brads in neat bins, rolls of steel cable for the elevators when they come, and steps for telephone poles. These last are the little iron supports you find sticking out of poles so the lineman can mount easily. They're precious to Sister William Marie.

"We got wooden poles to bring in the electric wires for the hospital but none of the cast iron steps to go with them. We used ladders, however, and managed to string the electric wires all right. But the South Korean Electric Company would not approve the job until we had cast iron telephone pole steps. It's a safety measure. Try to get them! We asked everywhere in Korea. Everywhere in the Orient. We shouted in letters to the Army. Months of delay. Then, at last we got them. And life goes on."

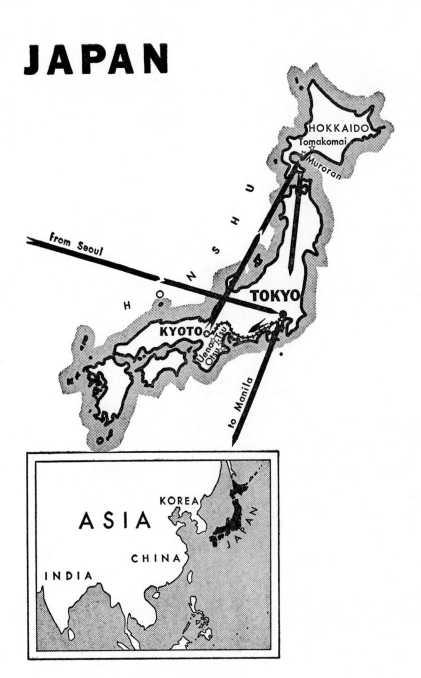

JAPAN

⫷ 20 ⫸ The Principle of Just Enough, No More

I LAST saw Japan as a country of bicycles. I came back to find it a nation on roller skates. And each roller skate takes five to seven passengers. One must be half pussycat and half snake to wriggle in or out of a Japanese automobile. But millions do it every day.

I cannot imagine that Japan was ever a nation on foot. Since the invention of the wheel, I suspect, they have been on the move. Away back in 1938, three of us went from Yokohama to Kyoto, and in every railroad station were swarms of children out on excursions, sometimes for days and weeks at a time. "They go as far as Manchuria," we were told. "This is to make our children empire-minded." Even then, a crowd of war widows in somber kimonos stood outside Tokyo's railroad station awaiting the urns which contained the ashes of their dead, killed in the Sino-Japanese war that began in 1937. In later years, during the Japanese occupation of the Philippines, I often thought of those war widows. How their number increased when Japan bled from a hundred wounds!

In 1949, when I next saw Japan, the people were desperate for food. Wheat grew between the railroad tracks all the way from Tokyo to Kyoto. Wheat grew in stone pots on people's front steps. Every inch of ground was used for food.

Now the winter wheat stands high in the fields. Patches of rice seedlings grow nearby waiting for the wheat harvest so that they can take over the fields. There is still poverty in Japan, of course, but even in Ant's Town where the ragpickers live in Kyoto, the TV aerials make a network in the sky. Sloshing through the muddiest alleys where each family has only a dank dark hole to call its own—in each of these you find the omnipresent TV set bought on the installment plan. Someone has estimated six million TV sets in Japan today. Also one radio for every six people.

After World War II, the Japanese had no money to travel on and no empire to travel to. But the children are on the march again, now. Swarms of boys and girls hang out of windows in chartered buses or special trains.

243

They all carry cameras; all have transistor radios in their pockets. Their luggage is plastic—cheap, light, durable and new. Every temple you visit, every palace, every park or reserve, every "national treasure" is overrun with boys in somber high-collared suits and girls in middy blouses and pleated skirts. Some are in their late teens; some have swarmed out of kindergartens. They all have that cohesive unity of a Japanese group out to appreciate nature, or history, or religion, or duty. I'd as soon buck a battalion of army ants as try to break through a crowd of Japanese children bound for a spot of aesthetic relaxation.

Much has happened to this dynamic nation, but the national flavor remains the same. Railroads are clean and on time; kimonos, although seen more rarely, are glorious in color and material; rock gardens are exquisite; flowers and vegetables without parallel; the people, wondrously polite.

In 1949, it was fun to decipher the katakana signs advertising foreign things—aisukureemu (ice cream), biru (beer), hotto dogu (hot dog), syeda (cider), ueesuki (whiskey) and so on. But now the katakana speaks of coresoteroru (cholesterol), ueekuendo (week-end) and supahmaketto (supermarket). Hoteru (hotel) signs are now moteru (motel). Terebi is everywhere short for television. Neon signs advertise washing machines, electric rice cookers and instant foods—instant soups, beverages, baby foods, fruit juices, gravies. One may even get an instant obi—that wide sash which Japanese women wear on kimonos. It sounds impossible but I asked a friend how she fixed the elaborate bow in the back. "Do you do it in front and then push it around to the back?"

"No," she said. "I used to get my husband to help me, but now I use an instant obi. The whole thing is made up in the store and I zipper it up the back."

Compared with the post-war era, the Japanese are well-dressed and well-fed. Their life expectancy is sixty-six; the rest of Asia can hope to live for thirty to thirty-five years, and Americans to seventy. I noted the taxi drivers in small towns as well as in Tokyo. They have no frayed collars or cuffs, no patches on their trousers. The last time I was in Japan, they were afraid to leave their seats to open the door for passengers.

The train from Tokyo to Kyoto was cleaner, swifter and more luxurious than anything I ever rode on in the States. Besides the usual modernities—adjustable seats, air conditioning, acoustic ceiling, picture windows, ash trays, carpeted floor, etc., there was a radio connection in each seat. The weary traveller could hook the device around his ear and enjoy news or music. Also, each seat had a detachable desk arrangement. And two boys appeared every hour or so; one went ahead and gathered up all papers, cigarette stubs, bits of rice from lunch boxes, etc. The other followed with a vacuum sweeper for the carpet.

It's hard to imagine from this that Taiwan has the densest population in the Orient.

TAIWAN

The temple is ancient, but the girl wears toreador pants, the oxen have plastic bridles and balloon tires finish off the wooden farm cart.

The Japanese baby buggy solves the baby-sitting problem for this Taiwanese mother. The toy zebra, too, is a legacy from Japan.

Rice fields, temples and mountains—that's Taiwan for the photographer.

The bicycle school bus takes the toddlers off to kindergarten.

The nylon-stocking factory girls are crowded but happy.

Lim Sui Sam's feet were bound according to old Chinese custom; her daughter, Jade Flower, rides her to church on a bicycle.

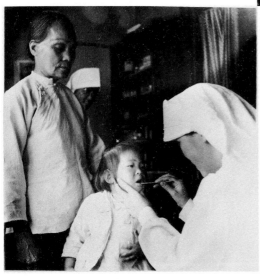

This Japanese Sister-doctor has a storefront clinic for the aborigines high in Taiwan's mountain area.

Quiet beauty at a leper colony near Pusan.

KOREA

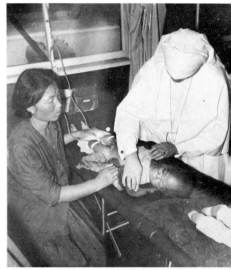

Malnutrition accounts for the rough, dark skin; meningitis brought on the coma.

Catholic Relief Services—NCWC gave this mobile clinic for use in Korea's war-ravaged village.

Harmony Alley is paved with misery, flowing down from the hill behind.

Mother Nature and Japanese artistry have made a serene and fruitful marriage.

JAPAN

This substantial farmer's wife is as proud of her concrete
stove in the kitchen as she is of her TV in the parlor.

A Japanese Maryknoll Sister teaches the blind by braille.

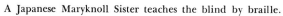

Seventy-six years old and a Buddhist
grim! I loved her.

Japanese students ponder Hokkaido's steel factories and busy harbor.

as modern as tomorrow, but she the old way of carrying the baby.

Organized outings to Japanese "national treasures" fill every railroad station with schoolchildren, each one equipped with plastic bag, new shoes, camera and intelligent questions.

Ah Sam, school janitress in Hong Kong

Iringi, chieftain's wife in Tanganyika.
She retains her tattoo and filed teeth;
as a Christian the ear plugs and brass
arm coils are gone.

Nishimura San, who cleans the public park in Kyoto

Hortensa on Yap with flower crown and
betel blackened teeth

THEY ALL SAID CHEESE!

Rammenike, neighbor in Ceylon

т. Pyong II, maker of Korean
chair hats

g Mei Lin, farmwoman on Taiwan

logio, homesteader in the Philippines

ABOVE. Negros, Philippines—Her country has not forgotten World War II.

UPPER RIGHT. Tanganyika, Africa—Imps of the altar!

RIGHT. Hong Kong—Brother does his share of baby toting.

BELOW. Ise, Japan—Tug-of-war in fancy kimono

ABOVE. Yap, U.S. Pacific Trust Territory—Small fry at the end of the dancing line.

LEFT. Kundasale, Ceylon—They'd stand on their heads if you asked them to.

LEFT. Miaoli, Taiwan—"He? Oh, he doesn't know you!"

BELOW. Pusan, Korea—Young sceptic

Draped in flowers, Mother sits with Jesuit Father Condon on the stone platform to watch the dancers on Yap.

YAP

The "bank" where Yap's stone money is stored. Steal it—if you can.

Harbor and causeway as seen from our front porch. The woman is a stranger from Ulithi and wears her own skirt of lave-lave, bark cloth.

"Hold still!" A mother makes up her son for the dance of the Joyful Mysteries.

his girl in the bamboo dance became a Sister a onth later.

The Abai or town hall on Koror. Pictures tell the island's history.

Hulks of big machines like this remind one constantly that Koror was once a great Japanese naval base. Sister wears a raincape; it's a bit of precaution, wise on Koror.

Christopher and his grandfather grate a fresh coconut for the chicks.

The boys were pudgy, cheerful youngsters—dedicated to the task of sparkling up that train. No doubt, they dreamed of owning the railroad someday. There's an Horatio Alger quality about the Japanese, refreshing in this cynical world. They honestly believe that the road from Rags to Riches opens to hard work, cheerful service and thrifty living.

A news item on TV one evening was that the Tsubome (The Swallow), a crack train, was twenty-five minutes late arriving in Tokyo. It was such terrific news that television cameras were hustled down to the station to record the event. Passengers were shown coming off the train in a daze. Our Sisters, as well as all Japan, were shocked. "What? A train late? And twenty-five minutes off? It's incredible!"

Even out on farms, the Japanese woman has refrigerators and deep freezes. Before going into the fields, the farm wife puts the rice for dinner into an electric cooker which turns itself on and off. Washing machines— they look like toys—are in every home. Propane gas eliminates fuel gathering. I went to many a farm in Japan. From a distance, you would certainly think they were sunk back in the Kamakura Shogunate, completely out of touch with our world. But don't let them fool you. Electric pumps bring up water; chemical fertilizers produce bumper crops. The farmer may still slosh through mud to plant his rice, but he has small machines to harvest and thresh it.

We went out to the Nakamura farm near Ueno. A long dusty bus ride, a walk over rice paddy dikes, and finally we were in the large courtyard where they dried rice and beans, fruits and grains in the sun. The house roof was massive—wood, thatch and tile at least eighteen inches thick. Heavy beams and posts had held it up for centuries. We found Nakamura San herself in the kitchen. She, at least, had no electric rice cooker. Her kitchen range was cumbersome concrete with deep holes for the heavy iron pots. She stoked it with wood from a pile in the corner. She showed off her ancestral shrine, a big affair strung with white papers and ropes. Shinto offerings of cakes and rice wine, a bit dusty and flyspecked, lay before the ancestors.

"Ah, old Japan!" I exulted. "Nothing can penetrate this bastion of the old civilization."

Grandma Nakamura was beckoning at the door to their main room. "Dozo! Please step into our humble living room." We took off our shoes and stepped. Nothing was in it, neither table, chair, ashtray nor spittoon. Tatami, rice-straw matting, on the floor, and in the corner, a TV set. Grandma, atwitter with delight, went on her knees and fiddled with the buttons. For some minutes, she sat on her heels in utter contentment while animated cartoons glorified "Instant Coffee," "Aspirin," and Somebody's Superior Garlic Powder. Grandma never turned to us again. After a few minutes we tiptoed out, disillusioned women.

The best TV story, however, happened in Nagahama, a town on the shore of Lake Biwa. Here the Catholic Church is a former bank building in the heart of town. Part of it is a recreation room where young people can play ping-pong, listen to TV or read magazines. One evening two brawny young fellows wanted to see the ballet, "Swan Lake," on the TV. A dear little old lady, with many apologies, would not let them change the channel. So sorry; so very sorry! Father intervened; why couldn't the boys see an artistic presentation such as Swan Lake? The eighty-pound Japanese lady bent over double with politeness. Oh, so very very sorry! But unfortunately, if they saw the ballet she would miss the baseball game broadcast at the same time.

I wonder if it could have happened twenty years ago. Would any woman have stood her ground then? Which brings us to the subject of women's liberation—or is it a new enslavement? The bus girls and factory girls are symbols of the New Woman, Japanese style.

"They make wonderful money," people tell you about the bus girls, "but they don't last more than a year at the job." Looking at the dapper young women in their cocky hats, you doubt that statement. However, take a ride in a city bus and you see why they wear out so fast.

The bus girl chatters in a squeaky voice every minute. She hops out at every stop to collect tickets and possibly to shove the last sardine into the can. She flings open the heavy doors; she goes through the bus collecting fares; she gives the driver an idea of what's coming behind him. When he has to back up, she's right there tweetling her whistle to clear a path behind him. The driver needs only his two ears to hear her and his two eyes to look in front; the bus girl does everything else.

Her high whine is in the very best Japanese, but ten hours of it a day must do things to her vocal cords. I listened attentively for five minutes of it once. It ran something like this:

> We're going to stop at Sanjo Street next. I'm afraid you will experience a bit of a jolt but don't let that disturb you or knock you off your feet. So here we are at Sanjo Street. Anybody who wants to get off may do so. Be sure you take all your bundles with you. Be careful where you put your feet; there's a mud puddle just under the step. I'll open the door now to let you out. There's quite a crowd waiting at this bus stop. Please excuse us for keeping you waiting. Let the others out, if you don't mind. Please enter quickly. One more can get in, I'm sure. Just one more. There now, let me get in too and we'll be off. All right, driver, you can start now. Everything is clear on the right but there's a fellow trying to pass us on the left. We'll be going around a curve soon so hang on to the straps. I'll have to bother you now to give me your money for the tickets. Thank you very much. Thank you very much. Go ahead, driver; everything's clear around. We'll be going over a bump soon; don't let it knock you off your

feet. And now we're nearing Takano Street, our next stop. Anybody off
at Takano Street? Be sure you take your bundles with you. I'm afraid you
will experience a jolt . . .

I got off at Takano Street, went into a store and bought ear plugs.
Small wonder these girls last no more than a year. They live in dormitories run by the bus company; moral conditions are often very bad indeed. Recently, a bus official, concerned about this, asked Sister Therese
Martin to give a class in morality to the girls. He said he had ten new
girls signed up but hesitated to put them in the dormitory until things
are better. All very good. But the few classes will not clear up a condition caused by long hours, exhaustion and lack of good companionship.

Factory girls, too, get good money. Recruited from farms, they are
herded into dormitories, perhaps one thousand in each. Nearly all have
finished ninth grade and may be as young as fifteen. They sign up for
a three-year period. Except for $4.05 a month for board, all expenses
are paid. Women mill hands at the rayon spinning factories get $32.27
a month; clerical workers get $87.76. This is about half what men get.
They have five paid holidays a year and two free days a month. Clinics
and a company hospital care for any ills; many factories are completely
air-conditioned. An eight-hour work schedule gives more free time than
these girls have ever had before. The company gives culture classes and
offers athletics, but many of the girls find the Catholic Church near their
factories and wander in. The difficulty is that when they return to their
farms they are caught up again in pagan households, unable to practice
their Faith.

Factory girls are given three weeks off-duty before and after the birth
of a baby. But with legalized abortion and government clinics all but
forcing contraceptives on women, there isn't much call for this type of
vacation. Among poor women, the ravages are most noticeable.

I went with Sister Marie Elise into Ants' Town where the "Fourth
Class People" live. These Untouchables of Japan are relegated to certain
sections; they are restricted to the meanest of jobs. The Japan Tourist
Bureau says nothing about them, but they are as distinct a Second-Class
Citizenship as are the Negroes in our own South. The outcasts look, act
and speak as do any other Japanese; three million of them live in six
thousand strictly segregated communities. For the past three hundred
and fifty years, as a result of wide-spread Buddhism which forbids the
taking of any life, their stigma has come from their occupation—butcher-
ing and allied work such as leather curing, saddle making, boot and
shoe manufacturing. By extension, those who make wooden clogs are
also outcasts. This is why they are called Fourth Class; not that there
are three higher classes, but they deal with four-footed animals. Outcast

women especially find it hard to get honest employment; they have to be factory hands at sweat labor wages, waitresses in cheap eating places, or attendants at "pachinko"—slot machine gambling joints of which there are hundreds in any city. Modern, large-scale industries will not employ them; thus ninety-nine percent have no welfare insurance, national health insurance or unemployment pay.

Since the schools are not segregated, outcast children get as good an education as others. More than one young girl cuts ties with the past and passes into normal society. But she rarely gets involved in marriage; it's too dangerous. The fiancé's family always does detective work on the intended. If she were discovered ever to have lived in an outcast section—that would be the end of her dreams of any sort.

The outcasts of Ants' Town live under feudal rule. They are in the pay of various junk dealers who provide barracks for them and require that they bring in a certain amount of junk each day. The barracks are of plywood; no cool tile roof, no smooth tatami, no sliding doors such as make a Japanese home a pleasant oasis. Even the factory dormitories have these things. The door of each one-family room opened out into a corridor so narrow that the open door blocked it entirely. Several times as we talked to Nobechi San, we had to close the door to let someone by. Once it was a drunken man, all but carried home by his pals; most often it was a neighbor woman hauling her buckets of water from the well downstairs to her bare plywood room at the end of the corridor.

Nobechi San was in pain. Physically and mentally. She had had an abortion four days before and was still bleeding. She rubbed her stomach again and again as the tears rolled down her face.

Nobechi San is one of two million women who had abortions performed —and registered—in Japan in a year. Dear only knows how many were not registered. Birth control and abortions have cut the national birth rate in half; it was thirty-four per thousand in 1948, seventeen per thousand in 1960. Japan will be a nation of old people not long hence. Already schools find their primary classrooms too big.

A woman who wants children has to fight for them. Relatives and friends pressure her; if she goes to a clinic for help, she is handed the name of an abortionist. What is desperately needed is a place where such women can go in peace and have their babies. For once a baby has contrived to get himself born, he is loved to distraction. His troubles vanish from that point on.

Japanese women have earned a fairly comfortable way in life. Sister Rose Ann and I came by train from Ueno to Kyoto. Across the aisle in a double seat were four middle-aged women with careworn faces and knobby hands. They wore their best kimonos of handsome light-weight wool in subdued colors. Snow-white tabi, those two-toed Japanese stockings, fitted into gaeta (wooden clogs) on the floor or were tucked under them when they sat on their heels on the seat. They were coming from Osaka where a temple celebrated the seven hundred and fiftieth anniversary of the founding of Zen Buddhism. It was a pilgrimage for them— and a picnic, too. One carried a furoshika with small boxes wrapped in it—probably lunch boxes with the fragments thriftily saved. Another carried a plastic net shopping bag. The third had gathered quite a bunch of flowers wrapped in newspaper. Number Four carried a PANAM airplane bag.

They really enjoyed themselves on their day off. Chattering at times and lapsing into silence, they were neighbors on a long-planned outing. They all had "pahmas"—permanent waves; they all had wrist watches. Probably during the week they wore Western clothes, a skimpy cotton dress or those long dark slacks working women go in for. But for a picnic? No, they wore a real kimono which cost each one maybe $20 to $25 US.

It was raining as we pulled into Kyoto. Two got ready with bright Japanese paper umbrellas. The youngest reached into her PANAM bag and brought forth a plastic tablecloth. She wrapped it around her like a shawl. Number Four liked the rain; she refused shelter for herself or her flowers. They stood in the aisle ahead of us chattering and laughing, glad to have had the outing and glad to have come to the end of it. Tomorrow they might be knee-deep in mud in the rice fields, or pulling a cart in the streets, and tourists would cluck in dismay at the hard lot of women in Japan.

Japan puzzles me. It won't stay still. There's no country so rooted in tradition, so immobile in the past like a prehistoric fly in amber; and none so fluid, so sensitive to every passing fad. No country has more restrained taste, lovely soft fabrics of subdued patterns, paintings in black and greys, table arrangements of a few dry twigs. And yet gaudy pinwheels, cheap statues, crazy plastic toys from Japan flood the markets of the world—their own included. At times, it seems their Westernization happened around 1910 and froze there; at other times, we see them whizzing away ahead of us, streaking past 1980 right now while we dawdle along in the 60's.

The Teddy Roosevelt era lives on in Japan. Hiking, field days, setting-up exercises, all the trappings of "keeping fit" are "great stuff." Turkish baths and massage are still all the rage. Yogurt—which plagued my puny childhood—is advertised everywhere. The children run around catching butterflies. The clothes often look like something from your mother and father's honeymoon album. It's as if the germ theory of contagious diseases just hit Japan; street cleaners and housewives wear gauze masks over their noses like operating room nurses. Black, high-collared suits such as German university students wore before World War I, are still standard for schoolboys; middy blouses and pleated skirts, for girls. Little boys wear long stockings and high button shoes.

Yet the slickest brochure I ever saw is put out by Toyo Rayon Company; a beautiful print job, luscious photography, models in tomorrow's fashions, and all put out, not for foreign, but for Japanese trade. Madison Avenue has arrived in Japan!

Still, even those Japanese girls, modeling extreme fashions, have only put on Westernization. The hard core is Japanese through and through. No matter how good the veneer, the wood remains the same.

Haruko was a student in a large public high school. She had her camera, played American records, danced Western dances and had, indeed, worn a kimono only two or three times in her life. One day, at school, she found that 3,600 yen had been stolen from her. Worth about $10.00 US, it was quite a loss. She reported the theft to the police. An investigation followed. Teachers and principal were incensed. They called her on the carpet. "You have given our school a bad name because you reported the theft to the police. You must apologize publicly to all the students." Haruko did. She humbly implored pardon for having cast a slur on the school's reputation. Then she went home and committed suicide.

Suicide is still the honorable way out of any difficulty. At Kujo I met Sadao with this story: He was a soldier stationed near Kyoto. A good Catholic, he came each Sunday to Mass and often during the week as well. One day, Sister Marie Elise found him white and tense in the last pew. Sadao was in love with a girl with a propensity toward suicide. The first time, she took sleeping pills because her stepfather was making advances to her. But she survived them. Then she met and fell in love with Sadao. The stepfather forbade him the house; the girl went for the sleeping pills again. Again, she survived. The stepfather relented a little but said she could not marry until she had repaid him for board and lodging for ten years. Seeing years of hard work ahead of her, the girl reached once more for sleeping pills. She was in the hospital now. What should Sadao do?

"Go away and forget her," Sister advised. "If she goes in for suicide at every hard spot, you will soon find yourself a widower, anyway."

The idea fell flat; he could not forget her.

"Then, you will have to change her views on life. Bring her here to the church, and if she becomes a Christian, you stand to gain a wife who is willing to live long enough to overcome her difficulties." He did and she did.

Many old customs survive. For instance, it is most unlucky for a hearse to back up, because then the spirit of the dead man will return to his house to plague his relatives forever. Likewise, a car bearing a bride must never back up; the marriage will go on the rocks and the bride will return to her father's house. Well, one day on a very narrow road, Father Murrett was accompanying a corpse to the cemetery and the hearse met another car. There was a bride in it. Both cars stopped; the drivers haggled. Neither was willing to back up.

"Why can't you let the bride sit by the road while you back up?" one asked.

"It would be better for you to take your corpse out and let him lie on the roadside while I pass," urged the other. They argued for some time. Then Father Murrett's party gave in. The man he was burying had no near relatives. Furthermore, he had been such a good man nobody would mind his spirit being around for ever and ever.

Years ago when Sister Gemma and Sister Rose Ann were assisting Japanese Sisters in Tokyo, one of the girls there brought them a half-dead cat. Her heart was touched; if Puss could not be healed, he should at least have tender loving care for his last days. Sister Gemma struggled with his malady for a week or so. Then she told the girl, "I don't think he is going to recover. Will you take him to the veterinarian and have him disposed of? Whatever the fee is, we will pay it." In due time the following bill came from the vet:

NAME OF ANIMAL	....	Pussu
PRICE OF INJECTION	....	450 yen
FOR BURIAL IN BUDDHIST CEMETERY WITH APPROPRIATE PRAYERS	....	500 yen

This was pretty awful—a convent cat gets a Buddhist funeral!

In Japan, religion has three main streams—Shintoism, Buddhism and Christianity—and any number of offshoots. Shinto is the old Japanese state religion; it embodies the best in Japanese character. Simple living, unadorned temple—in a word, love of the Just Enough, No More. It's dangerous to propound theories about any nation, but it seems to me that the truest thing about the Japanese is that they hate excess. The snug fit—that's their dish. Clothes wrap around neatly; no billowing skirts or ruffled top pieces. No excess room in cars; just enough to fit the human person. Doorways permit the normal-sized Japanese to pass through; Westerners can bump their heads, if they insist on growing so high. Lunch boxes are crammed with rice, fish, vegetables. Just enough for one meal, compact and convenient. The whole lunch fits into a pile of school books like just another book. On the road, too, they love the tight squeeze. Why miss a truck by three inches when a half-inch still leaves your paint intact? Maybe this principle is why the Japanese don't use chairs; think of all the space wasted beneath you. It's why they delight in little boxes that fit into little boxes that fit into little boxes ad infinitum. Affection is deep but it never overflows into kisses in public.

Flowers in a vase, too, are never profuse. A dry branch, one blossom, one leaf—that's enough to bring about beauty. Why be opulent?

Shinto temples are simple little houses with steep roofs. No bright paint, except a bit of gold on the crossed rafters. The subdued coloring of weathered wood is nicer. Shinto temples aren't meant to endure. You never find anything like the ancient Hindu or Buddhist sanctuaries of India, China or Ceylon. Rather, Shinto sacred places are built of wood, torn down and rebuilt every ten years or so.

Buddhism came from India through Korea in the sixth century; the two religions achieved a very happy marriage, each going its own way and yet taking on something of the other's personality.

The aoi, Hollyhock Festival, brings out hundreds and thousands to Kyoto's streets. This ancient capital of Japan (Tokyo has been capital a mere hundred years) boasts more than three hundred temples. Some are massive buildings, built of mammoth stones and added to through the centuries. Others may be just a torii gateway opening on a set of old steps to a pagoda-like summerhouse set under venerable trees. The smell of incense pervades the streets of Kyoto; head-shaven Buddhist nuns ride in her trolley cars and buses; many pedestrians nod respectfully as they pass a temple or a sacred place. The entrance to a shrine is ornamented with a thick rope strung with longish whisk brooms. The idea is that brooms brush off the world's dust as a worshipper enters the temple. Something like our idea of holy water fonts.

Small wonder, then, that Kyoto's very modern streets were packed to watch the Hollyhock Festival procession. We found ourselves behind rows and rows of children, the lucky ones in front sitting on the curb. Across the street were electric advertisements for cigarettes, whiskeys, banks, toys, toothpastes, automobiles and "pahmanettos," now further reduced to "pahma." A jeepful of policemen cleared the street with walkie-talkie loud speakers. Once they had gone, ancient Japan took over.

First the priests. Their long robes were a bit rumpled; their faces, tired; but the straw sandals paced deliberately as they had been doing since nine that morning and would keep on doing until six that evening. Each walked quietly with plenty of clear space around him, as if contemplating in isolation and yet as one of a group. Like the Cistercians—each alone in his cell and yet with the feeling of others doing the same thing nearby.

Several, most handsomely dressed, rode magnificent horses. Bulls festooned with orange silk ropes and tassels were led by; and girls, representing princesses, passed. Many walked. On the white painted faces were lines of weariness and I saw more than one turn impassive eyes from right to left and back again. But they stepped steadily forward. Others, in glorious white and gold kimonos, were mounted on horses. The Imperial Princess herself was borne by on a high palanquin on the shoulders of six men. They looked exhausted after five hours' marching. As they passed me, a new man exchanged places with one of the bearers, slipping up behind him and easing his shoulder into place. Throughout the hour-long procession, deep religious feeling kept paraders and the crowd silent.

During centuries-old pageantry, light green papers fluttered down on the tightly packed streets. One landed on my gadget bag. I took it home, loath to profane the silence of that hallowed procession. "What is it?" I asked Sister Sabina later.

"I'll read it for you," she said with an odd smile. "It says: You can win a transistor radio with three hundred wrappers from our Lucky Buy Ice Cream sticks."

Christianity is a late-comer, brought by St. Francis Xavier in 1549. For a short time it flourished, but before long smiles turned to frowns. By 1638, headlords were going around with nails and hammer posting proclamations such as the one we have on a wooden board preserved in Tsu. For being three hundred years old it has a very modern flavor:

> The Christian religion has been prohibited. Therefore, if anyone is suspected of being a Christian he should be reported. The rewards are as follows:
>
> To the accuser of a priest .... 500 pieces of silver
> To the accuser of a brother .... 300 pieces of silver
> To the accuser of one who has abandoned his faith and
> then repented .... 300 pieces of silver
> To the accuser of a Christian or his servant .... 100 pieces of silver
> The above list of rewards will be adhered to. If the accuser is a believer himself or a servant of a Christian, then he will be pardoned because of his own accusation and rewarded with 500 pieces of silver. If a Christian is hidden and found out by an outsider, then chief of the Five Persons Group which hides him, and every member of the Group, will be punished.
>
> (signed) Todo Daigaku no Kami
> Headlord of the Tsu clan

The technique of punishing every member of a group for the misdeeds of one is powerful, especially if the group has nothing much in common. Thus the "Neighborhood Groups" operating in Manila during World War II were designed so that the non-heroic would make sure no American or Filipino guerillas were harbored in their neighborhood. In certain prisons, ten men were executed if one escaped; this perfects a spy system operating among the prisoners themselves.

In ancient Japan, the "Five Persons Groups" gave each Christian four potential traitors. Paying tattletales is still in very good standing in certain quarters. Also the old bait, "Get yourself out of hot water by putting someone else into it." What with communists holding much of

Europe and all of China, the Christian who dies in his bed must feel a
bit odd about it. Why anyone thinks it peculiar to die for the Faith is a
mystery to me. Not so long ago, we saw Mexican Catholics lined up and
shot. In this world of the sixties, without putting it into words, many a
death sentence is levied for the Faith. Indeed, a Maryknoller who can't
talk about his prison days, is considered sort of underprivileged.

The latest religion to sweep over Japan is the Sokagakkai, a combination of politics and health-prayers with a large dash of aggression. "You
will recover from your illness," the proponents tell a victim, "if you get
three more to join Sokagakkai." Telephone calls, personal visits, button-
holing people on the streets—anything is done to secure another adherent.
We come across Sokagakkai when we instruct people who want to become
Christian. "If you go on with this," they say, "your child will die or you
will be killed." The Sokagakkai run out the back door when we come in
the front. And vice versa; they come in the back door as soon as we leave
the front. As a political party, Sokagakkai has elected one candidate to the
Diet; they claim they will take over the entire country in twenty years.
Well, we will see.

⋘ 21 ⋙ *Two Chips off the Old Heart*

OF course, I fell in love. There are bits of my heart left
all over the world, but two very considerable chunks fell off in Japan.
One fell at the feet of an old Buddhist pilgrim; the other I put into the
dying hands of a saint. "When you get up there," I asked her, "tell God
we love you because you love Him."

Oddly enough, I met both of them just after seeing the fabulous Toyo
Rayon Company's Shiga plant in Ishiyama—"fabulous" in the Hollywood
sense. This one plant employs seven thousand five hundred people, of
whom two thousand are girls averaging twenty-one years of age; it produces about twenty-five thousand tons of rayon thread a year. If you ever
held two hundred thousand feet of spun rayon hanging easily from your
little finger, you would realize that it takes a lot of rayon to add up to
twenty-five thousand tons. Toyo Rayon is one of the biggest and best of
the great post-war factory system which is changing Japan's social grades.
The idea is: How are you going to keep them down on the farm after
they've been factory girls?

Three of us asked to go through the factory. We did not expect VIP
treatment but we got it. Scarcely through the front gate, we were bowed

at by the uniformed policeman. Then the receptionist bowed too, and took us to what must have been the Board of Directors' room—huge soft chairs with a low table. Another girl appeared with hot perfumed towels and bowls of green tea. We sank almost out of sight in the cushioned chairs and, on coming up for air, saw four men enter the room. They bowed; we bowed. One of them handed out lush literature—coated paper, rich pictures, modern lay-out, sophisticated writing in English, and yet obviously intended for Japanese trade. They too got towels and hot tea. Naoyuki Minai, possibly twenty-six or so, formerly employed by the US Air Force at Tokyo's Flight Control Tower, was our guide. His English limped a little but there was no mistaking his American accent.

This Shiga plant is only one of eight such factories of Toyo Rayon Company. A reservoir holds water from Lake Biwa; the plant uses one hundred thousand tons a day, to operate three mills, a hospital, a research institute, a power plant and living quarters for 2,750 men and women in separate dormitories. The other half of the employees are "commuters" as Naoyuki called them; they live outside the plant but can buy their meals at company cafeterias. The company is owned and operated entirely by Japanese.

We went to South Dormitory where 623 girls live under the wing of Kasuko Utugi, twenty-three, a graduate Social Worker. All the "mothers" at Toyo Rayon must be graduates in Social Work, she said. The mill runs twenty-four hours a day, seven days a week. The girls work in eight-hour shifts—from 6 A.M. to 2 P.M., 2 P.M. to 10 P.M., and 10 P.M. to 6 A.M. They are recruited from country districts, but unlike many factories, Toyo Rayon does not bring them from distant islands. Most of their girls come from central Honshu, close to the factory. Applicants are tested, Kasuko said.

"What kind of a test? Intelligence test?" I asked.

"No," she said slowly. "For just common sense, I think you would call it."

They sign up for three years and many renew. The average girl at Toyo Rayon stays five years.

The dormitory itself, we would say, is a barn—a big wooden building with bare corridors wide enough to drive a fire-engine through. But when you know the furniture-less Japanese homes, you know the girls would want nothing else. At the entrance is what the British call a "tuck shop." The girls can buy odds and ends—candy, chewing gum, pencils, shampoo, slippers, laundry and toilet soaps, combs, letter paper, etc. The woman behind the counter was a cheerful, motherly type. She operated two such stores for the company. The girls at South Dormitory now were working in the morning shift, so the store was open in the afternoon. East Dormitory girls worked afternoons; they bought in the morning.

On the first floor were huge "common rooms" for washing and ironing, a beauty parlor, a ping-pong room, a bathroom more like a steamy swimming pool. Like all Japanese, the girls first wash themselves and then soak all together in a tank of very hot water. The Company provides all sorts of free-time activities. A cooking class occupied one room; a flower-arrangement class, another. Although every girl must have finished ninth grade before she can be hired—and that is an excellent education by Asian standards—she has a chance to continue her studies while she works. She may be short on Kanji characters (the complicated ones from China); she can learn more of them here. English, history, fine arts—many cultural courses are open. At the end of her three years, she may get a diploma. Not equal to a secondary school diploma, nevertheless it is worth something in Japan's education-hungry society.

Sleeping rooms were upstairs. Miss Utugi ran ahead to see if we might visit a room; the girls' privacy was not to be violated. Seven girls to a very large room; each roomful responsible for keeping some part of the house clean. The young "mother" came dancing down that long bare corridor. Yes, we could visit one of the rooms. She slid open a door and we stepped out of our shoes on to the tatami floor. It was very large and lined with sliding doors. Out of sight were shelves and cupboards and rolled-up mats and all the paraphernalia of living. The outside wall was really a series of picture windows; the room was bright and airy. Two girls sat on the tatami before a low table with a mirror, intent on the age-old feminine business of improving on nature. They leaped to their feet and bowed nicely. The low table, I saw then, was a knitting machine. Many girls make nice things for themselves or to sell to others. A light blue sweater, half done, hung from the machine. "It takes me ten days' spare time to make one," the girl said. "Smart people can do it in one day if they work hard at it. But I'm slow—and lazy."

Further down the hall, Miss Utugi slid open another door. "This is to give the girls a feeling of a small home." It was a typical Japanese vestibule leading to a number of small rooms; a complete Japanese house. "The girls can come here at night to study or to chat when the light or noise would disturb others in their dormitory rooms."

Factory girls at Toyo Rayon get about $20.00 a month to start with. They pay no rent, light, heat or electricity; $4.00 a month for meals and a trifle for insurance completes expenditures. Each year, they get $1.50 to $3.00 a month increase, depending on how efficient they show themselves to be. There are twenty-five work days a month but there is no day, such as our Sunday, when they are all free.

"Toyo Rayon is unusual," Sister Therese Martin told me. "The girls develop poise, independence and yet they keep the gentleness of the true Japanese woman. You can tell the difference between them and those from other factories. They are not so shy. They respond to friendliness.

We have asked if we might go through other factories, but have been refused. I think the management thought we would see things they would prefer to keep quiet about."

En route to the mill, we passed the gymnasium, auditorium and swimming pool. Landscaping was perfect. "Gardens keep the dust down, and the morale up," Naoyuki said.

Jinken (man-made silk), in spite of its name, seems to be made without man's help. We wandered through the huge air-conditioned rooms as through deserted cathedrals. An attendant here and there glanced through glass windows which let the eye in on the mysterious processes going on in the machines, but he was a supernumerary. One could almost hear the machines say, "Get along out of here! We are doing all right by ourselves." Nevertheless, we saw the blocks of wood-pulp from Canada as they are ground up, mixed with caustic soda, mushed, squeezed, rolled, shredded, churned, dissolved, filtered, until the poor stuff looks like Karo syrup on a chilly day. Then it is thinned and poured out of a tiny sieve with holes .07 mm. in diameter. You can punch 131,500 such holes in a single inch. Forty streams of liquid rayon are solidified at once in the sulphuric acid. All forty of them are caught up on the bobbin to make a single rayon thread.

It was a relief to get into the washing, drying, inspection and packing rooms where human beings made a comfortable shuffle and human hands were at work. Girls and men were swathed in coverall aprons; their heads covered by white caps. But they looked up and smiled at us and graciously let us see their work. Shipments were going off to Bulgaria, Pakistan, Canada, South Vietnam, not to mention India, China, the United States and Australia. Yet, only forty percent of Toyo Rayon goes out of the country. Most of it is destined for the socks, underwear, shirts, curtains, kimonos—light and dark, simple or gorgeous—of little old Japan. Synthetic fibers are a godsend to a nation so squeezed into its four little islands that there is no land left for cotton plantations, silkworms, sheep ranches and other means of producing natural cloth.

Naoyuki brought us back to the "main office" and we sank once more into the vastly overstuffed chairs. Hot perfumed towels again, and green tea; he bowed, we bowed; the party was over.

On to Ishiyama temple where I met one of the major loves of my life! I have learned by now that pagan gods never live on the level. Maybe that's why the Old Testament abominates the "high places." Ishiyama temple is very old—nine hundred years. I felt every bit that old myself when we reached the street again. Then I stopped dead in my tracks. Through the trees I saw a strange apparition. An old woman in wooden gaeta, with a pack on her back, a long stick in her hand and a black rosary twined around her left wrist. She was hobbling down the graveled path, very, very tired. She too stopped dead at the sight of us, far stranger than she in old Japan.

She smiled; we smiled. She was very ready to talk. Seventy-six years old. From Nagoya. Had never been on a pilgrimage before, but started off four days ago to tramp around from one temple to another. "Why?" she repeated our question. "Because I love God and this is how I can tell Him so."

She had a family. "Indeed, they gave me the chance to make this pilgrimage and I'm praying for them as I go along."

She turned to me. "And how old are you?" I laughed and owned up honestly. She beamed at me like my long-lost grandmother. "Now live long," she urged, patting my shoulder. "Live long and make lots of converts. Teach them to love God."

We walked out to the street with her. "Where will you stay tonight?" we asked.

She sighed a little. "I asked that young man in there (referring to one of the monks) and he told me that there's another temple in town which has rooms for pilgrims. I'll go there."

"But that's on the other side of town," Sister protested. "You can't walk that far."

The old lady looked a bit disheartened. After all, she was seventy-six and had never been a pilgrim before. Home and her own roll of bedding looked pretty good to her at that moment.

"Why don't you take a taxi?" Sister suggested. "Here's one coming right now."

The dear old face brightened. "It's not exactly right," she demurred, "but I'll do it."

We put her into it—pilgrim stick, straw hat, bundle, rosary, angelic face and all—and waved her off. Then we caught the bus home to Otsu. My heart has never been the same since.

That was hard enough, but Hirayama Sensei stole a bigger piece. When I saw her, she was lying on the tatami of a small house near the Tsu church. The room was cleared of furniture, as usual. Only an exquisite flower arrangement lay before a shrine where Hirayama Sensei's dying eyes could see Our Blessed Mother and tell her she was coming. Her white hair flowed over the small pillow. Her frail body made hardly a mound beneath the clean bedding. Her good friends and "children in the Faith" were always there, one or two of them sitting silently alongside, to tend her and pray for her.

For Hirayama Sensei was a catechist. Sensei means teacher; Teacher Hirayama had told people about God all her life. In fact, it *was* her life. As she lay dying for many weeks, her spiritual children practiced on her all the virtues she had taught them. Surely as she looked at them, her thoughts went back to the time she had deliberately put aside the chance of having natural children.

In 1893, she had been born Little Lady Unwanted, the seventh girl. When a boy was born after her, she was given away to a Catholic orphanage in Kyoto, and there saddled with the baptismal name of Pelagia. She was three at the time. Some years later when she was pretty well grown up, a childless couple named Hirayama adopted her with the idea, not unusual in Japan, that she would marry and her husband would take the Hirayama name. By this time she had conceived a great devotion to St. John Vianney, the Curé d'Ars, who spent his life as a parish priest in a humble corner of France. She used her confirmation name of Jeanne Marie, in his honor.

When it was time to marry, the girl threw a monkey wrench into the whole Hirayama plan. She refused to marry. "I intend to spend my whole life working for the Church," she declared. I can imagine how chagrined the Sisters at the orphanage were. The Hirayamas were even more embarrassed. They turned her out of the house. It was understandable.

From that time on, she was known as Hirayama Sensei—Teacher Hirayama. She used to go to Catholic families, preparing children for First Holy Communion and Confirmation, and instructing adults as well. She was a private tutor for religion subjects. At Tsu, I met Mrs. Yakota who remembers her very well.

"When I was around eleven," she told me, "Hirayama Sensei used to come to our house. We children were enthralled with her old-fashioned hair-do. We knew her as 'Auntie,' and were a little afraid we would break her. She seemed so frail, even then. There were few Catholics in Kyoto then and we all knew one another. My parents and grandparents knew her; my children too were instructed by Sensei. In my family, she has been a beacon of Faith for four generations."

Had she lived in Europe in the Middle Ages, Sensei would have been an anchorite, living in a stone cell up against the church wall with a window cut into the sanctuary. As it was, she lived in a tiny house, as neat as a pin, next door to the church. Father Barry and the Sisters knew much that she would never have made known to anyone else. Every night, she made a visit to the Blessed Sacrament; every noon, she and Yamaguchi San, a hunchback and a cripple, said the rosary together in church. They chose that hour because no one would be around to hear them. She was constantly making things for the church—little things like finger towels, altar linens, small cloths. She never gave vestments; she could not have afforded the materials for one thing and—she was so Japanese!—they would be seen and admired and people would say "Hirayama Sensei gave them."

She never kept money she received for private teaching; she gave it and most of her monthly salary as catechist, to the poor.

Had you passed Hirayama Sensei on the street, you would never have looked twice. Yet a second look would have been rewarding. She made her own clothing, exquisitely; her manners were perfect; her language without flaw. Her gentility was Japanese to the bone—no fanfare, no publicity, just devoted service.

She was wonderful in hospitals. She slipped in and out quietly, stopping by a bedside here and there, saying a few words and leaving whatever she had brought for that particular patient. When they were dying, she stopped to pray. Nobody could ease a parting soul as Sensei could.

And what a person for writing letters! She kept in close contact with any new Catholics she had taught. Some of them fell away; most caught her spirit of staunch Faith. Hirayama Sensei kept them all in her prayers and correspondence, no matter.

She was a silent worker, a lone ranger. She ferreted out the lonely, the old, the unfortunate. She found more than one leper hidden in a spare room, afraid to show his face; she brought sunshine and calm endurance to them all.

Her crowning achievement—but she would have called it, her best gift from God—came a few months before I saw her. Some years before, she had befriended a school boy, a brilliant student who could not study in the racket which went on in his home all the time. She suggested that he come to her house to study. He did. She never disturbed him, just let him use the light and the table as he wished. When he grew up, he asked to be a Catholic; later he asked her prayers to enter the seminary; and in 1961 he was ordained.

I took my turn with Sister Pastores and Sister Amelia at Tsu, watching beside the dying Sensei. The doctor who cared for her, the women who also took turns tending her, the youngsters who came in after school to see if they could do anything for her—they all were her spiritual children. She confessed once that when she made her great decision, what cost her the most was the thought that she would die without any family to love her. "And see!" she said, weakly waving to the people around her.

She made a will, she who had nothing to leave:

Dear Father,
    You told me to write my will for after my death. I started but I have nothing to write. I am passing every day in gratitude for God's love. In spite of old age and inability to work, I have lived until now, thanks to the mercy of Jesus. My only wish is to thank God and continue loving Him until I die.

She died on a Sunday morning after I left Tsu. It just happened—how can anyone use that phrase, "It just happened"?—that the Papal Internuncio to Japan, Archbishop Enrici, was in Tsu that morning. It just happened, too, that Bishop Furuya of Kyoto was there too. They bent over the wisp of a person as she lay on the clean tatami floor and gave her every blessing possible, from the Pope's on down. Possibly, she had even higher blessings. The night before, she stretched out, full length, the arms which had lain helpless for months. Her weak voice became strong. "Maria Sama, Maria Sama—ah, how beautiful!"

Maybe, up there with Maria Sama (Mary Queen), Hirayama Sensei is still working. Maybe by this time she has met that sweet old Buddhist pilgrim who stole my heart at Ishiyama. Maybe the two of them have had a good talk. Maybe, by this time, the pilgrim lady has learned that God loves her even more than she loves Him. I hope so.

≤(22)≥ *B-R-R-R! It's Cold Up Here*

THE Japanese are old hands at split-level living. Levels are split into a hundred parts in every house. Two steps up to the bedroom, one step down to the bath, dive down into the kitchen, take a ladder to the storage space. Not only steps, but half-steps and step-and-a-halfs lie in wait for the unwary.

Walls are non-existent. That is, as walls. Or is it that doors are non-existent as doors? But it all makes for gracious living. Walls slide away; rooms merge; a cozy bedroom turns into a wide-open balcony by sliding papered wall sections together like the blades of a Japanese flashbulb reflector. Very convenient. For instance, you are in tedious company. There is no need to start edging toward the door to make your escape. Everyone knows your wicked intent, that way. No. You merely slide a section of the wall open and back gracefully away—probably into a cupboard or down three steps to the bathroom.

I love Japanese living—from the ankles up. Quiet, serene, simple. No pictures on the walls; no tables, chairs, sofas, coffee tables, to fall over or walk around; instead, cushions to kneel on, tea to sip, gardens to view. But is life complicated below the ankles! You have shoes to walk the street—wooden gaeta in wet weather. At your doorway, you shed the shoes and step into slippers for wooden floors and corridors. But before you may tread on the sacred tatami (rice mat floors) you must shed the slippers. Only bare feet or stockings are permitted. Reversing the process, to go out you don slippers for wooden floors, take them off at the front door and do your best to get into shoes gracefully for the street. Heaven help you, if you try to leave the house by the back door when you came in the front! I tried to have shoes and slippers posted at every door, running around late one night to get them just where I'd need them. But by evening of the next day, five pairs were at the front door and none anywhere else. A shoe horn is standard equipment when you go out. Small wonder the Sisters go in for elastic shoelaces!

And the church problem. In the States, the worthy pastor estimates Mass attendance by a glance at his parking lot. In Japan, all he has to do is to count the shoes in his church vestibule. After Mass, doorways are clogged. Each parishioner has to step from the church floor into his shoes. What a hubbub! Who has stepped into whose shoes? Why aren't mine where I left them?

In the Philippines, during my ten years as a teacher there, we Maryknoll Sisters used to shake hands with one another when we read school-management magazines from the States. Thank God, we didn't have to provide lockers for coats, rubbers, galoshes, mittens, ski-pants. Goodie! Our kindergarteners did not have to be buttoned into their snow suits. The worst we had to put up with was the racket of wooden shoes running upstairs in typhoon weather, when nobody in his right mind would wear his one and only pair of sneakers, much less his Sunday-go-to-Mass leather shoes, if he had some.

But due to this complexity below the ankle, Japanese schools are not so easy. You should see the shoe rack room at the Muroran Catholic School, just put up by Benedictine Sisters from St. John's, Minnesota. Eight hundred girls attend. Each must have her locked compartment to store her outside shoes for the day.

Muroran, by the way, is just about the last place on earth that one would expect to find a Catholic girls' high school dominating a mountain and equipped with the latest gadgets for science labs, Home Ec kitchens, sewing classes, athletics and dramatics. For Muroran is a city on Hokkaido which was, until recently, something like Siberia. In other words, a place of bitter winters, few people, tremendous scenery and a wealth of natural resources frozen stiff.

Throughout Asia, it seemed to me, people were on the move. In Ceylon the Indians were being pushed out. In the Philippines, vast numbers of homesteaders were ripping up their roots to resettle in the wastelands of Mindanao or up in northern Luzon. In Hong Kong, five out of every six on the streets had fled from ancestral homes in China. Taiwan was full of Mandarin-speaking "mainlanders" who had been driven off the continent. And now in Japan, I met the restless ones again, seeking jobs in new factories, new fields to plow, new horizons to follow.

There is even a new mountain to play with. In December, 1944, the land near Muroran began to rise, oddly; helped along by earthquakes, the vegetable fields rose nearly eight inches a day. By July, 1946, things started erupting, and in February of the next year a new active volcano was formally recognized. They had to recognize it; it was right there. The government gave it a name, Showa, in honor of the Emperor's family, and declared it a "national treasure." This last alone will make sure that the baby mountain will be accustomed from its infancy to being visited, photographed, exclaimed over, wondered at, and tramped around, by thousands of school children who roll up in busloads to appreciate dutifully Japan's national treasures.

It takes most of two days to reach Hokkaido by train and ship. But we went in about four hours from Kyoto to Tokyo and on to Sapporo's airport in a very modern plane. Everything seemed as drably Western as a tourist might want. Hostesses in pert caps and suits; passengers slumped behind newspapers and nearly all in Western dress. But a young Japanese woman, attired in glorious zebra-striped kimono, was not satisfied. She surveyed the tourist seat with mistrust. Then she stepped out of her "zori" and, tucking her feet under her, sat on her heels up on the chair. For all her poise, she might have been on a tatami mat pouring tea. She made sure her obi would not be wrinkled on the chairback, rearranged a jeweled pin in her hair, and settled herself to enjoy modern transportation.

It was not for too long. The distance in mileage as well as in climate is like a trip from Wilmington, N.C., to Portsmouth, Me., or Toronto, Canada. Or from Los Angeles to mid-Oregon. Or from the northern edge of Mississippi up into Wisconsin. The air was chilly, even at the end of May. Trees were just beginning to bud. Snow stays on the ground for six months—a fine, powdery snow the Japanese are not wasting. Enthusiasts by the chartered plane-load come to ski and toboggan. In summer the crowds come for hot springs; a famous spa at Noribetsu attracts thousands. Hokkaido is a great honeymoon spot. In a railroad station, we walked behind a young couple getting off on the right foot for happy married life. He carried the camera and guide book; she, attired in her trousseau finery, walked behind with the suitcases.

Besides pleasure, Hokkaido has industry. Coal and iron mean steel; there are two huge steel plants at Muroran. Coal brings ships to refuel, even in this diesel age. Two-thirds of the island is covered by forests; that results in papermills and sawmills aplenty. More than seventy percent of Japan's newsprint comes from one mill in Tomakomai. What isn't forest, is good grazing land. So cattle, horses, pigs, goats and sheep flourish. The

Emperor's white horses come from Hokkaido, they say. Not so beautiful but more interesting to common people are the island's sardines and herrings. For a while, after the war, Japan hoped that farmers would rush up there to stake out homesteads, but few like the idea of only one crop a year. Japanese don't like cold countries. The only inducement to make them settle in Manchuria in the old Empire days, was the double wages paid for almost any type of work. Hokkaido is as far north as Manchuria.

So—five million people rattle around on the island. But they have big ideas for the future. Seven of us wedged into one of those itsy-witsy Japanese cars and whizzed along sixty miles of magnificent road from the airport to Muroran. Forty of them were along the beach; the waves practically washed us out to sea. Practically, that is. From Tomakomai to Muroran is a strip of ocean land which, they tell us, will be the industrial center of Japan in twenty years. The two towns will be merged into one great population center of more than a million—something like the Tokyo-to-Yokohama area, or the Kobe-Osaka district. Or, to translate it into our own megalopolises, like Chicago-Gary-Hammond-East Chicago; those in California around San Francisco and Los Angeles where one town runs into another with nary a cow nor a tractor to separate them; and of course the biggest of them all, which sprawls intermittently all the way from Boston to Washington, D.C.

It's hard to see, right now, that projected city of one million spread along this virgin seashore where tall grass waves on the undulating sand dunes. Fishermen's huts, nets drying, boats pulled up on beaches, seemed the only signs of life. But every few minutes we passed a new factory with a cluster of company houses around it. Not so many workers as one might think come with the company. Maybe eight hundred technicians from Honshu, the Japanese main island, and a few local helpers. Machines are run by automation, which doesn't help the local situation much. But the two steel mills near Muroran were erected before automation times. They employ eight thousand and four thousand people—which helps a lot. Later, when we went over it again by train, the whole area reminded me much of the stories I have heard of Manchuria; drab paintless houses, sometimes mere shacks, roofs of galvanized iron or tar-paper shingles, railroad tracks with factory sidings, a few soot-covered bushes, men and women in boots and dark clothes. Unlike Manchuria, however, a TV aerial sprouts on each shabby roof. There isn't always a TV inside the hut, the Sisters say, but keeping up with the Joneses demands at least the aerial. This strip in Hokkaido has the highest TV rate of Japan. In spite of this, there is a rawness in the civilization to match the rawness of the wind.

This is what amazes one in Hokkaido. It is so unlike Japan. The rice fields, the mountains, the ancient temples, the farmhouses bowed down under the weight of huge roofs—in other words, the national flavor—is not here. The houses have doors on hinges, built to withstand biting winds—not the casual sliding walls one is used to. There are not even tatami floors; one can hardly imagine a Japanese being happy without tatami. A fire hazard, so they say. Borrowing an idea from Siberia, to heat a house they build a furnace in a chest-high brick wall between two rooms so that the hot bricks heat both sides. That's for comfortable rooms. Most people—including us!—have small iron stoves and a pile of firewood. After all, Siberia is only 250 miles away—an icy swim over the Japan Sea which will get you nothing but a whopping good cold.

You have to pinch yourself from time to time, not only to keep the blood circulating, but to convince yourself you are not in Pennsylvania Dutch territory. Farms around Sapporo, the capital, are nothing like typical Japanese homesteads. Wide fields, red-painted barns, apple orchards, metal-topped silos, broad American-type farmhouses—can this be Japan? Back in 1871, President Grant sent one Horace Capron to Japan to teach American large-scale farming. Capron was then United States Commissioner of Agriculture. He resigned to take on the title Agricultural Adviser to the Japanese Government. He stayed in Hokkaido for four years. From where he is today, Horace can look down and see how faithfully his pupils still carry out his lessons. Evidently, sharing American technical knowledge has been going on for nearly a century.

Our Sisters are at work in both Muroran and Tomakomai. They have Girl Scout troops, choirs, English classes and even cooking classes which bring them in contact with the people. Their projects are varied. Anything and everything to make the Church known. One year they put on a fashion show of wedding gowns in Muroran's biggest department store; this was to emphasize the sacred character of marriage. Another time, they staged a Maypole dance; the Japanese love such outdoor festivals. Of course, it ended with crowning Our Blessed Mother. Father Alfred E. Smith tells about the time Sister Hostia made a huge rosary of ping-pong balls to hang behind the altar for October. Unwilling to pierce the balls, she put them together with scotch tape, which was fine—for overnight. Then they started to fall apart. During Mass and sermon, ping-pong balls were bouncing all over the sanctuary. Not so good for devotion.

Bishop Benedict Tomizawa, a bundle of energy, governs the Church from Sapporo. Besides, he teaches in a large secular girls' school and seems to have a finger in every worthwhile pie in the city. He has four thousand Catholics in the city, less than one percent of the population, but great hopes flood his breast as he notes progress in the last few years. In 1954, he had but nine Japanese priests; he has twenty now and more than twice as many foreign missioners as were in Hokkaido before. He ordains at least one priest every year for his diocese. The Bishop put his long lean frame behind the wheel of his small car and took us out to the ball park, the imposing City Hall, the TV tower in the center of town, the track stadium and his own very modest cathedral. The city was two hundred thousand in 1946; it is half a million now. Somebody with foresight laid out the side streets, the plazas, the landscaped public parks. Then we sat down to a good simple dinner with the most energetic Bishop I have ever broken bread with.

The Bishop himself took us to the air terminal but he kept glancing at his watch. "I have to leave now," he apologized as the plane was delayed. "My classes, you know. I have to be at school to teach." I smiled to myself. Thus might St. Paul have said, "I'm sorry, but we expect an important customer at our tent-making shop and I can't afford to lose the sale. I know you'll excuse me."

As Bishop Tomizawa waved his apostolic hand in farewell, I thought I saw on it the prickles made by pushing a needle through heavy canvas.

Back to Tokyo. The 1960 census places the population at more than nine million three hundred thousand, the largest city in the world. As you might expect, it is a welter of new and old, rich and poor, East and West.

Modern Japanese talk just about half in English now. But hearing the English words is like seeing your own face in a Coney Island mirror. It's a nasty shock to a language student to look up some obscure Japanese word and find that it is English, after all. Sister Deborah was on a TV show and the director said, "We have a nation-wide tie-up for this." It was all Japanese except the word "tie-up." Poor Sister spent hours poking through a Japanese dictionary until someone told her that tie-up means tie-up.

Reading English words is even worse. Katakana characters were devised in a kindly attempt to spell foreign words. The mistake was that they consist mostly of one consonant and one vowel—ka, po, yu, te, etc. Some consonants are missing; "b" stands for "v," "r" for "l." The short "u" sound doesn't exist. It comes out as a soft Italian "a." I learned Katakana during the war years, and tried to read the advertising signs. What a thrill when I could make out turansisutoru for transistor, durai cureeningu for dry cleaning! A taxi is a takusi; a bus is a bahsu; a truck a turaku and a tire is a tiya.

They have a thrifty habit of shortening words. In 1949 I spent some time deciphering pahmanetto waybu for permanent wave. Now I find the beauty shops advertising a simple pahma; I suppose it saves much on neon lights. Television is down to terebi; and a demonstration is just a demo. Apartments are merely apahto and a department store is a depahto. These are real Japanese words in common use. You have to use English this way if you want to be understood.

Phrases too have been lifted bodily into the language. Rezyah tymu (leisure time); Rahsu awa (rush hour); Beeru haru (beer hall), are seen on every billboard. No U tahn (no U turn); Uan ue (one way); cahbu (curve) and burayki (brake) are on every highway sign. Everybody uses "How about?" In a train away up in the wilds of Hokkaido, a girl comes through the coaches selling food, "How about some ice cream?" she calls. "Ah ri' " for "all right" is a favorite of the bus girls. "Ah ri' hidari; ah ri' migi" (all right on the left; all right on the right) they sing out to the bus driver telling him it's safe to go ahead.

Why modern Japan keeps on using the Kanji or Chinese characters is beyond me. They make the reading of even a newspaper a colossal task. Even educated Japanese are stumped by lettering on memorial bronzes or on gift wrappings. "I don't know this or that character so I'm not sure just what it means," they say. The Japanese typewriter, although greatly simplified, still has banks and banks of keys which must be shifted into correct position before you can strike a single character. Operating one makes you feel that you are getting tangled up in an IBM machine. In Muroran a printing shop is down our street. The walls are lined from floor to ceiling with tiny boxes, each containing a different character in type. The old printer putters around the room, shuffling from wall to wall to find the exact character he needs. He has only three fonts of two thousand characters each, a pitiful collection. "Calling cards, wedding invitations, thank-you notes are about all I can do," he told me. To set up a newspaper, he needs 8,200 characters. He can't use a linotype nor even a typewriter. Each character must be hand-set into the press. When once the job has been run, he must study each character with a magnifying glass and file it back in those small boxes which line his walls. Poor fellow! I felt I had been talking to Ben Franklin in his printshop in Philadelphia along about 1750. But Ben had to wrestle with only about 100 characters in a font, counting upper and lower case, figures and signs.

In spite of this difficulty, the Japanese are great readers. The literacy rate, at ninety-eight percent, is highest of any in Asia. Traveling book shops and newsstands ply their trade up and down the streets. The nation reads in buses, streetcars, trains and planes as well as at home. Everything from comic books to somber tomes comes out in Japanese. With this in mind, the Church is spouting out reading material constantly. Magazines for all ages, pamphlets, leaflets, posters, all well done and beautifully illustrated, are seen everywhere. Catechisms for every grade, and even in braille, spread the truth everywhere. Legion of Mary workers canvass every home with literature; they visit hospitals, old folks' homes and country poorhouses. The Sisters do the same. Japan is plentifully watered; it's up to God to give the increase.

Japan has always been a puzzle to me—and to more astute people as well. No other people love beauty so much. They diffuse it through everything. Vegetables in the market are laid out temptingly. Cheap plastic toys are displayed in charming strings. In the rest of Asia, a market woman may have her peanuts put up, twenty or so at a time, in little cones of newspaper piled in a drab heap on her stand—probably banged together of an old carton and rusty nails. She sits impassively behind, more occupied, it seems, with nursing her baby, making up more newspaper cones, peeling the vegetables for dinner, or arguing with her neighbor for more space. If you want desperately to buy her peanuts, she will take time off to accept your money. But don't expect fraternization. In Japan, on the other hand, the market woman is all smiles and bows. She dances around her pretty little bamboo cart eager to forestall your every wish. Her radishes are tied together with red string; her apples are polished and the bad spots turned away from the customers. She is a past master at Mr. Woolworth's policy: bright lights, music, gay crepe paper, fiesta spirit will wheedle the dimes out of your pocket.

Keen commercial instinct, yes, and a deep-rooted love of Mother Nature. It is hard to figure out whether the Japanese have bent themselves to Mother Nature, or whether they have bestowed Japanese citizenship on the great lady. I tried to think it out as our airliner slipped through the clouds to soar away to Manila.

Japanese love nature so much they are unwilling to efface her handiwork. Their houses and shrines are unpainted because well-weathered wood, dark and rough, is marked by the storms and sunshine, wind and snow of years. Why cover that beauty with paint? Stones should not be chipped and polished; that results in raw colors, unnatural glare. Old faces are lovely—grey hair against dark skin, all the wrinkles that living has pressed into them. In fine old Japanese houses, posts are not cut straight up and down; rather, the tree grows as it was, from floor to ceiling. My bed was beside a lovely trunk; the wall was made to fit around it. Rather than carve a banister, a Japanese will search the world over for a tree which bends to suit his staircase.

On the other hand, there's nobody like a Japanese to twist nature to suit his own ideas. Dwarf pines, odd shapes, hybrid flowers are everywhere. Children wear cosmetics up to their eyebrows. And black hair dye is a very salable item for both men and women. Nobody will have salt and pepper hair; it must be all black or all white.

So, which is the right theory? Perhaps this is right. The Japanese and Mother Nature are like man and wife. Each gives in to the other on some points. Long association and deep love have welded them into a happy marriage. Long may they reign!

TRUST TERRITORY
of the PACIFIC

Total island population ··· 75,836.
Inhabited atolls and islands ··· 97.
Ocean area ··· 3,000,000 square miles.   Land area ··· 700 square miles.
2,141 islands.

TRUST TERRITORY
of the PACIFIC

⫷ **23** ⫸ *The Grass Skirt Has My Vote*

"AN island," wrote the boy on his examination, "is a body of land entirely surrounded by water, except on top."

Flying over the Trust Territory in the Pacific, one gets the idea that it would not take much to put these islands under water. One good wave ought to do it without half trying. You fly so long over blueness before you see even a tiny spot of green, that every dot of an island seems mighty precious. More than half the world's water is in the Pacific. It doesn't seem possible that there is any at all left for the rest of the world.

One of the nicest of these dots is Guam. Just about dead center in what might be called the Asiatic Pacific, it has always been a way station to anywhere you might wish to go. If a swimmer were to start south from Tokyo, another to swim east from Manila, a third to struggle north from Australia, they would, after fifteen hundred miles or so, emerge dripping on the beach at Guam. They might be joined by another foolhardy young fellow who had swum fifteen hundred miles west from Wake Island.

Guam is a steppingstone to some place else. Such is her fate. Even the people who live there are always popping off to Saipan or Rota or up to Okinawa. The Chamorros, who form ninety percent of the stable population of around thirty-eight thousand, are themselves late-comers in racial strains. They are a blend of Filipinos, Spanish and the original Chamorro of the Mariana Islands. Their language is half Spanish; their color is light; the men play guitars; the women wear long skirts and blouses with the typical Filipino "butterfly sleeves." Ever since 1900 Guam has been a U.S. territory; the Chamorro is educated, sanitary, and well able to hold his own in any situation. Yet he retains the gentleness of his racial background.

I am thinking in particular of Sister Callista, a Mercy Sister. Twelve years ago, I stopped on Guam for two weeks, awaiting passage into the Trust Territory. The Mercy Sisters then were two, living with thirteen novices in seven quonset huts much the worse for wear. One, I remember, had been picked up by a Navy crane and moved twenty feet or so across a road. In the process, the quonset had buckled badly. There was still a dent in the curved roof, so bad that it knocked many a harmless nun in the head as she walked back and forth inside the hut. At that time they were the only Sisters ever to inhabit Guam. The thirteen novices were local girls, thrilled at the chance to begin religious life after years of waiting. One of them was Sister Callista, with rounded features, steady eyes and a devastating smile.

The years have dealt kindly with Sister Callista. She is Superior of the main convent now, winner of several college degrees in the States, and former principal of a one-thousand-pupil school. She is still calm, steady, humorous and not in the least hurried. She drives the convent car in the same leisurely way. It has a leaky radiator, so she keeps a gallon jug of water on the floor in the back seat and a box of black pepper under the rear window. When she fills the radiator, she sprinkles black pepper into the water. Why? Well, a service station attendant told her it would help the situation—and it does.

Manila to Guam is fifteen hundred miles. We covered it in little over three hours, seven miles up in the sky. That's what everyone does—rushes into Guam, so as to sit around and wait for transportation elsewhere. While we cooled our heels, I could note what twelve years have done to this tiny island.

Guam fell to the Japanese three days after World War II began. It was bought back with blood in August, 1944. Even five years after that, it was mostly a shambles of broken coconut trees and pulverized buildings. Business was done by jeeps chugging from one shabby quonset hut to another. But now! The new post office, the government buildings, the replanted parks and ocean driveways are a joy to behold. The cathedral, once a tattered patchwork of woven bamboo mats covering what was left of the old Spanish framework, has been rebuilt, gloriously. Enshrining Our Lady of Camelin, Guam's beloved patron, it is the religious center of the island. A hospital with the latest equipment dominates an escarpment overlooking the sea. Schools for girls and boys, secular and religious, are impressive. One is a large school for boys named for Father Duenas, a Guamanian priest shot during World War II for his part in leading the resistance movement. School Sisters of Notre Dame from Milwaukee are on the island with three schools; Franciscan Sisters from La Crosse operate a clinic with four doctors employed full time. Spanish Mercedarian Sisters from Kansas City make the island the center of their extensive missions in the Marianas, Carolines and Marshalls. In 1946, when three Mercy Sisters stepped off an Army transport, they were the strangest creatures ever to set foot on Guam. Fifteen years later, the island is generously sprinkled with religious habits on both Americans and Guamanians. There are no fewer than seventy-four Mercy Sisters. All in all, the Church

in Guam, under the guidance of the Capuchin Bishop Baumgartner, seems
to be forging ahead at a great rate.

Most of the heel cooling—and heart fluttering—is done around the
Transport Office. One plane, seating perhaps fifteen people, makes a trip
once a week to Yap and Koror. Usually, the plane stays overnight on
Koror and returns the next day. Therefore, if you are not chosen to be
one of the fifteen that week, you must wait on Guam to try your luck
for the next week. The issue is always in the balance for, at the last moment, someone "more honorable than thou" may get the seat assigned
to you. Priorities are terribly, terribly important.

While we cooled the heels and fluttered the heart, Mother and I went
shopping on Guam. That meant a trip to Moylan's. If ever there was a
fabulous General Store in an outpost of civilization, Moylan's is it. Quite
soon, I hear, Moylan's will put up a new store, air-conditioned, boasting
even an escalator—the first escalator ever to pervert the Guamanian people. One more step in the you-don't-hafta life. You don't have to walk;
you ride in your car. You don't have to heat water over the stove; you
turn on the water-heater. You don't have to wash dishes; or clothes; or
even play the piano. Machines do it all for you. And now Moylan's escalator enters the picture of decadence!

But all of that was blissfully in the future; we saw Moylan's in its native
charm. The floors were of ancient wood, pretty well splintered. The show-
cases were Edwardian, if not Victorian. The merchandise is piled up to
the ceiling. Every time you breathe, you knock something down. Signs
are posted everywhere, lettered by a haggard hand:

> ADULTS WHO BREAK THINGS
> MUST PAY FOR THEM, AND
> ALSO THE THINGS THAT THEIR
> CHILDREN BREAK.

So, you try to be careful. A partial listing of all the stuff Moylan's sells
would give a case of severe frustration to Sears Roebuck's catalogue: school
bags, cameras (from $14.00 to $679.50), buckets, hair ribbons, toys, type-
writers, clocks, cosmetics, business machines, cake mixes, Japanese socks
and zori, power tools, seeds, refrigerators, ladies' hats, cornflakes, lawn-
mowers, greeting cards, plastic dishes, lamps, candy. An organ with a
pricetag of $2,995 stood right beside a box of chiclets priced at 5¢. The
candy department was doing a rush business in chocolate bunnies and
marshmallow eggs although Easter was two months past. Even Valentine
boxes of candy were going well. The shipment for those two fiestas had
arrived only a few days before; Guam's sweet tooth did not care about
dates.

One of those miracles which punctuated this trip fairly often happened on Guam. Instead of making one flight to Koror that week, the powers-that-be decided to make two "turnabouts," meaning that the plane would make a round trip on Thursday and another on Friday. The Transport Office listed us among the lucky thirty for the week. Our hearts were young and gay once more. We rose with the larks; Sister Callista and her Sisters sat us down to a hearty breakfast and out we sped to the airport to board our Albatross.

It's a bulky awkward plane, more like a ship, built for dependable service on land or water. We were a motley passenger list—a few Americans, a writer for the *National Geographic Magazine* and his wife, some island men going back home, Antonio, seven years old, and his big sister going home after a year of school on Guam. A thermos jug of coffee and a pile of paper cups beside it provided refreshment for anybody wanting it. The door to the pilot's cockpit swung open most of the time. Once up in the blue there was little for anyone to do but watch the watery miles go by.

After two hours or so, the blue-green reefs and dark palm fringes of Ulithi passed underneath. A long curving string of yellow sand in the sea. Only ten feet above sea level, Ulithi is practically washed out to sea with every hurricane. Yet it is the center of Father Walter's parish; and any parish with Father Walter in it is solidly established.

The only trouble with being Ulithi's pastor is this: Once you leave the atoll on business, it's awfully hard to get back on it. The planes do not stop; the ships call infrequently because there is no real harbor, and often they are in no mood to take passengers. There are only two ships, anyway, serving the Trust Territory. Father Walter is the classic example of frustration in that line. He had to go to Truk to see his Bishop six hundred miles away. He got a boat to Yap, then took the plane to Koror and from there, another boat to Truk, thirteen hundred miles in all. This was rare good fortune for him. At that point Lady Luck flew off on other business. For four successive weeks he was bumped from the plane which would have taken him as far as Koror or Yap. So he persuaded some friends to let him hop aboard a Coast Guard plane to Anguar; from there, he took a native boat to Koror; from Koror to Yap he managed a seat on the plane; the home stretch from Yap to Ulithi was made on the Errol, one of the two trading ships. At Ulithi, after several months' absence, he had long been given up for dead; his loyal parishioners would have had a Mass said for the repose of his soul if there had been a priest to say it.

It would take more than that to do away with Father Walter. He is a big man, hewn out of rock with a hatchet, it seems. He feels most comfortable in lumberjack plaids, preferably up on a building repairing the grass roof. Still, he recognizes that the island people are better in such work, so he takes for his part cooking the meals for the workers. He likes

to talk about it on the few occasions when he can visit us Maryknoll
Sisters on some island or other.

Don't know just how I got into kitchen work on the missions, he says.
Was no good at it at home, I know. My mother always said, 'Get out of
here. You're all thumbs in a kitchen.' Couldn't stand me around. Well,
now I'm in great demand at cooking. When the men of my parish are
working on a building, I always cook their dinner for them. Have a good
time doing it, too. Guess I'm just a natural-born cook, but a case of
arrested development. It didn't show up when I was little, that's for sure.

The men all like what I cook. In fact, I have an idea that's why they
show up so regularly on parish projects. Or maybe I flatter myself, and
they only like it so's they can appreciate home cooking when they get it.
At any rate, they work hard and I feed them as best I can. They call it
'happy labor' when they work for the church. That's nice of them.

Americans too like my cooking—for their cats and dogs, that is. We
have two American families on Ulithi, the Buhls and the Dongans. Mrs.
Buhl had to go to Guam to get her teeth fixed and she made me a proposi-
tion. 'You can live in my house, Father,' she said, 'if you feed my cats.'
She's got six of them. Or rather she *had* six when she went away. Two of
them succumbed to my cooking. Only, you'd hardly call it cooking; she
left twenty cans of cat food and twelve of tuna fish. All I had to do was to
open them and dish it out. Very uninspiring work, I must say. When I got
into the house after a bout with a sailboat getting to one of the outlying
islands for Mass, there were the six cats looking at me with six deepening
shades of contempt. 'Get going, bus boy,' they glared. 'We've been waiting
quite a while for you.'

Then, while I was still tangled up in cats, the Dongans went off, too.
They left me with their dog to feed. He was to get Frisky dog food. He
couldn't wait, either. The cats just glared their contempt; they could do
it so well they didn't need to speak. But the dog yelped all over the place,
howling and whining, leaping up and getting in my way. I had to defend
myself with the can opener and he got the point after meeting the business
end of it a couple of times.

I was still enjoying memories of Father Walter and his menagerie when
we circled preparing to land on Yap, 461 miles from Guam. Yap is one of
those geographic names you can't forget. Like Hohokus, N.J., Tugue-
garao in the Philippines, Zamboanga, Timbuktu or Zanzibar. Kokomo,
Ind., is another. Some forty years ago, Yap was a name bandied across
the Versailles Treaty table. The question was, would Japan get it or
would it stay with Germany? Of course Japan got it. And with it virtual
control of the trans-Pacific cable. In 1905 the Germans had built an impressive cable station on Yap; here the main cable divided into three. One
branch went to Japan, another to Shanghai and the third to Manila. Yap
was a real war prize for Japan.

The people on Yap had nothing to say about the transfer. They were used to foreigners coming on their hospitable island and doing odd things with cement and steel. The Spanish came in 1884; the Germans took over in 1898; the Japanese were puttering around from 1917 until 1945. Now Americans were here and there with jeeps, motorcycles, trucks and Coca Cola. The Yapese takes them all in stride. The only incident that ruffled his calm came when the Japanese tried to make him and his good wife wear clothes. Western clothes, that is. For the Yapese are, in a sense, fussy about what they wear. For women, a grass skirt and possibly a black string around the neck to indicate married status are enough. The string might be an old typewriter ribbon, a shoelace or, more stylish, strands of black embroidery thread. To this scant apparel, the well-to-do add a wrist watch, a few bangle bracelets, or some bright plastic wire. Men are content with red loincloths, ornamented for gay occasions with strips of tree bark slung casually between their legs and pulled up before and behind into a series of loops like a badly-tied Christmas package. Others— the young fellows—wear gay bands of red, white and blue which fall down to their knees. Not a few have strings of flowers in their thick curling hair. Little boys supplement the red loincloth with a rosary around the neck; little girls wear the grass skirt held up, it seems, only by the grace of God.

Mother and I fell in love with the Yapese people. Knowing them you can well understand why Robert Louis Stevenson buried himself on Tahiti. If I had money to live without working, I too would set up a shack in little old Yap and watch the rest of the world go by. No, not even watch it go by.

Intelligent and deeply religious, the Yapese are so matter-of-fact about it that we needed no adjustment to their grass skirts and no blouses. It seemed a very practical outfit on an island where one moment it rains in torrents and in the next the sun toasts you crispy brown. And it's not realistic to say that a woman in a grass skirt is not dressed. Indeed, each skirt weighs something like five pounds. When you have five pounds of grass, weeds, coconut fibers and assorted flowers hanging down to your ankles, you are really wearing clothes. No woman is happy with only one grass skirt; she has several different kinds. The "working skirt" is of grass, wound around and knitted together with a coconut fiber rope at the top. Such a skirt takes about two days' full-time work to make; it lasts only a week or ten days. The "dancing skirt" is of hibiscus fiber, not the hibiscus so common in Hawaii, but a small tree with yellow-pink flowers. The inner bark is stripped and soaked for a week in the sea, weighted down by stones. The fibers come up from this a lovely creamy white, but the custom is to dye them various bright colors. The finished skirt is colored in stripes running up and down. When the dancing really gets going, the swirl of bright skirts is thrilling. A hibiscus skirt is prized; it may last a year.

"Where do you get the dye?" I asked Amalia (of whom more later).

"Oh, down at the Yap Trading Company," she said, indicating the one General Store on the island, established since the Americans came in.

"What did you do before there was a Yap Trading Company?"

She was puzzled, thinking back into the far-gone past, although she is old enough to remember that far back easily. "I don't know," she said slowly. "We forget those things fast."

On the whole, the grass skirt has my vote. There is no laundry problem; it pioneers in the field of Disposable Clothes. Again, no need for perfume; the sweet smell of new-mown hay wafts at every step. And one carries a soft haymow everywhere, ready to sit on at a moment's notice. Not only that, but Junior cuddles up on Mama's haystack and drops off to slumber while Mama sits on the floor during Mass. Also it is made with a generous bustle around the hips. This is convenient; it gives baby quite a footing when Mama carries him on her back. Older children get a free ride just by standing on the bustle and hanging on to her shoulders.

Properly speaking, Yap is not one island, but four, with the engaging names of Yap, Map, Rumung and Tamil-Gagil, so named because it is divided into two "counties" so to speak, each with a population of about four hundred people. Once, Yap and T-G were a single island but the Germans dug a canal between them to facilitate traffic to Map and Rumung.

The Japanese too were busy with stones and mortar. They built a railroad to bring lumber down from the interior. They made causeways and even, although it is hard to believe, are credited with constructing a bridge over the harbor so high that ocean-going vessels could go under it. Not that this is an impossible feat, but one can't imagine what there was on either side of the harbor to make such a bridge a good investment.

All four islands in the Yap group, it is estimated, had less than 2,500 people during Japanese times, although historians say there were 40,000 Yapese before the Spanish came. They judge this from the number of uninhabited villages found everywhere. These villages all retain their names. In any census count they are listed with a simple zero after them, as if a presage of better times to come. I remember twelve years ago, many people told me the Micronesian races were dying out due to diseases the white man brought and to abortions the Japanese taught them. Men who traveled from island to island reported very few children on some. One of the Sonsoral group had fourteen adults and one child.

The trend is reversing. The Yap group has well over three thousand and babies seem to be all over the place. And all very healthy. Mrs. Patrick, administrator and only American on the hospital staff on Yap, says that ninety-nine percent of the babies are born in the hospital. The only ones not born there are the impatient ones who could not wait.

Americans, so far as I could see, are doing a splendid work in the Trust Territory. They seem to be dedicated, conscientious workers who keep the island people's good in mind. Quite a few are Hawaiian-born or have lived there a long time; this gives them a common feeling for all South Sea islanders. In fact, more than once I thought, perhaps not too accurately, "Twenty-five years ago, when I first knew it, Hawaii was like Guam is now. Koror probably is like Guam then; and Koror then was like Yap, now. They form stepping stones in history."

Mrs. Patrick is administrator of the hospital on Yap. It is a most unprepossessing building—just a one-story brick structure erected on the foundations of a Japanese fort which in turn was built on the foundations for the Spanish administration building. The whole is painted black as a cure for the bricks' predilection for letting rain pass through. Although of solid structure, it looks like a tar shack, but is neat and clean on the inside.

Mrs. Patrick is sold on the Trust Territory policy of passing on responsibility to native-born people as soon as it is prudent. She administered the hospital on Truk and trained a Trukese to take over. Then she started out afresh on Yap. Now, she is the only American on the staff. "Like you missioners," she tells us, "my job is to work myself out of a job. When the Church can get Yapese priests and Sisters here, you feel happy to go. It's the same way with me. Many a time, it would have been ten times easier for me to do something myself, but I knew that it was more important to get the native to do it right, than to rush ahead on my own."

Besides running the hospital Mrs. Patrick keeps a wary eye out for diseases coming from afar. For instance, last year, she heard of several cases of flu in the Marshalls. Marshalls? Why, they are two thousand miles away over the water! "The flu will be coming here," she told the District Administrator (known as Distad in common parlance). "We ought to round up the people and give preventive injections. But we can't do it free; we haven't that kind of money in our budget. So ask the chiefs if they will subscribe the funds." They did. The people were inoculated. And when the epidemic struck, there were many mild cases but only three deaths—one of whom was a child and another an advanced TB case. However, hundreds died on less fortunate islands.

She has done much for the babies. Each mother gets a booklet telling of supplementary foods, proper care, and so on. That is why one sees on Yap what one never sees in Korea, Formosa, the rural Philippines, China or anywhere else in Asia—that is, babies with diapers (often disposable ones) and nursing bottles filled with milk formulas. They go even further, and this amazes Mrs. Patrick. "The women trot down to the Yap Trading Company and buy strained bananas for the babies," she says. "Strained bananas! On Yap! With all sorts of native fruits here which can be used and not cost a cent." So she makes lists of these for the prospective mothers. As a result, Yapese babies are gurgling pictures of health.

Her two greatest enemies, Mrs. Patrick estimates, are T.B. and intestinal parasites. T.B. accounts for half the patients in her fifty-bed hospital. It will be a long, slow process to rid the island of T.B. But only ten years' education through schools and the training of native doctors, nurses and technicians, she feels, should put an effective bite into the ravages of intestinal parasites. Mrs. Patrick has sighted her guns at the worms. I have a feeling they are done for.

Trust Territory officials are pushing the education program. Young students have top priority in transportation. More than once we have stood aside to let a student take our place on the weekly plane. I once went by launch out into Yap harbor to where the plane bobbed on the water. It was pouring as usual; I found myself hiding under a tarpaulin with a student. He was bound for Guam and the great wide, wonderful world, not to return until he had a nursing diploma to hang on the clinic wall. I sat on a carton; the student sat on his cardboard suitcase. He wore a white shirt embroidered in gold around the collar and down the front. His trousers were pressed—or rather had been pressed. The luscious waves of his black hair shone with hair oil. He wore, no doubt, the family fortune on his back. I did not recognize him, but I am sure that at least once in those days on Yap I must have passed him on the road, attired in red loincloth, with a bolo slung through a belt, looking like the Noble Savage of romantic fiction. "Good luck to him!" I thought. "I only hope that in the process of education he does not lose his pride in being one of a truly noble people."

Yap has many customs, some good, some bad. Family life is often broken up. The wife has to return to her mother's house for four to six months after a child is born. Further, the men all sleep in "the men's house"; the women and children are left in their own home. A rigid caste system disheartens the lowly. Stanislaus Kameng took us across the harbor once in his boat. He is of the slave class, and his sense of degradation, they say, is the basic cause of his constant drunkenness. He knows he can never be anything but the lowest class. All of one class live together in a village; that is, a village may be first class, second class or slave class. No one may move out of his village to advance to higher class; similarly, he cannot fall lower.

Stanislaus is not poor, however. He owns his own outboard motor and has a good job in the Yap Supply Department. However, he is still held in contempt. "After all," he told Sister Fidelis, "we're not much better than animals; we aren't really people."

Much of Yap history and customs I learned from Amalia, now thirty-seven years old, who is, so to speak, everybody's sister and everybody's mother rolled into one very helpful person.

When she was a child, back in Japanese times, Amalia came from her tiny village in Gagil to the main island, Yap, to enroll in the school. She was bright, industrious and entirely pagan. But one day between classes, she slipped into the church, a big white building overlooking the blue lagoon. It got to be a habit. Then Padre Juan noticed her, the slight young girl sitting in her grass skirt on the cement floor. She always wore western dress to school—the Japanese insisted on it. But after class, she found it easier to run around without it. Saved on laundry, too.

Padre Juan instructed her. She was baptized after several years to test her constancy. For her baptism, Padre Juan gave her—and her eyes shone as she told me twenty-five years after—yes, he gave her a white dress, a rosary and a harmonica.

"Why the harmonica?"

"He liked to hear me play it. He taught me how."

"Do you have it still?"

"Ah no. I lost it in the war. So many sad things happened then!"

"Would you play for me if you had one?"

Her plain face lighted with a flash of joy. "Yes! I could still play one. I know I could!" I made a memo to myself: Send Amalia a harmonica when I get to the States.

In 1944, she was twenty-one. She could read the letters of our alphabet and the Japanese characters as well. She was a teacher in the school and a catechist in the church. Padre Juan had left Yap some years before; he was on Truk as superior of the Jesuits in the Carolines and Marshalls. Padre Bernardo and Padre Luis were on Yap with a Brother. The war was on. Bombs demolished the church; then the two priests and Brother were taken away and executed. Their rectory, now our convent, was occupied by Japanese soldiers. All the Yapese, men and women, were organized as work squads to repair roads, put up new barracks and—most urgent—clear the ground for an airfield which was never finished. Life wasn't easy for the Japanese; it wasn't easy for the Yapese, either.

"Why don't you marry?" everyone asked. Her parents, most of all. They had picked out a man—high caste, friendly family—what more could a girl want? There was no priest on Yap to marry them; to quiet them all she went through the tribal ceremony. But she knew he had another woman and needed her not at all. Years later, when the unnatural marriage had long ago broken up, he came down with T.B. in the Yap hospital. Amalia dropped everything, went to his side and took care of him until he died.

After the war, she worked for many American families on Yap. Her place, as she sees it, is always to help other families, never to have one of her own. She showed me snapshots of this or that American baby she had cared for—"before" and "after" pictures often, where a puny fretful child grows strong as he is held tight in her slender brown arms and pulls the curly black hair down over her laughing face. Now she turns her helpfulness to Angeline, a widow with four children, who works in the hospital laundry. Amalia makes clothes for the children, takes care of the old grandfather, keeps an eye on baby Carlos. Many Americans have offered high pay; Amalia feels this is her work for now and turns them down.

She was the first Yapese woman to own a sewing machine. She paid fifty dollars for it, shipped from Guam. Many Yapese women wear western dresses when they work in the Trust Territory offices, and slip into a grass skirt when they get home.

"What do you charge for a dress?" I asked.

A cloud of incomprehension passed across her face. It was not that she did not understand my English. After all, she reads American magazines, uses an English missal and speaks the language quite well. But the idea of taking money from another Yapese was incomprehensible. We talked about property rights. This is how she explains them:

"If you want to go fishing and you do not have a canoe, you can borrow anybody else's canoe. You don't pay for anything, but you should leave a present of a fish or two to thank the owner. If you want to borrow his motor boat, you should use your own gasoline."

"What if the owner wants to go fishing too, and he cannot because you have his boat. Does he get mad?"

"No. He realizes that you needed the canoe or you would not borrow it."

"Suppose you borrow it and wreck it on the reefs?"

"Too bad, but that could happen to anybody. You do not have to pay for the canoe. Not money. We just don't."

The very idea of money is hazy to our way of thinking. Many things serve as money. The value has nothing to do with the size or commercial worth. It is measured by the care taken to make it or the trouble someone went to to obtain it.

First there is Mmbul which is a length of lava-lava, the cloth used for loincloths, three or four feet long and two feet wide, wrapped up in a betel nut sheath.

Then there is Gau, a necklace of shells, two to four feet long. The shells come from Canet, an island near Ponape, from Ponape itself and from Euripik. Since these come from a distance, Gau is worth more than Mmbul. The first pieces of Gau, ninety of them, were brought by a man named Angumang; these are the most valuable.

Yar is money made of shells about eight inches long, pierced and tied on a coconut rope. They come from afar, New Guinea, Palau and Ponape.

Yar is commonly used for marriage money but it is also good to buy a canoe, bananas or a fish trap.

Reng is the name of money made of turmeric, the yellow root of the guchol plant. The dried root is ground and mixed with water and the paste shaped into a ball. Turmeric as a dry powder is dusted on shoulders and palms for dancing. It is also, incidentally, the source of curry powder.

Most valuable of the Yap currency is the stone money—huge rings of stone with a hole in the middle. Each separate piece of Yap money has a name. Everybody on the island knows where it is and who owns it. Used chiefly for the sale of land for a sweet potato patch, there is no need for the new owner to take the great stone from "the bank"—a stretch along the shore where the stone money is set up leaning against rocks or trees. However, some *nouveaux riches* like to have their money arrayed around their houses, much as suburbanites in the States put wagon wheels all over their lawns.

This brings us to O'Keefe, who made a fortune making stone money. He was a shipwrecked sailor who landed in Yap around 1880. At first, he contented himself with trading coconuts and such. But eventually, as the Yapese charitably put it, he "borrowed" an island in the middle of Yap harbor where he set up business on a large scale. He grew quite rich, went to Hong Kong and bought a sea-going junk. Making sails from jute sacks, he brought it back to Yap. Commissioned by various chiefs and with a crew of Yapese, he organized expeditions to Palau, two hundred and fifty miles away, to make the huge discs of stone money. That type of stone does not exist on Yap; ergo, the money is valuable since making and bringing it to Yap over many miles of water was a very tricky job. One piece fell from O'Keefe's boat as it was being brought to shore. It is still at the harbor bottom and still negotiable. Everyone knows it is there, like the gold bars in the treasury at Washington. In fact, as security, it is safer there than in a bank vault. During German times, O'Keefe's junk went down in a hurricane and O'Keefe with it. His daughter and son-in-law tried to carry on the business but nothing is left on O'Keefe's island now but the foundations of his brick buildings.

The largest piece of stone money is twelve feet in diameter; most of them are around six or eight feet. Far from being cumbersome, stone money is handy. It's so big you can't lose it. A thief would be at his wit's end to hide it. As one of our pupils on Yap wrote:

> Yapese money is very hard to move from place to place. As you know, it is too big to put into your pouch. If you have a piece of money and you can't move it to the place where you want to put it, you ask some people to come to carry your money for you, or they can put it in a canoe, boat or raft. These are the ways we move our money.
>
> Yapese money is very good because we cannot steal the pieces because

they are so heavy. Even those small enough to steal, we cannot hide in
our clothes. It is also good because you will not have to keep it in a safe
place or in your wallet. You can keep it any place you want, in the house
or outside.

Yapese money has some disadvantages because we cannot take it from
store to store to buy things. Also, we cannot buy American things with it.
The people who were born recently don't like it very well because they
don't know anything about it. They depend on American money. During
the Yapese dances, many people give money to other people. They do
not want to buy anything. They are just happy.

Things are changing now fast. Ideas are penetrating the island, soaking
in like rain. The mail-order catalogues are passed from hut to hut. Outboard motors, sewing machines, fish nets and clothes come every time
the trading ships stop by. That is, every two months or so. Copra is the
main money crop. A man can earn five dollars a day drying copra. Another cash crop, not faring so well lately, is trochus shells. For two weeks
of the year, the trochus—a sea animal with a cone-shaped spiral shell—
swarms on the beaches. Everything stops—school, work, play—while whole
families go after the trochus. The shells used to be sold to Japan and
Germany for mother-of-pearl buttons. Of late years, the sale has gone
down. The poor trochi, so rudely evicted from their shells, retaliate by
smelling something awful in horrible piles on the beach. Once Sister
Fidelis wrinkled her nose at the smell. But Julita in Grade Two set her
straight. "Yes, it smells bad, Sister," she said solemnly. "But I like it. It's
the smell of money."

As elsewhere, there is a breaking down of the old morals. "In former
times," said Amalia, "when a man said he would do something, he did it.
When he took something that was not his—borrowed it—it was because
he really needed it. That is why we did not mind. But now . . ."—her
voice trailed off.

Parents come to us, too, with their woes. "I can't do anything with my
children," we hear on Yap as everywhere else. Adoptions from one family
to another take place for no reason at all. If a lad doesn't like his adoptive
home, he hies himself back to his real parents. And vice versa, playing
one off against the other. If school gets oppressive—well, the door is open
and out he goes.

Drink is becoming a major problem on Yap. Every bomb crater with
its stagnant water, is alive with tadpoles and beer cans. "When do the
boys start drinking?" I asked Father Bailey who has been here since 1946.

"At four or earlier," he said. "At Yapese banquets I have seen toddlers,
sitting right beside their fathers, down a can of beer in practically one
swallow. Their fathers did nothing—except to open another can and
place it before the child."

But let's not end this chapter on the dark side of the ledger. Angelina shows the bright side. She is a little woman who would be quite pretty if her teeth were not solid black. To see her gums so red and teeth so black is a shock. This comes from betel-nut chewing; everybody does it. Angelina works in the hospital laundry, ironing and folding up sheets. Her husband died a bit oddly. He had a serious heart condition and one day became very angry at his sister. He started to say something and dropped over dead. That left Angelina with four children. So she moved back with her father, a grandfatherly type—big, easy-going, kindly, the sort of old man children adore and will not obey. And she went to work in the hospital laundry.

She rose to be a leader among the women workers. At the beginning of 1961, Trust Territory officials decided it would be a good idea to organize the women into a club so that they would have the thrill of hearing themselves express an idea now and then. Angelina was elected first President of the Yapese Women's Club. They meet every first Monday of the month in the living room of what might pass for the Executive Mansion. That is, the modest but comfortable home of the Distad, under the hospitable care of Mrs. Roy T. Gallemore, who is teaching them how a women's club works.

Besides her civic duties, Angelina takes her domestic chores very seriously. When she comes home at night, she rescues the children from Grandpa's benevolent anarchy. They help her prepare the tapioca and taro and fish for dinner. Then they spend an hour or more under the kerosene lamp studying tomorrow's school lessons. This is something unusual for Yapese parents. And Angelina's youngsters, Christopher, Timmie and Juliana are "tops" in our fourth, third, and first grades respectively.

One evening around nine o'clock, a gentle knock brought us to our door. Outside in the velvet night were Angelina and Chris. Angelina was in her grass skirt and black typewriter ribbon about her neck, smiling her betel-blackened smile. Chris wore only the barest bit of apron fore and aft. They carried an American flashlight and a covered dish of delicate Japanese china. It was a gift for Mother, a chicken boiled with curry. Angelina had made it after her work in the laundry.

"But Chris caught the chicken," she said putting her hand on Chris' curly head. At this point Chris should have pulled on his necktie or dug his hands into his pockets, but having neither of those things, he could only twist his toes on the ground. "Yes," his mother went on with real pride, "he put some grated coconut on the ground and made a noose of rope around it. Then, when the chicken stepped in, he pulled the noose tight very quickly."

Mothers and sons don't change much from country to country, nor from age to age.

❧ 24 ❧ *They Dance the Bible on Yap*

"WHAT's the use of taking those?" I asked, pointing to rubbers and raincoat.

"Standard procedure on Yap," said Sister Irene Therese. "We never leave the house without rubbers and raincoat." And she rubbed more sunburn lotion on her face.

We started out to Tamil Island in blistering sunshine. Twenty minutes in an open boat across the harbor, an hour's walk on the island to the church and Mass on a treeless plateau in the late afternoon—such was the schedule. We would be baked a fiery red, there seemed no doubt, since God has provided us with no built-in suntan.

But . . . As we waited on the shore for Stanislaus' boat, dark clouds gathered. We stepped into it and the heavens opened. They stayed open until we returned four hours later. Rubbers and raincoat? Pfff! As well try to stop Niagara with an umbrella. Soaked to the skin after the first five seconds, I would not have missed it for the world.

The dock—if you want to call it that—at Tamil is a long mound of coral covered with slippery moss. But we managed to leap ashore and start the walk through virgin forest. The path is wide—a roadway, really, started by the Japanese for their projected airstrip on the island, begun in a rush during war years and never finished. The road has only big-stone foundations. Now covered with mossy slime, they are hard to negotiate. Also sharp. But at least they gave solid footing.

It had been a steady climb all the way from the sea. Now we emerged on a flat headland overlooking sea, sky and green jungle. A quonset added to on front, back and sides, served as school for the area. Domingo, the teacher, is a graduate of the Jesuit school on Truk and before that he was one of our boys on Yap.

Nobody seemed to mind the rain (I told you that grass skirts are practical) and certainly we were too wet to get any wetter. So we sat on a bench under a tree or roamed around talking to various groups and reveled in the scene. People were coming to the galvanized iron hut that served as a chapel, congregating in small bunches, exchanging gossip, greeting neighbors, while the children chased around. The women wore only grass skirt and black string; the men were content with very little. Rain ran down their hair and coursed in rivulets down their bodies, yet they conversed in polite groups quietly. Martina, a little charmer in a

287

sodden grass skirt, ran over to Mother on the bench, cupped her hands
on Mother's lap and looked into her face. The white skin, the eyeglasses,
the religious veil—she took them all in. Then she sighed contentedly and
leaned up against this strange creature.

A few months before, a typhoon had whipped away the chapel; a galvanized iron hut was a wretched substitute. Mass, planned on the flat
headland, had to be celebrated indoors. The shed was dark inside but
I could make out the massive tree trunks which formed the frame. Crude
though the shed was, the Altar Society ladies had prettied it up. Hibiscus
flowers leaned out of sections of bamboo tacked to each post, and on the
altar Mexican creeper burgeoned from metal vases made from brass car-
tridges of big-gun ammunition. The roof of corrugated iron pieces was
full of holes where nails had punctured them in previous uses. Funny—
but one is much more annoyed with a drip of rain from a hole in the roof,
than with a washout outside.

There were no seats, of course. Some few spread pandanus mats on
the ground. About one hundred and eighty adults and God-alone-knows
how many children filled the shed. Their bodies glistened with rain, and
the smell of wet grass from the skirts pervaded the chapel.

Mass began. Father Condon, a big Jesuit with bright red hair and
beard, began the Mighty Action. These one hundred and eighty innocent
children of God paid strict attention. When the children stared around,
Mama or Papa turned their heads resolutely toward the altar. There
was no talking or whispering. Sometimes a chant was struck up, sung
through and finished. Most of the time there was no sound except for
Father's murmur at the altar and the swish of grass skirts as the congregation sat down or stood up. During the Creed, as Father said "Et
homo factus est," the swish of grass skirts as the people genuflected was
a mission sound par excellence. After all, that is what we come for; so
that knees will bend to those words.

At Holy Communion, the reverence of these people over-awed us. Eyes
down, hands clasped before their bare bodies, they went forward to receive their Lord. A strong youngish man had stood in front of me holding
his little girl in his arms, so that her bright eyes peered at us over his
shoulder. Tired of that, she amused herself pulling out the long curls on
her daddy's head. After the "Domine, non sum dignus," daddy took her
little brown hand in his and led her up to the altar with him. Her grass
skirt hung by a thread on the very last promontory of her small torso and
swayed with every step. Daddy looked like the very image of primeval
man, completely bare except for the frill of hibiscus bark around his
loins. He and she moved forward, stepping over and around the other
men and women on the floor, the babies sleeping, the children sitting

calmly nearby. They were intent on something very important. They returned after Communion the same way. The little girl was looking at daddy; he was steering her by the arm through the same welter of humanity on the floor. But the very way he steered her showed that he was interested only in getting back to their place where he could talk to the God within him. He looked like Adam; like Adam too he "walked with God."

The Catholic Church in these islands—meaning the sprinkling of dots over the Trust Territory's three million square miles of water—has had an uncertain career. The marvel is that it ever took root at all. The Spanish came to Yap in 1884; they went the two hundred and fifty-three miles further to the Palau Islands in 1891. On Yap, Spanish Capuchins built a good-sized church and began mission work. There are few reminders of the Spanish now, but high on the hill in the island's center I came across three very substantial monuments, evidently over graves. The writing is moss grown and much has been obliterated. One is unreadable. The other two read in Spanish:

> DON FRANCISCO [last name illegible]
> OFFICER OF THE SHIP MAGALLANES
> HEADSTONE GIVEN BY CHIEFS AND OFFICERS OF THE SAME
> 1887

and:

> DON ALONSO
> DOCTOR AND NOTARY
> DIED 1885

When Germany bought the islands in 1898, German Capuchins took over the mission. When you think of the hazards of transportation in those days, especially in that unimportant corner of the Pacific, you realize there may have been months and even years when no priest was on Yap during interregna. In 1917, the Germans gave way to the Japanese. These were truly lean years. Five years after the Germans were sent away, Spanish Jesuits took the missions at the personal request of the Holy Father. Since the Japanese used the islands for military purposes, they wanted as few visitors as possible, and no foreign residents. Missioners cooled their heels for years waiting for visas. Brother Juan, a fiery Basque now on Koror, waited eight years in Yokohama and would probably still be sitting on benches outside government offices, if it were not that World War II came to his rescue.

Padre Elias and Padre Marino de la Cruz were on Koror during the war; Padres Bernardo and Luis on Yap with a Brother. Padre Elias went from town to town telling the people, "The Americans will come here. When they do, you should go forth to meet them and carry a white cloth on a stick. This do, and they will not harm you." During the war, all five missioners were arrested, held three months in prison and executed on Babelthuap, a large island near Koror. However, the people remembered Padre Elias' advice. There was no disturbance in the American take-over. On Okinawa, if you remember, waves of people rushed into the sea to drown themselves because they believed the Americans would massacre them without cause.

For two years there was no priest, except an American Navy chaplain now and then or some such chance visitor. But in 1946 Father Bailey, an American Jesuit, came to Yap.

"The Navy was here then," he told me. "Also a colony of Chamorros whom the Navy had brought from Guam. At my first Mass here, the Chamorros came and only three Yapese—two old women and a little girl. I remember the little girl because she held a pet pig in her arms. During Mass I could hear that pig grunting and snuffling. Couldn't make out what it was. Then, as I turned around for the last blessing I took a good look all around. There was the small child with the pig in her arms. It was my introduction to the Yapese custom of making pets of pigs.

"Gradually the Yapese came around. There was some feeling between the Chamorros and Yapese on the island, people told me, although I doubt that it was very severe. Anyhow, after a few months the Navy decided to move the Chamorros to Tinian. On the last Sunday morning, the Yapese brought a mountain of foodstuffs for the Chamorros because they knew they would have a hard time getting settled on Tinian. One of the Navy officers, surveying the pile, said to Uag, a Yapese, 'Did the priest tell you to bring this stuff?' Uag said, 'The Father did not. We are Christians together with the Chamorros.' "

Of Yap's three thousand people, about seventy-five percent are Catholic. Yet there had never been Sisters on Yap. Small wonder then that the island all but turned upside down when three Maryknoll Sisters arrived in 1953 to open a school. One was a nurse, as well as a teacher. The school itself could be Exhibit A in a How-To-Do-It book, "How to make the most out of what you've got." The school occupies the first floor of the convent which was built around fifty years ago, plus a very run-down quonset hut used for second and third grades. There are no partitions between classes, no blackboards bigger than two by three feet, no sign of anything like individual seats. Of course the lighting is not perfect and the floor is nature's own. None the less, the Sisters are able to operate a good school; "our children" take top honors when they go to Guam or Truk for high school. Each class, for one thing, has its own collection of library books. For another, the pupil-teacher relationship is very, very

solid. The Sisters have the valuable help of a lay missioner who, with his
family, has come out to Yap to give his services to the mission.

The Church, like the Mother she is, is a true woman. She has a thousand dresses and still is ready for a new one. The body of dogma wears
the arts and customs of all nationalities and all the ages of those nationalities. The same Church comes arrayed in medieval Spain and modern
Japan. She can speak all languages, but even more than that, she expresses
the same old dogma in a hundred ways—in paint and canvas, stone, dance,
poetry, drama, journalism, lithography and—well, you name it!

Thus, we were not too surprised when we were told that on Tuesday,
the boys would "dance the Joyful Mysteries of the Rosary" in Mother's
honor. The night before, Sister Francis Xavier and I went to the rusty
quonset for the final rehearsal. Benches and desks for the Second Grade
had been pushed to one side. Sitting crosslegged on the teacher's desk,
looking like an amiable Buddha, was Uag, combination catechist, pillar
of the Church, elder of the tribe and dance teacher. He was placid enough
under his honors, wearing his oldest loincloth, with white hair and beard,
his ancient skin hanging in festoons on his ribs. He chewed betel continuously. Every now and then, he opened his "betel bag" which every
man, woman and child in Yap carries, to replenish the blood-red juice
in his mouth. From the bag he took out a fresh green leaf of the pepper
vine, sprinkled some white powder on it and stuffed it into his mouth,
already filled with chewed betel nut. The white powder is lime made of
pulverized coral.

He seemed to have no part in the proceedings; nevertheless, everything
swung around him. For this show, Uag was scriptwriter, director, inspira-
tion, producer and umpire. A line of boys sat on the floor in a straight
row with their legs in "maple-leaf pattern," that is, with the left foot
up against the right thigh. This is standard; no one sits otherwise for
the dance. The line-up included boys of fifteen or so in the middle and
tapered down at the ends to little fellows. David, in the middle, gave a
low growl. He clapped his cupped hands and slapped his thighs in
rhythm. The two on either side joined in; the four beside them and finally
the whole line were clapping and slapping to David's growl. A small boy
whom the Sisters call Joe sat behind the line-up. He began the chant in
a high nasal voice. The boys had been joking before; there had been horse-
play and laughter; but now they were deadly serious.

They swayed forward and backward. Their arms, stiff at the elbows,
swept an arc above their heads, the fingers fluttering fast like a humming-
bird's wings. They clapped with cupped hands and slapped their thighs
to emphasize points in the whining chant.

"What's he singing about?" I asked.

Uag told us. "The Annunciation," he said briefly.

All at once David gave a blood-curdling yell. The others yelped in response. Then the line-up crossed left arm over chest and slapped the right hand over it. It was the end of that episode.

They finished the Five Joyful Mysteries. Then they rose and faced each other in double file. The slow pace of the dance changed to lightning. Advance, step back, leap forward, spring to the side. It was a lively thanksgiving for God's goodness in taking a human body. Our Lord's own body must have been like these in His boyhood—brown, smooth, perfect in proportion, graceful and quick.

Beside me, on the cement floor, another lad with a white ginger flower in his hair had been sitting against the school desks piled up to clear the dance floor. He was reading. Now he slapped the book shut and sighed profoundly, as one coming out of a book world. I glanced at the book now lying closed on his slender brown legs. It was *The Three Billy Goats Gruff*, a second grade reader. He gazed with dreamy eyes at the dancers, not seeing them at all. It was with him as it is with an American boy who has just finished *Kim* or *Treasure Island*. He was lost in the world of *The Three Billy Goats Gruff*.

Next morning practically everybody on Yap was congregating in our back yard. Boys and their proud mothers swarmed in the school and surroundings. Mamas were intent on making up their sons, smearing red swatches on forehead and chin, dusting yellow turmeric on shoulders and palms, tying palm fronds around arms and legs. Feathers waved high in the headdresses, supplemented with paper flowers, palm fronds and the glint of Lucky Strike wrappers.

Buzzing around were most of the sixteen American families on Yap. With cameras. Never before had there been such a concentration of photographic equipment anywhere at any time on Yap. Most Yap dances are done at night but because we wanted to take colored movies, Uag consented to let his boys dance in the sunlight. The weatherman cooperated and produced a glorious sun guaranteed to last for the whole day. We invited others to share in this chance to get good dance pictures. The writer-photographer for the *National Geographic Magazine* came on the double-quick. District Administrator Roy Gallemore and his wife were there. Mr. Middleton brought his tape recorder for the chant; the Shug family their Polaroid; Mr. Goss, official photographer for the district, had a ball for himself; every one who owned a Brownie of whatever vintage was shooting all the film he had. One of the best cameras on the field was David's. Standing like Hiawatha in loincloth and palm fronds, he took expert shots of his classmates. All this flurry was so much milk-and-honey to the Yapese; it pleased them that their dances were so important to the often-strange Americans. The boys trotted on the field in single file, sat on the ground and chanted the Five Joyful Mysteries of the Rosary utterly oblivious of the photographers sneaking up in front and behind. The sun beat down; their bodies streamed with sweat. But they were intent on the story they told in dance.

Later, when the people had gone and only we Sisters were around, they danced it again. This was "to bury the dance," they said. After long rehearsals and then the big affairs, one buries the whole business with a last performance. That dance will never be done again—at least, not in the same way.

That afternoon, Elvira—a beautiful woman—arranged for the women to dance. This was held at the village dance place, down near the shore.

We went from the convent by truck as far as we could go, Mother and Sister Maura Shaun in the cab with Father who drove; the rest of us in the open rear. All roads led to the Dance Place that afternoon and we picked up dancers and friends as we went along, until the truck body was an immense bouquet of flowers, coconut fronds, grass skirts and black veils. At the end, we had to walk about half a mile. The path of large stepping stones brought us through "the bank" where most people keep their money. The great stone circles were lined up along the path, leaning against trees or partly buried in the mud. They have been there for years.

We emerged to a cleared space. Practically all of it was filled by a "stage" maybe two feet high, built up and filled with large stones. Here and there on the platform were flat stones stuck upright; these were backrests for people sitting cross-legged. For the audience sat on the stage and the dancers performed on a strip of ground below it. They needed no backdrop. Behind were the huge cartwheels of money, the coconut palms, the bright flowering bushes and the Pacific stretching beyond the beyond, blue and glistening.

All Yap was having a picnic that day; the space was alive with family groups, coming to dance or to watch. As soon as our white habits appeared in the clearing, a young man ran up to sound the gong. It was a section of railroad track suspended from a tree; he banged it with an ordinary hammer many times. Another young fellow, quick as a wink, whacked the tops off some coconuts and handed them to us to drink. Mother sat on the stage in the place of honor; the rest of us roamed around. Sister Francis Xavier spent the time with some of her pupils in school, who dragged her off to see something. Sister Irene Therese was in deep consultation with a couple of women under the trees. Sister Fidelis was with Elvira lining up the dancers for the grand entry. Not knowing much Yapese, I wandered around asking questions and trying to understand the answers. The Americans were out in full force again, shooting any film left from the morning's orgy.

The women danced much as the boys had done, but their story told the Creation. The same hand gestures, the same high chanting, the same shout at the end. Their brown bodies and grass skirts, dyed in glorious colors, the red spots and streaks from lipstick, the yellow turmeric powder sprinkled on shoulders, the betel-blackened teeth—these people seemed close to Primal Innocence as they chanted the story of Creation.

> *God created heaven and earth;*
> *All was an empty waste,*
> *And darkness hung over the deep;*
> *But the breath of God stirred.*
> *'Let there be light,' God said.*
> *And there was light. . . .*

One on the line-up was a very pretty girl; the photographers crowded around her. She seemed "the type," with her wealth of black hair, languid eyes, lithe body, swaying grass skirt and red and orange streaks on face and shoulders. One of the American women pointed out the beautiful dancer to Mother. "That's Francisca whom I told you about, Mother," Sister Fidelis said. "She's going up to Saipan to begin her training as a Mercedarian Sister, next month." The American woman gasped. "She? A nun? Well," she conceded, "I suppose she's having her last fling now."

Later, as the sun sent long streaks of shadow from the coconut trees across the dance place, the younger girls did a bamboo dance, with no religious significance at all. It was fast and furious.

Then came the Yapese dinner. The Americans had all gone and most of the Yapese as well. Only Elvira and her friends stayed to direct the banquet. For several hours I had noticed four boys taking turns at waving branches over a number of fresh-woven baskets covered with banana leaves. They were keeping the flies off our dinner. Each Sister now settled in front of a basket and the banana leaf was removed. Inside was fish, chicken, boiled sweet potato, boiled taro, boiled ubi and baked tapioca, the latter rolled up in a coconut leaf like the Philippine suman. We ate with fingers; afterwards, the whole Pacific Ocean was our fingerbowl. We went down to the sea where the men were stringing out their nets to prepare for night fishing, and dabbled our greasy, fishy hands in the water.

It was, as romanticists are wont to say, a night to remember.

⫷ 25 ⫸ *Koror, the Magnificent*

THE banquet cloth was plain wrapping paper, but the dishes were of exquisite Japanese lacquerware. The food? Truly cosmopolitan. For this banquet was given by the Palau Catholic Club, of Palauan blood and Japanese education, for Mother Mary Colman, an American. On the buffet table (an American touch), serving plates of little strings of raw fish, balls of boiled tapioca, something like potato salad, seaweed in various guises, wonderful crabmeat, coconut in chunks and bits of squid tempted the guests.

I found myself at table with three influential citizens, Indalecio Rudimch, formerly chief magistrate of Koror and now Vice-President of Micronesian Council; Felipe Bismark of the Palau Council and Sheriff as well; and David Ramarui, also of the Council and now Assistant Education Administrator. They were good examples of the Trust Territory policy as outlined in the 1960 Report of the High Commissioner: "The goal of our trusteeship is to employ and develop further the human and physical resources of the region for the benefit of the territory and its people. Emphasis is placed on utilizing Micronesian abilities in the current administrative, political, social and economic programs and preparing the Micronesian citizens through education, training and experience for greater responsibilities."

So here I was, eating raw fish, seaweed and potato salad, vis-à-vis three Micronesians high in the government offices of their native island. They all spoke English quite well. It was a golden opportunity.

"Tell me," I said. "You all lived in Japanese times. Your fathers were here under the Germans and your grandfathers must have talked about the Spanish. So you are used to changes in administration. What did you think of all these different people?"

The three men looked at each other. "I myself know only the Japanese. Many were good men," said Rudimch cautiously. "Yes, Japanese built up the place. They made Koror, you might say, the capital of Micronesia. It was the nerve center for their operation in the Southwest Pacific."

"Koror was a Japanese city of twenty thousand," said Bismark. "The main road that you see now full of holes and rocks, bordered only by slim jim, hibiscus bushes and a drainage ditch, was then a paved street lined with hotels, stores, concrete homes and pleasant gardens. Gas and water mains ran under it."

"True," commented Rudimch again. "We had large ships in the harbor, tied up to piers a quarter-mile long. Airfields and radio towers brought the news of the world. Yes, one felt that Koror was alive."

"But I have this to say," put in Ramarui. "If the Japanese had stayed, we three right at this table would not be here tonight. They were pushing the Palauans out. We had to go to other islands, far from Koror. Only six hundred remained of the four thousand who were here when the Japanese came." The others agreed with him.

"Many Japanese were intelligent men with good characters," he went on. "Individually—yes, they were good. But the policy of the nation kept the Palauans out of anything important."

"But I hear they gave a good education to everyone," I commented.

"A Palauan child would have three years at school. If he was very bright, perhaps five. Only a very few went to Japan to study. Also, every subject was taught in Japanese; we were not permitted to learn our own as a written language. A meeting like this tonight would be impossible."

He was referring to the speeches given just before. Father Roszel, the pastor, had welcomed Mother, giving one sentence in English and translating into Palauan as he went on. And, Judge Morei, a Palauan in charge of the local court, had spoken for the parishioners. He spoke in Palauan and translated into English as he went along. "In former times," the three men agreed, "the Japanese would not have come to such an affair and if they ever did, the whole program would have been in Japanese."

No doubt about it, Palauans look back upon Koror-that-was in much the same mood as that of the ancient Pompeians prowling around the ruins of their former glory after Vesuvius had finished with it. A picture taken in 1937 of Koror's main street shows it lined with shops, advertising "beer-u" and "tabaca," people in Japanese kimonos and western dress, a child with a school bag strapped between his shoulders, several men in military uniforms and a sailor arm in arm with a native girl. It was, to the empire of Japan, something like Hawaii was to us at the time—a naval center firmly established among an enchanting island people. There were hotels, nice homes, paved streets, public buildings of dignified, if not imposing, size. The sort of place that rings with joy at the glad cry, "The fleet's in!"

For everything swung around the Japanese Navy in those days. The Western Carolines, including Ulithi, the Yap group, and the Palau group (of which Koror is the main island), were Islands of Mystery. Foreigners got short shrift when they asked for visas to the islands. On the other hand, Japanese colonizers were encouraged; each boat brought families ready to set up housekeeping, not on Koror but on the other islands, now practically uninhabited. I remember shortly after World War II going along an agonizing road to the center of Babelthuap, one of the Palau group of islands miles and miles from anywhere. There we found the bombed remains of an immense radio station and airfield. People in large numbers must have lived there in Japanese times.

The Palauans saw all this, although they had small part in it. They were domestics and laborers. They worked in the officers' clubs, the restaurants and hotels; they tended the gardens; they swept the offices. Some attained to white-collar work as interpreters and clerks. The milieu was a bustling frontier town, booming with colonists, alive with transients coming from ships and hurrying off to other islands. All the gears meshed with the Japanese genius for infinite paperwork. The Palauans stood by and watched it all.

To them, American rule was a great letdown at first. To the "new people," Koror was a mere backwater. Where twenty thousand Japanese bustled along Koror's paved main street, fifty Americans now run their jeeps up and down the country road it is now. The iron inlets to the gas and water mains below the street are just bumps to be jolted over. A plane bearing twelve to fifteen passengers comes once a week to land in the harbor and waddle up a ramp to shore. Two ships, the Errol and Gunners Knot, ply among the islands bringing food supplies, parcel post, household things from mail-order houses, and the most outlandish foods to stock the empty shelves of the commissary. But the ships must anchor out in the harbor; the quarter-mile piers have not been rebuilt.

Still, there is a bustle about Koror you don't find on Yap. The one big project you can't help seeing was set up by Paige Communications, a $7,000,000 maze of radio antennae, iron scaffolding and lights that go on and off. Also the Court of Justice is a nice looking building, called "The Taj Mahal" by some Americans. The one and only hotel bears a sign almost as big as itself proclaiming its name, The Royal Palauan; rain and wet salt have robbed it of its pristine glory. Some one hundred and fifty jeeps are on the island, one bus, and forty-some trucks. Most of the buildings—including our own school—are ex-quonsets. Even American personnel live in quonsets adapted to family life. No doubt about it, Koror is shabby.

Some of the best buildings on the island are the Catholic mission works. We were lucky. We inherited them from the German regime and they were not destroyed in the war. New ones have been built too—Maris Stella School where six Mercedarian Sisters—three Spanish, two Palauan and one Saipanese—teach three hundred and fifty children from Grade One through Grade Six. Our own Mindzenty School is a quonset hut nicely set up in landscaped grounds. Here one hundred and fifty pupils from all the nearby islands go through high school. Three new classrooms of concrete block have been erected to relieve congestion; three more are going up now. Then the quonset can be used as an auditorium. After that,

a new church is planned; the present one holds only four hundred people
and there are two thousand Catholics here. After that, perhaps the ancient
rectory can be replaced. So you see the Catholic Church has plans.

It has to have plans, if it is to keep pace with the rest of the island.
Americanization goes on apace. Sister Loretta Marie finds that her driver's
license is No. 567. The last year or so, even the Palauan women are driving. The estimate is that some two hundred vehicles tear up and down
this little island which is six miles long and only half a mile wide. One
wonders where they are going in such a hurry. A good guess is that they
are rushing to get under a roof before it rains again. Rain is just one of
Life's Constant Companions here. The local newssheet makes the following announcement of a championship baseball game.

> Once again, the game between the Peleliu winners of the North Palauan
> League, and the Airai Champions of the South League, was postponed
> because of too much water, both on the field and in the air. At 3 P.M.
> yesterday, the sky was clear, the sun was out, the field was dry and both
> teams were ready to go at it, when a squall moved in from the north and
> drenched the field just at game time.
>
> The teams will have a try at it again next Friday, June 30, at 3:30 P.M.;
> if there is too much water, then they will try again, Sunday, July 2; and,
> if as usual there is rain, the game will be scheduled for the holiday, July 4,
> at 2 P.M. It is hoped that this part of the Pacific will run out of water
> one of these three days, so that the Palauan Baseball Championship for
> this year can finally be decided.

Probably the rush and tear also is to get a little business done before
the heavens open up again. Another good guess is that the jeeps are rushing down to Transportation Office to see Mr. Bean. "Mr. Transportation"
on any of the Trust Territory Islands is a harried man. He is charged with
getting passengers arranged for the Friday plane. His little job is to sort
out the fifty-some people who want to go and to allot the ten or twelve
seats to the most deserving, the most persistent, or the most honorable.
This leaves us out entirely, but usually we find Mr. Transportation does
his best for everyone. If he were not on an island surrounded by gobs of
water, he could leave town for the three days preceding Friday. As it is,
he must long to hide behind one of those tufty islets which stick up like
cupcakes all over the harbor, and stay submerged until the plane is off
ground.

"Getting bumped" is the Trust Territories' greatest outdoor sport. It's
dangerous and suspenseful. The rules are simple; the element of chance
adds zest.

We start with the assumption that you want to get somewhere. You are
on Koror, say, and you want to get to Guam. You have no boat or plane
of your own; it has been many years since you did marathon swimming

and 843 miles is long even for champions. You are a lowly #3 priority, from which you can fall no lower. It is Friday morning and you hear the weekly plane going off into the blue. You rush to the telephone to be first on Mr. Transportation's mind for next week's plane.

The phone is Early American. It is attached to the wall, and two batteries hang beneath it; once painted brown, then black, blue and green, it shows all these layers at worn spots. I asked for the phone book and Sister Loretta Marie with a knowing look slipped a mimeographed piece of paper from under the phone and handed it to me. It lists forty-six phones, twenty-six of them in offices—the weather bureau, commissary, docks, public works, hotel, hospital, police and District Administrator. The other twenty are residential; they are listed under one name—the first, last or in the case of Palauans the only name.

The frustration of it is that these few people are the only ones you can call. There is no Long Distance nor even another City exchange. Of course, you see all the other subscribers several times a day walking past your door, but a phone is a help anyway.

So in the Getting Bumped game, you wind up the telephone and get the operator.

"Hello, Sister," says the operator. "Want somebody?"

"Will you give me #19, please, Elise?"

"I don't think anybody's there, Sister. Who did you want to talk to?"

"Mr. Bean, the Transportation Officer."

"Oh, he left some time ago. I think he's at the hotel now. Do you want me to try there for him?"

Business of plugging in and plugging out several times.

"He's left there, too. Probably at home. Want me to try him there?"

"No thanks, Elise. It's not that important. . . ."

"Okay, Sister. If he comes on the line, I'll tell him you are looking for him."

An hour or so later he calls. He's heroic to call; he knows right well why you want him. He groans. "I'm awfully sorry. We have nineteen Priorities #1 already for next week. The week after? That's full, too. But," with a helpful lift to his voice, "I'll let you know if anything happens."

From then on, it's a chain reaction. Every day you inquire. Perhaps you meet Mr. Transportation in church, or Mrs. Transportation at the commissary, or both at a party. It's no, no, no in all sharps and flats. Hope rises; hope fades; hope revives; hope clings to a straw. You hear the Errol is coming in; maybe you can get on that? Sure you can—but it's going to Truk, not Guam, this trip. How about the Gunners Knot; that's due, isn't it? No, they're cutting out the Koror stop this time.

Sometimes the nicest things happen to #3 Priorities. Once I was definitely to be bumped. The plane would go at 10 A.M. that day. At break-fast, I resigned myself to God's Holy Will and took another piece of toast. Then the Transportation Officer came bounding up our back stairs. "Bring your baggage down at any rate," he said. "There's a wisp of a chance." I did. I walked on that plane with no one to say me "Nay."

But most of the time, if you're to be bumped, you are well bumped. Sister Maura Shaun once had her foot over the plane's threshold when one more honorable than she came running up and was accorded the seat. There was nothing to do but take her little satchel out of the baggage compartment and go home for another week.

On that same plane, an American from the Deep South suffered a like bump. He had a habit of calling anyone in religious dress, "Reverend." As they stood on the ramp watching the plane grow smaller in the distance, the Southerner turned to Sister Maura Shaun and sighed. "Well, Reverend, all I can say is: My thoughts at the present moment are strictly Old Testament."

Weight is important. Once, Brother Juan, who might tip the scale at one hundred and twenty, and Father Roszel, who is much larger, both asked for seats. "There is only one seat available," said Mr. Transportation. "Brother may go."

Brother demurred. "Let Father go. He is essential to the business."

"No," said the imperturbable official. "Father's too heavy. It's Brother or nobody."

Thelma was a bright young thing in the Transportation Office on Guam. She made an art of squeezing the last passenger in. At last Thelma got married. She knew so many people that she had loads of wedding presents for her new home on Truk. Her last act was to squeeze her wedding presents, her dog, her new husband and herself on the weekly plane to Truk. The other passengers were boys en route to school. The plane encountered difficulties on the way. The first ballast sent overboard was the boys' suitcases. Then the wedding presents went, one by one. Thelma pointed them out: Take the lamp. Now the table linen. And the wedding trousseau. The silverware. This was killing; she knew the next item would be the dog. But before poor poochy was dumped overboard, the wind abated and the plane was able to land on Truk. That's how Thelma started her married life with a dog and a husband and nothing else.

Speaking of weddings, we had a very formal one while I was there. It was the very first wedding with wedding invitations, no less. Usually, you meet the bride or her mother down in the commissary, buying the makings for the wedding feast and they ask you to come.

"When?" you ask.

"We don't know yet, but you'll see the wedding party going down the road, so just join in."

Or, someone runs up to the convent and announces, "Maria is marrying Juan over at the church right now. They want you to come."

But Bonita's wedding to Dr. Jorge was something special. The groom
has a medical degree from the Philippines; he is the only Palauan doctor
on Koror. The bride had lived on Truk with the Mercedarian Sisters for
a year or more. So they knew a thing or two about the world. The wedding
invitation was a piece of yellow Manila paper neatly folded into fourths.
On the outside was typed:

TO ALL THE MARYKNOLL SISTERS

Inside it read:

We want you to know we will be married at tomorrow's Mass
and we want you to come and pray for us. Bonita and Jorge.

Another milestone of civilization was passed while I was there. A
daily newspaper was born. The *Newsflash* is unpretentious—just two
mimeographed sheets 8½ x 13 inches—but it serves the basic needs of a
newspaper. If ever some fresh young student of journalism wants to dig
down through the superstructure of comics, political commentators,
household hints, gossip columns, advice to the lovelorn, sob-sister stories
and the junk emanating from Hollywood's fertile publicity offices, to find
the foundations of a newspaper, let him come to Koror. You editors,
snowed under by the handouts from Madison Avenue, come to Koror.
All ye feature writers, told to write ten inches on nothing at all, come
to Koror. For news evaluation, succinct style, consideration of the reader's
time, I recommend the Koror *Newsflash*.

Volume One, Number One, tells us, first, that the *Newsflash* is born,
says who publishes it, how often it will come out and gives a deadline
for any items you want to get into it. Transportation news says that the
Gunners Knot will go to Truk on Friday and will be back at Koror
maybe in three months' time. Passengers on the weekly flight are listed.
Meetings of the Palau Congress, the Landscaping Committee, the Fisher-
man's Cooperative are outlined. Boat builders on the island are asked
to come to a meeting to discuss plans to organize a Boat Builders' Association. Restaurant owners are to meet with the District Administrator
and talk about a new liquor law. There will be a baseball game next
Sunday between the people on Airai Island and Peleliu Island, if the
Peleliu team can somehow wangle a boat to bring them to Koror. The
weatherman reports showers are on the menu for the next few days. Three
or four items of world news boiled down to less than fifty words finish it
off.

What more does anyone want to read over his coffee in the morning?
We went shopping on Koror. Not so simple as it sounds. The day

before—indeed for weeks—news seeped in, "The Gunners Knot is on the way." Then one day the cry was raised, "The Gunners Knot is in!" For the first time in four months, fresh vegetables and meat would be available. Now begin the calls to the commissary.

"Is the ship unloaded yet?"

"No. Too rainy."

Then, "Yes, but the stuff isn't on the shelves yet. Come down this afternoon."

We hopped into Father's pick-up truck and hurtled down Koror's main road, bent on shopping that first day or everything would be gone. The supply would have to last until August or so.

The Koror Commissary is a quonset hut with additions. A paint-peeled sign proclaims it with no great pride. Arranged on a plan faintly resembling a supermarket, the shelves are not stacked high with bright labels. Rather, the empty spaces are dusty; the cans and packages look tired of waiting for customers. Only on days like this is there much traffic. Then the excitement centers around the lettuce and carrots; fresh oranges, apples, frozen meats, cauliflowers, cabbages and—oh, joy!— grapes. Soaps, detergents, steel wool, mops find quick sales. But the dusty cans are untouched.

I wondered why. Then I took a prowl through the alleyways; it was a gastronomic tour of the world in half an hour.

> *Prepared seaweed from Japan.*
> *Dundee cakes from Ireland.*
> *Antipasto from Italy.*
> *Biscuits from West Germany.*
> *Wafers and candy from Holland.*

That was just the start. China sent dried pineapple rings; India contributed hot chutney. Hawaii was there with ready-mixed poi (on Koror where you grow taro just by sitting on your doorstep and twiddling your thumbs!). Coconut syrup from the Philippines; Irish stew from—of all places—England; crepes suzette from France; fruit salad from Australia; and bubble gum from You-Know-Where. Cans and cans of lobster tails, crabmeat, clam juice and shrimp—on an island where the sea food walks out of the ocean and knocks at your kitchen door.

The labels range from odd foods to the higher levels of existentialism: champagne jelly, whole guinea fowl in aspic, Bombay duck (which isn't a duck at all but some sort of fish), buffalo stew, and reindeer steak prepared in Lapland style and imported from Norway. You could buy if you ever wanted to, smoked rabbit from Australia or from California. Also cat and dog food although I can't imagine a Palauan cat patiently waiting for somebody to open a can while juicy rats skip by with im-

munity. Pancake flour in rows of packages showed its age in successive
price marks—62¢, 43¢, 36¢ and now 28¢. No doubt, by now, the "protein
content" was high—you know, the proteins who walk around on ten or
twelve little feet.

How did such exotic foods get to this rugged outpost? Possibly they
did not go well in American supermarkets and some enterprising merchant palmed them off on the Navy for overseas commissaries. Who
knows? As a result, a family in grass skirts can sit down to champagne
jelly and reindeer steaks.

On Koror, however, they don't go in for grass skirts. You see youngsters
in shirts without pants and in pants without shirts, women in Mother
Hubbards or in slacks, men in pajamas going down the street or in nicely
fitted shirts and long trousers. Down on the main road is an "abai," a
sort of community house, a meeting place or town hall, bright with
painted symbols on the outside. The roof is tremendously high-pitched,
and the whole building is set on large stones on the four corners. Inside,
you can read the history of Palau painted on the transverse beams. Events
are recorded in childlike drawings: battles among the island tribes; the
Spanish galleons; the coming of missioners in 1887; the erection of the
church and school; the arrival of the Germans and a peace treaty they
signed with the islanders in 1898; then the coming of Japanese in 1914.
Right after that is a crude picture of a Japanese standing before several
men in loincloths and women in grass skirts.

"What is this?" I asked.

"Soon after they came," explained old Julito who was showing me all
this, "the Japanese called a meeting of the chiefs and told us that we
should wear clothes."

"The Japanese made you wear clothes?" I asked.

"Yes, it was their rule," he affirmed.

It always amuses me when writers assume that it was the missionaries
who clamped the gay carefree natives into clothes. They paint a picture
of the happy girls dancing on the beach in primeval innocence. Then
along come some nuns, draped in funereal black, who smother the girls
in corsets and Mother Hubbards, and drape a guilt complex around
their minds.

I would like to take these writers to Yap where, after seventy years of
missioners of three different nationalities, the pillars of the church attend Sodality meetings in grass skirts. The piety of men and women, in
or out of clothes, is apparent to the most jaundiced eye. As Father
Bailey once said to a reporter from *Holiday Magazine,* "I don't care
what they wear or don't wear, so long as their lives are good."

Koror's missioners, indeed those throughout the Trust Territory, are
American Jesuits from the New York province. The Jesuits are noted

among religious orders for their extra-curricular activities, so to speak. The order can produce an expert in just about any special field of knowledge you could name. You will find Jesuits steeped in meteorology, labor relations, French cuisine, and the fine points of atomic fission. Father Hoar, curate on Koror, for instance, is a radio ham.

The first sight of Koror's Jesuit rectory as you come up the hill is a mass of wires and poles, like a ship at sea peeping up over the horizon. These are the outside gadgets of Father Hoar's station, KC6AQ. KC6 tells all fellow hams that the station is in the Caroline Islands; the AQ is Father's individual call number.

He is a martyr to the cause. Radio has pushed him out of his own room. The wires, batteries, coils, tubes and what-not which make up his transmitter and receiver take up so much space he hasn't room for a bed. So Father "sleeps out" using any bed available in the rectory. If one of the other priests or a Brother is on a mission trip—which is most of the time—Father Hoar's lanky frame is laid to rest on that bed. If luck would have it that they are all home, Father betakes himself to the parish hall, usually used for meetings, play rehearsals, choir practice and what-you-will.

Of course compact sets are on the market. But they cost real money. The kind of money Father has, helped him to accumulate the parts and his own ingenuity put the parts together. Not so hard for him, because since he was a gangling lad away back in 1946, he has been fiddling around with radio. As a student at Woodstock, Md., he built a station, not once but several times. One of his stations, I heard, is in use now in the Philippines. So when he came to Koror—(remember? 834 miles from Guam, which is 1,500 miles from Wake, which is 3,000 or more miles from Hawaii, which is 2,500 from California)—he came with his wire, rods and tubes under his arm. Lucky thing he did. In a few years, he has set up what amounts to a public utility and a private joy.

For one thing, he keeps his mission in touch with Truk, center of this tremendous watery vicariate of the Marshall and Caroline Islands, with a water area larger than that of the whole continental United States (3,000,000 square miles), and a land area less than half of Rhode Island (516 square miles). All he has to do to talk to his Bishop is to toss a message up to the ionosphere and have it bounce down on the tiny island of Truk. That's all he has to do. Or, he might bounce it down to Majuro or Kwajalein where fellow Jesuits are stationed two thousand miles away. They're a chummy lot, these sons of Ignatius! As one remarked, "What this vicariate needs is a good bulldozer to push it all together."

Father uses his radio to help Trust Territory personnel. Often a man on one of the islands needs beds, let us say, or shovels or tires or paint or you-name-it. He could write to a store on Guam, of course, and send the letter by weekly plane or now-and-then boat. Maybe the answer is "Sorry. We don't have it in stock." That takes a week or more to come back, and the poor man is desperate for his shovels. He writes again. But Father can contact Guam and, through an obliging ham at the other end, canvass the stores by phone in half an hour until he finds the beds or bolts, tents or toothpicks.

The third use of KC6AQ is to contact a certain home in Buffalo, New York, where Mrs. Hoar can hear her son's report on his doings in his own words and in his own voice.

Sometimes, it isn't simple to call across the watery wastes. Antennae have to be turned in your direction; not many people expect a call from the Palau Islands. When his persistent CQ, CQ, CQ (which is radio jargon for Seek You) fails to reach a receptive ear on Guam, Father Hoar shoots farther afield. He figured one night that all Guam's radio hams were tuned toward the States. So he overshot Guam by six thousand miles and had an answer in Michigan. The Michigan ham called back to Guam, "There's a fellow just down the block from you, who wants you to call him."

They tell the story of a Maryknoll priest in the hinterlands of Chile who wanted to make an appointment with a dentist in Santiago, Chile. He could rouse nobody there, so he shot to New York where a fellow ham contacted a ham in Santiago who called the dentist.

There's a radio ham Call Book, not at all unlike a telephone directory of the whole world. Just leafing through the 250-page volume takes you off for parts unknown where many a devotee sits long hours before his set, shooting out signals and hoping to hear a friendly tap-tap in return. There is a Japanese ham down in Antarctica; several in Basutoland and dear knows how many in Tasmania and New Zealand. Men and women are listed; some claim to have been on the air since 1913. Others are high school lads; some are seminarians. A diligent young Capuchin in Hudson, N.H., has compiled a directory of clerics around the world who operate radio stations. There are—I counted!—996 of them, including five Sisters. One is in Rhode Island, another in New York, two in Minnesota and one up in Copper Valley, Alaska.

They're a friendly lot, these radio amateurs. They like one another. When the airwaves go swirling around the globe, they hate to think that this precious touch with another soul has come and gone. So they send postal cards to that lonely voice which spoke so wearily out of the blue. Thus it is that Father Hoar gets about seventy-five cards a week. They come from New Zealand, Italy, Sweden, Ecuador, the Bahrain Islands (know where they are?) and all parts of the United States, mostly Texas.

But none from Communist-dominated countries. In the Radio Amateur

Call Book, where other countries list each ham's call letters, his name and address, the Iron Curtain countries permit no fraternizing. Czechoslovakia says merely, cards may be sent to Cekslovenchi Amateur Vysilaci, Praha 1, Czechoslovakia. The Soviet Union wants all cards sent to Central Radio Club, Moscow. Brrr! It's a cold world behind that curtain.

Home to Mass on Koror! You will have to get up early, of course— maybe at 5:30. But already the night has lifted a little, the air is fresh, the world is quiet. You leave the house stepping on the soft green carpet of Japanese grass, that perfect lawn which never needs mowing nor weeding. You step over or on (depending on your feelings toward them) the giant African snails who are already up and about, intent on their god-given task of destroying your garden. You set out on the road, so strangely still. The moon, worn paper-thin after a night time of brilliance, is dying in the west. You walk down our rocky road, turn to the left and set your eyes toward the white church crowning the rise.

Others are going with you. Children, little and big. Men who carry a rosary in their hands and say it as they go along. Heavy-bodied, full-hipped women with regal smiles proper to those who rule their households with an easy hand. Nobody speaks to you. It's not a social time. Each is intent on bringing himself to God for a good-morning talk.

You dip your fingers into the huge shell which rests casually on an unpainted wooden stand, and bless yourself. It's not a fancy church, inside. The floor is concrete, the pews are debilitated, the underside of the galvanized iron roof is painted blue. No one pays attention to you; the people slip into pews here and there or half kneel, half sit on the floor. One of these is Clemente, born deaf and consequently dumb, who speaks reams and reams to God in his heart. Someone, long ago, was able to put deep into his mind the idea that God loved Clemente, came on earth, died for him and now stays on the altar especially to be with him. Clemente kneels bolt upright with his hands clasped before him and talks to God by the hour. Outside, he is cheerful in the practical affairs of life, but this early morning time is dedicated to his Best Friend.

Brother Juan, tall, skinny, wiry and very Spanish, hurries up the side aisle. His many-patched cassock flaps about his legs; his rough hand clutches the stem of a tuberose. He all but leaps the altar rail, goes to the altar, and thrusts the flower in among others in the brass casing of a howitzer shell, picked up after the war and polished to a fitting bright-ness for service as an altar vase.

Then Brother retires to his shabby prie-dieu and folding chair and is heard of no more. This is his hour of respite. All day, he is in khaki and flapping straw hat, out on the site for the new school buildings—fixing the concrete mixer, testing the new windows, telling truck drivers where to put a load of sand, pawing over the plans. Or he may be looking with pained eye at first one worker, then another, as he tries to figure out which of them walked off with his hammer. But all those things have dropped from Brother, now. He is a young man again in the Jesuit monastery in Spain, dressed in religious habit, kneeling before God and swearing that he will serve Him forever. And the Lord God says to him, "All right, Brother Juan, we'll sit together for an hour quietly. Then, I want you to get on with that building."

A bell tinkles. Two altar boys walk out followed by Father Hoar. He looks like a high school lad, really. But there is a determined way he puts down his bare feet, clad only in Japanese zori, which tells you that this boyish-looking man has made great decisions for himself. He walks up the altar steps to put the chalice on the altar. The nuns in the front pews appraise him. Sister Margaret George's eyebrows contract; she is worried. "I wonder if he is getting enough to eat. Or the right kind of food. That boy in his kitchen could stand a few lessons, if we only had the time—and patience!—to teach him. Maybe we could send Father a good meal. Hmmmm. . . ." Business of leafing through missal. "Oh yes, Thursday this week, St. Aloysius. Isn't that his middle name? Good enough excuse."

With that settled, she's ready for Mass. So is Father. He has come down the steps and, bending between the boys, is now reciting the Confiteor. He too has his thoughts, try as he might to shut them out. Last night, he talked to his mother in Buffalo, N.Y., which accounts for the reddish rim around his eyes. A kindly ham in Rochester, N.Y., got his signals loud and clear enough to relay the voice by telephone to Buffalo. He hadn't much to say; neither had she. But it was a satisfaction to repeat the same old inanities. "How are things?" "Where's Jim now?" "Sure, Mom, sure! I'm all right. Don't worry about me."

"She's probably at Mass now, too," he thought. Then—"Oh no, I forget. It's eight o'clock tonight, over there."

He cleared his mind of everything but thoughts of the Great Action he was to perform. My own mind, I confess, was off on a tangent. This tiny island of Koror I knew was the final stop on our world tour. From here, we would go to Guam, to Hawaii, to California and back to New York. In less than a week, I would be back at my old typewriter in the Motherhouse.

All the Masses I had heard crowded in upon me. All the holy souls in so many different bodies, in such odd clothes, speaking such queer tongues, streamed across that church on Koror. The heat at the equator, the chills at Hokkaido. The colonizers and the "colonized." Black, brown, white and yellow, with no unity among them except the one bond: That Christ was born, lived and died for each one.

This is the thought that lifts a man from torpor and drives him, often with stumbling feet and half-closed eyes, along deserted streets to Mass. Sleep is sweet in any land. It is no easier to rise from a mat of rags on the floor of a Chinese family boat, than from a warm quilt over a tatami floor in Japan. Look along the streets of Chicago on a winter morning; those people holding their hats on their heads are hurrying into a church for Mass. Watch the African swinging his rungu as he walks through grass tinged with the rising sunlight; he will turn in the mission gate and drop on his knees in chapel. In the high Andes, Indian women in llama wool shawls and derby hats, come to the ruined Spanish church. In Taiwan, aborigines with bells on their clothes walk the mountain paths. On "The Rock" of Hong Kong, a construction worker lays his shoulder pole along the pew where he can get it right after Mass as he goes off to work for the day. In the Philippines, a woman carries her wooden clogs in her hand as she slips quietly down the bamboo ladder of her nipa hut, lest she wake the other members of her family. In New York, a traveling salesman leaves Pennsy Station, crosses 31st Street and goes into the Capuchin church there.

They are all members of a strong brotherhood. They never saw one another; they never write; they have no idea of names. Yet each as he goes his often lonely way to Mass in the morning, feels the breath of his brothers panting beside him. He sees the sun rise behind skyscrapers, or palm trees, or over a limitless horizon of sea and knows that as the earth swings around to greet it, an army of Christ's brothers are on their way to start another day of knowing, loving and serving God.

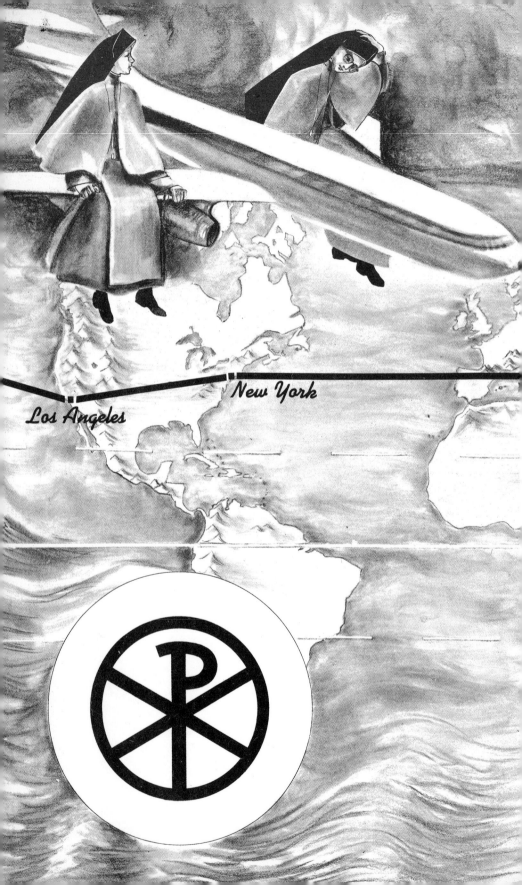